THE INTERNATIONAL DIPLOMACY OF ISRAEL'S FOUNDERS

During the early to mid-twentieth century, the Zionist Organization secured a series of political victories on the international stage leading to the foundation of a Jewish state and to its ability to expand its territorial control within Palestine. *The International Diplomacy of Israel's Founders* provides a revisionist account of the founding of Israel by exposing the misrepresentations and false assurances of Zionist diplomats during this formative period of Israeli history. By comparing diplomatic statements at the United Nations and elsewhere against the historical record, it sheds new light on the legacies of leaders such as Chaim Weizmann, David Ben Gurion, Abba Eban, and Shabtai Rosenne. Including coverage of little-discussed moments in early Israeli history, this book offers an important new perspective for anyone interested in the history of the Israeli-Palestinian conflict.

John Quigley is Professor Emeritus at the Ohio State University Moritz College of Law and a leading expert on the Arab-Israeli conflict. His recent publications include *The Six-Day War and Israeli Self-Defense* (2013) and *The Statehood of Palestine: International Law in the Middle East Conflict* (2010).

The International Diplomacy of Israel's Founders

DECEPTION AT THE UNITED NATIONS IN THE QUEST FOR PALESTINE

John Quigley
Ohio State University Moritz College of Law

CAMBRIDGE
UNIVERSITY PRESS

CAMBRIDGE
UNIVERSITY PRESS

32 Avenue of the Americas, New York, NY 10013-2473, USA

Cambridge University Press is part of the University of Cambridge.

It furthers the University's mission by disseminating knowledge in the pursuit of education, learning, and research at the highest international levels of excellence.

www.cambridge.org
Information on this title: www.cambridge.org/9781316503553

First published 2016

A catalog record for this publication is available from the British Library.

Library of Congress Cataloging in Publication Data
Names: Quigley, John B., author.
Title: The international diplomacy of Israel's founders : deception at the United Nations in the quest for Palestine / John Quigley.
Description: New York : Cambridge University Press, [2016] | 2016 |
Includes bibliographical references and index.
Identifiers: LCCN 2015038561| ISBN 9781107138735 (hardback) |
ISBN 9781316503553 (paperback)
Subjects: LCSH: United Nations – Israel – History – 20th century. |
Israel – Foreign relations. | Palestine – History – Partition, 1947. |
Arab-Israeli conflict. | Propaganda, Zionist. | Propaganda, Israeli. |
BISAC: LAW / International.
Classification: LCC JX1977.2.I83 Q85 2016 | DDC 327.5694–dc23
LC record available at http://lccn.loc.gov/2015038561

ISBN 978-1-107-13873-5 Hardback
ISBN 978-1-316-50355-3 Paperback

Contents

Preface

Lev Nikolaevich Tolstoy mastered the writing of fiction by portraying life events in a way that challenged the common perception of them. He would descend to great detail to explain situations that at first blush did not seem to require elaboration. Events that seemed simple became complex. Tolstoy's technique has acquired a description in literary analysis. Tolstoy is said to have "made strange." He took what appeared simple and mined the surface to show a more complex reality.

Tolstoy's technique can be applied in nonfiction as well. Events that have become part of history, events explained typically in a sentence or two, may hide a reality that sheds a different light. The Zionist movement has made a history for itself, a history remarkable in many respects. From ideas generated by a handful of individuals, it inserted itself onto the world stage. It functioned in the realm of international diplomacy. It arrived in that realm as Europe and the Middle East were tearing themselves apart in a world war. And a few years later it navigated through another conflagration that consumed even greater swaths of the planet in another world war.

Zionism achieved great feats in the realm of diplomacy, feats that have been depicted in heroic terms by its proponents and acknowledged with chagrin by its detractors. What has received less attention is the means by which Zionist diplomacy gained its successes. This book approaches Zionist diplomacy using Tolstoy's technique. A close reading will be given to key diplomatic forays that put Zionism in a position to succeed in its effort to gain territory for a Jewish state.

I must mention several technical matters. When an English language rendition is given from a source in another language, the translation is mine. Transliteration into the Latin alphabet from Arabic, Hebrew, and Russian is not uniform. As a result, a reader may find variances in the spelling of place names or other terms, particularly in quotations.

The text at many points contains statements of persons who spoke at United Nations meetings. The UN records typically paraphrase, as recorded by a rapporteur. So even if quotation marks appear at the beginning and end of a statement, the words may not be exactly those of the speaker.

Names can be confusing for two diplomats who are referenced frequently in the text. Each made a name change mid-career. In the text I have given the name as it was at the particular time. Thus, Moshe Shertok is "Shertok" in early references to him but "Sharett" after he adopted that surname. Aubrey Eban is "Aubrey" in early references to him, but "Abba Eban" after he began referring to himself that way. For the names of member states of the United Nations, the more colloquial names are used in the text, even though in quotations from UN documents the reader will see the more formal name. Thus, "Britain" is used instead of "United Kingdom of Great Britain and Northern Ireland." "Soviet Union" is used instead of "Union of Soviet Socialist Republics." "Egypt" is used instead of "United Arab Republic," which was the formal name of Egypt from 1958 to 1971 as result of a merger with Syria.

I had help from a number of sources in preparing this book. Dr. Anis F. Kassim provided helpful comments on an early draft. The Cambridge University Press readers pointed out avenues for additional research. Dr. Avi Raz provided direction on Israeli cabinet documents. John Vincent Quigley assisted on literary references. Jana Al-Akhras (JD 2017) and Michael Dewey (JD 2017) at the Moritz College of Law of The Ohio State University checked source references. Research librarians at the Law Library of the Moritz College of Law located materials in archives and libraries around the globe, allowing me to access critical primary sources. As always, I am grateful to the Moritz College of Law for providing an environment conducive to scholarly endeavors.

A Note on United Nations Committees

During the early years of the United Nations, a number of UN committees dealt with issues covered in this book. Some were permanent, part of the UN structure. Others were temporary, set up for a defined task. With names that sound similar one to another, these committees can easily be confused. This Note provides a brief guide.

Ad Hoc Committee on the Palestinian Question: set up by the UN General Assembly in September 1947 to consider the recommendations of the Special Committee on Palestine. Composed of all member states of the United Nations, it met during October–November 1947. It made a recommendation to the General Assembly in November 1947, after which it ceased to function. Its documents begin with the designation UN Document A/AC.14/SR.

Ad Hoc Political Committee: a standing committee of the UN General Assembly composed of all member states of the United Nations. As a committee that handles a variety of issues, it was tasked in May 1949 with dealing with Israel's application for membership in the United Nations. It made a favorable recommendation in that month. Over the next several years, it discussed a variety of matters relating to Palestine and Israel. Its documents begin with the designation UN Document A/AC.

Conciliation Commission for Palestine: established by the UN General Assembly in December 1948 to promote a negotiated settlement. Composed of three member states (Turkey, France, United States), it actively pursued a settlement for four years but thereafter focused on more limited issues. Its documents begin with the designation A/AC.25.

First Committee: a standing committee of the UN General Assembly that deals with issues of international security. Composed of all member states of the United Nations, it held much of the discussion at the United

Nations 1947 to 1949 relating to the status of Palestine. Its documents begin with the designation UN Document A/C.1.

Palestine Commission: created by UN General Assembly Resolution 181 in November 1947 to oversee the implementation of the partition of Palestine. Composed of representatives of five member states (Bolivia, Czechoslovakia, Denmark, Panama, Philippines), it was disbanded by the General Assembly in May 1948 when it became clear that partition would not be implemented. Its documents begin with the designation UN Document A/AC.21.

Special Committee on Palestine: set up by the UN General Assembly in April 1947, when the United Nations took up the Palestine Question. Composed of representatives of eleven states (Australia, Canada, Czechoslovakia, Guatemala, India, Iran, Netherlands, Peru, Sweden, Uruguay, Yugoslavia), its task was to make recommendations for Palestine's status. It made a final report and ceased to function in September 1947. Its meetings begin with the designation UN Document A/AC.13 but are cited from the Special Committee's report to the General Assembly, which is UN Document A/364.

Abbreviations

A/	Document of the UN General Assembly or of an entity subordinate to it
AC.	An ad hoc committee of the UN General Assembly (will be followed by a number to designate a record of a particular committee during a particular session)
A/PV.	Provisional Verbatim Record of a meeting of the UN General Assembly (will be followed by a meeting number)
C.1	First Committee of the UN General Assembly
CAB	Cabinet (UK National Archives, document of the British Cabinet)
Cmd.	Command Paper (UK, Parliamentary Paper)
ES-	Emergency Special Session (of the UN General Assembly) (will be followed by a session number)
FCO	Foreign and Commonwealth Office (UK)
FO	Foreign Office (UK)
FRUS	*Foreign Relations of the United States*, a publication of the Department of State of the United States. In citations in this book, the year indicated is the year of the documents included in the particular volume, not the year of publication of the volume
GA	General Assembly (UN)
IDF	Israel Defense Force
S/	Document of the UN Security Council or of an entity subordinate to it
S-	Special Session (of the UN General Assembly) (will be followed by a session number)

S/PV.	Provisional verbatim record of a meeting of the UN Security Council (will be followed by a meeting number)
SR.	Summary record of a meeting of a permanent or ad hoc committee of the UN General Assembly
UK	United Kingdom of Great Britain and Northern Ireland
UN	United Nations
UNEF	UN Emergency Force
UNTSO	UN Truce Supervision Organization

1

A Public Relations Imperative

Hasbara is a Hebrew term that one hears frequently in public parlance in Israel. Literally, *hasbara* means "explanation." In its usage in the public realm in Israel, *hasbara* relates to explanations given about Israel's policies and actions, explanations aimed at an audience abroad. It is how Israel explains itself to the world. *Hasbara* can be carried out by individuals. It can be carried out by government agencies. *Hasbara* in the realm of Israel's explanations of itself is sometimes defined as "public diplomacy." To some, Israel's practice of *hasbara* is a benign way of gaining acceptance abroad for actions and policies that fall within the realm of acceptable behavior but may not be immediately understood without explanation.[1] To others, *hasbara* is "the Israeli euphemism for propaganda," a deceptive practice that is used to give a false explanation for actions and policies for which there is no valid justification.[2]

All peoples and governments have a public face. They try to show themselves as worthy citizens of the planet. This function may be performed by any governmental official or ministry that has occasion to comment on an issue. It may be performed by an official press office. In some countries, one finds a cabinet-level ministry, sometimes called a ministry of information.

In Israel, one finds particular emphasis. Israel has been subjected to frequent criticism over the way it deals with the Arab population in the Palestine territories it occupied in 1967. That criticism has heightened a felt need to explain Israel to a world audience. Some say that *hasbara* is a national obsession in Israel. Government ministers are often criticized for failures in *hasbara*. They have not, it is said, adequately explained to the world why Israel engaged in one or another action. Israel acts correctly and justly in the world, so the criticism runs, but others do not understand. If only our government gave a better account of itself, the world would love us more.

The government of Israel has devoted considerable bureaucratic effort to *hasbara*. At various times, *hasbara* has been carried out by a cabinet-level ministry devoted to it, a ministry that has borne different names. As a governmental function, the term *hasbara* carries in Israel a positive connotation. The Ministry of Foreign Affairs has a public diplomacy division that deals with issues that yield negative public relations. In 2015 that division spearheaded Israel's effort to counter a move by the Palestinian football association to have Israeli football teams suspended from the International Federation of Association Football (FIFA in its French acronym). The basis for the Palestinian move was that Israel's football leagues included teams from Israel's settlements in the Palestinian West Bank occupied by Israel, an occupation said to be illegal. The Palestinian association further charged that Israeli officialdom impeded travel by Palestinian footballers, through restrictions at border crossings and at internal highway checkpoints.

The prospect of being unable to field football teams in international competition was one that the government of Israel did not relish. A ban on Israeli football teams would have highlighted the settlement issue to the international public. Under the direction of Yuval Rotem, who headed the Ministry's public diplomacy division, personnel at Israeli embassies in a number of countries lobbied local officials, arguing that politics should be kept out of sports activity. The Ministry was ultimately successful in gaining support for its view, and the Palestinian football association decided to drop its effort to exclude Israeli teams. However, even the raising of the issue highlighted the issue of Israel's settlements and their legality, as well as Israel's restrictions on travel by Palestinian Arabs. Those aspects of Israel's policy were ongoing topics of criticism of Israel by human rights organs at the United Nations.

They were also matters that increasingly were being raised by nongovernmental groups in various countries who urged a boycott of Israel. Criticism of Israel from such diffuse sources required expansion of the scope of public diplomacy. "I know what to do in the United Nations," said Rotem, in a reference to Israel's efforts to influence opinion in its direction at the United Nations. "I know what to do in Geneva," he continued, in a reference to Israel's efforts to influence opinion in the UN human rights organs based in Geneva. Those organs were inclined not infrequently to issue strong condemnations of Israel for one policy or another. "Now I need to build a base of power," Rotem bemoaned, "to deal with a trade union in Ireland or a church in Panama." Israel's public diplomacy had to contend with opinion at "campuses and universities, and all those conferences of sciences, all museums and art exhibitions. Every element of Israeli activity," he said, "is basically challenged."[3]

Hasbara has come to occupy such a prominent role in Israel's public agenda because of Israel's atypical history. Most countries do not need to justify their existence. China is accepted as a country because it has been on the map for so long. We may be vague on the names of China's ancient dynasties, but we know of China's lineage. Particular policies of China's government may be questioned, even condemned. The extent of China's territory may be debated – does it include Taiwan, or does it not? China may disseminate information to justify its policies, or to substantiate its claim to Taiwan, but it does not need to convince anyone about its status in the world. No one disputes that China is a state that should be allowed to continue to function as such. China is accepted as a fact.

The modern Israeli state, to the contrary, appeared only recently in historical terms on the international stage, and in circumstances of great controversy. It was formed through the efforts of an association of Jews in Europe, beginning at the turn of the twentieth century. Taking its name from Mt. Zion in Jerusalem, the World Zionist Organization aimed at a state for the Jews of the world. In 1948, those efforts were crowned with success, with the declaration and subsequent international acceptance of a state in the territory of what at the time was Palestine. The propriety of the World Zionist Organization's efforts was questioned, given that the existing population in Palestine fiercely objected and was not prepared quietly to acquiesce. Israel's early twenty first century Prime Minister Benjamin Netanyahu is at pains to condemn criticism of Israel as aimed at "delegitimizing" it.[4] His government mounted an effort to counter "delegitimization."

One of Israel's most successful early practitioners of *hasbara* was Abba Eban, who gave voice to Israel's story when it sought support to establish itself in the years that followed the end of World War II. Eban said that Israel was unusual as a state in its extreme concern over the opinion of others. "Other sovereign nations do not continually ask themselves what others think of them," said Eban in 1972, when he was serving as Israel's Foreign Minister. "We never relax," he explained, "to improve and expand on what is called our 'image.' "[5] For Israel, *hasbara* plays a central role in its relationship with the rest of the world.

AN UPHILL BATTLE

Eban was not alone in Israel's first years as a state in identifying the importance of burnishing Israel's image as it sought its place in the world community. From early on, *hasbara* has been seen as crucial in gaining the acceptance of a Jewish state. In 1951, the World Zionist Organization, which was instrumental in bringing Israel into being, set out a series of tasks for itself. One was "Organization of propaganda, and political aid for Israel in cooperation and coordination with the State."[6] The World Zionist Organization, originally called simply Zionist Organization, pre-dated the modern state of Israel. In part through successful efforts in the realm of *hasbara*, it was able to gain territory for a Jewish state. At the turn of the twentieth century, much territory in the world was controlled by outside powers, so the logical approach to gaining territory was to gain agreement from powers that controlled territory abroad. These powers needed to be convinced of the worth of the Zionist project. The Zionist Organization sought to establish territorial control in Palestine, a land inhabited by a population with long-standing roots there.

Success in this endeavor was by no means a foregone conclusion. The Zionist Organization could point only to a few settlements initiated there in the previous decades by handfuls of Jewish farmers from Russia. Even counting them, Jews constituted less than 5 percent of Palestine's population. The numerically dominant sector of the population was at that point in time referred to as Arab. That designation stemmed from conquest in the seventh century by Arabs invading from the east. Those Arabs spread their language and culture to a population that had inhabited the area from ancient times. At the turn of the twentieth century, the territory was under the political control of the Ottoman Turkish empire, which had been in place there since the sixteenth century. There was little reason to think that it would readily cede territory to the Zionist Organization.

Moreover, the Arab population of Palestine harbored its own aspirations for political control, so even if the Turkish government could somehow be convinced to acquiesce, the Zionist Organization would not be the only contender. Palestine had enjoyed a certain level of autonomy under Ottoman Turkish rule. The Arab population was predominantly rural. By the turn of the twentieth century, it had developed a commercialized agriculture with exports being shipped out to Europe and elsewhere from three Mediterranean ports. Olive production thrived on the hillsides, while grain crops flourished in the valleys. Orange groves dotted the coastal area. The major towns – Acre, Jerusalem, Hebron, and Nablus – housed a bourgeoning urban middle class. The Zionists harkened back to their predominance in a portion of Palestine in ancient times, asserting self-determination as their battle cry. Yet they confronted a strong claim to self-determination of the Arab population. Palestine in the late Ottoman Turkish period was a thriving territory that would not readily be displaced.

The sources of Zionism's eventual success were several. The Zionist Organization was Europe-based, hence might seek support from European governments. European powers would replace the Ottoman Turkish empire in the territory of Palestine after the Great War. Europe would come to call the shots on territorial disposition there. The Zionist Organization personnel were of European origin, while spokespersons for the opposing Arab side were not. The Zionist Organization prevailed at key junctures. At major turns, as the European powers made the decisions, the Zionist Organization outmaneuvered the Arabs.

A major factor in these successes was the Zionist Organization's ability to frame the issue for debate. In turn, the framing not infrequently involved convincing key international actors of underlying facts in a direction favorable to the Zionist Organization's positions and objectives. Its diplomacy has rested in large part on shaping facts in its favor. The Zionist Organization benefited from astute spokespersons who projected an image of integrity and credibility. Nonetheless, the task they faced was daunting. And it remained daunting even after the Jewish state was established.

A STATE UNDER SIEGE

"Ever since its creation in 1948," writes Aharon Klieman, a student of Israel's foreign relations, "Israel has had to counter diplomatic isolation deriving from the basic fact of Arab enmity."[7] Klieman says, "Israel still sees itself as besieged."[8] Whether one views that enmity as a product of anti-Jewish sentiment, or as a reaction to the actions of the Zionist movement, and of Israel itself, the enmity nonetheless colors Israel's international relationships.

In the diplomatic arena, the self-image that Israel projects is that of a state that may need to take extraordinary action to protect itself. An example is Israel's ratification in 1991 of the International Covenant on Civil and Political Rights. One provision of this instrument prohibits arbitrary detention. A person taken into custody must be informed of the reasons for the detention and must be brought promptly before a judicial officer holding the power to determine if the detention is justified.[9] Though desirous of joining the Covenant, the government of Israel said it could not be expected to comply with this provision. Under the Covenant, a state may enter a formal derogation from the provision on detention "in time of public emergency which threatens the life of the nation."[10]

A state of emergency was in fact authorized by Israel's parliament, the Knesset, within days after Israeli statehood was declared in May 1948, allowing for the nullification by the executive authority of any provision of law.[11] That state of emergency, declared at that time by the provisional government of Israel, remains in effect. Israel's derogation statement, filed with the United Nations in 1991, is instructive as an official self-portrayal of Israel's situation in the world. "Since its establishment," the derogation statement reads, "the State of Israel has been the victim of continuous threats and attacks on its very existence as well as on the life and property of its citizens. These have taken the form of threats of war, of actual armed attacks, and campaigns of terrorism resulting in the murder of and injury to human beings. In view of the above, the State of Emergency which was proclaimed in May 1948 has remained in force ever since." The statement recites that this situation constitutes a "public emergency," hence that Israel has "found it necessary" to take measures "for the defence of the State and for the protection of life and property, including the exercise of powers of arrest and detention."[12]

In 1999, the state of emergency was challenged before the Supreme Court of Israel by Israelis who said it was no longer necessary, and that it led to violation of human rights by the government. In 2012, however, the Supreme Court upheld the emergency as still being required. Judge Elyakim Rubinstein explained that "Israel is a normal country that is not normal." It is "not normal," he clarified, "because the threats to its existence still remain."[13]

One of the ways that the government of Israel has coped with the perceived threats and with having to prove itself to the international community is to devote considerable attention to portraying their actions and aims in terms that show Israel in a favorable light. This orientation in its diplomacy grew out of a body of diplomatic practice by the Zionist Organization. The story of *hasbara* in Israel's diplomacy begins with the diplomacy of the Zionist Organization.

2

Promises, Promises

For Jews in Europe who wanted territory for a Jewish state, the range of possible strategies was limited. They had no army to take territory. They focused on the states that controlled territory that might potentially serve the purpose. They hoped to convince some sovereign to cede territory. Theodor Herzl, a Viennese journalist, developed contacts with various governments and traveled widely in pursuing this endeavor. "I cling to the hope," Herzl wrote to the Grand Duke of Baden in 1896, "that the truly high-minded sovereigns of Europe will bestow their gracious protection on the cause."[1]

To have any chance of success, Herzl needed to provide some quid pro quo, or at least a potential quid pro quo. Giving territory for a Jewish state had to be in the interest of a sovereign.

Herzl explored a number of possible sites but early on focused on Palestine, then part of the sprawling Turkish empire in the Middle East. He approached Turkish officials, offering to buy Palestine. Herzl did not have ready access to the funds that would be necessary, but he hoped to raise cash from wealthy Jews in Europe. Herzl did have some leverage. Turkey was in dire straits, its economy faltering, hence the term "sick man of Europe" that came to be commonly applied. Turkey was heavily in debt to European countries, which had set up a debt administration system to manage repayment by Turkey. Herzl's idea was to pay off the debt. He planned, as he explained it, "to liberate Turkey from the Debt Control Commission."[2] This desperate situation opened the possibility that Sultan Abd al-Hamid might be receptive to the financial assistance Herzl was dangling.

Herzl's offer was attractive. It got the attention of Turkish officialdom. "The benefits in money and press support which you promise us are very great," one Turkish official told Herzl.[3] As discussions continued, Herzl came to realize that Turkish officials were not prepared actually to allow the carving out of territory for a Jewish state, so he modified his terminology with them. Even though Herzl did seek an actual state, he stopped calling what he wanted an "independent Jewish state" and instead told them he wanted an "autonomous vassal state" that would be "under the suzerainty of the Sultan."[4]

Herzl tried one other tack with the Sultan. Herzl suggested that Jews would help prevent an Arab uprising against the Empire.[5] Throughout Turkey's Arab territories, the population was chafing against Turkish rule. So this offer too was potentially attractive to the Turkish government. Jews would help the Sultan keep the Arabs quiet. Just how they would do that was not clear. Herzl had trouble selling the idea. Turkish officials were skeptical just what a population of Jews could do. Herzl never succeeded in convincing them that a Jewish population could curb an Arab uprising. The Sultan was unimpressed by the argument.

To make matters worse for his scheme for gaining territory from the Sultan, Herzl encountered difficulties on the financial front. He was promising vast sums of money to the Sultan, but without knowing if he could get it. In 1896 Herzl approached two wealthy financiers, Baron Maurice de Hirsch and Baron Edmond de Rothschild, asking for funds to bail Turkey out of its debt as a way of acquiring territory for a Jewish state. These two men had funded colonies to settle Russian Jews in Argentina and Palestine from the early 1880s. A Russian organization called Lovers of Zion promoted settlement outside Russia, in reaction to longtime discrimination against Jews in Russia. Jews were restricted both as to area of residence and as to occupation. The situation of Jews deteriorated after the 1881 assassination of the relatively liberal Tsar Alexander II. The new tsar, Alexander III, tightened restrictions on Jews. At that period as well, organized assaults (pogroms) were carried out against Jews in Russia.

The two financiers had been willing to provide financing for Jewish colonies, but neither took to Herzl's scheme of buying territory. They declined to commit funds. Despite this setback, and with only slim hope of acquiring the necessary funds, Herzl went on visiting Constantinople and promising funding to Turkey, whose officials did not realize Herzl might not have money behind him.[6]

Herzl was in any event making little headway. With his idea of buying territory producing no results, Herzl saw a need for a public-participation organization to agitate for a Jewish state. If he had a base of public support, Herzl surmised, he might be better able to make the case for a Jewish state. He wrote a small book to explain his concept. Published in German and in English, its title was *The Jewish State: An Attempt at a Modern Solution of the Jewish Question.* A founding congress was held in Basle, Switzerland, in 1897. It sent a message of greeting to Sultan Abd al-Hamid. From this conference was born the Zionist Organization. The name, taken from Mount Zion in Jerusalem, indicated which territory was contemplated for a Jewish state. The Russians who were already promoting settlement called themselves Lovers of Zion.

A BOON TO GERMANY AND TO EUROPE

Seeking a new way of approaching the Sultan, Herzl hit on the idea of enlisting one or another European government to lobby the Sultan on his behalf. He would try to convince them that a Jewish state in Palestine would benefit them. Germany figured most centrally in Herzl's thinking because it held influence in Constantinople. Kaiser Wilhelm II was keen on Germany pursuing economic penetration in Turkey, and German industrialists were already actively involved in his project.[7] Herzl approached Philipp Eulenburg, a German diplomat and a confidante of the Kaiser. Herzl asked Eulenburg to arrange a meeting for Herzl with Kaiser Wilhelm. To Eulenburg, Herzl stressed the importance such a meeting could have. "One word from the Kaiser," Herzl wrote to Eulenburg in a letter of September 21, 1898, "can have the greatest consequences for the shaping of things in the Orient." To Eulenburg, Herzl listed five points to show that a Jewish state in Palestine would benefit both the Turkish Empire and Europe.

First on Herzl's list was "The relief for the internal situation of the different countries if those parts of the Jewish population that are considered superfluous are diverted. At present they are supplying the revolutionary parties with leaders and lieutenants." Jews were prominent in antimonarchist and socialist movements. If they left for Palestine, Europe's monarchs would be secure.

Second, Herzl averred, the "drainage" of Jews from Europe would eventually "come to a standstill along with anti-Semitism itself." European governments would no longer have to cope with anti-Semitism. "For the stimulus to emigrate, which, as it is, is lacking or only slight in the upper economic strata, would then be eliminated." So the Jews who would leave for Palestine would be the poor Jews, and with anti-Semitism diminished the wealthy Jews would be more secure in Europe.

Third, Herzl focused on what he said were advantages that would flow to the Turkish empire. "For Turkey," he wrote, "the influx of an intelligent, economically energetic national element would mean an unmistakable strengthening." Financial benefits would flow: "Turkey would have direct benefits (a large payment of money on our part, and possibly a further improvement of her finances) as well as indirect benefits, through the general increase in commerce."

Fourth, "[t]he return of even the semi-Asiatic Jews under the leadership of thoroughly modern persons must undoubtedly mean the restoration to health of this neglected corner of the Orient. Civilization and order would be brought there. Thus the migration of the Jews would eventually be an effective protection of the Christians in the Orient." European powers had long shown concern about the status of Christians in the Turkish Empire. The Jews would be a counterweight against the Muslims, with resultant benefit to the Christians.

Fifth, Herzl turned to transportation. "The needs of all of non-Russian Europe call for the creation of a direct Southern route to Asia: that is, a railroad from the Mediterranean to the Persian Gulf. The Jews could and must build this great road of the nations, which, if undertaken differently might call forth the most serious rivalries."[8] A possible rail connection to the region, extending east to Baghdad, had been on the agenda of European governments for some time. The Sultan too was interested, because rail lines could move troops quickly if needed to suppress unrest in the Empire's Arab territories.[9] Herzl was promising Jewish help in the construction.

Herzl prepared a letter for the Kaiser, in which he elaborated on how Zionism would benefit Turkey economically. Herzl was giving the Kaiser arguments that Herzl hoped the Kaiser would use with the Sultan. "We are honestly convinced," Herzl wrote, "that the implementation of the Zionist plan must mean welfare for Turkey as well. Energies and material resources will be brought to the country; a magnificent fructification of desolate areas may easily be foreseen; and from all this there will arise more happiness and more culture for many human beings. We are planning to establish a Jewish Land-Company for Syria and Palestine, which is to undertake the great project, and request the protection of the German Kaiser for this company."[10] Herzl met the Kaiser in 1898 while the Kaiser was visiting Jerusalem. The encounter ended with no commitment on Germany's side. The Kaiser did raise the issue with the Sultan but with little result.

Even though his promises were making no dent with Turkish officials, Herzl kept up his efforts. Herzl visited the Sultan in 1901 and renewed his offer to find funds to pay off the debt the Turkish empire owed in Europe.

Herzl recorded his efforts in his diary. "The thorn, as I see it," Herzl told the Sultan, "is your public debt. If that could be removed, Turkey would be able to unfold afresh its vitality, in which I have great faith." When the Sultan said that such help would be welcome, Herzl averred, "I would have this operation carried out by my friends on all the stock exchanges of Europe."[11] Herzl had no commitments from any friends in the stock exchanges.

The Zionist Organization came in for ridicule at the time from Zionists who doubted that the approach of offering money to the Sultan would produce results. Ahad Ha'am, a Russian Jew who espoused Zionism, regarded Herzl as overly materialistic in his approach. Ha'am castigated the Zionist leadership for having let rumors spread in 1901 that the Sultan had given Herzl a favorable reception, but only after a time did they let it be known that a huge amount of money would be required, an amount not likely to be raised. "Leadership on these lines," Ha'am wrote, "cannot satisfy those who have a liking for the plain truth."[12]

Even though his prospect for a large infusion of capital from Jewish sources was dim, Herzl kept telling the Sultan that a Palestine under Jewish control would prosper. Unlike the normal outside investor, he told the Sultan during his 1901 interview, Jews would not only invest in Palestine but would remain permanently. "All this beautiful land needs is the industrial skill of our people. The Europeans who usually come here enrich themselves quickly and then rush off again with their spoils. An entrepreneur," Herzl said, "ought to remain in the country where he has acquired his wealth."[13] In the end nothing came of Herzl's approaches to the Turkish empire by the time he died in 1904. The Sultan would not be persuaded to give up territory.[14]

A "TURKISH-GERMAN GIBRALTAR"

During World War I, Zionist Organization representatives made a renewed effort with the Turkish empire. To Jamal Pasha, the Turkish commander, they made the same arguments that Herzl had tried unsuccessfully. The Turkish empire, after its anticipated victory, would profit from Jewish financial assistance and colonizing activity. Turkey was still coping with rising nationalism on the part of the Arabs over whom Turkey ruled. Zionist envoys argued that a population of Jews would provide a pro-Turkey counterweight to the Arabs.[15]

As well, Zionist representatives again courted the Kaiser, who was Turkey's ally in the war. To the Kaiser they argued that they could "establish, on the eastern shore of the Mediterranean, a modern cultural and commercial center which will be both directly and indirectly a prop of Germanism." Robert Lichtheim, the Zionist Organization's agent in Turkey, explained his strategy to a colleague in Berlin. Lichtheim said that, in approaching the Turkish authorities, he "brought every argument to bear – the German language and business connections of the Jews; their pro-Turkish sentiment, their possibilities as a counterweight to the Arabs; their international influence in the Press and finance; the gratitude of all Jews – for example, in America – towards Germany if she supports us; the political significance of a cultural base for Germany as the future leading Power in the Near East." A "Palestine by Jewish immigration," he asserted, "could become a politico-commercial base, a Turkish-German Gibraltar, on the frontiers of the Anglo-Arab ocean."[16]

It was even suggested by Lichtheim that ten thousand Polish Jews could be recruited to come fight for Turkey if Jewish colonization of Palestine after the war could be promised. However, this project was soon abandoned on the Zionist side along with the entire effort with the Turkish empire. The Zionist leadership calculated that they had a better chance of getting backing from Britain than from Turkey.[17] A Jewish corps was formed to fight instead on the British side in the ill-fated incursion at Gallipoli in 1915, and, later in the war, in the more successful campaign in Palestine itself.[18]

BRINGING BACK CIVILIZATION

Making promises and predictions became a staple of Zionist diplomacy. The situation in which the Zionist Organization found itself required this approach. The Zionist Organization had to project concrete advantages to governments it solicited. Its diplomats engaged in what in the advertising industry is called puffery. They made promises that might or might not have been possible to keep. They pushed to the limit their predictions of the benefits that would accrue to a potential sponsoring power. With European governments, Zionist diplomats had the argument that the Jews who would settle in a Jewish state were European. Putting them in territory under the control or influence of a European power might enhance that power's status there.

As the world war unfolded, the focus of Zionist diplomacy shifted from Germany and Turkey to its enemy, Great Britain. Britain was seen as a potential new force in Palestine as it battled Turkey. In Britain, the Zionist Organization enjoyed the benefit of an influential spokesperson in

Chaim Weizmann, a transplanted Russian Jew who was doing important war work for Britain. In 1914, Weizmann lobbied C. P. Scott, editor of the influential newspaper *Manchester Guardian*, to the Zionist cause. In a letter to Scott, Weizmann argued how Zionism would benefit Britain. Weizmann projected a British victory over Turkey and the possibility that Britain might take over Palestine. "Should Palestine fall within the British sphere of influence," he wrote, "and should Britain encourage a Jewish settlement there, as a British dependency, we could have in twenty to thirty years a million Jews out there, perhaps more; they would develop the country, bring back civilization to it and form a very effective guard for the Suez Canal."[19]

In Weizmann, Zionism found a powerful advocate. During the war, Weizmann worked in biochemistry for the British Admiralty. Weizmann developed a propellant for artillery that made a significant contribution to Britain's war effort. This work earned Weizmann honor in Britain and ready entrée to the upper echelons of the British government.[20] Weizmann enjoyed access to David Lloyd George, who in 1915 was Minister of Munitions, and who in that capacity benefited directly from Weizmann's contributions in biochemistry. Weizmann took advantage of that connection to press Lloyd George on the advisability of a Jewish Palestine and how it would benefit Britain. In 1916, to Weizmann's good fortune, Lloyd George became prime minister. By that time, as result of Weizmann's ministrations, Lloyd George was firmly committed to Zionism.[21] A practical man, Weizmann understood that Britain would not support Zionism unless British interests would be served. So he framed his arguments in terms of British national interests. Weizmann was gifted in the art of persuasion. One chronicler of Weizmann's work describes him as "the most potent advocate Zionism ever had," possessing "an instinctive gift for diplomacy." Weizmann's "charm of manner captivated those who he wished to seduce." "He knew what the other man most wanted to hear."[22]

LEVERAGING A WAR

Chaim Weizmann wanted Britain to commit itself to promoting Zionist aims in Palestine when, as he anticipated, the Turkish empire would be driven from Palestine. But it was unclear how the Zionist aim should be framed. The Zionist Organization wanted Palestine as a Jewish state. But calling for a state would be controversial, as it would threaten the position of the existing Arab population of Palestine. So Weizmann downplayed the

Zionist Organization's aim. In a May 1917 speech to the English Zionist Federation, Weizmann cautioned against calling immediately for a Jewish state in Palestine. Weizmann noted that "one hears from our friends, both Jewish and non-Jewish, that it is the endeavor of the Zionist Movement immediately to create a Jewish State in Palestine." Zionists, said Weizmann, should practice "safe statesmanship." A Jewish state was their "final ideal," he said, but it should be achieved in stages. Weizmann anticipated that, after a successful conclusion of the war, Palestine would be "protected" by Britain. "Under the wing of this Power Jews will be able to develop, and to set up the administrative machinery which, while not interfering with the legitimate interests of the non-Jewish population, would enable us to carry out the Zionist scheme." "His Majesty's Government," Weizmann predicted, "is ready to support our plans."[23] A statement calling for a state might backfire. A pledge couched more ambiguously would suffice.

Weizmann pulled out all the stops in telling the British government how support for Zionism would benefit Britain. His main argument went to an immediate and compelling British interest – winning the war against Germany. In the early months of 1917, the prospects for British and Allied troops were bleak. Britain needed any advantage it might gain over Germany. Articles in the German press called for Germany to retain Palestine under its protection, should it prevail in the war. The issue of Zionism had already come up in Germany. The German Government was contemplating a pro-Zionist declaration, to rally support among Jews for its cause in the war. Weizmann urged the British Foreign Office to gain the march by declaring for Zionism before Germany did.[24]

Political upheaval in Russia provided Weizmann with an additional line of argument. Russia was Britain's ally in the war and kept Germany's forces engaged in the east. But in 1917, the tsar was overthrown, and Russia's willingness to stay the course was in doubt. The Bolshevik Party, which was vying for power, threatened to pull out of the war completely. By mid-1917, British officials sought ways to convince the Jews of Russia to look more favorably on Britain, and thereby hopefully pressure the Russian Government to stay in the fight. Russian Jews might be willing to stand firm against Germany if they thought they were fighting for a Jewish state in Palestine. There was a base of support for Zionism among Russian Jews that could be exploited. Britain decided to use Zionism to counter pacificism. According to Arnold Toynbee, who then worked in the Foreign Office, Britain saw Zionism as a "trump card" against Germany.[25]

Weizmann plotted a strategy to exploit Britain's desire to woo Russia's Jews. A Zionist congress was scheduled for June 1917 in Petrograd.

Nahum Sokolow, who headed the London Zionist office, was a Russian.[26] Weizmann and the British Zionists wanted Sokolow to go to Russia for the congress to speak favorably about Britain and to say that Britain favored Zionism.[27] For various reasons, Weizmann's plan did not come to fruition. In the event, Sokolow did not attend the congress. The conference adopted resolutions referring vaguely to a national center in Palestine but with no mention of Britain as a potential sponsor.[28]

Despite this setback, Weizmann pressed the situation in Russia on the British government. He promised to mobilize Russian Jews to back Britain, if Britain would declare for Zionism. The promise impressed David Lloyd George, who by then was Prime Minister. "The Zionist leaders gave us a definite promise that if the Allies committed themselves to giving facilities for the establishment of a National Home for the Jews in Palestine," Lloyd George would later recall, "they would do their best to rally to the Allied cause Jewish sentiment and support throughout the world."[29]

The British government began planning for a declaration on Zionism, with war aims as the motivating factor. Drafts were circulated. A. J. Balfour, the Secretary of State for Foreign Affairs in Lloyd George's government, told the War Cabinet that "the vast majority of Jews in Russia and America, as, indeed, all over the world, now appeared to be favourable to Zionism. If we could make a declaration favourable to such an ideal, we should be able to carry on extremely useful propaganda both in Russia and America."[30]

A declaration was issued on November 2, 1917, calling for a "Jewish national home" in Palestine. The declaration would come to bear Balfour's name. Weizmann conferred with British officials to plot how to use it. A mission to Russia was planned. Zionist leaders of Russian background would go to Russia to convince Jews to support Britain.[31] Britain airdropped Yiddish-language translations of the declaration over German and Russian territory, proclaiming, "The Allies are giving the Land of Israel to the people of Israel."[32] The German government, understanding that Britain had scored a coup, reacted by calling in Jewish representatives and promising to make improvements for Jews in their lives in Germany. Balfour feared a pro-Jewish move by Germany.

The Balfour Declaration did find resonance in some sectors of Jewry in Russia.[33] And Weizmann did make some effort to carry through on his promise to rally Russia's Jews for Britain. He wired Israel Rosov, a Zionist functionary in Petrograd, noting the "providential coincidence of British and Jewish interests" that brought about the declaration. By so saying, Weizmann underscored his understanding that Britain had issued the Balfour Declaration for the reasons he had urged upon it, namely, that it would help Britain win the war. Weizmann urged Rosov "to strengthen pro-British sympathies in Russian Jewry."[34]

But just at this time, the government in Russia that had taken power from the tsar was in turn ousted by the Bolsheviks, who were intent on leaving the war. The Bolsheviks opened peace talks with Germany and signed a separate peace, the Treaty of Brest-Litovsk. The treaty declared "that the state of war between them has ceased."[35] Russia was out of the war. Russia's Jews had not kept it in.

At a Zionist gathering in 1927, Weizmann reflected on the Balfour Declaration, saying again that Britain had issued it in response to his argument that it would help against Germany. "We Jews," he said, "got the Balfour Declaration quite unexpectedly; or, in other words, we are the greatest war profiteers." Weizmann also acknowledged that in 1917 he had no way to follow through on the promises he made to Prime Minister Lloyd George to help Britain win the war. Jewish support for Zionism was simply too thin. "The Balfour Declaration of 1917 was built on air," he said. Weizmann admitted that Zionism's backing among Jews was uncertain. "I trembled lest the British Government would call me and ask: 'Tell us, what is this Zionist Organisation? Where are they, your Zionists?'" Said Weizmann, "The Jews, they knew, were against us; we stood alone on a little island, a tiny group of Jews with a foreign past."[36]

CAPITALIZING ON BALFOUR

Even as the world war continued, Weizmann began planning for the post-war disposition, to ensure that the promise of the Balfour Declaration would not be forgotten. In a January 1918 letter to Louis Brandeis, the US Supreme Court justice who had headed the Zionist organization in the United States, Weizmann assessed the chances for a favorable outcome in Palestine. Weizmann looked ahead to peace negotiations that would follow the war. "Much will depend," he wrote to Brandeis, "upon our activity and achievements in Palestine between now and the Peace Conference." Weizmann saw a need to avoid doing anything that "might be construed by the world as a hidden desire of Great Britain to *annexe* Palestine by simply using the Jews as a blind." So, he told Brandeis, the Zionist Organization had to be cautious until it got what it wanted out of the anticipated peace conference. In particular, that meant going slow on land purchases. "Any acquisition of land on a large scale at the present moment," he wrote, "would probably present great difficulties."[37]

Purchase of large tracts of agricultural land from Arab owners was a sore point with the Palestine Arabs, as purchase typically resulted in the eviction of long-term Arab tenant farmers, depriving them of their livelihood.[38] The Jewish National Fund, the Zionists' land-purchasing organization, was actively seeking agricultural land. Ahad Ha'am had noted already in 1912 that "many natives of Palestine," by whom he meant Palestine Arabs, "look askance, quite naturally, at the selling of land to 'strangers.'"[39] Weizmann wanted large tracts as a precursor to a territorial claim, but it was agreed within the Zionist Organization that for the time being, Zionist land purchases in Palestine would be limited to outlying areas that would not infringe on tracts currently being cultivated by Arab farmers.[40] The British authorities realized the negative impact of Jewish National Fund land purchases. In 1918, as they took control in Palestine from Turkey, one of their first measures was a moratorium on land sales, in order to protect tenant farmers from eviction.[41] They worried that these sales could create a sizable landless class among the Arabs.[42]

Weizmann conceived a plan to solidify implementation of the Balfour Declaration. He convinced the British Government to set up a quasi-governmental agency to promote Zionism. It would be called the Zionist Commission, and it would be attached to the British army as it took full control of Palestine. The commission would serve as a link between the Jewish population and the British authorities in Palestine. Weizmann argued to the British Government that such a commission would enhance the propaganda value for Britain of the Balfour Declaration.[43] The war was not yet over, and its outcome remained an open question.

Beyond the reasons Weizmann posed to the British government for the commission, Weizmann hoped that a Zionist presence in Palestine would push Britain in a Zionist direction. He also thought that a Zionist presence backed by the British government would show the Jews of Palestine that Zionism was a viable force, and that the British were committed to it. This was no small matter, because the sympathies of Palestine's Jews were by no means on the side of Zionism.

Britain complied with Weizmann's entreaties and appointed a Zionist Commission, naming Weizmann as its head.[44] Weizmann and the Zionist Commission departed for Palestine in March 1918. Weizmann still worried about a backlash from the Zionists' aim of Jewish statehood. Weizmann instructed his colleagues in the Zionist Commission to soft-pedal statehood.

While Weizmann made clear to them that the aim of Zionism was a Jewish state in Palestine, the less they spoke of it the better.[45]

While in Palestine as head of the Zionist Commission, Weizmann came face to face with the negative view that the Palestine Arabs held of the Zionist enterprise. Palestine's Arabs were fearful of what Zionism might mean for them. Weizmann gave the impression of being solicitous of the Arab population of Palestine, but he viewed the Palestine Arabs as a population to be managed. While still in Palestine with the Zionist Commission, Weizmann revealed his attitude to the Palestine Arabs in a letter he wrote to Balfour. In the letter, Weizmann analyzed the attitude of the Palestine Arabs toward the Turkey-Britain hostilities, which were still ongoing. Weizmann provided advice for Britain on how to convince the Arabs to back Britain over Turkey. He said that the fact that the Arabs were not firmly committed to one side or the other "has naturally made the British authorities rather nervous, and, knowing as they do the treacherous nature of the Arab, they have to watch carefully and constantly that nothing should happen which might give the Arabs the slightest grievance or ground of complaint." He said that "the Arabs have to be 'nursed' lest they should stab the Army in the back." "The Arab," he wrote, "screams as often as he can and blackmails as much as he can."[46] Weizmann saw no need for or purpose in negotiating with the Arabs.[47] In a letter written from Palestine to his wife, Weizmann indicated he did not expect to negotiate. "I feel that I do not have to concern myself with the Arabs anymore," he wrote. "We have explained our point of view publicly and openly: *c'est à prendre ou à laisser*," he concluded in French.[48] The Arabs could "take it or leave it." In public, Weizmann gave no hint of his opinion of the Arabs or how he planned to disregard their wishes.

Others within the Zionist movement took a more nuanced and conciliatory approach to the Palestine Arabs. They had an appreciation for the fear of the Palestine Arabs of losing their country. Weizmann was not of that stripe. Like those speaking for many human groups that have suffered serious wrongs, Weizmann focused solely on protection of his group. Ahad Ha'am, who visited Palestine in 1891, criticized his fellow Russian Jews who had come as settlers for this orientation, even before Herzl and Weizmann appeared on the scene. Ha'am wrote of the settlers, "slaves they were in their diasporas, and suddenly they find themselves with unlimited freedom." Ha'am said they treated the Arabs as they themselves had been treated. "They deal with the Arabs with hostility and cruelty."[49] Whatever may have been behind Weizmann's inclinations as he plotted how to deal with the Arabs of Palestine, Zionism was in a precarious political situation as it sought major power support for its aspiration to territory. Weizmann needed to depict Zionism's aims as being consistent with the well-being of the Palestine Arabs.

3

Pranks in Paris and Geneva

By mid-1918, the fortunes of war turned against Germany and the Turkish empire. By year's end, armistices were signed with the Allies, and British forces were in control of Palestine. Plans were aired for an international organization of states that would preside over the hopefully peaceful world emerging from the devastation of trench warfare. A central element of those plans was an anti-colonialist plank. The victorious allies, in particular France and Britain, would not take as colonies the Arab territories they were now occupying. But neither would they set them free. Instead, France and Britain would remain in control, but subject to the scrutiny of the new international organization.

A conference was called in the Paris suburb of Versailles that would lead to the formation of a League of Nations. Peace treaties would be elaborated, and a mechanism arranged for oversight of the territories changing hands, including Palestine under British administration.

The Zionist Organization, having gained endorsement for Zionism from Britain, now maneuvered to see that endorsement solidified in the arrangements being made at the Paris Peace Conference for the future of the Arab territories.

Success for the Zionist Organization was far from assured. Palestine Arabs convened in a Palestine Arab Congress in January 1919 and made plans for Palestine to become independent, either by itself or together with Syria.[1] Were those plans to materialize, Zionism would have little role in Palestine. The Allies conferring in Paris, moreover, were writing a covenant for the League of Nations that would enshrine self-determination as a watchword. The wishes of local populations were to occupy center stage in the administration of the territories that were changing hands, in particular the Arab territories being carved out of the Turkish empire.

That orientation might be the death knell for the efforts of the Zionist Organization at gaining territory in Palestine.

At the same time, Britain's desire to retain control in Palestine, even if under oversight by the League of Nations, gave the Zionist Organization an opening. A Jewish deputation was granted a hearing at the Paris Peace Conference. The Zionist Organization was invited to testify before what was called the Council of Ten, a committee made up of two representatives each from Britain, Italy, France, Japan, and the United States. The Zionist Organization marshaled arguments to make its case. It submitted a written memorandum, asking for recognition of "the historic title of the Jewish people to Palestine and the right of the Jews to reconstitute in Palestine their National Home." The memorandum suggested that the League of Nations should take charge of Palestine. Using a term that was only just then entering the international lexicon, the memorandum asked that a "mandate" be established by the League over Palestine, with Great Britain as "mandatory." The Balfour Declaration would be written into Britain's obligations, the memorandum recited.[2]

PUFFING UP THE RANKS

A small group of Zionist Organization representatives converged on Paris in February 1919 to make their case. The Zionist Organization needed to convince the Council of Ten of the advisability of Zionist aims for Palestine. One element of the argument was that they had a movement behind them. If there were no interest among Jews in enhancing a Jewish presence in Palestine, it would make little sense for the League of Nations to back Zionism. The Zionist Organization representatives tried to convince the Council of Ten of high numbers of Jews who supported Zionism. Nahum Sokolow, one of the leading figures in the Zionist Organization, introduced himself to the Council of Ten as representing "the Jewish population of Palestine."[3] Fortunately for Sokolow, he was not challenged on this claim. Sokolow had never lived in Palestine. He had no connection to the Jews there. Zionism had no base of support in Palestine. To the Jews of Palestine, the Zionists were outsiders. One segment of the Jewish population of Palestine was ultra-Orthodox and opposed secular Jewish autonomy.[4] An influx from Europe, many Palestine Jews feared, might engender resentment against them.[5] Sokolow's claim to represent the Jews of Palestine was a wild mis-characterization.

Chaim Weizmann, who was part of the Zionist Organization delegation, had written down his impressions of Palestine Jews during a visit he made to Palestine in 1907. Zionism was not on their agenda. Half the Jewish population of Palestine," Weizmann wrote, "were pious Jews living on money sent to them from Jews elsewhere. Weizmann called them a "useless and retarding element." They focused solely on their individual endeavors. "They had not envisaged a process of national development, in which Jewish workers and Jewish landowners would form harmonious parts of a larger program." Their "few colonies were detached and scattered; they did not form blocks of territory."[6] These Jews were hardly represented by the Zionist Organization.

Sokolow did not limit his claim of representation to the Jews of Palestine, however. He purported to represent world Jewry. He declared that the Zionist delegation at the Paris Peace Conference was fulfilling a role of historical magnitude. With the Zionist participation in the conference, he told the Council of Ten, "the solemn hour awaited during 18 centuries by the Jewish people had, at length, arrived." The Zionist delegates "had come," he said, "to claim their historic rights to Palestine."[7] So Sokolow claimed to be voicing the desires of "the Jewish people" as a whole. This depiction was a gross exaggeration. At the time, Zionism was in its infancy, despite the promotion it gained from Britain with the Balfour Declaration. Most Jews saw no need to give up their lives in Europe or elsewhere to move to an uncertain situation in a distant territory.

Another dubious claim of support was made by Menachem Ussishkin, another Zionist Organization representative, when he spoke to the Council of Ten. Ussishkin was from Russia.[8] He introduced himself as "President of the National Assembly representing 3,000,000 Jews of South Russia, an Assembly which, in the month of November last adopted a resolution proclaiming the historic rights of the Jewish people to Palestine."[9] So Ussishkin was claiming three million favoring Zionism. The group Ussishkin headed was of Ukrainian Jews. The group had formed only a few months earlier, in 1918, in the city of Kiev.[10] The overthrow of the tsar in Russia had allowed Zionist activity to come out in the open, with street demonstrations in major cities, so there was some growth in support for Zionism.[11] But the Jews in Ukraine in total numbered only 1.5 million by one estimation,[12] two million by another.[13] Of these, perhaps 300,000 supported Zionism.[14] Ussishkin's claim of three million adherents of Zionism had no basis in reality. Ussishkin was not questioned by the Council of Ten on his claim.

THE "EMPTY SPACES" OF PALESTINE

Among the Zionist Organization representatives at the Paris Peace Conference, Weizmann made the most extended speech. Weizmann did not take a back seat to his colleagues in exaggerating to the Council of Ten the support that Zionism enjoyed among Jews. Like Sokolow, Weizmann claimed to represent world Jewry. He announced that he "spoke for 96% of the Jews of the world, who shared the views which he had endeavoured to express."[15] How Weizmann came up with such an exact percentage one can only guess. Most Jews at the time rejected Zionism.

Weizmann was no more forthright in what he related to the Council of Ten about what Zionism would mean for Palestine. In his presentation, Weizmann focused on Russia, painting a dire picture of life for Jews at that time in Russia. Zionism, he said, presented the only solution.[16] But that point did not substantiate the advisability of a Jewish state in Palestine. Weizmann was asked by US Secretary of State Robert Lansing, who sat on the Council of Ten, what he envisaged for Jews in Palestine. Weizmann was quick to answer that the Zionist Organization was not asking for a state. "The Zionist organization," he replied to Lansing, "did not want an autonomous Jewish government." This response was in line with the admonition Weizmann had given to his colleagues in the Zionist Commission to avoid talking about a Jewish state.

Weizmann answered cautiously. He told Lansing that for the present he hoped there would be a mandatory power administering Palestine "which would render it possible to send into Palestine 70 to 80,000 Jews annually." Gradually, a "nationality" would build up "which would be as Jewish as the French nation was French and the British nation British." Later, "when the Jews formed the large majority, they would be ripe to establish such a Government as would answer to the state of the development of the country."[17]

As of 1919, Jews formed only 10 percent of the population in Palestine. So a transition to a Jewish majority would have seemed difficult to accomplish without displacing Arabs. Aware that the League might balk at Zionism because of its threat to Arab self-determination, Weizmann tried to convince the Council of Ten that Jewish migration would not harm the Arabs. Weizmann's approach was to say that "Zionists wished to settle Jews in the empty spaces of Palestine."[18] He said that the population of Palestine was sparse. He gave figures.

Weizmann claimed that there were only 10 to 15 persons per square kilometer in Palestine. To arrive at that figure, Weizmann had to be including in his calculation the Negev Desert, only sparsely inhabited, which constituted a major segment of the territory of Palestine. That meant that the figure he gave on population density was highly misleading. He was grossly understating population density in the settled, arable areas of Palestine. Jews migrating to Palestine were not going to "empty spaces." Many went to urban centers like Jerusalem. In the rural areas, as we saw in the last chapter, the Jewish National Fund sought prime agricultural land to purchase but had temporarily drawn back in these purchases precisely to fool the League of Nations.

Despite Weizmann's obfuscation, he scored points with the Council of Ten. A recent Israeli writer was able to say that Weizmann's appearance in Paris was "the pinnacle of Weizmann's diplomatic achievements."[19] Weizmann met with Italian and British representatives privately and got the impression, doubtless correct, that his group's statements were favorably received.[20] Weizmann and the Zionist Organization got what they wanted from the Allies. Britain would remain in Palestine with a mandate to implement Zionism.[21] This was no small achievement, because the League's Covenant, as finalized at Paris, provided for a system of mandates and purported to give a central role to the populations involved. The Covenant provision on the mandates in the Arab world recited, "Certain communities formerly belonging to the Turkish Empire have reached a stage of development where their existence as independent nations can be provisionally recognized subject to the rendering of administrative advice and assistance by a Mandatory until such time as they are able to stand alone." Then followed an important proviso: "The wishes of these communities must be a principal consideration in the selection of the Mandatory."[22]

But Weizmann and the Zionist Organization succeeded in getting the League to violate its own principle in that regard. The population of Palestine was desperate to keep Britain out. The Arabs did not want Britain in control, because of Britain's commitment to Jewish migration to Palestine. The Arabs of Palestine were surveyed by a commission sent by US President Woodrow Wilson. They were asked about their preference for a mandatory power, if a mandate were established over Palestine. The clear choice was the United States.[23]

The Zionist Organization, aware that the United States might be a candidate for mandatory, took a strong stance against it. A tract published in 1919 by the Zionist Organization in London asserted that the United States would be inappropriate as mandatory in Palestine. The reason, it was explained, was that United States follows the principle of majority rule in politics. That principle, the tract continued, would be devastating to Zionism, because the numerical majority in Palestine was Arab.[24] This was a strange argument to make in so public a fashion. The Zionist Organization was saying that for its aims to be accomplished, democracy had to be ignored.

Despite the clear disregard of the League Covenant, Britain was nonetheless installed as mandatory. The mandate instrument that would shortly be issued to Britain by the League did not simply leave it to Britain to decide what to do about Zionism. Rather, it required Britain to implement the Balfour Declaration. The Palestine Mandate made explicit reference in a preamble paragraph to "the declaration originally made on November 2nd, 1917, by the Government of His Britannic Majesty," and then recited that Britain "shall be responsible for placing the country under such political, administrative and economic conditions as will secure the establishment of the Jewish national home, as laid down in the preamble, and the development of self-governing institutions, and also for safeguarding the civil and religious rights of all the inhabitants of Palestine, irrespective of race and religion."[25] The League of Nations, subject to manipulation of facts and deception on the part of the Zionist Organization, had handed the Zionist Organization a clear victory.

CONCEALING THE TENSION

To keep Britain and other mandatory powers to their obligations, the League of Nations set up a monitoring mechanism. Called the Permanent Mandates Commission, it was asked to ensure that the interests of the populations under mandate were being served. Mandatory powers were required to file reports, which were then examined by the Commission in an oral proceeding in which a representative of the mandatory power could be cross-examined. These proceedings were published and were made available to the public.[26]

The legal instrument that formed the basis of these proceedings with respect to Palestine was the Palestine Mandate. Under this document, Britain was to govern in the interests of the population and prepare it for independence. Because of the clause about a Jewish national home, the Palestine mandate provided for a role in the governance of Palestine to a body that would represent the Jews, both those in Palestine and those elsewhere. The Palestine Mandate recited, "An appropriate Jewish agency shall be recognised as a public body for the purpose of advising and co-operating with the Administration of Palestine in such economic, social and other matters as may affect the establishment of the Jewish national home and the interests of the Jewish population in Palestine, and, subject always to the control of the Administration to assist and take part in the development of the country." The Palestine Mandate gave the Zionist Organization this role. "The Zionist organization, so long as its organization and constitution are in the opinion of the Mandatory appropriate, shall be recognised as such agency. It shall take steps in consultation with His Britannic Majesty's government to secure the co-operation of all Jews who are willing to assist in the establishment of the Jewish national home."[27] In its relations with the League, the Zionist Organization would be called the Jewish Agency for Palestine. Securing this role was a major coup for Weizmann, since the Zionist Organization, as already seen, had little base among the Jews of Palestine, and only marginal support among Jews living elsewhere.

The arrangements for oversight by the Permanent Mandates Commission suffered from serious flaws that the Zionist Organization was quick to exploit. The Commission was ill-equipped to assess the impact on Palestine of the Zionist project. As one historian of the Commission said, it "was handicapped in that none of its members had an extensive background of experience in the Middle East."[28] In addition to the former Ottoman territories, the Commission dealt with territories in Asia and Africa. For those regions of the world, European governments had functionaries who had served there, administering European colonies. The states chosen to appoint to membership on the Commission were in the main states possessing colonies.[29] Most of the individuals appointed to the Commission had experience in colonial administration.[30] But the Arab territories had been under the Turkish empire, so there were no Europeans with hands-on experience. As a result, the Commission included no "real specialists on the Middle East."[31]

No provision was made for the Commission to conduct on-site visits, so even as the Commission conducted its business, it did not develop expertise on Palestine.[32] When a visit to Palestine was suggested by one Commission member, other members objected that a visit would be an affront to Britain as mandatory, or that a visiting delegation would draw protest from locals unhappy with the way Britain was carrying out its mandate.[33] Reliance solely on the written documentation supplied by the mandatory powers and the affected populations, however, limited the Commission's knowledge of the situation on the ground.[34]

Representatives of the populations of mandate territories could send written communications, and they were not prohibited from establishing informal contact with Commission members. Chaim Weizmann early on sought informal contact.[35] He cultivated connections with individual Commission members, to urge them to pressure Britain to promote Zionist settlement in Palestine.[36] He sought them out on a social basis.[37] He visited often with Pierre Orts, the Commission's long-time chair, at Orts' home in Brussels. Weizmann reported that Orts had "a sympathetic and critical appreciation of our efforts, and a deep understanding of the bearing of the Jewish problem on the National Home."[38]

Weizmann established a critical connection with the League's central figure in the administration of the mandates.[39] William Rappard served in the League Secretariat as Director of the Mandates Section.[40] In that capacity, Rappard oversaw the establishment of the Permanent Mandates Commission and organized its sessions.[41] In 1925, Rappard resigned from the Secretariat, but his role had been so crucial that the Commission decided to add him as a member of the Commission.[42] Rappard helped Weizmann maneuver through the League bureaucracy. Weizmann wrote that Rappard served as "a helpful guide to us, and to me in particular, in the inner workings of the League."[43] Through his contact with Weizmann, Rappard became a supporter of Zionism and would serve as an informal advisor to him on strategy.[44]

Weizmann took advantage of the deficit of knowledge of the Commission's members. Reprising his pitch to the Council of Ten, Weizmann painted a rosy picture for the Commission about what Zionism would mean for Palestine. The Zionist project was compatible, he averred, with the interests of the Arab population of Palestine. In a 1930 memorandum to the Commission, the Jewish Agency had to acknowledge Arab actions that occurred in 1929 to express opposition to Zionism, but the Agency asserted that "up to the middle of 1928, Arab-Jewish relations had for some years been steadily improving."[45] The Jewish Agency was trying to minimize Arab opposition to Zionism. But as European Jews migrated into Palestine, the Palestine Arabs increasingly feared losing their country.[46]

Arab discontent with the Mandate and with Zionism was constant and intense. Overt opposition surfaced from time to time on the ground in Palestine, leading Britain to conduct inquiries about the impact of Jewish migration on the Arab population. Zionist Organization functionaries argued that the immigration of Jews to Palestine benefited the Arab population. In 1930, the Histadrut, the Jewish labor organization in Palestine, affiliated with the Jewish Agency, claimed to a British commission of inquiry that "our immigration and settlement, far from ousting other elements, has actually spelt more plentiful employment and a higher standard of life for the rest of the population."[47] At the same time, however, the Zionist movement discouraged the hiring of Arabs by Jewish employers and enterprises, insisting instead on a policy of "Jewish labor." It was considered that a Jewish economy could be created in Palestine only if Jewish employers hired exclusively Jews.[48]

The 1929 constitution of the Jewish Agency specified that only Jews were to be hired on land purchased by the Jewish National Fund, which held much of the Jewish-owned land in Palestine. The constitution stated that "the Agency shall promote agricultural colonization based on Jewish labour, and in all works and undertaking carried out or furthered by the Agency, it shall be a matter of principle that Jewish labour shall be employed."[49] This policy was enforced by the Histadrut, the Jewish labor organization in Palestine, which picketed Jewish employers who hired Arabs. Actions taken to menace such employers led the government of Palestine to adopt a law in 1927, titled the Prevention of Intimidation Ordinance.[50]

HELP FROM BRITAIN

The British government reinforced the Jewish Agency's representations to the Permanent Mandates Commission. It too told the Commission that all would be well in Palestine. But the British government knew that trouble lay ahead. As early as 1921, the British government understood that the Zionist project could not be carried out in Palestine in a way that would be accepted by the Arabs. The minutes of a Cabinet meeting held August 18, 1921 reflected cause for concern. "The Cabinet were informed that recent reports from Palestine were of a disturbing character. Arabs and Jews were armed, or were arming, and a conflict might shortly ensue, particularly if the Moslem Christian Delegation, now in London, returned without having secured the withdrawal of Mr Balfour's pledge to the Zionists." As the minutes also reflect, the Zionists were lobbying Britain to stay the course. They "were naturally anxious as to their position, and wished to be reassured as to the government's support. Two courses were open to the Cabinet. They could withdraw from their Declaration, refer the Mandate back to the League of Nations, set up an Arab National government, and slow down or stop the immigration of Jews: or they could carry out the present policy with greater vigour and encourage the arming of the Jews with a view later on of reducing the numbers of the British garrison and cutting down expenses."[51] For the Zionist Organization, the lobbying that preceded the Balfour Declaration would have to continue.

The British government was aware that the Zionist project was leading Palestine down a path to violence, even as it said the contrary to the Permanent Mandates Commission. In 1923, a new government came to power in Britain, replacing the government that had issued the Balfour Declaration. Victor Cavendish, the new secretary for the colonies, wrote a stinging assessment of the Balfour Declaration as it was being put into practice. He said that Jewish immigration could not be successfully implemented in Palestine. The Arabs of Palestine would not accept further settlement of Jews from Europe, given the declared aim of the Zionists to take the country as their own. The consequence would be bloodshed. The Jews and Arabs would be at each other's throats. There was little the British government could do to reconcile the Arabs to a takeover of their country. There was little likelihood that the Arabs would accept outsiders who claimed rights to the territory.

Cavendish's conclusion raised the obvious question of whether to continue implementing the Balfour Declaration. Remarkably, Cavendish advocated staying the course, even though he had no hope of an acceptable outcome. He thought that if Britain repudiated Balfour, it would have to give up the mandate. "We should be placed in an intolerable position," Cavendish wrote, "if, after breaking a promise made to the Jews in the face of the whole world, we were to retain any connection with Palestine from which we derived, or could be held to derive, any conceivable benefit."[52]

Cavendish recited reasons why it was in Britain's interest to retain the mandate.

"There are Imperial considerations," he wrote, "that favour the retention of Palestine by Great Britain. Recent developments have profoundly modified our position in Egypt and circumstances might easily arise, under the new conditions, that would seriously affect our hold upon the Suez Canal. In such a contingency the control of Palestine might be of vital importance to us."[53] The Cabinet went along with Cavendish's recommendation. Even though it knew that what the Zionist Organization was telling the Permanent Mandates Commission was not true, it would continue to implement Balfour. And, like the Jewish Agency, it would continue to tell the Permanent Mandates Commission that the Balfour Declaration could be successfully implemented.

Successive British commissions of inquiry would substantiate Cavendish's fears. One such commission, the Peel Commission, found in 1937 that Arabs were being displaced from land. The Commission concluded that "the further displacement of Arabs from the land may intensify political discontent, as evidenced by the demand now made by the

Arabs for a complete stoppage of the sale of land to the Jews."[54] The Peel Commission proposed dividing Palestine into an Arab state and a Jewish state.

The Jewish Agency enjoyed more success with the Permanent Mandates Commission than with British inquiries. Weizmann's lobbying with the Commission paid off. The members of the Commission knew less than the British commissioners about what was occurring in Palestine, hence were more receptive to the Jewish Agency's claim that Zionism posed no threat to the Arabs of Palestine. The members of the Permanent Mandates Commission persistently pressured Britain to ensure that it was implementing the Balfour Declaration.[55]

The Arab community of Palestine, though not given a role in the text of the Palestine Mandate, was allowed by the Commission to send communications, but the Arab community viewed the mandate system as one set up to keep it in its place. For it the Permanent Mandates Commission was hostile territory. Arab representatives did record their objections to the Zionist project. In a 1926 letter to the Commission, the Palestine Arab Congress wrote: "Now and forever, any Arab of reason and love to his country in any territory of the Arabic-speaking countries is bound to oppose Zionism as being most detrimental to the Arab national cause."[56]

Arab representatives could not hope to convince the Permanent Mandates Commission of the futility of implementation of the Balfour Declaration, while both Britain and the Jewish Agency were telling the Commissioners that Jewish immigration could be carried out successfully. But once the Palestine Mandate was confirmed by the League of Nations, the Jewish National Fund resumed purchases of prime agricultural land. Through the 1920s and 1930s, it purchased land in key areas of Palestine, with a view to establishing a Jewish presence on contiguous tracts, as a basis for making a claim to territory.[57] The Jewish Agency successfully concealed this aim from the Permanent Mandates Commission. But the land purchases paid off in 1937 when Britain's Peel Commission floated the idea of partition in 1937. The plan designated areas in which the Jewish National Fund had purchased land as territory that would constitute a Jewish state.[58]

4

Courting the Commissar

During the years of World War II, the Zionist Organization gave attention to the international environment as it expected it to develop after the war. By then, Britain had taken a turn in its Palestine policy that did not sit well with the Zionist Organization. In May 1939, the British government decided that rather than working towards partition of Palestine into two states as recommended by the 1937 Peel Commission, it would instead limit Jewish migration into Palestine to a specific number per year.[1] The Zionist Organization took that move as a repudiation of the Balfour Declaration. The bloom on the relationship between the Zionist Organization and Britain faded. At the same time, the Soviet Union was allied with the major Western powers against Germany, and the Soviet advances in industrialization in the 1930s were propelling the Soviet Union towards becoming a major actor at the international level. In particular, the Soviet Union might play a role on war and peace issues after an anticipated defeat of Germany.

The Soviet ambassador in London, a hub of activity for the Zionist Organization, was an erudite diplomat named Ivan Maiskii. In 1939, Moshe Shertok, who headed the Jewish Agency's Political Department, approached Maiskii and held a series of meetings to try to incline the Soviet government towards a pro-Zionist position. Shertok's effort produced no immediate result.[2] It was an ambitious undertaking. The Soviet view of Zionism was distinctly negative. Jews had been the object of discrimination in tsarist Russia, and Zionism had been suppressed. The Bolsheviks promoted the assimilation of Jews in Russian society.[3] Zionism went in the opposite direction from assimilation. Early Soviet policy on Zionism was hesitant. Zionist organizations were tolerated, but within a few years, Zionists were subjected to arrest and their activities thwarted.[4] By the 1930s, Zionists were unable to organize, with many of their number imprisoned.[5] So the Zionist Organization faced an uphill battle if it wanted the Soviet Union on its side.

In January 1941, Shertok's effort was resumed by Chaim Weizmann, then serving as President of the World Zionist Organization. Maiskii's notes of their encounter found their way into the Soviet archives. As Maiskii recorded, Weizmann adopted the approach of telling Maiskii that the Jews of Palestine were at odds with the British administration. The sub-text was that the Jews of Palestine would find the Soviet government more compatible. Playing on the Soviets' traditional criticism of colonialism, Weizmann told Maiskii that Britain's administrators in their colonies were accustomed to subservience on the part of the population. They could build "a few roads," provide "a little medical care," and the population would be happy. In Palestine, the Arabs are "the guinea pigs the administrators are used to." But the Jews there, Weizmann said, explaining the British attitude, are "discontented with everything, they ask questions, they demand answers."

A British victory in the war would not benefit the Jews of Palestine, Weizmann said. The Zionist movement needed to save the Jews of central Europe, in particular those in Poland. Four or five million could be settled in Palestine, but only if Arabs could be moved out. Weizmann anticipated resettling one million Palestine Arabs in Iraq. But, he acknowledged to Maiskii, Britain would not countenance this approach. "The British are hardly likely to agree to this," he said.

Maiskii, again according to his account, reacted to Weizmann's numbers with skepticism. How could four or five million be settled in place of one million? Weizmann explained that Jews are more productive. For the Arab, "his laziness and primitivism turn a flourishing garden into a desert. Give me the land occupied by a million Arabs, and I will easily settle five times that number of Jews on it."[6]

Weizmann recorded his own account of this meeting with Maiskii, in a report to the Jewish Agency Executive. Weizmann's account of what was said was consistent with Maiskii's. Weizmann reported that he mentioned the desirability of resettling Palestine Arabs out of Palestine, "into Iraq or Transjordan." Maiskii replied that the Soviet Union had some experience with population exchanges. Weizmann said the exchange he was contemplating would be easier than what the Soviets did, because the distance to Iraq or Transjordan was short. Weizmann said that he told Maiskii that "if half a million Arabs could be transferred, two million Jews could be put in their place." These numbers Weizmann characterized as "a first installment." Again by Weizmann's account of the meeting, Maiskii agreed that "there would have to be an exchange of populations."[7]

Weizmann was telling Maiskii that getting Britain out of the picture was essential to Zionist aims in Palestine. The Soviet Union would be a better ally for the Zionists, because it did not object to population exchanges. For Weizmann, this approach to the Soviet Union was little short of remarkable. Weizmann had always attached the Zionist cart to Britain. From his time working in Britain's war industry, Weizmann saw Britain as providing the Zionists a path to Palestine. Now he was badmouthing Britain. But now Britain was retrenching in its support, and the Zionist movement would need the support of the major powers. The Zionists might need to cast their net wider.

Weizmann's statement to Maiskii about removing the Arabs was quite the opposite of his assurance to the Council of Ten at the Paris Peace Conference in 1919 that the Zionists would settle only the empty spaces of Palestine. But it was consistent with a consensus reached within the World Zionist Organization in the 1930s on the advisability of removing the Arabs from Palestine.[8] A so-called Transfer Committee was set up within the Jewish Agency in 1937. The immediate aim was to examine transfer of Arabs out of the bounds of the Jewish state that was proposed in that year by Britain's Peel Commission, into the territory of the proposed Arab state. But the Transfer Committee also examined the feasibility of transferring Arabs out of Palestine entirely. A subcommittee was formed. Moshe Shertok asked the subcommittee to investigate suitable vacant land in Transjordan and Syria. Committee members were split on whether transfer should be done only with the consent of the Arabs involved, or without their consent.[9] Weizmann at the time was urging Britain to buy out Palestine Arabs and relocate them elsewhere in the Arab world.[10]

Joseph Weitz, who headed the Jewish Agency's Colonization Department, wrote in 1940 that Zionism required getting the Arabs out of Palestine, but that this aim could not be disclosed publicly. "Between ourselves it must be clear," Weitz said, "that there is no room for both peoples together in this country. We shall not achieve our goal if the Arabs are in this small country. There is no other way than to transfer the Arabs from here to neighboring countries - all of them. Not one village, not one tribe should be left."[11] Weitz developed plans to acquire tracts of land in Arab countries.

Britain opposed transfer. In late 1937, as the British government was considering partition of Palestine's territory, it declared its opposition to the removal of Palestine Arabs, even to other territory within Palestine.[12] Britain's opposition to transfer gave Weizmann an opening to argue to

Maiskii that Britain was not serving Zionist interests, hence that a connection with the Soviet Union made more sense.

WE ARE ALL COMRADES

On the other side of the Atlantic Ocean, Zionist representatives began working the Soviet embassy in Washington, also in search of Soviet support. In 1941, Konstantin Umanskii served as Soviet ambassador in Washington. Emmanuel Neumann visited him on behalf of the Emergency Committee for Zionist Affairs, a coordinating body for Zionist groups in America. As Neumann described the exchange, Umanskii pointed out that the situation of Palestine would be determined after the war and that the Soviet Union would be involved. Neumann replied that the Zionists "would be glad of course to have as many friends at the peace conference as possible."[13]

The focus of the lobbying continued, however, to be Maiskii in London. A further approach was made by David Ben Gurion. Born in Poland with the surname Grün, Ben Gurion hebraicized his surname when he migrated early in life to Palestine. He became one of the leading lights in the Zionist movement. In 1941, Ben Gurion chaired the Executive Committee of the Jewish Agency. In October of that year, Ben Gurion met with Maiskii and built on Weizmann's foundation. In his written notes, Ben Gurion described his aim in holding the meeting with Maiskii as being "to remove the unfortunate misunderstanding which had existed in regard to Palestine," by which he meant a misunderstanding on the part of the Soviet government about Zionism. Ben Gurion understood the antipathy of the Soviets to Zionism but thought he could work through. Ben Gurion told Maiskii, "I was not criticizing the past; but we were concerned about Russia's attitude towards Palestine in the future." Rather than dwell on the Soviets' negative view towards Zionism, Ben Gurion focused on possible cooperation going forward. Ben Gurion looked ahead to the post-war period, anticipating an Allied victory. "At the end of the war," Ben Gurion told Maiskii, "Russia would at the least be one of the three leading powers which would determine the fate of the new world."

Whereas Weizmann in his approach to Maiskii had focused on distance between the Zionists and Britain, Ben Gurion pitched a similarity of interests between the Zionists and the Soviets. Ben Gurion depicted the Zionist movement to Maiskii as holding a philosophy close to that of the Soviets. Ben Gurion came out of the labor movement in Palestine. He stressed to Maiskii the role of labor and communalism in the Zionist settlement activity in Palestine. "Labour was the leading group in the Jewish community in Palestine," he told Maiskii. The "chairman of the Jewish community," he said, "was a labour man." This was a reference to Yitzhak Ben Zvi, a leading member of the Zionist labor organization, the Histadrut. Ben Zvi chaired the Vaad Leumi (National Council), a political organization of Palestine Jewry, established in 1920. Ben Gurion assured Maiskii that the Zionist movement was "very serious about our socialist aims, and we meant to achieve those." Ben Gurion averred, "In fact we had already built up in Palestine the nucleus of a socialist commonwealth."[14]

A SPECIOUS ARGUMENT?

Despite the prevailing Soviet view of Zionism, Maiskii proved open to discussion. Weizmann and Ben Gurion did well to choose him as their primary conduit to Moscow. Maiskii was well established in London. He had lived there in exile from tsarist Russia in the years just before the First World War. He knew European languages and possessed a familiarity with the international scene that other Soviet diplomats lacked. Maiskii, moreover, was a person who gave serious thought to the international order. He focused in particular during the war on what a postwar order might be, and what role the USSR might play in it. After the war he would retire from the diplomatic service and devote himself to historical writing.

With Maiskii based in London, the Zionist leaders had ready access to him. Weizmann kept up the contact. In March 1942, Weizmann picked up on Ben Gurion's arguments to Maiskii. Weizmann sent Maiskii a document he titled Memorandum on the USSR and Zionist Aims. "Past misunderstanding should not be allowed to bar a new orientation of the USSR towards Zionism," recited the Memorandum. Weizmann stressed the importance of the USSR to Zionism, "as itself containing almost one-third of world Jewry, and as the closest neighbor of the countries in which the problem is most acute, and as one of the Great Powers which will be responsible for the peace settlement." Weizmann's reference to the problem being acute was, of course, a reference to anti-Semitism in Eastern Europe. His reference to the USSR as a "Great Power" was a bit of flattery. Weizmann urged Maiskii to "take an interest in the Zionist solution of the Jewish question." The Memorandum also touted the economic achievements of the Jewish migrants living on land purchased for them. The Arab population of Palestine, it recited, "has derived great benefits from this vast economic development."[15]

Meeting with Maiskii, Weizmann tried to counteract the Soviet antipathy to Zionism. He averred to Maiskii that "the Zionist movement has never felt antagonistic to the Soviet social philosophy." He said there were "no fundamental psychological barriers to mutual understanding."[16] He depicted the Zionists' approach to economics as similar to the Soviet. Both "construct their economy according to plan, for both have to build up in backward countries a fully developed modern society." The similarity extended to political thinking as well. "Three of the most fundamental aspects of the Soviet social philosophy," he told Maiskii, "are embodied in the national system which is being built up in Palestine by the Zionist movement: collective welfare and not individual gain is the guiding principle and goal of the economic structure; equality of standing is established in the community between manual and intellectual workers; and consequently the fullest scope is provided for the intellectual life and development of labour."

To what extent Weizmann believed what he was telling Maiskii when he argued that the Zionists and Soviets shared values, one can only guess. A biographer of Weizmann thought that Weizmann was pulling Maiskii's leg. Norman Rose cited the quoted passage from Weizmann's memorandum to Maiskii and called it "Weizmann's speciously argued community of purpose."[17]

Weizmann also stressed personal connections. "The vast majority of adherents of Zionism have close personal and family relations with the USSR," he told Maiskii, "and a special interest in and sympathy for the Soviet people."[18] It was true, of course, that many of the leading figures, like Weizmann himself, were Russian.

In May 1942 Weizmann took his lobbying effort to Washington. There he visited Maxim Litvinov, who served as Soviet ambassador. Weizmann promised to send Litvinov Zionist literature, so that Litvinov "would be well informed at the time of the peace conference, at which the Jewish question would be finally resolved."[19] In August 1942, a visit to Palestine was arranged for a Soviet delegation, hosted by the Jewish Agency and by Ben Zvi. In his diary, Ben Zvi recorded that the main topic discussed was Jewish refugees in the Nazi-occupied countries, particularly those in Poland. "We need these refugees," he reported telling the visiting Soviets. "Our human reservoir is limited and small, we need more manpower. It is inconceivable that hundreds of thousands of Jewish refugees and emigrants should be lost [to us] when we have an acute need for manpower. You must permit these emigrants to immigrate [to Palestine]."[20] Ben Zvi reported his impression, based on private remarks he attributed to the visitors, that they understood "that the Jews have prepared the ground here for a *Jewish state*."[21]

It was being suggested to Maiskii that the Zionist Organization, if it were to achieve territorial status in Palestine, would be close politically to the Soviet Union. The leading force in Zionist politics was the Mapai party, with Ben Gurion at the helm. The Mapai leadership was Western-oriented and anticipated that the state they aspired to form would be pro-Western.[22] Convincing Maiskii to the contrary was a difficult task. One hopeful sign for the Zionist Organization in its effort to cultivate the Soviet leadership was the fact that during the war, the Soviet government gave Zionists in the Soviet Union greater latitude than they had in the 1930s. The change was likely related to a Soviet effort to enlist all sectors of Soviet society in the war effort.

Another was that Maiskii was sufficiently interested in what he was hearing that he agreed to visit Palestine in 1943, hosted by the Jewish Agency. Ben Gurion drove him around and found that Maiskii had a favorable impression of the Zionists' agenda for the country.[23] In February 1945, a Soviet delegation attending the World Trade Union Conference in London backed a resolution stating that "the Jewish people must be enabled to continue the rebuilding of Palestine as their National Home."[24] In March 1945, Sergei Kavtaradze, deputy commissar of foreign affairs, urged Foreign Commissar Viacheslav Molotov to open a Soviet consulate in Palestine. The Soviet Union had never had representation in Palestine. As background for his proposal, Kavtaradze gave Molotov his read on the political situation in Palestine. Kavtaradze noted Zionist efforts to connect with the Soviet Union. "Even Zionist circles with an anti-Soviet outlook, in light of the general situation," he said, "are now trying in every way to arrange official links with the USSR."[25]

Despite these developments favorable to the Zionist initiative, at war's end there was no firm indication which direction Soviet policy on Palestine might take. In July 1945, with the war in Europe concluded, the Soviet government began working on a position it might adopt. The Ministry of Foreign Affairs drew up a position paper that focused on easing Britain out of Palestine by replacing its mandate with a collective trusteeship administered jointly by the USSR, USA, and Britain. According to the position paper, the collective trusteeship would not be bound by the Balfour Declaration or any promises Britain made but would consider "the Palestine problem justly in accordance with the interests of the population as a whole."[26] The position paper was submitted confidentially to Communist Party General Secretary Joseph Stalin.[27]

A year later, another memorandum that circulated quietly within the Foreign Ministry modified the trusteeship idea. Instead of collective administration by the USSR, USA, and Britain, it suggested administration by the United Nations.[28] Neither the 1945 paper nor the 1946 paper went beyond the walls of the Foreign Ministry, so the Soviet Union was taking no public position. In June 1946, Nahum Goldmann, the Jewish Agency's representative in Washington, asked Andrei Gromyko, the Soviet representative at the United Nations, if the Soviet Union would support the partition of Palestine. Goldmann asked Gromyko to arrange for a Jewish Agency delegation to visit Moscow to lobby the Soviet government in that direction. Gromyko declined, saying that the Soviet government already had the information it needed.[29] The Soviet government was keeping its counsel.

5

Saving Europe's Jews – Our Way

As Germany drifted in the 1930s toward Kristallnacht and the Nuremberg laws, the danger to Jews grew more and more apparent. In other countries, Jewish organizations, and non-Jewish organizations as well, urged their governments to give Jews refuge in their territory. One might have expected Zionist organizations to take up this demand on Western governments. But the Zionist movement did just the opposite. It discouraged Jewish migration to Western countries. Instead, it worked to channel European Jews to Palestine to the exclusion of other destinations. The Zionist movement took this stance on the basis of the principle that the only way to protect Jews in the long run was to gain territory for a Jewish state. The Zionist Organization regarded the dispersal of Jews to various countries that might accept them as a serious threat to its goals. For the Zionists, Palestine had to be the only destination for emigrating Jews.

The Zionist position became clear at a meeting of Western leaders in Evian, France, in 1938. US President Franklin Roosevelt called the meeting to encourage Western countries to take in anyone from Germany or Austria who felt threatened "by reason of the treatment to which they are subjected on account of their political opinions, religious beliefs or racial origin."[1] Some thirty nations attended. The British delegation avoided mentioning Palestine as a possible destination, Britain being painfully cognizant of the conflict that Jewish migration to Palestine was creating. That omission drew criticism from Zionists as the meeting proceeded. Britain finally averted to Palestine on the final day of the meeting, saying that Palestine could not be the venue for resettling European Jewish refugees.[2] Representing Britain, Lord Winterton (Edward Tournour) noted, "It has been represented in some quarters that the whole question, at least of the Jewish refugees, could be solved if only the gates of Palestine were thrown open to Jewish immigrants without restriction of any kind." That was an obvious reference to the Zionist view. But Lord Winterton explained that "Palestine is not a large country," and "there are special considerations arising out of the terms of the mandate." That was a reference to the need to protect the existing population of Palestine. Lord Winterton told the delegates that "the question of Palestine stands upon a footing of its own and cannot usefully be taken into account at the present stage in connection with the general problems that are under consideration at this meeting."[3]

Weizmann's approach was precisely the opposite of Britain's. Addressing the Zionist-oriented World Conference for Palestine a few weeks after the Evian conference, Weizmann said that Palestine must be the destination for emigrants leaving Europe. "Our position today has become so acutely critical," said Weizmann with reference to the Jews of Europe, "we must demand a permanent solution to our problem. That solution can be found only in Palestine – the national home of a homeless people."[4] For Weizmann, the immigration of displaced Jews into Western countries was no solution.

Ben Gurion feared that resettling Jews outside Palestine would erode support for Zionism among world Jewry. In a December 17, 1938 letter to the Zionist Executive, Ben Gurion wrote, "If Jews will have to choose between the refugees, saving Jews from concentration camps, and assisting a national museum in Palestine, mercy will have the upper hand and the whole energy of the people will be channeled into saving Jews from various countries." In that eventuality, Ben Gurion wrote, "Zionism will be struck off the agenda."

In the letter, Ben Gurion castigated Britain for seeking to deal with the issue of Jewish refugees separately from the issue of Palestine. "Britain is trying," he wrote, "to separate the issue of the refugees from that of Palestine." Ben Gurion feared, "If we allow a separation between the refugee problem and the Palestine problem, we are risking the existence of Zionism."[5]

A leading Zionist who after the Second World War would chair the American Section of the Jewish Agency, Rabbi Abba Hillel Silver, was of the same mind. Shortly after the Evian conference, Rabbi Silver was approached by James McDonald, whom President Roosevelt had appointed to advise him on refugee issues. McDonald asked Rabbi Silver, who then headed the United Jewish Appeal, for help in resettling European Jews in the United States. Rabbi Silver turned him down flat. "I was shocked," McDonald recounted, by his attitude "toward the Evian effort." Rabbi Silver told McDonald that he saw "no particular good" in what Roosevelt was trying to do at Evian.[6]

The refusal to encourage the West to take in Jews at risk in Europe continued even as wartime atrocities unfolded. At the Extraordinary Zionist Conference held at the Biltmore Hotel in New York in 1942, Nahum Goldmann expressed alarm at what the Nazi government might do to the Jews if it were to find itself on the edge of defeat. Goldmann spelled out a doomsday scenario. "Who can foretell what the Nazi regime, once brought into the position of the surrounded killer, will do in the last moment before it goes down to shame?"[7] Like Ben Gurion in 1938, Goldmann focused exclusively on Palestine as a venue for Jews seeking to leave Europe. Historian Aaron Berman, recounting Goldmann's Biltmore speech, commented, "Surprisingly, Goldmann didn't propose any program to come to the immediate aid of those threatened with annihilation. Instead, he called for the establishment of a Jewish Commonwealth that could absorb two million Jewish refugees in the decade following the war."[8]

There was logic to the Zionist Organization's position if one accepts the premise that Jews would be safe only if they had their own state. At the Biltmore Hotel conference, a coalition of Zionist groups came out publicly to declare their aim as being a "commonwealth" to encompass the territory of Palestine. This became the position of the Zionist Organization. But Palestine was clearly not large enough to handle more than a small percentage of the world's Jews, even if they all felt the need to settle there. Even so, the Zionists could argue, a safe haven should be available for Jews.

At the same time, the position of the Zionist leadership opened them to the criticism that they were leaving Jews to die in Germany, for lack of an immediately available destination for their resettlement. The Zionists purported to be champion of world Jewry, yet their policy arguably left Jews in unnecessary jeopardy. To be sure, the Western governments were not anxious to take in large numbers of Jews, even as the clouds of genocide were gathering in Germany. But the Zionist movement contributed to the reluctance of the Western governments. In upholding strict immigration quotas, those governments could take comfort in the fact that their policy was approved by the Zionists.

SACRIFICING JEWS FOR PALESTINE?

The Second World War changed the context in which the Zionist Organization operated in its effort at statehood in Palestine. Only a minority of Europe's Jews survived the killing at the hands of the Third Reich.

This mass killing would have a profound impact on Zionist diplomacy. The Zionist argument that Jews could be protected only by having their own space gained resonance. The logic of that argument could more readily be grasped by those to whom Zionist diplomats appealed for support. The resolve of the Zionists themselves to carry out their project was reaffirmed, even as many Zionists were among those killed. Within world Jewry, Zionism had remained a minority view before the war, but now it commanded the support of most Jews.

The international context in which Zionism operated changed as well. The United States and the Soviet Union emerged as arbiters of world politics, marginalizing the formerly dominant Western European powers. With the decimation of European Jewry, US Jewry became the dominant element in Zionism. At the practical level, many of the Jews who survived the genocide in Europe wanted to emigrate, especially from Germany and Poland. This population of Jews could make a compelling case for being taken in by other countries.

US President Franklin Roosevelt explored the possibility of accepting large numbers of Jews into the United States, while encouraging other countries to do the same. Roosevelt's advisor Morris Ernst was tasked with the project. Ernst communicated with Jewish organizations in the United States to see if they would be supportive. But Ernst, as he describes, met a brick wall. "I was amazed and even felt insulted when active Jewish leaders decried, sneered and then attacked me as if I were a traitor." They objected that his plan would "undermine political Zionism." Ernst surmised that Jewish leaders who supported Zionism thought they would have difficulty raising funds for a Jewish state if they could not say that the Jews of Europe have no place to go except Palestine. Ernst thought that if offered the option of multiple destinations, "only a minority of the Jewish DP's would choose Palestine."[9] Roosevelt abandoned the resettlement project. Ernst reported that Roosevelt did so because he thought he could not admit Jews in substantial numbers over and against the opposition of leading Jewish organizations.[10]

American Zionists worked instead to pressure Britain to expand Jewish migration into Palestine. The American Zionist Emergency Council solicited state governors in the United States to endorse a petition calling on President Roosevelt to work to "open the doors of Palestine to Jewish mass immigration and colonization and to bring about the earliest transformation of that country into a free and democratic Jewish Commonwealth."[11]

The Jewish Agency considered a task it identified as "salvation" of European Jews. The task meant directing displaced Jews to Palestine and to Palestine only. In June 1945, the Jewish Agency asked Britain to admit 100,000 immediately into Palestine.[12] It directed no call to other governments to admit displaced Jews. In August 1945, the World Zionist Conference, meeting in London, similarly set its sights on Palestine as the only destination for emigrating European Jews. The Conference declared in a resolution, "The remnants of European Jewry cannot and will not continue their existence among the graveyards of the millions of their slaughtered brethren. Their only salvation lies in their speediest settlement in Palestine." And more, a Jewish state must emerge in Palestine. In his 1941 State of the Union address, President Roosevelt had famously used the phrase "freedom from fear" as something all peoples should enjoy. The Conference applied that phrase to their demand for a Jewish state in Palestine. "The vast majority of the Jewish people throughout the world feel that they have no chance of 'freedom from fear' unless the status of the Jews, as individuals and as a nation, has been made equal to that of all normal peoples, and the Jewish State in Palestine has been established."[13]

Shortly before his death in April 1945, Roosevelt asked Earl Harrison, who had been his Commissioner of Immigration, to serve on an inter-governmental commission to assess the situation of displaced persons in Europe. When Harry Truman became President upon Roosevelt's death, he asked Harrison to visit the displaced person camps in Europe. Harrison's assignment was to ascertain the sentiment of displaced persons about their future. Harrison did not do sophisticated sampling, but he reported back to Truman that most said they wanted to go to Palestine. For some, it was out of a belief that only in Palestine could they be safe. For others, Harrison found, it was "because they realize that their opportunity to be admitted into the United States or into other countries in the Western Hemisphere is limited, if not impossible."[14]

On December 22, 1945, Truman issued a directive to allow Jewish immigration to the United States from American zones of occupation in Europe.[15] Arrivals began in May 1946, but by April 1947 only 12,401 were admitted.[16] While seeking ways to admit more Jews into the United States, Truman also thought that Britain could admit more into Palestine. After receiving Harrison's report from the displaced person camps, Truman asked Britain, in line with the Jewish Agency's request, to allow 100,000 Jews to migrate to Palestine.[17] Truman's rationale was different from that of the Jewish Agency. Truman thought that allowing increased Jewish immigration to Palestine would relieve the pressure for a Jewish state, not that it would facilitate the creation there of a Jewish state.[18]

Weizmann obtained a meeting with President Truman on December 4, 1945. The conversation turned to the advisability of a Jewish state in Palestine. Truman asked Weizmann what the status of the Arabs would be in a Jewish state. Weizmann reverted to the line he had pushed since the Paris Peace Conference. He told Truman that the status of the Arabs would not suffer. He said that reports that the Arabs hated the Jews were "highly exaggerated." He said that such reports were "being used as an excuse to prevent a pro-Jewish solution." Truman was far from convinced that a Jewish state was a good idea for Palestine. He challenged Weizmann, suggesting that the Jews wanted to set up a theocratic state.[19]

President Truman did not support the Jewish Agency position that Palestine should be the sole destination for Jews migrating out of Europe. Dean Acheson, who at the time was Acting Secretary of State, wrote in an internal State Department communication in August 1946 that "the solution of the Palestine question will not in itself solve the broader problem of the hundreds of thousands of displaced persons in Europe. The President has been giving this problem his special attention and hopes that arrangements can be entered into which will make it possible for various countries, including the United States, to admit many of these persons as permanent residents. The President on his part is contemplating seeking the approval of Congress for special legislation authorizing the entry into the United States of a fixed number of these persons, including Jews."[20]

The Jewish Agency was promoting partition of Palestine. In the United States the Zionist movement was lobbying Truman to issue a statement in favor of partition. Truman resisted.[21] The United States at that point was working with the British government on the possibilities for the continuation of a central government in Palestine with Arab and Jewish sectors. Issuing a statement in favor of partition would have undermined that effort. Truman was inclined toward a solution in Palestine that would involve autonomy for the Jews under a central government.[22] But he informed British Prime Minister Clement Attlee that this idea enjoyed insufficient support within the United States. He thought that the Jewish Agency's proposal of a Jewish state in an "adequate area of Palestine" might enjoy support in the United States, and that perhaps "the gap between the proposals" might be bridged.[23] So Truman was open to the idea of partition, even if not as his favored solution.[24]

The World Zionist Congress continued to promote Palestine as the sole destination for emigrating European Jews. Meeting in December 1946, it again demanded that Britain admit more Jews to Palestine but did not call for other states to accept Jews.[25] Shortly, however, Britain would no longer be the addressee of the Zionists' demands. The fate of Palestine would be decided elsewhere.

6

Smoke and Mirrors at the YMCA

On February 25, 1947, British Foreign Secretary Ernest Bevin stood before the House of Commons in London to say that Britain had failed to find any solution for Palestine. "The course of events has led His Majesty's Government to decide that the problem of Palestine must be referred to the United Nations," Bevin announced. "The problem of Palestine is a very vexed and complex one. There is no denying the fact that the Mandate contained contradictory promises," Bevin conceded. "In the first place it promised the Jews a National Home, and, in the second place it declared that the rights and position of the Arabs must be protected. Therefore, it provided for what was virtually an invasion of the country by thousands of immigrants, and at the same time said that this was not to disturb the people in possession. The question therefore arose whether this could be accomplished without a conflict, and events in the last 25 years have proved that it could not."[1] The only respect in which Bevin's statement was not forthright was contained in this last sentence. Bevin made it appear that it took the British government twenty-five years to realize that it had taken on contradictory and irreconcilable obligations. As we saw in Chapter Three, it had known that since at least 1923.

Britain's solution was to ask the newly formed United Nations to devise a solution for Palestine. In April 1947, Britain asked the United Nations to formulate proposals on Palestine.[2] The Charter of the United Nations did not make it entirely clear what powers the United Nations had to deal with Palestine, but Britain had run out of solutions on its own. As a permanent member of the UN Security Council, Britain would not be entirely out of the picture. The Security Council deals with threats to the peace, and Palestine appeared headed for trouble.

The Jewish Agency immediately geared up to encourage the United Nations, in line with the Biltmore Program, to make Palestine into a Jewish state. Realism required, however, that it allow for the Arabs to have a state as well, so Palestine would have to be split. The matter would go to the General Assembly in the first instance, and votes on what were considered "important questions" required a two-thirds majority.[3] The Jewish Agency realized that its chance of gaining two-thirds of the members of the General Assembly for partition was slim if it did not have the two major power blocs. If either the United States or the USSR went against partition, it would take with it other states in sufficient numbers to block passage.[4] Despite Zionist diplomacy to that point, neither the United States nor the Soviet Union had publicly committed to any particular position on Palestine.

Jewish Agency officials worried that they had no official role in the United Nations. A number of Arab states were UN members, and they would argue for the Arabs of Palestine, who opposed partition. But the United Nations was set up as an organization of states, and it had made no provision to allow nonstate entities any involvement in its proceedings. Weizmann relished the opportunity for a Jewish Agency voice at the United Nations. Weizmann told a colleague that the fact that the United Nations would debate the Palestine situation presented "a great chance."[5] The Jewish Agency mounted an intense lobbying effort in Washington to pressure the United States to push at the United Nations for Jewish Agency participation.[6] The United States agreed, resulting in a resolution at the United Nations to afford a hearing to "the Jewish Agency for Palestine" in the General Assembly's First Committee. The First Committee dealt with security and political affairs and was expected to play a role in consideration of the Palestine question.[7]

A RUSSIAN SURPRISE

With the United Nations moving to take up Britain's request, the government of the Soviet Union moved toward formulating a stance. To many in the Soviet foreign affairs establishment, the logical choice was to oppose Zionism and support the Arabs. On April 15, 1947, an internal document was drafted titled "Memorandum by the Middle East Department of the USSR Ministry of Foreign Affairs on the Palestine Question (for the forthcoming discussion of the Palestine question at the United Nations)." The Memorandum, circulated within the Ministry only, stated: "The United Nations must draw up a constitution for a single, independent and democratic Palestine which will ensure that all the peoples living there will enjoy equal national and democratic rights." Continuing, it recited, "The United

Nations must also act as guarantor for the implementation of its own prerequisites for an independent and democratic Palestine state. The independent and democratic State of Palestine shall be included [as a member] in the United Nations."[8]

This was support for the Arab position. The Arabs wanted a Palestine state upon Britain's withdrawal. That was the view of the Arab Higher Committee, which regarded itself as a government-in-waiting for Palestine. The Soviet position, as yet confidential, was moving away from the trusteeship proposed in the earlier Soviet paper, in the direction of outright independence for Palestine. Under this approach, the Arab-Jewish hostility would be resolved through democratic processes. Migration to Palestine would presumably require the consent of the Arabs. So the USSR would oppose the Zionist desire for a Jewish state.

On May 14, 1947, however, Andrei Gromyko as Soviet representative made a statement in the UN General Assembly as the formation of a committee to make proposals on Palestine was under discussion. To the surprise of many, Gromyko did not limit himself to the details of committee formation. He spoke to the heart of the matter, namely, what the outcome might be in Palestine. Gromyko started out with the approach outlined in his Ministry's April memorandum. "The solution of the Palestine problem by the establishment of a single Arab-Jewish State with equal rights for the Jews and the Arabs may be considered as one of the possibilities and one of the more noteworthy methods for the solution of this complicated problem," Gromyko told the delegates. "Such a solution of the problem of Palestine's future might be a sound foundation for the peaceful co-existence and co-operation of the Arab and Jewish populations of Palestine, in the interests of both these peoples and to the advantage of the entire Palestine population and of the peace and security of the Near East." To that point, Gromyko was following the Ministry's memorandum.

But what Gromyko said next went in a different direction. "If this plan proved impossible to implement, in view of the deterioration in the relations between the Jews and the Arabs – and it will be very important to know the special committee's opinion on this question," he said, "then it would be necessary to consider the second plan which, like the first, has its supporters in Palestine, and which provides for the partition of Palestine into two independent autonomous States, one Jewish and one Arab. I repeat that such a solution of the Palestine problem would be justifiable only if relations between the Jewish and Arab populations of Palestine indeed proved to be so bad that it would be impossible to reconcile them and to ensure the peaceful co-existence of the Arabs and the Jews."[9]

It was becoming increasingly clear, in the Spring of 1947, that reconciliation was a distant hope. So Gromyko's suggestion of partition as a second choice seemed to be, in practical terms, support for partition. Supporters of Zionism were elated. Gromyko's statement portended a change in the dynamic at the United Nations in favor of the Jewish Agency.[10] David Horowitz, who at the time was a junior Jewish Agency official focusing on economic issues, wrote that Gromyko's May 1947 speech came "out of a clear blue sky after so many years during which our cause had been ostracized by the Russians."[11] While Gromyko's statement was the first from the Soviet Union to show possible support for a Jewish state, the Jewish Agency was not totally surprised, given the intense lobbying by Weizmann and Ben Gurion during the war years. Gromyko's statement was seen within the Jewish Agency in light of their lobbying effort, and as an occasion for quiet self-congratulation.[12] Publicly, however, the Jewish Agency never advertised the approaches to Maiskii or to other Soviet officials. To do so might jeopardize its relations with the Western powers. Even in the memoirs that a number of Zionist Organization and Jewish Agency figures would write in later years, one finds no mention of the wartime effort to lobby Soviet officials.

Had the efforts of the Zionist leaders borne fruit? Shertok's biographer concludes that the meetings in London with Maiskii "laid the groundwork for the USSR's favourable policy toward the Yishuv and the Jewish state later during the war and after it."[13] "Yishuv" is a Hebrew term used to refer to the Jewish community of Palestine. Arnold Krammer, an historian of Soviet-Zionist relations, agrees with Shertok's biographer. "There is a strong indication," writes Krammer, "that Jewish overtures during these early meetings between Palestinians [by which Krammer means Palestine Jews] and Communist leaders included a variety of personal promises and prophesies regarding the future political direction of the Israeli government. The Soviet Union, in effect, entered the United Nations debates on the Palestine Question in May and November of 1947 with a number of personal assurances from relatively important, though left-wing, individuals who might have risen to prominent positions in the future government of the created state."[14] Krammer's reference to left-wing Zionists was to interaction between Zionists of that stripe and Soviet officials during the war that included visits by Soviet officials to Palestine. But as we have seen, the contacts included Shertok, Weizmann, and Ben Gurion, all leaders of mainstream Zionism. The Soviet leadership had been given reason to believe that a Jewish state would be friendly to them.

BUGS IN HOTEL ROOMS

The importance of the Soviet move was immediately apparent. The day after Gromyko's speech, the United Nations General Assembly appointed a committee to make recommendations. If Palestine were simply to be regarded, upon Britain's withdrawal, as an independent state, in line with the Arab position, no such recommendations would be needed. Palestine would become independent and accepted as such by the United Nations, just as other two formerly Turkish mandate territories in the Arab world – Syria and Iraq – had been accepted as independent by the League of Nations. With the Jewish Agency pushing for partition, the Soviet announcement enhanced the likelihood that partition would become the United Nations' approach, even if the United States remained uncommitted.

The topic the committee was to address was "the question of Palestine," according to the General Assembly's resolution setting up the committee. A UN Special Committee on Palestine would analyze the situation, consult the interested parties, and report back to the General Assembly. This Special Committee was to be composed of representatives of eleven states, which were named in the resolution. The states chosen would include no major powers, on the theory that the major powers had interests of their own. Nor would they include Arab states, on the theory that they were partial. The Special Committee would hold hearings before formulating recommendations. Interested parties from the populations concerned were to be invited to testify. The Special Committee was asked to file its final report with the General Assembly in three and one-half months, by September 1, 1947.[15]

The Special Committee began preparations to hold hearings in Jerusalem. On June 13, the Arab Higher Committee cabled UN Secretary-General Trygve Lie to say it would not participate. It told Lie that Britain's mandate should simply be terminated, so that Palestine would become independent. The "natural rights" of the Palestine Arabs, it wrote, "cannot continue to be subject to investigation."[16] The Arab Higher Committee doubted that the Special Committee would back its position.[17] To the Arabs of Palestine, the situation was obvious. Britain had taken control of Palestine on the understanding it would bring it to independence. If Britain was now to leave, Palestine would become independent. There was no need for a committee of outsiders to come to their country to say what it should become.

On June 16, the Special Committee set up shop in Jerusalem's YMCA building, which had facilities appropriate for the event. Unlike the Arab

Higher Committee, the Jewish Agency seized on the opportunity to testify. On June 18, the Jewish Agency's Executive met and resolved to support partition, and to try to enlist the Special Committee to do so as well.[18] The Jewish Agency knew it could not gain a recommendation to turn all of Palestine into a Jewish state. Its aim would be partition.

RIPE FOR PICKING

The Special Committee was friendly territory for the Jewish Agency from the cultural standpoint.[19] Like the Zionist diplomats, most Committee members were European, either from Europe itself (Sweden, Yugoslavia, Netherlands, Czechoslovakia), or from states settled by Europeans (Australia, Canada, Guatemala, Peru, Uruguay). Only two members, those from India and Iran, lacked a connection with Europe.

Ralph Bunche, a US diplomat, was appointed by Secretary-General Lie to facilitate the Special Committee's work. Bunche, who would later take a major position in UN work on Palestine, was not impressed by the caliber of the Special Committee. As the hearings began, he wrote to his wife that he found a number of them to be "petty," "vain," and "stupid." He said that they were "just about the worst group I have ever had to work with. If they do a good job it will be a real miracle."[20] The members of the Special Committee were not, overall, committed at the outset to a particular outcome.[21] But they lacked background on the Palestine situation.[22] And they were working against an incredibly short deadline. Even if they made their best effort, and even if Bunche's assessment of them was overdrawn, they were not in a position to give critical examination to factual information they would be given by those who testified.

The Jewish Agency pulled out all the stops to gain the outcome it sought from the Special Committee. The Jewish Agency's intelligence arm, the Mossad, researched personal information on the background of each Committee member to ascertain their proclivities. As Committee members arrived in Jerusalem, the operatives installed listening devices in their hotel rooms to catch their private conversations. The Mossad arranged for its own female agents to serve as cleaning staff at the YMCA building, to eavesdrop on Committee members.[23]

Leading figures in the Jewish Agency testified. They took the opportunity to make their case for a Jewish Palestine, in as strong terms as they could. Ben Gurion made the Jewish Agency's basic point. He urged the Zionist agenda. "Only by establishing Palestine as a Jewish state can the true objectives be accomplished: immigration and settlement for the

Jews, economic development and social progress for the Arabs," he told the Special Committee. A Jewish state would be good for the Arabs of Palestine. "Nothing will further the Jewish-Arab alliance," he predicted, "more than the establishment of the Jewish state."[24] The attitude of the Arabs, who still constituted a large majority of Palestine's population, was a critical matter for the Special Committee. If the Arabs would not accept having the territory, or part of it, taken for a Jewish state, then a recommendation for a Jewish state would be a recipe for war.

Ben Gurion's statement that Palestine should be established as a Jewish state seemed to be a claim to the entirety of Palestine. Ben Gurion was pressed on whether the Jewish Agency would settle for partition. Ben Gurion replied in the affirmative, in line with the decision of the Jewish Agency. "We would be ready," he said, "to consider such an offer as a Jewish State in an adequate area of Palestine."[25]

FANCY FIGURES ON MIGRATION

Arguments to support the Jewish Agency position would be spelled out by other Jewish Agency figures, and by Ben Gurion himself. A central theme was that Jewish statehood would find acquiescence from Palestine's Arabs and would even benefit them.

Testimony before the Special Committee would be much more extensive than the presentations to the Council of Ten at the Paris Peace Conference. A series of Jewish Agency speakers took up different aspects of the Zionist argument. Moshe Shertok gave an overview presentation. Shertok focused on the connection of Jewry to Palestine, to show the strength of the Jewish attachment. Shertok started from the presence of Jews in Palestine in ancient times, and the dispersal of many of them out of Palestine. He told the Special Committee that since that time in the distant past, the Jews "had attempted to return to Palestine" repeatedly, "in every century and in every generation."[26] Shertok was not challenged on his recitation, even though he provided no substantiation for his claim that Jews had persistently tried to return since ancient times. Nor did he explain why, if the Jews had "attempted" to return, they were unable to do so.

In fact, Shertok's claim was pure fiction. A concentrated effort within European Jewry to migrate to Palestine dated only from the nineteenth century. Shertok's claim that Jews in any significant numbers had been trying to get there since ancient times was simply untrue. This claim, which other Zionist figures repeated in other contexts, was addressed some years later by historian Hugh Trevor-Roper, who undertook an assessment of the migration patterns of European Jews. Trevor-Roper wrote that it was not the case that the Jews "for nearly two thousand years, were constantly prepared for a return to the Holy Land, or that the Zionist solution was the end to which all creation, in those two thousand years, had been groaning and travailing."[27]

Shertok claimed especially high levels of Jewish migration in the decades around the turn of the twentieth century. He referred to what he called "the present phase of Jewish resettlement in Palestine, which," he said, "had begun in 1881." "The Jews, driven by suffering and peril to seek refuge elsewhere, had been drawn to Palestine," Shertok claimed, "because this was the only country where they could hope to rebuild their lives on secure foundations and become a nation again."[28]

Like Shertok's previous statement, this one was false. Palestine was not "the only country" where Jews sought to rebuild their lives. Trevor-Roper would address this claim as well. Whatever might be "the terrible persecutions and pogroms in Russia or Poland," Trevor-Roper wrote, when Jews felt the need to leave, "their feet carried them" not to Palestine, but to "Germany or England or America."[29] Jews seeking a new life understandably were drawn to countries where they could expect upward economic mobility. Most Jews leaving eastern Europe in the late nineteenth century went not to Palestine but to the United States.

Only a year before the Special Committee hearing, another hearing was held on Palestine by a panel set up by the British and American governments. Chaim Weizmann testified before this Anglo-American Committee of Inquiry. Like the Special Committee, it held hearings in Jerusalem. Weizmann addressed Jewish migration at that hearing. But Weizmann supplied figures far different from Shertok's. Weizmann gave the 1946 inquiry panel a figure of 2.5 million for Jews emigrating from eastern Europe between 1880 and 1914. Of these, Weizmann said that two million went to the United States, and another 300,000 to Britain, South Africa, and Canada combined.[30] That would leave only a small minority heading to Palestine. So Shertok's statement that the Jews leaving eastern Europe in the main migrated to Palestine was at odds with Weizmann's 1946 statement.

Precise figures on Jewish emigration out of eastern Europe are elusive, but the numbers Weizmann gave to the Anglo-American Committee of Inquiry were close to the mark. Only a fraction of the Jews leaving eastern Europe – well under 5 percent – went to Palestine.[31] One scholar who tallied Jewish migration to the United States (from anywhere) for the period 1880 to 1914 gives a figure of 2.5 million.[32] Most were from Eastern Europe. As many as 75,000 may have gone to Palestine during that period, a significant number to be sure, but hardly showing that Palestine was "the only country" for emigrating Jews.[33] Shertok's false claim was a serious misrepresentation of reality.

Shertok attributed the exodus from eastern Europe to a desire to escape suffering and peril. To be sure, that was part of the picture. According to Israeli economist Jacob Metzer, who analyzed Jewish emigration out of eastern Europe, however, economic factors predominated in the decision to emigrate. Of the Jews who left eastern Europe, wrote Metzer, "some sought security and freedom from persecution, but most made the move in expectation of material betterment in the relatively labor-scarce countries of destination."[34] Despite the higher prospects for material betterment in the United States than in Palestine, the decision to opt for Palestine may have been made by some because the cost of a boat ticket to Palestine was far less than one to the United States.[35]

No member of the UN Special Committee on Palestine challenged Shertok on the figures he gave on Jewish migration to Palestine. The Anglo-American Committee of Inquiry that heard Weizmann's figures on Jewish migration was composed of individuals who had a background on Palestine. The members of the Special Committee did not.

In addition to his falsehoods, Shertok omitted one crucial fact about Jewish migration to Palestine, a fact that the members of the Special Committee doubtless did not know. Shertok left the impression that Jews who migrated to Palestine remained there. But integrating into the economy of Palestine proved difficult for Jews entering Palestine at the turn of the twentieth century. As many as half of them left Palestine within a few years.[36] Jewish migration to Palestine caught up with Jewish migration to the United States only in the 1920s, and the cause for the shift related not to Palestine but to the United States. At that time the United States clamped down on immigration, which had previously been allowed with little restriction. "Mass immigration to Palestine," writes an Israeli historian specializing in migration patterns, "only began when American immigration quotas came into effect, closing the gates of the United States to Eastern European immigrants in general and to Jews in particular."[37]

WE ARE HELPING THE ARABS

Shertok also played fast and loose with facts in describing the impact of Jewish migration on the Arab population of Palestine. He was at pains to make the Committee think that the Arabs were not disadvantaged by the influx of Jews. He told the Committee that Jewish migration into Palestine had caused no "economic dislocation."[38]

Shertok's approach in the hearing, in the words of his biographer, was "to employ an old Zionist tactic, that is, to underline the spectacular economic development of the country and community, including its benefits to the Arabs."[39] But that account was far from accurate. Rural Arabs were losing their livelihood. The eviction of Arab tenant farmers that had caught the attention of the British occupation authorities in 1918 resumed once Britain re-opened land sales in the 1920s. Land purchases by the Jewish National Fund for incoming European Jews led to Arabs being moved off land they tilled. Purchasers were free to evict Arab tenant farmers.[40]

Moreover, once land was purchased by the Jewish National Fund, it was closed in perpetuity against use by Arabs.[41] A 1930 British inquiry, the Hope Simpson Commission, noted that Jewish National Fund land, by the terms under which it was held, could not be sold or leased to Arabs. Fund land, the Commission, said, "ceases to be land from which the Arab can gain advantage either now or at any time in the future. Not only can he never hope to lease or to cultivate it, but, by the stringent provisions of the lease of the Jewish National Fund, he is deprived forever from employment on that land."[42] Shertok, of course, was aware of the British inquiries but made no mention.

Further excluding Arabs, the Zionist Organization followed a policy called "Jewish labor" Arabs were not to be hired to work on farms, or in shops or factories. The Anglo-American Committee of Inquiry of 1946 found that the Jewish labor policy kept Arabs from many jobs.[43] Historian Arnold Toynbee wrote that the result of the land-purchasing and Jewish labor policies was the creation in Palestine of "an exclusive preserve for the Jews, what in South Africa is called segregation."[44]

After Shertok spoke, Committee member Sir Abdur Rahman of India acknowledged, on his own behalf and on behalf of his colleagues, that the Committee "did not know most of the facts which have been related by the witness, we should like to have time for studying them."[45] Unaware of the accuracy of what they were being told, Committee members did not mount any cross-examination of Shertok.

Despite Rahman's expressed hope that the Committee could study the facts, time did not permit. The Committee was working under a September 1, 1947, deadline. One Committee member, Jorge García-Granados, seemingly accepted Shertok's statements at face value. In a book García-Granados later wrote, he lauded Shertok, saying that Shertok "had apparently an encyclopedic knowledge of his subject."[46] Had García-Granados done independent research on the topics Shertok addressed, he would have learned that there was little reality to what Shertok related about immigration and about the economic impact of Jewish settlement.

WE FINANCED PALESTINE

David Horowitz, the Jewish Agency economist, addressed government finance in his testimony before the Committee. Horowitz told the Committee that two-thirds of government revenue in Palestine came from the Jewish economy, but that government expenditure went to the population as a whole, which meant predominantly to the Arabs, since they were in the majority.[47] Horowitz thus gave the impression that the Jewish community, by the taxes it paid, was subsidizing the Arab community.

A comprehensive analysis of government finance in Mandate Palestine was undertaken in 1998 by Israeli economist Jacob Metzer. By his study, government expenditures at both the central and local levels went more to Jews than to Arabs. At the central government level for Palestine under Britain's mandate, Metzer found, "the average Jewish inhabitant of Palestine utilized 1.4–2.1 times more public services and aid." The differential was even greater at the local government level. In Mandate Palestine's localities, Jews received more benefit than Arabs from government expenditures by three to one.[48]

One of the facts the Jewish Agency pushed in relation to the economic situation in Palestine was that Jews brought capital into the economy. Horowitz described for the Special Committee the capital that Jews were importing into Palestine and claimed that "a considerable proportion of this capital is percolating, naturally, into the Arab community and the adjacent Arab countries." Metzer would later examine Jewish capital coming into Palestine. He concluded that some Jewish capital was indeed entering the Arab economy, but that the transfers were "minor."[49] Horowitz's claims about benefits to the Arab economy were greatly overblown. The Special Committee's members had little knowledge of the matters Horowitz addressed. Like Shertok, Horowitz was not challenged on his claims.

WE WERE PROMISED A STATE

David Ben Gurion gave extensive testimony. One of his approaches was to tell the Committee that Palestine had already been promised as a Jewish state by the Balfour Declaration as incorporated by the League of Nations.

Hence, were the Special Committee to recommend any solution that did not include a Jewish state, it would be reneging on a commitment already made by the international community. Ben Gurion told the Committee that "an international undertaking was given to the Jewish people some thirty years ago in the Balfour Declaration and in the Mandate for Palestine, to reconstitute our national home in our ancient homeland." Ben Gurion told the Special Committee that the commitment made in the Balfour Declaration and in the Mandate for Palestine was to give Palestine to the Jews. "It will be to the everlasting credit of the British people," he said, "that it was the first in modern times to undertake the restoration of Palestine to the Jewish people."[50] That formulation suggested that Palestine was to be given to the Jews as a state, not only in part of Palestine, but in its entire territory. In support, Ben Gurion cited passages from the Royal Palestine Commission of 1937 (Peel Commission), which had recommended the creation of two states in Palestine – one Arab, one Jewish – and had cited the Balfour Declaration as at least not precluding a Jewish state.[51]

But Ben Gurion failed to mention to the Special Committee that two years later, in a White Paper, the British government said that no Jewish state had been promised. "It has been urged," read the 1939 White Paper, "that the expression 'a national home for the Jewish people' offered a prospect that Palestine might in due course become a Jewish State or Commonwealth. His Majesty's Government do not wish to contest the view, which was expressed by the Royal Commission, that the Zionist leaders at the time of the issue of the Balfour Declaration recognised that an ultimate Jewish State was not precluded by the terms of the Declaration. But, with the Royal Commission, His Majesty's Government believe that the framers of the Mandate in which the Balfour Declaration was embodied could not have intended that Palestine should be converted into a Jewish State against the will of the Arab population of the country."[52] The British government thus read the Balfour Declaration to preclude Palestine becoming a Jewish state without the consent of the Arabs. That consent was never likely.

NOT QUITE THE WHOLE TRUTH

Ben Gurion did mention the reaction of the Permanent Mandates Commission to the analysis of the Balfour Declaration reflected in the 1939 White Paper. The Permanent Mandates Commission had addressed the question of whether the White Paper, which imposed numerical limits on future Jewish migration to Palestine, violated Britain's obligation to implement the Balfour Declaration as incorporated into the Palestine Mandate. Ben Gurion quoted to the Special Committee a statement of the Permanent Mandates Commission in a report to the League Council that "the policy set out in the White Paper was not in accordance with the interpretation which, in agreement with the Mandatory Power and the Council of the League of Nations [the] Commission had always placed upon the Palestine Mandate."[53] Ben Gurion left the impression that the Permanent Mandates Commission had decided that the restrictions on Jewish immigration called for by the White Paper violated the Balfour Declaration.

In fact, the Permanent Mandates Commission had come to no such conclusion. The statement of the Permanent Mandates Commission that Ben Gurion quoted is found in a report filed by the Permanent Mandates Commission with the League Council in 1939, shortly after Britain issued its White Paper. Ben Gurion omitted a critical passage appearing later in that report. After saying that the White Paper's limitations on Jewish immigration were inconsistent with the interpretation it had previously placed on the Palestine Mandate, the Commission then asked itself whether the previous interpretation might be incorrect. "The Commission," recited the Permanent Mandates Commission in its report to the League Council, "went on to consider whether the Palestine mandate might not perhaps be open to a new interpretation which, while still respecting its main principles, would be sufficiently flexible for the policy of the White Paper not to appear at variance with it."[54] So the Commission's earlier view was only half the story.

The way the Permanent Mandates Commission carried out that consideration was that each of its seven members took a turn to state whether the White Paper violated the Palestine Mandate. Four members said that the White Paper violated the Palestine Mandate, whereas the other three said it did not. The four-member group included Orts and Rappard, the two members Weizmann had cultivated most assiduously. They found the White Paper's limitations on Jewish immigration to violate Britain's obligation under the Mandate. The other three members of the Commission thought that the circumstances in which Britain found itself as mandatory in 1939 justified the restrictions on Jewish immigration reflected in the White Paper, and that these restrictions did not violate the Palestine Mandate, hence did not violate the Balfour Declaration.[55]

Given that split of view, the Permanent Mandates Commission issued no statement on the matter. It reported to the League's Council the "inability of the Commission to submit on this point conclusions which would be both definite and unanimous." It said that "it can only refer the Council to the Minutes of its meetings for an account of the individual views of its members."[56]

After hearing Ben Gurion's testimony, the Special Committee consulted the Permanent Mandates Commission's report and found the passage that Ben Gurion cited. In its own Report, the Special Committee noted that each of the seven members of the Permanent Mandates Commission had expressed a view whether the interpretation reflected in the White Paper was consistent with the Palestine Mandate, and that four had said it was not, while three said it was.[57] Thus, the Special Committee understood that the Permanent Mandates Commission had not taken a position on the consistency of the White Paper with the Balfour Declaration, hence that Ben Gurion's portrayal of the Permanent Mandates Commission's view was a misleading half-truth.

JEWS WERE "EXTERMINATED?"

Historical issues also arose in a question to Ben Gurion from Abdur Rahman, the Special Committee member from India. Rahman asked whether the Jews "have always been here," meaning in Palestine. Ben Gurion answered, "Yes, except in the period of the Crusades, when all Jews were entirely exterminated."[58]

This was an astounding statement. Crusaders coming from Europe had killed Jews in Palestine, but the Jews were not "entirely exterminated." Some Jewish communities were untouched by the Crusaders. Jews in other Jewish communities were forced out of their home areas, but when Muslim forces under the Kurdish military leader Saladin defeated the Crusaders, ending the Second Crusade, Jews were invited to return to their former homes. Ben Gurion's statement was obviously aimed at eliciting sympathy for the Jews, but there was no historical basis for it.[59]

Rahman also asked about peoples other than Jews. He asked Ben Gurion if there was anyone in Palestine prior to what Rahman called "the Israelites." Without conceding that there was anyone prior to "the Israelites," Ben Gurion said, "There were a large number of people who came here." This answer prompted a further question from Rahman. "All of them have died out?" Ben Gurion replied, "Yes, all of them." Rahman was skeptical. "All of them and their descendants," he asked, "have died out?" To which Ben Gurion replied, "Yes, they disappeared." Rahman put one last follow-up question. "And the fellaheen who exist in Palestine today, are they descendants?" By "fellaheen" Rahman meant the rural Arab population. Ben Gurion replied, "I do not think so."[60]

Rahman, still not satisfied, asked Ben Gurion about the Old Testament story that Abraham had two wives, one of whom bore Isaac, and the other Ishmael, with the Jews descending from the former and the Arabs from the latter. Ben Gurion replied that in the Bible it is said with regard to these two children that to "Isaac and the seed of Isaac I will give this land."[61] Ben Gurion, who never purported to be religious, was relying on a supposed divine gift of Palestine to the Jews.

Their Biblical disagreement apart, Ben Gurion was telling the Committee that the twentieth century population of Arabs in Palestine did not descend from any population group that inhabited the area in ancient times. While one does find disagreement on the roots of Palestine's modern population, there is little doubt that the twentieth-century Arabs of Palestine descended from populations that inhabited Palestine before the start of the common era. That population became Arabized with the Arab conquest of the seventh century.[62]

The fact that Rahman's learning derived from the Old Testament bespoke the limitations on his knowledge of the populations that inhabited Palestine. Throughout the dialogues in the Special Committee hearings, Special Committee members posed basic questions that showed that they knew little about Palestine. The Jewish Agency representatives were free to recite facts without concern that their facts would be seriously scrutinized.

THE ARABS WILL LOVE US

The point on which Ben Gurion dissembled the most, however, was on the question of what would become of the Palestine Arabs if a Jewish state were established. Emil Sandstrom, Chair of the Special Committee, asked Ben Gurion whether there was any conflict between Arab and Jew in Palestine. Ben Gurion replied, "We have no conflict with the Arabs on our side. As far as this country and the Arabs are concerned, what we say is that we were dispossessed from our country, although it was a considerable time ago. But we did not give it up. It is our home."

Then Ben Gurion addressed the status in Palestine of its Arabs. "We admit that all those who are living in this country have the same right to it, just as we," he said. "We do not say, as in the case of other dispossessed people, that the people who are there ought to be removed. There was such a view held by the Labour Party, adopted only two years ago by the British Labour Party, just before the election, that in order to make more room for Jews the Arabs should be encouraged to transfer to other countries. We did not accept it even then; we did not approve of it. We do not claim that any Arab ought to be removed."[63]

What was remarkable in this exchange is that Sandstrom had not asked about transfer. Sandstrom posed only a general question about whether Jews and Arabs got along well in Palestine. Ben Gurion went out of his way to address transfer and to deny that it was part of the Jewish Agency's program. Ben Gurion, evidently fearing that the Special Committee might learn that the Jewish Agency's had actively discussed transferring Arabs out of Palestine, wanted to tell them it was not so.

The Jewish Agency was being circumspect in 1947 about any mention of its idea to transfer Arabs. Israeli historian Benny Morris commented on the Jewish Agency's concern that if it were thought they wanted to get rid of the Arabs, they would not receive favorable treatment at the United Nations. "Talk of transfer would only torpedo the passage of the Partition resolution," Morris explained that "the Yishuv leaders usually ignored the subject."[64]

As we saw in Chapter Four, transfer was very much on the Jewish Agency's agenda. Of the Jewish Agency team speaking for the Jewish Agency before the Special Committee, two members had served on committees exploring transfer. Shertok, whose testimony we have seen, was one of them. The other, who also testified, was Eliezer Kaplan, Treasurer of the Jewish Agency.[65] But the work of the transfer committees, and the participation of Shertok and Kaplan on them, was probably not known to members of the Special Committee. Ben Gurion was able to take advantage of their lack of familiarity, since the work of the transfer committees had not been publicized.

Chaim Weizmann also testified before the Special Committee, but only briefly. Weizmann argued that if the territory of Palestine were to be divided, the Negev desert should fall to a Jewish state. The Negev was not heavily populated. There were a few Jewish settlements, but its population was predominantly Bedouin Arab. The Jewish Agency argued that it was better equipped to develop agriculture in the desert environment. "Give us a chance of developing the derelict part of Palestine which is today the Negeb [Negev]," Weizmann implored in his testimony.[66] Importantly, the Negev at its southern tip opened into the Gulf of Aqaba, which gives access to the Red Sea and the Indian Ocean.[67]

7

The Ship that Launched a Nation

The Jewish Agency did not confine itself to testifying and telling the Special Committee what it thought its members might believe. It appointed two young Jewish Agency representatives as liaison officers to the Committee. One was David Horowitz, the economist who testified. The other was a young linguist named Aubrey Eban.[1] Horowitz and Eban were tasked by the Jewish Agency with shepherding the Committee members on field trips. They took them on what Eban called "an encyclopedic sightseeing tour" of Palestine. "Between tours, conversation and hearings," recalled Eban, he and Horowitz "were required to fill the minds of committee members with some ideas on a future solution."[2] So they pushed partition as the desired outcome, reinforcing what the Jewish Agency spokespersons said in the formal sessions.[3]

They particularly focused on Ralph Bunche. They figured out early on that his role would be central, and that, in fact, it would be he, not any member of the Special Committee, who would draft its findings. "The Jewish Agency boys," Bunche would relate, apparently referring to Horowitz and Eban, "obviously have it figured out that I will prepare the first draft of the report and are cultivating me steadily." Shertok as well buttonholed Bunche privately to make the case for partition.[4]

As further reinforcement of the Jewish Agency's testimony to the Committee, the Mossad staged a dramatic publicity stunt for the Special Committee.[5] It organized a ship to sail from France to Palestine, with 4500 European Jewish refugees on board. Mossad had been arranging such voyages since the end of the war, over and against the wishes of the British government, which was trying to limit migration into Palestine to the numbers it specified in the White Paper of 1939. The British authorities tried to keep these ships from unloading passengers in Palestine.

This particular voyage had a special purpose. The arrival in Palestine waters was timed to the presence in Palestine of the Special Committee. A ship purchased in the United States was specially outfitted. It was renamed *Exodus 1947*, to dramatize its purpose. It was provisioned in a port in Italy, overseen by Ada Sereni, who was Mossad's chief operative in Italy. Sereni later wrote about her experiences shepherding refugee ships to Palestine. "At that very time," Sereni explained, "came information about the imminent arrival in Palestine of the Committee of Inquiry appointed by the United Nations to propose a solution." This was a reference to the Special Committee. "The Jewish leadership in Jerusalem wanted the committee to be present for the arrival in Palestine of a ship, because this would give the best account of the drama of the boarding and of the desperate resistance by the immigrants. Shaul Avigur, the head of Mossad Illegal Immigration, was given the task of ensuring the arrival on time of one of these convoy ships."[6]

The logistics of the voyage were far from easy. Getting the ship out to open sea proved an obstacle. The Haganah, the military organization affiliated with the Jewish Agency, paid a bribe to a French boat pilot to steer the ship out of port. (He pocketed the cash but did not show up to steer the ship.)[7] Few of the passengers on the *Exodus 1947* had valid travel documents. Haganah officials arranged for forged documents and handed them out. The *Exodus 1947* passengers held entry visas for Colombia.[8]

Mossad's goal, as Sereni wrote, was not to get the 4500 displaced persons to Palestine. It was to show the Special Committee the strength of the desire of Jews to migrate to Palestine, and the need for more open migration to Palestine. But at the same time, as we saw, the Zionist movement was working to prevent the acceptance of these persons by other states.

The British government, aware of Mossad's plan to send the *Exodus 1947* to Palestine while the Special Committee was on site, made its own plan for interception and boarding.[9] The Jewish Agency knew that if the ship got as far as Haifa, British authorities would prevent docking.[10] *Exodus 1947* took on its load of refugees in France and exited into the Mediterranean Sea. The Royal Navy shadowed it all the way to Palestine.[11]

OFF-SHORE BROADCASTS

The Haganah had an underground radio station that could broadcast into Palestine from the ship. While the *Exodus 1947* was in transit, Mossad agents in Palestine sent communications instructing the crew to broadcast messages that would stress the suffering of the refugees and their desire to settle in Palestine, and specifically directed to the Special Committee, asking the Committee to board the ship and interview refugees.[12]

One of the passengers on the *Exodus 1947* was Reverend John Grauel, an American Methodist cleric who had joined the Haganah in the United States as one of very few of its non-Jewish members.[13] As the vessel approach Palestine, Reverend Grauel broadcast a call to the Special Committee. "Gentlemen," Reverend Grauel said, "we request you, in assembly in Eretz Israel, that you appear to gather testimony from the forty-five hundred Jews who are coming to Palestine in a few hours aboard the *Exodus, 1947*. We remind you that no committee was called to witness the death of six million Jews in Europe. This is your opportunity to fulfill the requirements of your declared justice in these matters."[14]

British vessels intercepted the *Exodus 1947* offshore opposite Gaza, and in a confrontation wounded scores of the prospective immigrants, killing two teenage boys and one crew member.[15] The captain thought that he could nonetheless sail to shore and disembark passengers, but the Jewish Agency official on board, Yosi Harel, thought it better to surrender and let the Royal Navy escort the vessel to shore. Harel's aim was to maximize publicity, because the spectacle of the refugees being reloaded onto other vessels, as Harel anticipated, "fulfilled long-range political goals of far greater consequence than the immediate welfare of 4,500 Jewish DPs."[16] The Royal Navy then escorted the *Exodus 1947* into port in Haifa. Israeli historian Idith Zertal wrote that "the Zionists had never intended to actually bring the 4,500 refugees onto the shores of Palestine, and such an effort had no chance of success since the *Exodus* was a show project from its inception."[17]

AN OCEAN VIEW

Special Committee members, as it turned out, knew about the *Exodus 1947* well before Reverend Grauel broadcast his message to them. From the time it left France, the Palestine press covered its progress. By July 18, with the *Exodus 1947* arriving in Haifa, the Committee had completed most of its hearings in Jerusalem but had not yet departed for Beirut, where it would hear from Arab governments. So the timing of the arrival was perfect. Horowitz and Eban, as Eban explains in his memoir, "decided to try to get some of the committee to see the ship with its human cargo."[18] After consulting with Shertok, Horowitz and Eban composed a letter to Emil Sandstrom as Chair of the Special Committee about the impending arrival.

Sandstrom, as he reported, "received a letter from the Jewish Agency in which it was suggested that some Members should go to Haifa to witness the arrival of the ship (the Exodus 1947) carrying Jewish refugees, to ascertain the exact conditions on board and to hear a first-hand account of the occurrence."[19]

Sandstrom agreed. He and Special Committee member Vladimir Simic of Yugoslavia went to the Haifa dock to visit the *Exodus 1947*. There they were taken aboard and spoke to passengers. Sandstrom related his impression to the Committee. He told them that "the people looked very poor and tired." Simic reported seeing "twelve people gravely wounded lying on stretchers."[20] They described to the other Committee members accounts they heard of the violence on board that led to the passenger deaths and injuries.[21] They also observed the passengers being reloaded onto other ships to be deported.[22] Eban described Sandstrom as "pale with shock" over his experience with the *Exodus 1947* passengers.[23]

After debarking in Haifa, Reverend Grauel was briefly detained by British police, then released. Haganah operatives were keen to get him to see members of the Special Committee. As a non-Jew and a cleric, Reverend Grauel possessed objectivity, as well as moral authority. Teddy Kollek, a future mayor of Jerusalem who at the time was the Haganah representative in the United States, was anxious to keep the British police from finding Grauel before he could be delivered to the Special Committee. "We engineered his escape from the British police," Kollek would recall years later, "and brought him before the United Nations Commission then meeting in Palestine." By "Commission," Kollek meant the Special Committee.

Reverend Grauel referred to his Haganah guides as "nursemaids" planning his mission to Jerusalem.[24] There he was taken to the apartment of Special Committee member García-Granados. Grauel described to García-Granados the horrors of the *Exodus 1947* voyage and especially the British boarding off Gaza. The next day, at García-Granados' invitation, Grauel went to Sandstrom's apartment, where he met with three other Special Committee members. There Grauel repeated his account of the voyage. Grauel also made a point of saying that the Jews in the displaced person (DP) camps in Europe wanted to settle in Palestine.[25] The Jewish Agency wanted the Special Committee to connect the issue of the displaced Jews in Europe with that of the status of Palestine.[26] The aim of the *Exodus 1947* voyage and its timing to the stay of the Special Committee in Jerusalem was to convince the Special Committee to make that connection.

Horowitz and Eban kept the Special Committee members busy in their off hours. Some members of the Special Committee met privately with

Ben Gurion and other Jewish Agency personnel at Shertok's apartment in Jerusalem.[27] There Ben Gurion pressed the point that the Jewish Agency would accept partition only if the Jewish state got the Negev.[28]

García-Granados relates these events in a book he published in 1948 titled *The Birth of Israel: The drama as I saw it*. García-Granados indicated that he had scant knowledge of Palestine or Zionism at the outset, but after the fact he described his work on the Special Committee as involvement in "a people's fight for freedom."[29] By "people," he meant the Jews as represented by the Jewish Agency. From the accounts by García-Granados and by Committee Chairman Sandstrom, the arrival of the *Exodus 1947* had the intended impact, inclining Committee members toward the need for a Jewish state that would allow immigration for victims of Nazi persecution.[30]

Reverend Grauel was also taken to meet with Golda Meir, a leading figure in the Jewish Agency, along with other Jewish Agency personnel.[31] Meir attributed great significance to the *Exodus 1947* episode. She considered it to have been key to the Special Committee's partition recommendation. She said that Reverend Grauel's graphic account of the voyage of *Exodus 1947* marked a turning point in the thinking of Committee members.[32]

Meir was not alone in this conclusion. Historian Idith Zertal wrote that the *Exodus 1947* episode "undoubtedly contributed to the final draft of the UNSCOP conclusions."[33] Bartley Crum was another. Crum was an American lawyer appointed by President Harry Truman to serve on the 1946 Anglo-American Committee of Inquiry. Crum was thus close to the international work on Palestine. Crum considered the voyage of the *Exodus 1947* a key event in the partition of Palestine. "No other event in 1947," Crum wrote, "was as important as the odyssey of the *Exodus*. It made possible, in fact, the United Nations vote for a democratic state in Palestine, a Jewish state in that land."[34] Crum called the vessel "the ship that launched a nation."[35] The voyage was fictionalized a few years later by Leon Uris in his best-selling novel *Exodus*.[36]

The American Council for Judaism, a group that opposed Zionism, denounced the Jewish Agency over the *Exodus 1947*. A Council leader, Rabbi Morris S. Lazaron, emeritus rabbi of the Baltimore Madison Avenue congregation, delivered a sermon in which he called the episode the most recent chapter "in a long story of Zionist extremist hypocrisy, unscrupulous propaganda and exploitation of our brothers' misery." In refusing to debark in France after being denied entry to Palestine, Rabbi Lazaron thought, "the miserable people on these ships did not act spontaneously."

Rather, he said, "They were instructed to make martyrs of themselves by men who used their pitiful helplessness to create a situation which would evoke world sympathy for Zionist ends."[37] The passengers had little chance of getting into Palestine, with the Royal Navy tailing them. Rabbi Lazaron viewed the passengers as having been deceived and victimized.

LINKING THE ISSUE OF DISPLACED JEWS

Even though the Arab Higher Committee declined to testify in Jerusalem, a number of governmental figures from neighboring Arab states did agree to appear. A session was held for that purpose by the Special Committee in Lebanon, near Beirut, after it departed Jerusalem. Only two brief sessions were held there, however.[38] The Special Committee did get enough from the Arab side to realize, according to García-Granados, "that if we finally recommended any form of Jewish independence, which was later accepted by the General Assembly, bloodshed might result."[39] So the Special Committee understood that a proposal of partition would not be accepted on the Arab side.

The scant participation on the Arab side left the Jewish Agency with a great advantage. The Special Committee never got a point-by-point refutation from the Arab side of the factual information the Jewish Agency gave the Committee in Jerusalem. Ben Gurion's story about the Jews being totally exterminated, Shertok's account of Jewish migration to Palestine, Horowitz' statement about Jewish migration benefiting the Arab economy, all this went unchallenged.

After completing its hearings, the Special Committee retired to Geneva to finalize recommendations. Sandstrom was so impressed with Horowitz and Eban that he invited them to accompany the Special Committee to Geneva.[40] Shertok went as well, taking a whole staff with him. Consulting there with the Committee, these Jewish Agency personnel were able to influence the Special Committee in shaping recommendations.[41]

Once in Geneva, the Special Committee decided that a visit to displaced person camps should be made.[42] This was a critical decision, because it meant that the Committee was considering the DP situation as it fashioned recommendations for Palestine. The *Exodus 1947* incident had served its purpose. The visits to the camps had the effect the Jewish Agency intended. They solidified the Committee's view that the issue of Palestine should include the issue of the Jews seeking to leave Europe. The making of that link was key to the Committee's formulation of its proposed partition borders that envisaged a Jewish state with territory much larger than was warranted by the then present demographic breakdown in Palestine. The General Assembly's resolution creating the Committee directed it to report on the "question of Palestine." Shertok had asked the General Assembly, when it was establishing the Committee, to include the interests of Jews outside Palestine who might wish to immigrate, and several delegates of member states had concurred. Rabbi Silver had suggested to the General Assembly that the Committee visit the DP camps.[43] But no reference to Jews outside Palestine had been written into the Committee's terms of reference by the General Assembly.[44] Now the Special Committee itself added this aspect to its work.

A sub-committee made the visits. What the Special Committee did not know was that the Jewish Agency was working feverishly, as we saw, to keep Jews who sought to emigrate from being accepted by the countries to which many of them wished to go. The Jewish Agency continued that effort as the Nazi concentration camps opened at the end of the Second World War. It was in particular Jews in Germany, Austria, and Poland who felt a need to leave. The Jewish Agency saw that population as a boon to its efforts at gaining territory in Palestine. It used them effectively to that end, bringing the Committee along in that process.

By the time of the sub-committee's visit, many DPs had been in the camps already for two years. The sub-committee found that propaganda work was being conducted in the camps to promote Palestine as a destination. It did not attempt to quantify the impact of that propaganda. A confidential assessment by the Jewish Agency made about the same time as the visit of the sub-committee concluded that it was questionable if the sentiment for Palestine was very strong among the DPs.[45] As we saw earlier, the report solicited by President Truman in 1945 found that the West was the preferred destination. A lower level of enthusiasm for Palestine had also been found by the Anglo-American Committee of Inquiry in 1945.

The sub-committee surmised that the orientation to Palestine among the DPs had increased since then. "Various persons who were in a position to compare the state of feeling as between this year and last," the sub-committee wrote, "were all disposed to agree that there had been an intensification of sentiment in favour of immigration to Palestine since, for example, the time of the visit of the Anglo-American Committee of Inquiry."[46] Through this time period, as the sub-committee found, Zionist organizations were lobbying the refugees to choose Palestine.[47] Ben Gurion visited DP camps in October 1945 and again in January 1946, using those visits to propagate Zionism among the camp residents and to encourage them to express a desire to settle in Palestine.[48]

In August 1945, Ben Gurion addressed a Zionist conference in London and advocated getting one million Jews from Europe to Palestine over the coming months.[49] In Autumn 1945, Ben Gurion set up a Zionist underground, headquartered in Paris, that planted Zionist operatives in communities of Holocaust survivors, to agitate in favor of their migration to Palestine.[50]

The Harrison report, recounted in Chapter Five, from late summer 1945 found many displaced Jews desiring to migrate to Palestine, but that many of these named Palestine only because they knew they could not gain admission to the United States. The Anglo-American Committee of Inquiry in winter 1946 did a more intense survey and found most of those desiring to leave Europe indicating migration to Palestine as their aim, but again against the background of doors being closed to countries in the Western world.[51]

The Special Committee's sub-committee, now in Summer 1947, found an increase in expression of a desire to migrate to Palestine over what the Anglo-American Committee of Inquiry found, though the sub-committee acknowledged that propaganda conducted by Zionist organizations accounted for some of the increase. The sub-committee thought, in any event, that a desire for resettlement in Palestine was strong. It reported, "there exists among the Jewish displaced persons in Germany and Austria today a mass urge toward settlement in Palestine."

The sub-committee drew a further conclusion that the Anglo-American Committee of Inquiry had not made. The sub-committee thought that the desire among the displaced Jews to migrate to Palestine needed to be taken into account in devising a future status for Palestine. "We were left in little doubt," the sub-committee wrote, "that if only because of the extraordinary intensity of the feeling displayed in this direction, such a situation must be regarded as at least a component in the problem of Palestine. This is true whether the state of mind among the Jews is to be regarded as spontaneous or whether it is to be attributed to deliberate indoctrination; in either case the situation seems to us to be unavoidably an element in the shaping of the policy of organized Jewry in relation to Palestine."[52]

A RESOUNDING SUCCESS

The Report the Special Committee gave the UN General Assembly showed that the Jewish Agency had done well for itself. The Special Committee accepted the most crucial Jewish Agency argument, namely, that Jewish economic activity in mandate Palestine had benefited the

Palestine Arabs. The Special Committee accepted the dubious picture of economic activity in mandate Palestine that Shertok and Horowitz had painted. The Special Committee would mention nothing of the ways identified by the Anglo-American Committee of Inquiry or the Hope Simpson Commission in which the Palestine Arabs were being disadvantaged. The Special Committee accepted as fact what Shertok and Horowitz told them.[53]

The only point on which the Special Committee found fault with what the Jewish Agency told it was Ben Gurion's statement that the Permanent Mandates Commission had found the British White Paper of 1939 to be in violation of the Balfour Declaration. On that point, the Special Committee did research into the records of the Permanent Mandates Commission and uncovered the falsity of Ben Gurion's account.

The Special Committee was unable, however, to agree on a single recommendation. Ralph Bunche did the drafting in Geneva, writing both a majority view and a minority view.[54] The two non-European members (Iran, India) plus Yugoslavia favored a federation between an Arab sector and a Jewish sector. This variant was far from what the Arab Higher Committee wanted but would have left Palestine as a single state. However, seven members did what the Jewish Agency asked by recommending a division of Palestine's territory between a Jewish state and an Arab state, albeit joined in an economic union with Jerusalem under UN supervision.[55] Australia abstained, supporting neither approach.

In regard to division of territory, the majority of seven was quite generous to the Jewish Agency. The majority recommended putting enough territory in the Jewish state to accommodate an anticipated influx of Jews from Europe, even though by so doing it called for a Jewish state in territory that at the time had as many Arabs as Jews. The majority acceded to the demand by Ben Gurion and Weizmann for the Negev. This was one of the Jewish Agency's greatest successes with the Special Committee.[56] After being escorted to Jewish settlements in the Negev by the Jewish Agency, Special Committee members were impressed by efforts to cultivate crops in the desert environment.[57] The Committee even recommended placing Jaffa, the largest Arab city, in the Jewish state. When Britain's Peel Commission had suggested partition of Palestine in 1937, neither Jaffa nor the Negev was to be part of a Jewish state. The majority recommended giving a Jewish state even more of Palestine than the Jewish Agency had dared request.[58] This discrepancy was rationalized by the expectation that displaced Jews in Europe would immigrate. "The proposed Jewish State," read the majority recommendation, "leaves considerable room for further development and land settlement."[59] The majority linked the issue of Europe's displaced Jews with that of Palestine, as the Jewish Agency urged it to do, giving a Jewish state the lion's share of Palestine.

8

Cocktails at the Consulate

The Special Committee on Palestine submitted its report to the UN General Assembly on schedule, on September 1, 1947. The Jewish Agency was heartened by the outcome. It had lobbied for partition, and that was the recommendation of the Special Committee's majority. The Zionist General Council, a body functioning under the World Zionist Organization, adopted a resolution applauding the majority recommendation and denouncing the minority recommendation.[1]

The Arab reaction was predictably negative. The Arab Higher Committee, as we saw, distanced itself from the Special Committee precisely because it sought a single state in Palestine and feared a recommendation aimed at dividing it. The Arab Higher Committee reacted to the Special Committee's report by calling for a one-day commercial strike for October 3 to "protest against the schemes and recommendation of the UNSCOP." "The Arabs of Palestine," declared the Arab Higher Committee, "refuse definitely to acquiesce in any solution entailing the partitioning of Palestine."[2] Arab businesses throughout Palestine shut their doors on October 3.[3] Absent acceptance on the Arab side, any proposed solution for Palestine would be difficult to implement. As a result, the Special Committee report was not seen as providing a solution for Palestine. Rather, it was regarded as giving the Jewish Agency a base from which to work.[4]

The General Assembly decided to have the Special Committee's report considered first by an *ad hoc* committee of the whole of the General Assembly.[5] Called the Ad Hoc Committee on the Palestinian Question, this committee was to decide what to recommend to the General Assembly itself: whether to adopt the partition recommendation of the majority, whether to adopt the federal state recommendation of the minority, or whether to take some third approach.

AN "IGNORANT MAJORITY" IS UNDESERVING

The Ad Hoc Committee on the Palestinian Question held its first meeting on September 25, 1947.[6] The effectiveness of the Jewish Agency's performance in Jerusalem was quick to reveal itself. Some individuals who had served on the Special Committee participated on behalf of their states. One was Jorge García-Granados, who represented Guatemala. García-Granados had supported the majority plan in the Special Committee. Not surprisingly, he spoke in favor of it. For García-Granados, it was unthinkable that the Jewish community would be part of a country in which the Arabs, as the numerical majority, might hold the keys to power. "What would happen," he asked, "if the demands of the Arabs were yielded to and an independent State of Palestine were created? The Arab population," he said, was characterized by "its simple religiousness and rudimentary political sense."[7] Because of these defects in the Palestinian Arab polity, said García-Granados, the country was not theirs even though they constituted a numerical majority of the population. "What characterized a nation," he said, "was its culture and not the number of inhabitants. In twenty-five years, the Jewish people had left upon Palestine the indelible mark of an outstanding culture, which characterized the country even more than the Arab culture: Palestine was no more Arab than certain Spanish countries of Latin America were Indian."[8] "An ignorant majority," he said, "should not be allowed to impose its will. A million progressive human beings should not be the plaything of a few ringleaders supported by millions of human beings of less advanced ideas."[9] So in García-Granados' analysis, the Palestine Arabs could be discounted as a recommendation for the status of Palestine was being fashioned. They might be physically present in Palestine, but they did not constitute a "nation." Because the Jews had a superior culture, Palestine was theirs.

García-Granados' reference to Latin America was telling. His own country, Guatemala, had an indigenous majority, but the government was in the hands of settlers from Spain. García-Granados did not elaborate on his reference to Latin America, but the obvious logic of the reference was that just as the Spaniards were entitled to govern Guatemala, so the Jews were entitled to govern Palestine.

This characterization of the Palestine Arabs as a backward people of low culture showed the extent to which the Jewish Agency delegation had succeeded in Jerusalem. The Jewish Agency had gone to great lengths to show the superiority of their polity. Much of the information it had presented was misleading or untrue. The Jewish Agency had done well in drawing García-Granados into their corner. His condescending references to the Palestine Arabs were as fully racially-laden as Weizmann's in his 1918 letter to A.J. Balfour. García-Granados' view that the majority could be overridden mirrored the 1919 Zionist tract that we saw in Chapter Three, where the same argument was made to justify the Balfour Declaration. And as we also saw in Chapter Three, the British government ignored the view of the majority of Palestine's citizens by inserting itself as mandatory.

The most disturbing aspect of García-Granados' denigration of the Palestine Arabs in the Ad Hoc Committee on the Palestinian Question is not that he himself had imbibed such a view. The more disturbing aspect is that García-Granados must have thought that expressing this view of the Palestine Arabs would be persuasive with the membership of the United Nations. The League of Nations had made inroads on colonialism with its mandate system. And the UN Charter provided protections for non-self-governing peoples. But as of 1947, most UN member states either held colonies or, as was the case in Latin America, had been formed through colonial settlement that left the colonizers ruling over an indigenous population.

García-Granados advocated adoption of the majority recommendation. But he found few delegates willing to express any optimism that partition would be good for Palestine. Some challenged the decision of the Special Committee to link the question of displaced Jews with that of Palestine. India affirmed, "the problem of the displaced Jews in Europe was not one with which the Committee should be concerned. Nor should it be linked to the issue of the future government of Palestine, with which it was totally unconnected." For India, the question of the displaced Jews in Europe should be addressed by the United Nations, but as a self-standing matter. India also questioned giving any present significance to the Balfour Declaration. India, agreeing with the Arab view, thought that Palestine should simply become independent. Palestine, said India, "should be recognized as an independent State, with wide autonomy for Jews in areas where they were in a majority."[10] China, like India, thought that the issue of the displaced Jews was separate from that of Palestine. Like many other member states, China worried that the Arab opposition to partition meant that a partition recommendation would lead to armed conflict.[11]

QUALMS ABOUT PARTITION

The United States had struggled with the Special Committee's two recommendations. Loy Henderson, Director of the Office of Near Eastern Affairs in the US Department of State, said in a confidential meeting of the US delegation at the United Nations that the Special Committee report was "not based on any principle," but was "full of sophistry."[12] "It is probable," read a confidential assessment of the report prepared within the US Department of State, "that the Arab States will reject any solution that creates a Jewish State or province or permits further Jewish immigration into Palestine." Further, "It is difficult to predict whether any solution short of immediate independence would obtain even the reluctant acquiescence of the Arab States." Without such acquiescence, the Department, like the government of China, anticipated "armed strife in the Near East."[13]

Despite these concerns, the Department of State decided on the eve of the first session of the Ad Hoc Committee on the Palestinian Question to support the Special Committee's majority plan for partition. The only modifications the United States would suggest were territorial adjustments to be made in favor of the projected Arab state over what had been suggested in the Special Committee majority recommendation.[14] The United States told the delegates that it supported partition.[15]

A number of states expressed support for partition in principle but nevertheless voiced reservations about the majority recommendation. Haiti supported partition but rejected two of the considerations that had influenced the Special Committee's majority. Haiti thought that "the suffering of the Jewish people, distressing as it had been, was not an argument for the partition of Palestine or for their claims on a land inhabited for thousands of years by another people." Haiti also objected to the fact that the Special Committee had given weight to financial investment in Palestine by the Zionists. Haiti said it did not think that the "material contribution during the preceding twenty-five years" by Jews in Palestine created "a vested interest in Palestine."[16]

Yugoslavia, whose representative had supported the minority recommendation in the Special Committee for a federated Palestine, spoke up for that recommendation.[17] Delegates from the Arab states opposed partition. Saudi Arabia said that Palestine should simply be declared independent.[18] Argentina spoke against partition, proposing instead that a committee composed of Jews and Arabs be formed and tasked with arriving at a compromise.[19] Britain said it would take no position on proposed solutions for Palestine.[20] Cuba expressed concern that not everyone on the Jewish side would settle for only a portion of Palestine, hence, the majority plan "would only lead to subsequent Jewish demands for more living space."[21] Although the Jewish Agency lobbied for partition, that was, as we saw, a position it took only as a compromise, understanding that the Special

Committee would not give it the entirety of Palestine. Ben Gurion regarded partition as a first step toward control of all of Palestine.[22]

Moshe Shertok, representing the Jewish Agency for Palestine, spoke in the Ad Hoc Committee on the Palestinian Question in favor of the majority plan. Shertok did not shy from highlighting the fact that the majority plan was premised on linking the issue of displaced Jews with that of Palestine. He said that the majority recommendation would "provide a complete solution" to "the problem of the Jews of Europe."[23]

Responding on behalf of the Arab Higher Committee, Jamal Husseini spoke for "a unitary and democratic State including the whole of Palestine."[24] Chaim Weizmann spoke as former Chairman of the Jewish Agency, reiterating Shertok's advocacy of the Special Committee's majority plan and, like Shertok, saying that it would "solve the problem of the Jewish displaced persons." Weizmann rejected "the accusation of conspiracy in regard to Jewish immigration into Palestine," a reference to the charge that the Jewish Agency was forcing displaced Jews to Palestine. Weizmann spoke against Jewish migration to states other than Palestine. "To suggest that they should rebuild their ruined homes or ask refuge of countries reluctant to receive them," he said, "was mere mockery."[25]

As in the Special Committee, the Jewish Agency was successful in keeping out any mention of its plans for getting rid of the Arabs. Ben Gurion, as we saw, went out of his way in his testimony before the Special Committee to deny plans to "transfer" Arabs out of Palestine. No delegate in the Ad Hoc Committee on the Palestinian Question raised transfer as a criticism of the partition proposal. But the idea remained on the Jewish Agency's agenda. In a speech he made to the Executive of the Jewish Agency on November 2, 1947, while the Ad Hoc Committee on the Palestinian Question was still in session, Ben Gurion addressed the issue of Arabs in a Jewish state and said that Arabs might form a fifth column. If that happened, he said, "they can either be mass arrested or expelled; it is better to expel them."[26]

Some effort was made in the Ad Hoc Committee on the Palestinian Question to arrange for Jewish-Arab conciliation, but when nothing was done in that direction Britain said it would not assist in implementing partition if partition were to be the recommendation. Britain called partition "a scheme which was not acceptable to both Arabs and Jews."[27] If Britain as mandatory power was not prepared to aid in implementing partition, the chances for successful partition were bleak.

A subcommittee of the Ad Hoc Committee on the Palestinian Question worked with the territorial division in the majority plan. By a United

States-sponsored amendment,[28] the subcommittee made modifications favorable to the projected Arab state, putting Jaffa in the Arab state along with Beersheba and some land in the northern Negev.[29]

Syria said that the Arabs opposed "the very idea of partition." Moreover, they rejected the particular territorial division. It "cut off the port of Jaffa from its hinterland." It put "the people of Jerusalem under trusteeship." It "put 60 per cent of the territory of a country at the disposal of a third of its population." In a reference to the Negev, Syria said that the plan would "give the Jews territory where not a single Jew lived." "The League of Nations had already perpetrated an injustice in accepting the terms of the Mandate; the United Nations would be perpetrating an even graver injustice in recommending the plan for partition."[30]

The debate took an odd direction. Most states said they would vote for partition, since the two sides could not agree on another outcome. But at the same time, most said that the very disagreement meant that partition would not work. States expressed concern over the possible consequences of recommending partition. Belgium said it would abstain in a vote on partition. The plan for partition, it said, "was not calculated to achieve the essential aim of the United Nations, namely, the maintenance of peace."[31]

SOVIETS LAUD PARTITION

A major unknown as the Ad Hoc Committee on the Palestinian Question began its deliberations was what position the Soviet Union would take on partition. Despite Gromyko's statement in May, the Soviet government had made no further pronouncements on whether its sympathies lay with the Arab Higher Committee's position or with the Jewish Agency's. The US Department of State was guessing, given the longstanding Soviet antagonism to Zionism, that the Soviet Union would back the Arabs. "The Soviet Union has thus far avoided taking a position," recited a September 30, 1947 Department assessment, "but the Embassy in Moscow and other observers are convinced that, in the final showdown, the Soviet Union will support the Arab States."[32]

To the surprise of many, the Soviet delegate, Simon Tsarapkin, in his first statement in the Ad Hoc Committee, said that partition was an acceptable approach, and that the Soviet Union approved the Special Committee's majority plan.[33] So the US assessment of the Soviet leaning was off the mark. Even more surprising was the enthusiasm Tsarapkin showed for partition. Most of the states that spoke in favor of partition were pessimistic about its chances for peacefully resolving the Palestine situation.

They spoke of the Arab opposition to the plan. They saw partition as a last ditch measure in light of the impossibility of gaining agreement between the parties.

Tsarapkin's approach was different. He made no reference to Arab opposition or to problems of implementation. Alone among the delegates, he said that partition was a principled approach that would benefit both Jews and Arabs. The partition plan of the Special Committee majority as modified in regard to territory, Tsarapkin said, "gave both the Arab and the Jewish people an opportunity to organize their national life as they desired. It was based on the principles of the equality of peoples and the right of self-determination." The plan "was perfectly practicable and its adoption by the General Assembly would be of benefit not only to the Arab and Jewish peoples but also the United Nations and all peace-loving peoples."[34]

This was a remarkable statement, given what other states were saying about the prospects. The Arab states were all saying they would oppose partition if it were recommended by the General Assembly. Britain was saying that it would not implement partition. The Soviet statements ignored the realities that troubled the other delegations.

During the time of the Ad Hoc Committee's sessions, the Soviet Union began privately conferring with the Jewish Agency. In informal settings, they discussed strategy. Tsarapkin sought out meetings with Shertok. He invited Jewish Agency representatives to meet with Soviet diplomats at the Soviet consulate in New York. There, Tsarapkin served wine as they conferred. The Jewish Agency team asked Tsarapkin to support territorial modifications favoring the prospective Jewish state.[35] The Soviet delegation did promote modifications favoring the Jewish State, principally in sectors of central Palestine.[36]

The fact that both the United States and the Soviet Union came out in support of partition had an impact on smaller countries. Bolivia said that partition was not ideal for Palestine, but Bolivia gave "weight to the views of those countries which were most directly involved in the implementation and the consequences of whatever solution was decided upon. Among those countries were some of the great Powers which had agreed to guarantee the peace in the world, and they believed that the partition plan which they supported would bring peace to Palestine."[37] For the Arab Higher Committee, the fact that the Soviet Union and United States were on the same page was nothing short of disaster. "The two great champions of freedom, the USSR and the United States," bemoaned Jamal Husseini, "had joined hands – prompted, they said, by humanitarian motives – to support the monstrous perversion of the principle of self-determination in Palestine."[38]

The partition plan was approved by the Ad Hoc Committee on the Palestinian Question by a vote of 25 to 13, with 17 abstentions.[39] Four days later, it was approved by the General Assembly in plenary session by a vote of 33 to 13, with 10 abstentions. It was denominated Resolution 181.[40] The plan included an economic union between the projected Arab state and the projected Jewish state. Jerusalem was to be administered by neither state, but rather by the UN Trusteeship Council, a main organ of the United Nations that dealt with non-self-governing territories. A Palestine Commission was set up by Resolution 181 to administer the transfer of control from Britain to the two projected states. Jewish immigration without limitation as to numbers was to begin almost immediately, even prior to either of the two states coming into being, under a provision calling on Britain as mandatory to make available a port facility for that purpose.[41]

A TRIUMPH FOR THE AGES

UN General Assembly Resolution 181 was a major diplomatic success for the Jewish Agency. It has been called "the first concrete success of international, Zionist, diplomatic efforts to establish a state for the Jews in Palestine."[42] Ben Gurion publicly welcomed Resolution 181 as the first explicit statement at the international level that Jewish statehood was appropriate for at least some of the territory in Palestine. Ben Gurion lavished praise on Shertok, depicting Shertok's success in gaining adoption of Resolution 181 as a triumph in "the greatest political battle in the history of any nation for at least the past two thousand years."[43]

On the Arab side, Resolution 181 was denounced and led almost immediately to civil disobedience in protest. Ralph Bunche said that for the Arabs, Resolution 181 "was considered just about a complete defeat," because it envisaged dividing Palestine and eliminating restraints on Jewish immigration.[44] Resolution 181 drew boundaries that, even with the modifications over the Special Committee's majority recommendation, attributed to the Jewish state slightly more than half the territory of Palestine. At the time, the Jewish percentage in the population, even counting recent immigrants, stood at one third.

Soviet backing was key to the Jewish Agency victory. David Horowitz, the Jewish Agency economist who testified before the Special Committee, gave credit to Tsarapkin and to his deputy in the Soviet UN delegation, Boris Stein. "The unremitting aid that Zarapkin [Horowitz's spelling] and

Stein gave our cause, and their sharp, direct logic, played an important part in the long series of gains we made and in the sum total of our triumph."[45] So in Horowitz' estimation, the strong statements of the Soviet delegation swayed other delegates.

The strength of the Soviet support for partition befuddled the United States. Through State Department channels, Walter Bedell Smith, the US ambassador in Moscow, was asked how this came about. Smith thought that the Soviet Union decided to support partition for reasons related to the Zionist efforts to show Maiskii that a Jewish state would be a political ally for the Soviet Union. In a confidential telegram to Secretary of State George Marshall, Smith wrote that the Soviet government decided to back partition because they thought that the Jews were more susceptible than the Arabs to what he termed "Soviet penetration." The "Arab East," wrote Smith, was difficult for the Soviet Union to "penetrate" because it was squarely in the Western camp by virtue of the US predominance in neighboring states – Greece, Turkey, and Iran. There were "strong US and British interests and commitments" in the Arab states, which, moreover were "controlled by [a] feudal anti-Communist ruling class." Indigenous Communist movements in the Arab states were weak. As a result, said Ambassador Smith, the Soviet calculation was that "Jews and other minority groups provide Kremlin's only immediately useful tool to 'soften up' [the] area for eventual straight Communist cultivation."[46] Whatever the designs of the Soviet Union may have been in the region, a Jewish state was regarded as potentially friendlier territory for it than were the Arab states. The view that a Jewish state would be on close terms with the Soviet Union had, as we have seen, been cultivated by Weizmann and Ben Gurion.

9

Causing Chaos

Resolution 181 brought more than verbal denunciation on the Arab side. The Arab Higher Committee resorted to the same tactic as it had after the issuance of the report of the Special Committee on Palestine. It called for a three-day commercial strike. But this time the call for a strike was taken up seriously. Violence ensued. Groups of Arabs attacked buses carrying Jews, killing a number of them.[1] Zionist militias responded quickly. On December 10, Ben Gurion approved a policy of intimidation aimed at Arab civilians, to be implemented by the Haganah.[2] The policy was implemented immediately. "The Jews again appeared today to be on the offensive," wrote the *New York Times* on December 12, 1947, "roughly two-thirds of the incidents being initiated by them, and in their operations they showed evidence of planning, something absent in general from the Arab attacks."[3] A primary actor was the Irgun Zvei Leumi (National Military Organization in the Land of Israel), a well-organized Zionist force that had directed violent attacks against the British. It now shifted its attacks to the Arabs. "The day's total casualties were twenty-one Arabs and three Jews killed, reported the *Times* on December 13. "More than eighty Arabs were wounded and three Jews were seriously wounded."[4]

The UN Palestine Commission, the body that was given the unenviable task of convincing the parties to implement Resolution 181, met in January 1948 to figure out what was happening in Palestine in the wake of that resolution. Britain's UN representative, Alexander Cadogan, appeared before the Commission and characterized the situation as he saw it. "In present circumstances," Cadogan told the Commission, "the Jewish story that the Arabs are the attackers and the Jews the attacked is not tenable. The Arabs are determined to show that they will not submit tamely to the

United Nations Plan of Partition; while the Jews are trying to consolidate the advantages gained at the General Assembly by a succession of drastic operations designed to intimidate and cure the Arabs of any desire for further conflict."[5]

Cadogan addressed these same incidents in responding to charges that the Arabs were blockading Jerusalem's Old City, thereby cutting off residents in its Jewish Quarter. "The facts," Cadogan said, "are that on 13 December, bombs were thrown into Arab crowds immediately outside the Damascus Gate of the Old City by Jews passing in motor cars. In the explosions which followed seven Arabs were killed and fifty-four injured. These casualties included women and children. As a result of this outrage, credit for which was later claimed by the Irgun Zvei Leumi, the Arabs set up road blocks outside the Old City to check the identity of passers-by. These road blocks were cleared away by security forces. On December 29, the Irgun Zvei Leumi carried out an exactly similar indiscriminate bomb attack at the Damascus Gate, killing eleven and wounding thirty-two Arabs, many of whom were women and children."[6]

Cadogan's analysis captured the reality of the moment. The Irgun Zvei Leumi and another Zionist military force, LEHI (Fighters for the Freedom of Israel), operated outside the Jewish Agency. They threw bombs at Arab shops and street crowds and attacked Arab civilians in their villages.[7] The *Times* correspondent described Irgun Zvei Leumi attacks against Arabs in villages as "terrorist bombings of Arabs."[8] Menachem Begin, leader of the Irgun Zvei Leumi, wrote proudly of these attacks in his memoir. "For three days, from 11th to 13th December," Begin said, the Irgun Zvei Leumi "hammered at concentrations of rioters and their offensive bases... we attacked at Haifa and Jaffa; at Tireh and Yazar. We attacked again and again in Jerusalem... Enemy casualties in killed and wounded were heavy."[9] These locations were Arab-populated towns, located all over Palestine. Begin's recitation of their names was intended to show the scope of the Irgun Zvai Leumi's attacks.

Attacks from the Arab side focused largely on convoys to Jewish-populated points, as Jewish populations were dispersed and used road transport for supplies.[10] The *Times* of London reported, "While the Jews are suffering mainly through sniping at their road convoys, the Arabs have lost many lives through Jewish assaults on their villages."[11] The Haganah directed attacks at villages from which convoy attacks were staged.[12] By mid-December 1947, the Haganah, like the other Zionist militias, was attacking Arab civilians.[13] In one village, the Haganah dynamited the house of the village elder, with inhabitants inside.[14]

"TERRORIST RAIDS": CIA

The Palmach was an elite unit of the Haganah. It had received training from the British Army during the war. One of its trainers had been Aubrey Eban, who at the time was a British officer. One Arab village that was attacked by the Palmach was called Khissas. A dozen Arab civilians were killed in that operation.[15] With the Haganah falling under Jewish Agency leadership, the attack on Khissas was laid at the door of the Jewish Agency. David Ben Gurion, in a cable to Shertok in New York, said that the attack had not been authorized by the Jewish Agency.[16] Whatever may have been authorization for the attack on Khissas, a leadership meeting was called by Ben Gurion on December 31, 1947 to discuss tactics. The consensus reached at this meeting was to use military force not only to retaliate for particular Arab actions, but to attack more broadly, to drive the Arabs out.[17]

By the turn of the year, in any event, the three Zionist militias were attacking in a way that was sending Arab civilians to flight out of fear. The British Army was still nominally responsible for security in Palestine, but it provided little protection. Arab militias were organized in neighboring countries and entered Palestine about this time, focusing attacks on outlying Jewish settlements, and on supply convoys to them.[18] The Zionist militias sought to counter these Arab militias, and to defend supply convoys.

In January 1948, attacks by the Zionist militias on Arab civilian populations picked up in intensity.[19] LEHI bombed a municipal government building in the city of Jaffa where Arab villagers had taken refuge to escape attacks on their villages.[20] On January 4, the Haganah bombed a major Arab hotel in west Jerusalem, the Semiramis, killing 26 persons. The British government called this attack a "dastardly and wholesale murder of innocent people."[21] Whole neighborhoods in west Jerusalem began to empty of Arab residents.[22] Ben Gurion was called on the Semiramis attack by Alan Cunningham, Britain's high commissioner in Palestine. Ben Gurion expressed regret. Arabs in the vicinity of the hotel fled Jerusalem in panic.[23]

While Ben Gurion in his public utterances denied any intentionality behind the flight of Jerusalem's Arabs, he sounded a different tone behind closed doors. At a meeting of his Mapai party on February 7, Ben Gurion expressed elation at the panic flight. "Since Jerusalem's destruction in the days of the Romans," he told his colleagues, "it hasn't been so Jewish as it is now." In "many Arab districts" in Jerusalem, he said, "one sees not one Arab. I do not assume that this will change." He expressed hope that the Arab flight from Jerusalem would be followed by Arab flight elsewhere. Looking ahead to the military action that would follow, he said, "Certainly there will be great changes in the composition of the population in the country."[24] The Jewish Agency was calling its strategy defensive, but the US Consul-General in Jerusalem, Robert Macatee, informed Washington that the Jewish Agency was misrepresenting its military strategy. Macatee described military operations by the Zionist militias. "In the field of offense, which the Jewish Agency prefers to term 'preventive defense,' " he wrote, "we have seen all three Jewish armed groups in action, Haganah, Irgun and the Stern Gang [This was another name for LEHI]. Their offensives generally consist of demolitions of Arab strong points, and forays into Arab villages which they believe to have been used as bases for Arab guerrillas. The blowing-up of the Old Serail [municipal building] in Jaffa (by the Stern Gang), the same type of action against the Semiramis Hotel in Jerusalem (by the Haganah), and the shooting of Arabs in Tireh Village (by the Irgun) are all examples of Jewish offensives."[25]

There were enough abandoned houses in Arab neighborhoods of Jerusalem by this time that Ben Gurion issued a directive to settle arriving Jewish migrants in them. On February 12, a Haganah loudspeaker van drove through a west Jerusalem neighborhood where a Jewish woman had been shot, ordering the Arab residents to evacuate.[26] On February 19, Ben Gurion called another leadership meeting. Ben Gurion counseled Haganah forces "to continue to terrorize the rural areas." Destroying housing, he said, helped in inducing flight. "A destroyed house – nothing. Destroy a neighborhood, and you begin to make an impression." Ben Gurion applauded a recent attack on a village because it caused "the Arabs to flee."[27] The US Central Intelligence Agency was tracking developments and reported that at this period, the "Hagana adopted a policy of 'active' defense and carried out terrorist raids against the Arabs similar in tactics to those of the Irgun Zvai Leumi and the Stern Gang against the UK forces."[28]

"FLEE FOR YOUR LIVES"

Arab irregulars from neighboring states entered Palestine through the winter of 1948. While they occasionally engaged Haganah forces, they did little to stop the Zionist militia attacks on Arab villages or urban neighborhoods. A Haganah tactical plan for taking Palestine, developed in early 1948, called for the occupation and levelling of Arab villages, and the expulsion of inhabitants.[29] The Haganah called it Plan D.[30]

By this time, it was obvious that partition by consent of the parties, as contemplated in Resolution 181, would not work. In February, the Palestine Commission reported to the Security Council that implementation of

Resolution 181 would require armed force supplied by the United Nations. The Commission's Chair told the Security Council that because of "chaotic conditions of violence and lawlessness" in Palestine, "the only way of implementing the plan of partition as it has been envisaged by the General Assembly, consists in providing for assistance by non-Palestinian military forces available not in some symbolical form but in effective, adequate strength."[31]

With the Palestine Commission saying it could not implement partition, the United States asked the Security Council to suggest a different approach to the General Assembly. The United States proposed a temporary trusteeship in Palestine until the two parties could reach a settlement.[32] Trusteeship was viewed by the Jewish Agency as a threat to its aims. Trusteeship would keep power out of its hands. Trusteeship would bring in a new governing authority that might protect the Palestine Arabs.

The Jewish Agency got immediate support from the Soviet Union. It backed the Jewish Agency in opposing trusteeship.[33] Andrei Gromyko criticized the Security Council for failing to support the Palestine Commission. He reiterated the Soviet Union's view that partition would be a just solution, in the interest of both parties. He criticized the United States for abandoning partition in favor of trusteeship.[34] On April 1, 1948, at the urging of the United States, the Security Council asked Secretary-General Lie to call a special session of the General Assembly to "consider further the question of the future government of Palestine."[35] It was understood that this meant to explore trusteeship.

On the ground, the expulsion of Arabs from Palestine accelerated.[36] Arabs from many sectors were fleeing in large numbers.[37] Ben Gurion took heart at the flight. On April 6, at a closed meeting of the Zionist Executive, Ben Gurion exulted, "Villages have been emptied in panic, even from Haifa one-third of its Arabs have fled."[38] A few days later, the Irgun Zvei Leumi and LEHI killed scores of civilians in the village of Deir Yassin, near Jerusalem. The Irgun Zvei Leumi claimed that the civilian villagers they killed died in combat operations, but eyewitnesses told news reporters that the killing occurred after the Irgun Zvei Leumi and LEHI were in full control of the village.[39] A group of surviving "Arab men, women and children captured in the village, were paraded through some quarters of Jerusalem in open trucks."[40] This was done apparently as a demonstration to Jerusalem's Arabs.[41] Fear instilled by the Deir Yassin killings accelerated the flight from all over Palestine.[42]

The Deir Yassin killings potentially jeopardized the position of the Jewish Agency at the United Nations by showing the Zionist militias as perpetrators of atrocities. The International Committee of the Red Cross had just begun operating in Palestine.[43] Jacques de Reynier of the ICRC managed to visit Deir Yassin the morning after the killings. De Reynier confronted Jewish Agency officials at their office in Jerusalem over what had occurred. They sought to distance themselves by disclaiming any ability to control the Irgun Zvei Leumi or LEHI.[44] The Jewish Agency Executive issued a statement expressing "horror and disgust at the barbarous manner" of the killings, which it said were "utterly repugnant to the spirit of the Yishuv."[45] Ben Gurion sent a letter to King Abdullah of Jordan, placing the blame on the Irgun Zvei Leumi and LEHI.[46]

At this same time, the Jewish Agency's Haganah was capturing numerous towns and villages, expelling residents in the process. In Tiberias, one of the major towns of Palestine, the Haganah used barrel bombs and loudspeaker warnings. One Haganah officer later explained how barrel bombs were used, in Tiberias and elsewhere, to frighten Arab residents into fleeing. The barrels went "crashing into the walls and doorways of Arab houses," he recounted, exploding "with a furious sound, like an erupting volcano, sending up sheets of flame and pillars of nauseating smoke." Loud tape-recorded horror sounds would be broadcast, and a voice recorded in Arabic, shouting "Flee for your lives."[47] The British helped evacuate Tiberias' Arabs, who were undefended and too frightened to remain.[48] The *Palestine Post*, the Yishuv's English-language newspaper, reported, "A hasty exodus of Arabs from Tiberias continued all day long, and scores of Arab trucks, carrying panic-stricken foreign Arabs and local families, moved out in long convoys."[49]

On April 17, 1948, the Security Council called for a cessation of violence. In the hope of gaining cooperation between the two communities toward a political settlement, the Council asked them to "refrain, pending further consideration of the future government of Palestine by the General Assembly, from any political activity which might prejudice the rights, claims, or positions of either community."[50] The call had little effect.

A PLAN TO STOP THE EXPULSION

The United States kept pushing its trusteeship proposal. "The Assembly," said Warren Austin, the US delegate, "should consider the establishment of a temporary trusteeship which would provide a government and essential public services in Palestine pending further negotiations. If the Mandatory Power actively co-operated, the General Assembly would thus be able to establish United Nations governmental authority in the country."[51] The

United States drafted a detailed document for a trusteeship. The United Nations would be trustee.[52] Trusteeship would be temporary. Agreement between the Arab and Jewish communities would be sought on a long-term plan of governance.[53]

Trusteeship would have created a major obstacle for the Jewish Agency. It would bring in an administration that might stop it from expelling Arabs. The ongoing expulsion was a motivating concern for the United States as it proposed trusteeship. Along with Arab-state delegates, Austin denounced the continuing attacks on civilian Arab populations by "certain elements in the Jewish community" as "widespread terrorism and wilful murder which had shocked the entire world."[54] The Haganah and Irgun, attacking the major Arab town of Haifa a few days after Austin spoke, lobbed mortars into densely-populated neighborhoods and rolled barrel bombs into alleys. In an assessment written in June 1948, the Haganah Intelligence Branch found that the "barrages making loud explosive sounds" and "loudspeakers in Arabic" were effective in encouraging flight.[55] As the Haganah took control of Haifa, Palestine's major port city, residents fled in "whatever transport they could find, many of them on foot – men, women, and children – moved in a mass exodus toward the port area."[56] A Haganah commander at Haifa recalled, "we manned the biggest mortar which our forces had at that time–a three-inch mortar – and when all the Arabs gathered in this area we started firing on them. When the shells started falling on them, they rushed down to the boats and set off by sea for Acre."[57] Acre is another port city farther north from Haifa.

NO EXPULSIONS HAVE OCCURRED: SHERTOK

The exodus of Arab population was raised in the UN Security Council. Shertok put the onus on the Arab leadership in Palestine and on the neighboring countries. Shertok said that on the Arab side, "the policy is for Arabs to be evacuated or to evacuate themselves from Jewish areas." He said that the Arab flight was the result of "a deliberate policy aimed at representing us, or, rather, misrepresenting us as the aggressors, using this as a slogan to stir up feeling in the Arab countries, to move people to volunteer and to impel governments to intervene in the fighting in Palestine in order, as it were, to save the Arabs from the danger of being persecuted and even exterminated by the Jews. There was no pressure whatsoever exerted by the Jews which would have forced the Arabs to evacuate."[58]

But the expulsions were hard for the Jewish Agency to conceal. News reporters had access to the areas in which Zionist military forces were operating. Expulsion continued, despite the denunciation and publicity. In a few instances efforts were made to evacuate the Arab population in an organized fashion. These efforts opened the way to the Jewish Agency to argue that the departures were voluntary. However, these were evacuations under the gun by Arabs who had no protection from the Zionist militias and who feared being killed.[59]

The United States kept up its push for trusteeship. Again the Soviet Union jumped in on the side of the Jewish Agency. The United States, it charged, was "attempting to wreck partition." Partition, it said, repeating its prior stance, "constituted a just and correct decision and met the deep-rooted national interests of the Arab and Jewish peoples of Palestine."[60] The Arab Higher Committee said it would accept a trusteeship, so long as it were short-term, and so long as it would lead to "the independence of Palestine as a single democratic State in which the legitimate rights of the different sections of the citizens would be safeguarded."[61] Shertok continued to insist on implementation of partition.[62]

As Arab flight mounted into the tens of thousands, Shertok continued to deny expulsions. "It was not the policy of the Jews," he said in the General Assembly on April 27, "to drive Palestinian Arabs from their homes. The Zionists desired that Arabs should be perfectly secure within the Jewish State." Shertok had to acknowledge the extent of the flight. He referred to it as "mass evacuation." Repeating his earlier claim that it was the Arab leadership that was telling Arabs to flee, he said, "The mass evacuation had, in fact, been dictated by Arab commanders as a political and military demonstration."[63] This version of the reasons for the Arab flight gained much acceptance.[64]

As if to give the lie to Shertok's words, just at that time, Jaffa was emptied by force. The Haganah had shelled Jaffa intermittently.[65] The Irgun Zvei Leumi, engaging in military operations of its own, attacked Jaffa in a major assault.[66] The Irgun Zvei Leumi commander, briefing troops in preparation for the assault, told them that the aim was to "cause chaos among the civilian population in order to create a mass flight."[67] The *Palestine Post* reported a "mass exodus" from Jaffa by overland and by sea.[68] As many as 50,000 Arabs were forced out of Jaffa.[69] Many of those leaving by sea fled south to the Gaza Strip.[70]

Menachem Begin, the Irgun Zvei Leumi leader, would describe the shelling in his memoir. "I do not know exactly how many shells we sent into Jaffa," Begin wrote. "The total load was certainly very heavy. We went all out." That brought "confusion and terror," Begin related. Then, he recounted, "the great flight began, by sea and land, on wheels and on foot.

It started with thousands, but very quickly tens of thousands were sucked into the panic flood."[71]

John Ross, a member of the US delegation at the United Nations, confronted Shertok a few days later over both Jaffa and Jerusalem. During a private meeting with Shertok and Rabbi Silver, as related by Ross, Rabbi Silver complained about aggression on the Arab side. Ross reacted by posing a question. "I inquired how recent affairs in Jaffa and Jerusalem squared with the idea that only Arabs were aggressors." The question reflected Ross' understanding that these attacks had not been defensive. Ross reported the response of Rabbi Silver and Shertok. "They replied with [the] well-known line re protecting their people and positions, somewhat embarrassed, however, re Jaffa."[72]

Shertok and Rabbi Silver should indeed have been embarrassed for billing the taking of Jaffa as a defensive operation. Their assertion of defense was belied by the statement of the Irgun Zvei Leumi commander in his prebattle briefing. Alan Cunningham, the British high commissioner, wrote shortly afterward that the Irgun Zvei Leumi's mortar attack on Jaffa "was indiscriminate and designed to create panic among the civilian inhabitants."[73]

At this time, Shertok was joined at the United Nations by Aubrey Eban. Eban added his voice in opposing trusteeship. Eban suggested to the General Assembly that partition was preferable to trusteeship because it was not possible "to bring about collaboration between the Arabs and the Jews without first creating equality." Eban's point was apparently that partition would give each party a territory, and that collaboration would follow. Eban also addressed the flight of Palestine's Arabs. He referred to what was occurring in Palestine vaguely as "the present disorders" and laid the blame at the door of the United Nations. Eban said the "disorders" could have been averted if the Palestine Commission had been given more assistance in its task of implementing partition. "The Jews," said Eban, "wished to co-operate and contribute to the well-being of the Near East as an independent and free nation."[74] Arabs fleeing as a panic response to Zionist militia attacks would have been hard pressed to understand how those militias were contributing to their well-being.

SUCCESS OF JEWISH ARMS

As the conversation continued in the General Assembly, the Zionist militias expelled more Palestine Arabs. The Palmach managed to force thousands of Arabs out of the Galilee. In capturing the Galilee town of Safad, the Palmach shelled residential neighborhoods. As many as 8000 Arabs fled.[75]

Palmach commander Yigal Allon later acknowledged that the Palmach intentionally drove the Safad residents out of their city. "The Arab population fled," he said. "We did everything to encourage them to flee."[76] In Beisan, another town in the Galilee, residents fled as the Palmach shelled the town. Most of the remaining Arabs were forced out by the Palmach when the town fell.[77]

Ben Gurion was more candid than Shertok or Eban in describing the Arab flight. Ben Gurion was jubilant. On May 6, he was quoted in the *Palestine Post*, gloating over the flight. Ben Gurion said that "the Arabs had left 100 villages," and that "150,000 of them were on the move." This showed, Ben Gurion exulted, "the success of Jewish arms."[78] So Ben Gurion was saying that it was the Zionist militias that were precipitating the Arab exodus. A few days later, the *Palestine Post* reported that the Arabs of Palestine were "in panic flight."[79] Ben Gurion, it will be recalled, had told the Special Committee on Palestine that the Jewish Agency had no plan to transfer Arabs out of Palestine. Now Ben Gurion's troops were forcing Arabs out and he was celebrating.

The expulsions created a major headache for Shertok and Eban, who had to reply to condemnation from the Arab states at the United Nations. The matter was particularly delicate for an agency purporting to represent world Jewry. Only two years earlier, the World War II allies who set up the International Military Tribunal at Nuremberg had identified mass expulsion of population as a crime against humanity.[80] Nazi leaders were convicted for mass expulsion of Jews. To manage this problem, the Jewish Agency simply denied expulsions. The expulsions were being reported in newspapers and by the International Committee of the Red Cross, but the situation in Palestine was being viewed at the United Nations as generalized unrest and violence. No serious inquiry was made at the United Nations. By the month of May 1948, upward of 300,000 Arabs had fled from their home areas.[81] On that day, the Haganah drove loudspeaker vans through streets in the western sector of Jerusalem, urging the remaining Arabs to leave. A journalist who did radio broadcasts at the time for the Haganah reported that the loudspeaker message advised Jerusalem Arabs to leave by the road leading eastward toward Jericho, and adding a threat, "If you stay, you invite disaster."[82]

EXPULSION A WAR AIM

Britain was projecting to withdraw from Palestine on May 14. The Jewish Agency approached US President Harry Truman and asked if he would recognize a Jewish state if one were declared. Jewish statehood would be a repudiation of the United States' proposal for a trusteeship. Truman was in the throes of a difficult election campaign. The advisor who had Truman's ear was Clark Clifford, his guru on domestic politics. Clifford pushed Truman toward recognizing a Jewish state if one were to be declared. Secretary of State George C. Marshall on the other hand wanted to pursue trusteeship. Marshall urged Truman to ignore Clifford's advice.[83]

A US presidential election is based on a state by state count, rather than a national popular vote. While Jews were a small minority overall in the country, they were a key constituency in certain states, notably New York. By the end of the Second World War, American Jews had in the main come to a favorable view about Jewish statehood in Palestine. Catering to them made electoral sense. On May 14, as the British troops completed their withdrawal from Palestine, the National Council, the political organization that was the domestic counterpart to the Jewish Agency for Palestine, declared statehood for a state to be called Israel.[84] Truman immediately recognized it as a state.[85] With partition having failed, the special session of the UN General Assembly disbanded the Palestine Commission. In its place, the General Assembly arranged for the appointment of a UN mediator, who was asked to "promote a peaceful adjustment of the future situation of Palestine."[86]

With Truman's recognition of Israel, the United States stopped pushing for trusteeship, and the idea was dropped at the United Nations. Success in averting trusteeship was, for the Jewish Agency, a major diplomatic coup. Instead of having to deal with an administration in Palestine that might impose law and order, the Jewish Agency was now able to do as it liked with the Palestine Arabs. By this time, a Haganah officer would later write, "the evacuation of Arab civilians had become a war aim."[87] The Haganah's Intelligence Branch wrote up a tally sheet on Haganah operations. In regard to the Haganah's ability to force Arabs out, the intelligence branch said, "British withdrawal freed our hands."[88]

10

Denying the Undeniable

The United Nations remained in the picture, but, having given up first on partition, and now on trusteeship, it would assume a reduced role. The Jewish Agency, now operating as the State of Israel, benefited from disinclination on the part of the major powers for any on-the-ground involvement that might have stemmed the expulsions. On May 15, 1948, the first day after the declaration of Jewish statehood, military forces of the Arab League entered Palestine, vowing to stop the expulsions and to restore order. Egypt's foreign minister justified the Arab League troop entry in a statement to the Security Council. "The Royal Egyptian Government declare, now that the British Mandate in Palestine has ended, that Egyptian armed forces have started to enter Palestine to establish security and order in place of chaos and disorder which prevailed and which rendered the country at the mercy of Zionist terrorist gangs who persisted in attacking the peaceful Arab inhabitants, with arms and equipments amassed by them for that purpose." The foreign minister elaborated. "Horrible crimes, revolting to the conscience of humanity, have been perpetrated by these Zionist gangs." Invoking the concept that had been used at the Nuremberg trials in Germany, he called these acts "crimes against humanity" and said that it was Egypt's duty "as a Government of an Arab State and a civilized nation to intervene in Palestine with the object of putting an end to the massacres raging there and upholding law and principles recognized among the United Nations." He said that the troop intervention "has no other object in view except the restoration of security and order to Palestine particularly after the British Mandate has ended, and until a just and equitable solution is reached."[1]

China, as a Security Council member, found the Egyptian analysis persuasive. On the day after the declaration of Jewish statehood, China challenged the Jewish Agency, blaming it for a breakdown of order in Palestine.

In a reference to the efforts toward establishing a trusteeship, China criticized the statehood declaration, saying, "The prompt proclamation of the Jewish state last evening reduced considerably the prospects of peace in Palestine."[2]

Shabtai Rosenne was the Jewish Agency's chief lawyer. Rosenne, writing some years later, derided the Arab League explanation for its entry into Palestine. "Scarcely was the Union Jack lowered from Government House in Jerusalem in May 1948," Rosenne would write, "when these Arab States began their armed 'intervention' in Palestine and formally notified this to the United Nations, proclaiming their objective to be the establishment of 'security and order in place of chaos and disorder'– they even expressed their confidence that they would 'receive the support of the United Nations'. Such frankness when embarking upon armed aggression is surely unequalled in the annals of the United Nations."[3] Rosenne ignored the expulsions as a factor in the Arab League intervention.

The Arab states did, to be sure, hope to forestall the implementation of a Jewish state. From the Arab standpoint, as we have seen, Palestine should simply have become independent upon Britain's withdrawal. Speaking for the Arab Higher Committee in the Security Council, Isa Nakhleh explained that under the Covenant of the League of Nations, "the people of Palestine were recognized provisionally as an independent nation. Now that the Mandate has ended, the people of Palestine consider themselves to be an independent nation." Nakhleh brought up the population figures: "The majority of the population of Palestine, the 1,300,000 Arabs, considers that the Jewish minority – whether the 300,000 Palestinian citizens or the 400,000 foreigners – is a rebellious minority which has revolted against the sovereignty of the majority of the population of the country." By "foreigners," Nakhleh meant Jews who had migrated to Palestine but had not been naturalized as citizens. "We, the Arab Higher Committee, representing the majority of the people of Palestine," Nakhleh intoned, "consider that any attempt to create any foreign government in Palestine is nothing but an act of rebellion which will be put down by force."[4]

KUDOS FROM THE KREMLIN

When statehood was declared for a Jewish state, a Provisional State Council was formed as a legislative body, and a provisional government as an executive arm. The declaration of May 14 set United Nations membership as a goal in a clause promising that the new state "will be faithful to the principles of the Charter of the United Nations."[5] The first step in that direction was gaining recognition from the United States and the Soviet Union. That support was forthcoming, and it gave the Jewish Agency a leg up as it sought acceptance for the new state.

The US recognition came first, because it had been prearranged. The Soviet recognition was requested only on May 15. The United States and Soviet Union differed in the way in which they accorded recognition to Israel. In international practice, one finds two kinds of recognition that states extend. One is recognition of an entity as being a state. The other is recognition of the government of a state as being the legitimate government. The United States phrased its message as follows. It first recited that it had been informed that a Jewish state had been proclaimed in Palestine and that recognition had been requested by the provisional government. It then affirmed, "The United States recognizes the provisional government as the *de facto* authority of the new State of Israel."[6] This statement did not directly say that the United States recognizes Israel as a state, but the recognition accorded to the provisional government as that of Israel, and the reference to Israel as a "new" state implied that Israel was being recognized as a state. The provisional government was, however, being recognized only in a *de facto* sense, meaning that the United States understood that the provisional government was operational but was reserving judgment on its legitimacy.[7]

The Soviet recognition came on May 17.[8] The Soviet message was quite different in tone and in substance. It came from Viacheslav Molotov, who was now called Foreign Minister, since Soviet officials had dropped the appellation "commissar." Like the US message, it recited that recognition had been requested. Molotov wrote that "the Government of the Union of Soviet Socialist Republics has adopted a decision officially to recognise the State of Israel and its Provisional Government." So Israel was being recognized as a state, and the provisional government was being recognized as its lawful authority. The recognition of the provisional government thus was unqualified.

The United States' message was framed in sparse diplomatic language. But Molotov added a note of congratulations, saying, "The Soviet Government hopes that the creation by the Jewish people of its own sovereign state will serve the cause of the strengthening of peace and security in Palestine and the Middle East, and expresses its confidence in the successful development of friendly relations between the Soviet Union and the State of Israel."[9]

The Soviet recognition thus was more complete and robust. An American lawyer, commenting at the time on the difference between the two messages of recognition, wrote, "The Soviet Union, acting as a kind of godfather, accorded a diplomatic baptism to the newborn infant and thus assumed by implication a benign interest and responsibility for the child's welfare. President Truman did not imply anything more than the acknowledgment of the child's existence and of its *de facto* guardians."[10]

The more enthusiastic Soviet reaction to the declaration of a Jewish state was consistent with the greater support the Soviet Union had given the idea of Jewish statehood starting in 1947. As partition was being considered by the UN General Assembly in 1947, as we saw, the Soviet Union had lauded partition as a solution that accorded rights to all parties and would promote peace while the United States saw it as simply better than other alternatives. When trusteeship was floated by the United States, the Soviet Union backed Israel's resistance. Now again the Soviet Union put itself forward as the principal champion of Jewish statehood. The Soviet stance was not lost on the provisional government and was seen as critical to the Jewish Agency's success in bringing Israel into being. Rosenne, writing some years later, commented that "the Soviet support in 1947 and 1948 for Israel was probably one of the decisive factors in its establishment."[11]

Shertok sent a cable to Secretary-General Lie on May 15 that included the National Council's declaration, which asked the "United Nations to assist Jewish people in building of its State and to admit Israel into family of nations." In the cable, Shertok signed as "Foreign Secretary" of the "Provisional Government of Israel." The text of the cable was published in the UN official records with those designations.[12] The Soviet government was a focus of attention as well, as part of the strategy to gain acceptance for Israel as a state at the United Nations. A trip by Shertok to the United Nations was being planned, and the nascent Israeli delegation at the United Nations cabled him to say that the trip would be significant. It would not likely lead just then to any advance for Israel as a state, they thought. However, the Soviet representative Andrei Gromyko would be present, and Shertok could have "direct conversation with Gromyko" that "could have important bearing [on] future relations [with the] USSR."[13] The chance to schmooze with Gromyko would make the trip worth while.

RETURN OF ARABS "UNTHINKABLE"

Whatever the aims of the Arab League, its forces failed to protect the Arabs of Palestine. They continued to be pushed out. On May 18 the Security Council directed a series of questions to the Arab and Jewish authorities about their military activity. Eban forwarded back replies on May 22. One question directed to the Jewish Agency was, "Do you have armed forces operating in areas (towns, cities, districts) of Palestine where the Arabs are the majority?" Eban answered in the name not of the Jewish Agency but of "the Government of the State of Israel," to make the point that statehood had been declared. Eban said that its forces were operating in areas that "formerly for the most part, contained Arab majorities. These areas have, however, been mostly abandoned by their Arab population."[14] So Eban was acknowledging the Arab flight but as to its cause he answered in a way that did not indicate the reason. By saying that the Arab population "abandoned," he was denying any responsibility of the Zionist militias.

A few weeks later, however, the Intelligence Branch of what by then was being called the Israel Defense Force completed an analysis for internal distribution about the reasons for the Arab flight. After May 15, 1948, the three Zionist militias had merged under this new name. The Intelligence Branch reported "hostile operations" as "the main cause of the movement of population," accounting for 55% of the population flight. "Hostile operations" meant the attacks by the Zionist militias. Another 15% of those fleeing, according to the report, were motivated by fear engendered by prior military attacks.[15] If these figures were accurate, it meant that 70% of the Arabs who departed were either forced out or left for fear of being forced out. So Haganah intelligence was saying that the Arab flight was substantially caused by the Zionist militias.

The mass departure raised the question of whether the departure was permanent. Most of those fleeing went only far enough to get away from the Zionist militias. Some alighted in sectors of Palestine not yet taken by the Zionist militias. Others stopped in neighboring states, just across the border from Palestine. The Jewish Agency had no intention of allowing the Palestine Arabs to reoccupy their home areas. On June 15, Shertok wrote a personal letter to Nahum Goldmann in which he raised the issue of what should become of the Arabs who had left.[16] Shertok was ecstatic over "the wholesale evacuation" of Palestine's Arab population." As to whether the Arabs should be allowed to return, Shertok wrote, "The reversion to the *status quo ante* is unthinkable," meaning that the Arabs would not be repatriated. "The opportunities which the present position opens up for a lasting and radical solution of the most vexing problem of the Jewish State, are so far reaching as to take one's breath away. Even if a certain backwash is unavoidable, we must make the most of the momentous chance with which history has presented us so swiftly and so unexpectedly."[17] The provisional government's way of dealing with the "backwash" was to deny responsibility for the exodus.

GODFATHER TO THE RESCUE

Eban made every effort to convert the status of the Jewish Agency for Palestine at the United Nations into a status for Israel. He tried to get UN officials to refer to him as the representative of Israel. Eban told Shertok that the Security Council presented good possibilities for gaining acceptance for Israel as a state. "High priority should be devoted to the Security Council powers," he said. "We have a certain momentum in the Security Council which can be developed."[18] Eban also worked the Secretariat. Eban wanted to apply for UN membership and consulted Secretary-General Lie about the chances. When Lie said more work was needed to secure the requisite number of votes in the Security Council for admission, Eban backed off.[19] Eban sent Secretary-General Lie a letter on June 10 relating to truce proposals in the name of the provisional government of Israel. Lie obliged by circulating the letter as being from the "Provisional Government of Israel."[20]

Soon Eban saw an opening in the UN Security Council. The Security Council was holding frequent meetings on the Palestine question, and the Jewish Agency was being invited to participate in them. Eban conceived the idea of getting the Security Council to accept him as the representative of Israel. Eban knew that he might get help from the Soviet Union. So he consulted Andrei Gromyko, who was the Soviet representative in the Security Council. Gromyko was open to the idea but advised Eban to wait until they could be certain of sufficient support in the Security Council.[21]

A fortuitous circumstance worked in Eban's favor. As it happened, in 1948 the Ukrainian Soviet Socialist Republic was a nonpermanent member of the Security Council. The Ukrainian SSR held a UN seat separate from that of the Soviet Union, even though it was part of the Soviet Union. Being part of the Soviet Union, the Ukrainian SSR typically aligned its actions at the United Nations with those of the Soviet Union. So Eban was virtually assured of two votes in the Security Council for his plan to be designated the representative of Israel.

Even more fortuitously, the Ukrainian SSR was up for the presidency of the Security Council for the month of July. The presidency of the Security Council rotates every month among the Council's members. The president chairs the Security Council's meetings. So if Eban made a move in July, he might get help from the chair. Eban decided to wait until July. "We believe problem can now be speedily solved," he wrote to Shertok, "by awaiting Ukrainian chairmanship first July. He," Eban predicted, "will invite [the] representative [of] Israel to [the] table if [the] Government applies."[22]

A meeting on the Palestine question was set for July 7, to which Eban would be invited as a representative of the Jewish Agency. The Ukraine representative was Dmitri Manuilskii. Eban approached Manuilskii privately. He asked if Manuilskii would refer to him at the July 7 meeting not as a representative of the Jewish Agency, but as a representative of Israel.[23] Manuilskii agreed. Eban also consulted privately with Philip Jessup, who served as the US alternate representative in the Security Council.[24] Jessup told Eban that the United States would not oppose the move, but neither would it take the initiative to get the designation Eban sought.[25]

On July 7, the meeting was indeed held. Manuilskii opened the meeting and announced that he was inviting to the table the representatives of four states that were not members of the Security Council but that had an interest in the day's topic. He referred to them as "the States of Israel, Iraq, Egypt, and Lebanon."[26] So Manuilskii was referring to Israel as a state, the first time that had occurred at any UN meeting. Several members objected when they heard this, not wanting to prejudge the question of sovereignty in Palestine. France said that it had not recognized Israel as a state and feared that an invitation to Eban "couched in these terms might complicate a situation which is in itself already very delicate."[27] At one point in the discussion that followed, Eban asked to speak. As Manuilskii recognized him, he referred to him as "the representative of the State of Israel."[28]

In light of the objections, Manuilskii as chair of the meeting announced that he would call a vote to ask the members of the Security Council if they approved his ruling that Eban was being invited as a representative of Israel. The Security Council at that time had eleven member states, and under the UN Charter any motion proposed in the Security Council required a qualified majority of seven for passage. The discussion to that point suggested that the matter divided the Security Council almost evenly, hence Eban would not get seven votes.

Andrei Gromyko made a quick mental calculation and saw that Eban would lose. Gromyko asked to be recognized. Manuilskii recognized him. Gromyko suggested that Manuilskii frame the question the other way around, namely, to ask for a vote to overrule his ruling, rather than to uphold it.[29] Seven votes would be required to overrule. Manuilskii obliged. He rephrased the motion as one to overrule him. He put that motion to a vote. Only five member states – Belgium, Canada, China, Syria, and Britain – voted to overrule, so Manuilskii's ruling stood.[30] Had the vote been taken in the way Manuilskii originally proposed, Eban would have lost. Thanks to Gromyko's ploy, Eban was seated as a representative of Israel.

Jamal Husseini, the Arab Higher Committee representative at the meeting, objected. Husseini said that the Arab Higher Committee could not participate in the Security Council "as long as that designation is being used by the Chair." He stood up and left the room.[31] But for the first time, the state declared on May 14 by the National Council was dealt with as a state at the United Nations. In the transcript of the meeting, when Eban's remarks were recorded, he was identified as "Mr. Eban (Israel)."

Eban had scored a major coup for Israel. He prevailed only because of the compliance of the Ukraine representative and the timely intervention by Gromyko with his proposal to change the motion to be put to a vote. Again, the Soviet Union was stepping in and supporting the Jewish Agency in its pursuit of statehood. The promises made to the Soviet Union by Shertok and Ben Gurion seemed again to be reaping rewards. Whatever the Israeli delegation sought to achieve at the United Nations, the Soviet Union helped to achieve. At this time Count Folke Bernadotte, a Swedish diplomat appointed as the UN mediator, made a proposal that would have involved Israeli losing the Negev.[32] The Soviet delegation helped keep the proposal from being adopted.[33]

BARREL BOMBS OVER GALILEE

In July 1948 the Haganah, the Israel Defense Force (IDF) captured two adjoining Arab cities in central Palestine, Ramleh and Lydda. Aerial bombardment and artillery shelling panicked residents who were only too aware of what the Zionist militias had done elsewhere in Palestine. An Arab Legion contingent present in Ramleh was too undermanned to mount a defense. The IDF occupied the two towns without a fight. As the IDF entered, its personnel shot randomly at civilians, resulting in the killing of upward of 200 persons.[34]

Ben Gurion was at operational headquarters a short distance away. There he conferred with Yitzhak Rabin and other officers. A suggestion was made to expel the entire populations of Ramleh and Lydda. Ben Gurion said to expel them. Rabin signed an order for Lydda, reading, "The inhabitants of Lydda must be expelled quickly without attention to age. They should be directed towards Beit Nabala... Implement immediately." Rabin issued a similar order for Ramleh, and the IDF forces executed the orders, forcing out 60,000 Arab residents.[35] The IDF marched them eastward toward Jordan, firing mortars to keep them moving down the road.[36] Many of the Lydda Arabs died en route, from exhaustion, dehydration, or disease.[37]

Many years later, Israeli journalist Ari Shavit would interview commanders who carried out the Lydda-Ramleh expulsion. Shavit concluded that the reason for the expulsion was the geographic centrality of the two cities in the area over which control was sought. Shavit wrote "that Zionism could not bear Lydda. From the very beginning there was a substantial contradiction between Zionism and Lydda. If Zionism was to be, Lydda could not be. If Lydda was to be, Zionism could not be."[38]

Concerned over IDF gains like those in the Lydda-Ramleh area, the Security Council declared a threat to the peace in its Resolution 54 on July 15 and ordered all parties to "desist from further military action." Military advances by any party would be considered a breach of the peace, requiring "such further action under Chapter VII of the Charter as may be decided upon by the Council."[39] One of the concerns was the expulsion that accompanied the taking of territory by the IDF. Chapter VII of the UN Charter allows for the Security Council to mount a military campaign to stop aggression.[40]

Despite the concern of the Security Council, the IDF expelled thousands more Arabs during Summer 1948, particularly from the Galilee.[41] By now the IDF had airplanes, and it used them to bomb Galilee villages.[42] It dropped barrel bombs and metal fragments. This tactic induced flight from the Galilee.[43] The IDF was able to continue taking territory and to continue expelling population without more than verbal objections from the United Nations. In a letter he wrote to Chaim Weizmann, Shertok was jubilant over being able to advance territorially in central Palestine. "For the time being we have the best of both worlds – we have behaved like good boys *vis-à-vis* the United Nations and proved that we are good soldiers on the field of battle."[44] Convincing the United Nations that they were "good boys" was being achieved largely by disguising the magnitude of what the IDF was doing to get the Arabs out of Palestine. Soviet support was another factor. Eban had a long conversation with Yakov Malik of the Soviet delegation and reported to Shertok that Malik "evinced appreciation [at] our military successes." Eban also asked Malik about applying for UN membership, and Malik promised Soviet support.[45]

A CALL FOR JUSTICE

When Count Bernadotte raised the repatriation issue, Shertok replied that it could be considered by Israel once a general peace settlement with the Arab states was on the table.[46] In towns and villages that it captured, however, the IDF demolished houses so that the inhabitants would have nothing to which to return.[47] Repatriation of the displaced Arabs quickly became a priority agenda item for the major powers. The United States threatened sanctions against Israel for keeping the displaced Arabs out.[48] The international pressure prompted Ben Gurion to call a meeting of his top advisors for August 18. The advisors were clear on how they thought Israel should react. It should ignore the pressure. The consensus reached at the meeting was "to do everything possible to prevent the return of the refugees." Ben Gurion said they should look for ways to have these Arabs "resettle abroad."[49] Shertok, who attended the meeting, wrote a few days later to Weizmann on the subject. Shertok told Weizmann that it was imperative to prevent any immediate return of Arabs. "Once the return tide starts, it will be impossible to stem it, and it will prove our undoing." But equally, return should be prevented long-term. "As for the future," Shertok continued, "we are equally determined – without, for the time being, formally closing the door to any eventuality – to explore all possibilities of getting rid, once and for all, of the huge Arab minority which originally threatened us."[50] Demolishing houses was one way of reducing the possibility that they might ever be repatriated. At the August 18, 1948 meeting, it was decided that refugees should be prevented from returning, and that the buildings of empty Arab villages should be destroyed.[51]

In September 1948, Count Bernadotte filed a report dealing with the overall situation in Palestine. Bernadotte addressed the refugee issue. Bernadotte expressed concern over the demolitions of houses in Arab villages, saying they were being done "without apparent military necessity." Bernadotte could see that the aim was to make the departures permanent. Bernadotte wrote that the "exodus of Palestinian Arabs resulted from panic created by fighting in their communities, by rumours concerning real or alleged acts of terrorism, or expulsion." Bernadotte called for repatriation. "It would be an offence against the principles of elemental justice," he wrote, "if these innocent victims of the conflict were denied the right to return to their homes while Jewish immigrants flow into Palestine, and, indeed, at least offer the threat of permanent replacement of the Arab refugees who have been rooted in the land for centuries."[52] Bernadotte highlighted the extent of the exodus, writing that "almost the whole of the Arab population fled or was expelled from the area under Jewish occupation."[53] Bernadotte was unable to follow up to gain action on repatriation. The day after he filed this report, he was assassinated in a street in Jerusalem by LEHI.

AN IMPLAUSIBLE DENIAL

Armed with what was now a policy of keeping the Arabs out, the IDF continued expulsions. As it advanced southward into the Negev in Autumn 1948, it forced out most of the Arabs there.[54] Population fled from Beersheba, the Negev's largest town, as Israeli aircraft bombed it.[55] One episode in the IDF campaign in the south drew international attention. It involved an allegation of an atrocity in a letter the Arab League sent to Secretary-General Lie. The letter said that the IDF "ruthlessly massacred Arab women, children and old people" in the town of Dawayma in the Upper Galilee sector of Palestine.[56] The next day in the Security Council, Egypt's delegate called attention to the Arab League letter,[57] and Lebanon's delegate suggested that the Security Council set up a commission of inquiry to look into the allegation.[58]

Eban responded by a letter of his own, saying that the Arab League had invented a fictitious atrocity. "It is obvious that lurid and sensational events, such as those described by the Secretary-General of the Arab League, could not take place without there being some knowledge of where they took place. The Security Council should therefore be informed that no such place as Dawayma exists anywhere in any part of Galilee. The Secretary-General of the Arab League, by inventing a record of non-existent events in non-existent places is frivolously using the Security Council as a platform for irresponsible propaganda." Eban did acknowledge the existence of a village of that name in another part of Palestine. "The only locality in Palestinian territory known as Dawayima," he wrote, "is in the south of the country between Beit Jibrin and Dahariya, east of Hebron." As to that locality, Eban wrote that it "had been completely abandoned by its civilian population before it was occupied by Israeli forces."[59]

Eban was correct as to the location of the town. Dawayma was in the south of Palestine. The Arab League had erroneously written that it was in the Galilee, which lies in the north of Palestine. Realizing the error, the Arab League sent an apology and a correction. It explained that the error stemmed from the placement of a dot in the Arabic rendering of the word "Hebron," a town near Dawayma. In Arabic, the name for Hebron is "Khalil," which is very close to the Arabic for Galilee, which is "Jalil."[60] So Dawayma had been identified incorrectly as being in the Galilee. Eban as it happened had specialized in Oriental languages as a university student at the University of Cambridge.[61] As a result, he knew the Arabic language well. Eban doubtless understood the error stemming from the placement of the dot. He took advantage of the error to portray the Arab League as perfidious.

Eban's claim that there was no civilian population at Dawayma was untrue. Dawayma was a thriving town in southern Palestine when the IDF entered. Its normal population of 2000 had been augmented by an additional 4000 who had fled IDF advances in neighboring areas. Dawayma's economy was agriculture-based. A market held weekly on Fridays drew from neighboring villages.[62] Dawayma was in no way abandoned. An IDF unit had occupied Dawayma on October 29, encountering little resistance. As it entered, the IDF shot indiscriminately, causing villagers to flee.[63] A group of about 80 men who fled into a mosque for safety were killed there by the IDF.[64] Upward of 400 were reported killed during the time the IDF was in the village.[65] The atrocities were investigated internally by the IDF.[66] The IDF investigation attributed the killings to the presence of Irgunists and others "who tend to bad behavior" within the IDF contingent.[67]

After Eban sent his letter, Lebanon's delegate raised the issue again in the Security Council. He chided Eban for focusing on the Arab League's error on the village's location and for ignoring the substance of the allegation.[68] Nevertheless, the Security Council took no action.

Just at the time Dawayma was being discussed in the Security Council, the General Assembly's First Committee was discussing Count Bernadotte's September report. Shertok was keen to counter Bernadotte's finding of mass expulsion perpetrated by the Zionist militias. He claimed reasons for the flight that did not implicate the Zionist militias. He attributed the Arab flight from Haifa to supposed urging by the Arab Higher Committee.[69] Shertok did not mention the shelling of the Arab population, recounted above, that induced panic in Haifa's Arabs and immediately led to their flight. Shabtai Rosenne, the Jewish Agency's lawyer, would later generalize Shertok's point to say that the Arab flight from all over Palestine was organized by Arab leaders as part of their war plan.[70]

Shertok did, perhaps inadvertently, admit the truth of Count Bernadotte's analysis. Shertok sought to place the onus for the exodus on the Arab rejection of partition. He said in the UN General Assembly "that if the Arabs of Palestine had accepted partition and cooperated with the Jewish State, the latter would never have attempted to reduce its large Arab minority."[71] Shertok did not explain by what means "the Jewish State" had "attempted to reduce" the Arab population. But the only means it had used was force and intimidation. This statement contradicted his overall denial of responsibility for the Arab exodus.

The Arab Higher Committee replied to Shertok. Its representative Henry Cattan listed attacks by Zionist militias on civilians in a number of towns he named. His list included Deir Yassin. Cattan characterized these attacks as terroristic. He said that "the aim of Jewish terrorism against the Arabs was to drive the Arabs out of their homes and their country."[72] Cattan cited figures. "Some 750,000 Arabs living in Palestine for centuries," he said, "had been driven out, stripped of their possessions and reduced to the status of refugees, whilst their houses had been destroyed and pillaged." Responding to Shertok's argument that the Arabs had abandoned their localities without compulsion, Cattan asked, "Who would believe that hundreds of thousands of people had left the country of their own free will, abandoning all their goods, because they had been asked to do so by the representatives of the Arab Higher Committee or of certain Arab States?"[73]

Eban in turn replied to Cattan. Eban said that Cattan "had conjured up a terrible picture of the plight of the Arab population fleeing from alleged atrocities, but did not attempt to refute the fact that the Arab population had found itself in imminent danger of being caught in a clash between the invading Arab armies and those of its Jewish neighbours."[74] This explanation differed from Shertok's. Eban was saying that the Arabs simply feared being caught up in the fighting. This explanation too avoided the evidence of mass expulsions.

Shertok also addressed the possible readmission of the displaced Arabs. "It was unthinkable," he said, for Israel to readmit these refugees while the war lasted." "The Government of Israel," he said, "was ready to discuss this question at a peace conference."[75] So Israel was willing to talk about repatriation. This public statement stood in stark contrast to his statement in private to Nahum Goldmann on June 15, when Shertok said the Arabs were gone for good.

11

A Peace-Loving State?

The Soviet Union would be the Jewish Agency's most ardent supporter at the United Nations as the Jewish Agency pressed for acceptance of the statehood of Israel. The support would show when admission of Israel to the United Nations was requested. In September 1948, Moshe Shertok urged the provisional government to let him apply for membership for Israel.[1] The provisional government agreed.[2] Shertok chose November 29, the first anniversary of Resolution 181, to send a letter to Secretary-General Lie, signing it as Foreign Minister of Israel, and applying for the membership for Israel in the United Nations. Shertok wrote to Lie that Israel's admission to the United Nations would be "an act of international justice to the Jewish people." So Shertok was justifying UN membership as a means of reparation for the Holocaust. It was a risky strategy, because he was putting Israel forward as a state that saw itself representing not only its present inhabitants, but a people scattered around the world. As an indication of Israel's consolidation as a state, Shertok recited in his letter that Israel had gained diplomatic recognition from nineteen states.[3] Whether Israel could be considered a state in part of the territory of Palestine while UN mediation was still taking place was unclear, however.

An application for UN membership for Israel faced the further problem that the situation on the ground in Palestine remained unsettled. Military action was continuing. Armistices had yet to be concluded with the Arab states. A rival All-Palestine Government had been declared by an Arab administration in Gaza City in October 1948 and had proclaimed itself as the governing body of Palestine, to replace the departing British. So there was a rival claim to Palestine, one premised on the League of Nations mandate, which was supposed to lead, in principle, to a government for all of Palestine.

Making the situation more uncertain still for a membership application, the Israel Defense Force was not acting in ways that most UN member states considered necessary for peace. The IDF was on the offensive to chase out the Arab League forces that had intervened. The National Council had declared statehood by reference to Resolution 181, but the IDF was taking territory well beyond the lines drawn in that resolution. The IDF was fighting in contravention of the July 1948 Security Council prohibition contained in Resolution 54 against any further territorial conquest in Palestine. Just at the time Shertok filed the application for admission, the IDF was pushing to the south, in the offensive that had included its entry into the village of Dawaymeh. It was also pushing northward in the Galilee. This new military offensive led the Security Council to adopt Resolution 61 on November 4, 1948 to reinforce its Resolution 54 that no further territory in Palestine be taken by force.[4]

The UN Charter, in Article 4, specifies that a state, to be admitted as a member, must be "peace-loving." The Autumn military offensive in disregard of the Security Council's mandate, left doubt whether Israel could qualify. But UN membership was greatly prized by the new state. Walter Eytan, who served as Director-General of the Foreign Ministry, explained that UN membership was avidly sought to solidify Israel's status. UN membership would, said Eytan, "set the seal of international recognition on her independent statehood."[5]

Gaining UN membership had long been an aim. At the hearings of the UN Special Committee on Palestine, Weizmann had been asked why he opposed proposals for arrangements that might not involve Jewish statehood. In a written response, Weizmann said that those proposals did not assure "the Jews of the political status enjoyed by surrounding Arab countries – that of independence and U.N. membership."[6] Referring specifically to proposals being made for a federal structure for Palestine, Weizmann said, "Federalism does not offer the Jewish people a place in the United Nations. That is a grave disability for the Jewish people in its political life."[7]

Shertok's letter to Secretary-General Lie requesting Israel's admission was transmitted to the Security Council for a recommendation. By UN protocol, admission applications go first to the Security Council, which decides whether to recommend admission. The General Assembly can then vote to admit the applicant state. The Security Council referred Shertok's letter to its Committee on the Admission of New Members, a committee of the whole in the Security Council. When this committee discussed Israel's application, only two member states – Ukrainian SSR and the Soviet Union – advocated admitting Israel. So again the Soviet Union was the Jewish Agency's champion. The Soviet and Ukrainian delegates both said that they "saw no reason whatever for delaying Israel's admission to the United Nations." Most member states on the Security Council, however, did see a reason for delay. They were not ready to act because "the General Assembly itself had not yet reached any conclusion on the Palestine question as a whole." The United States had indicated it would back Israel's application, but it stayed with this majority. The committee reported back to the Security Council on December 7 that it was not recommending admission because it lacked enough information to act on Israel's application.[8]

This episode in the Security Council demonstrated the strength of the Soviet support for Israel. The provisional government was keeping in the good graces of both the United States and the Soviet Union under a policy it called non-identification, meaning that it would maintain a certain distance from both East and West, so as not to alienate the other. Ben Gurion as Prime Minister of the provisional government saw the support to date from both as having been critical for Israel. He told the Cabinet on September 27, 1948, "We have friends both in the East and in the West. We could not have conducted the war without the important help we received from several States of East and West."[9] In a December 1948 meeting with Andrei Vyshinskii, who was Soviet Deputy Foreign Minister, Shertok was effusive in expressing Israel's appreciation for Soviet support at the United Nations.[10]

TWO ISSUES LOOM

Before the Security Council could deal with the report of its Committee on the Admission of New Members, the UN General Assembly adopted a resolution that seemed to set back Israel's chances for membership further still. By Resolution 194 of December 11, 1948, the General Assembly marked a path toward possible peace in Palestine that did not necessarily envision a Jewish state. Resolution 194 called for a commission to be set up to negotiate with the contending parties on all outstanding issues. It would be called the Conciliation Commission for Palestine. It would be made up of three states: Turkey, France, and the United States. A commission of this composition was thought to carry more weight than a single UN mediator. The post of mediator had been assumed by Ralph Bunche after the assassination of Count Bernadotte, and Bunche would continue to function. The appointment of the Conciliation Commission for Palestine was hoped to improve the possibility of a successful outcome to negotiations.

Resolution 194 also identified key issues to be resolved, issues on which the policy of the provisional government of Israel was questionable. Jerusalem was mentioned specifically in Resolution 194. Jerusalem was to be placed under international administration, overseen by the United Nations, as called for in Resolution 181. Jerusalem would fall under the sovereignty of neither side.[11] But it was no secret that the provisional government had its eye on Jerusalem. In June 1948, Ben Gurion said that there was no legal distinction between Jerusalem and other territory Israel controlled.[12] In August 1948, Ben Gurion issued a proclamation specifying that "the Law of the State of Israel shall apply to the occupied area," which the proclamation defined as the part of Jerusalem that the IDF by then controlled.[13] Moshe Shertok informed his delegation at the United Nations that the provisional government had decided to make a claim on the sector of Jerusalem that Israel controlled.[14] In September 1948, a Supreme Court was opened for Israel, situated in Jerusalem.[15] In December 1948, Chaim Weizmann, who was President of the Provisional State Council, gave an address in Jerusalem in which he said that it was "utterly inconceivable that this Jewish city should be placed under foreign rule."[16]

Repatriation of the displaced Arabs also merited attention. Resolution 194 recited "that the refugees wishing to return to their homes and live at peace with their neighbours should be permitted to do so at the earliest practicable date, and that compensation should be paid for the property of those choosing not to return and for loss of or damage to property which, under principles of international law or in equity, should be made good by the Governments or authorities responsible."[17] Ralph Bunche, as UN mediator, viewed repatriation as "the big, outstanding issue" in the conflict.[18] In the area the IDF occupied in 1948, there had previously been 900,000 Arabs. According to the first Israeli census, conducted in November 1948, only 120,000 to 130,000 remained.[19]

These issues of Jerusalem and repatriation posed major obstacles to Israel's membership. The General Assembly well knew that Israel was not readmitting the refugees. The bulk of Palestine's Arab population sat in refugee camps just outside the reach of the IDF, hungry and in need, anxious to resume their lives. The existence of such a beleaguered population of refugees was a disaster if one sought an overall settlement. Their repatriation was regarded as a necessary first step. Of the major powers, only the Soviet Union failed to press Israel on repatriation. Shertok reported to Golda Meir, who was serving as ambassador in Moscow, that he perceived a lack of interest on the Soviet part in the fate of the displaced Arabs.[20] For the Soviet Union, the failure to repatriate was of no concern in relation to Israel's admission to the United Nations.

The Western powers did press Israel on repatriation. It was being seen that the IDF not only was denying repatriation for the moment but was seeking to render it less feasible in the long term. The policy that we saw being followed in Summer 1948 of destroying Arab villages was so general that other governments were aware of it. France's Foreign Minister, Robert Schuman, said in the General Assembly, "Many of the villages which they [Palestine Arabs] had been obliged to leave had been partly demolished by systematic action which was still continuing." Schuman found it "unthinkable that the horrors perpetrated during the war against the Jewish populations in Europe should be repeated or should be reproduced in respect of the Arab population." He called this effort to prevent repatriation "a disgrace to mankind" that "must be brought to a close."[21]

Shertok and Eban were under instructions from the provisional government to say that repatriation could be considered by Israel only in the context of arranging a general peace with the Arab states.[22] But connecting repatriation to a peace settlement was raised when Resolution 194 was being debated, and had been rejected by the General Assembly. Guatemala, still a strong backer of Israel, had proposed to add in paragraph 11, the paragraph on repatriation, the words "after the proclamation of peace by the contending parties in Palestine, including the Arab states," so that repatriation would have been contingent on peace agreements.[23] Eban, speaking for Israel, supported the Guatemala amendment.[24] Egypt objected that the amendment "gave the Jews an opportunity to use the status of the Arab refugees as a bargaining point in the settlement of the Palestine question."[25] The United States agreed. Dean Rusk, speaking for the United States, said that the Guatemala amendment would make the refugees "pawns in the negotiations for a final settlement."[26] The Guatemala amendment was voted down.[27] So the General Assembly was rejecting the proposition that repatriation could await the conclusion of peace agreements. Repatriation was a humanitarian issue requiring immediate action regardless of whatever outcome might develop as to Palestine's status.

The status of Jerusalem also proved problematic. As Resolution 181 was being drafted in 1947, the Jewish Agency representatives had tried to prevent the internationalization of Jerusalem, the *corpus separatum* concept as it was being called. They preferred dividing Jerusalem.[28] Now the provisional government was making moves that appeared to be leading to a claim to the city, a step that was regarded by the General Assembly as erasing any possibility of peace. Shertok told the General Assembly in

November 1948 that while the walled city of Jerusalem could be under an international regime because of the holy sites there, Israel "must claim the permanent inclusion in Israel of modern Jewish Jerusalem."[29] Shertok threw cold water on the *corpus separatum* proposal. Questioned about Israel's intentions on Jerusalem in the General Assembly, Shertok averted to the hostilities that had left the city divided between sectors of control by Israel on the western side, and Jordan on the eastern side. Shertok told the General Assembly "that he could fully understand the feelings of those representatives who had expressed themselves in favour of the principle of an international regime for the whole of Jerusalem. But after the experience of the past year this matter was no longer an academic question of principle. The lamentable reality was that at a time of crisis the United Nations had not been able to discharge its responsibilities under the Assembly's resolution of 29 November 1947, and it could not be assumed that such a situation would not again occur."[30]

Draft resolutions were introduced to reiterate the *corpus separatum* idea. Shertok spoke against them. "The draft resolutions attempted to reaffirm the principle of international rule without taking account," he argued, "of the facts of the situation."[31] This statement by Shertok on Jerusalem did not bode well for Israel's membership application. Israel's stance both on Jerusalem and on repatriation cast doubt on whether the member states would consider Israel to be a "peace-loving state."

KEEPING THE HOLY CITY OFF THE RADAR SCREEN

Despite the cautious report of its Committee on the Admission of New Members, the Security Council held three meetings in mid-December 1948 on Israel's application. The majority sentiment in the Security Council remained that admission was not appropriate while the UN was pursuing reconciliation in Palestine.[32] Syria, a non-permanent member of the Security Council, raised the repatriation issue. The authorities that declared Israel as a state have, Syria said, "expelled the Arab population, massacred the people, looted their property and oppressed them to such an extent that they have been compelled to leave their own country."[33] Syria referred in particular to Jaffa. "Seventy or eighty thousand people have been expelled from Jaffa," he said, "cast out naked into the desert of Sinai or forced to take to the sea in small boats."[34]

The ongoing IDF military action in the south of Palestine was also raised. Britain said in the Security Council that the "southward movement" of IDF forces was "flagrantly contrary to the resolution of

4 November which provided for the withdrawal of forces and not for their continued advance."[35] Again, the Soviet Union spoke up in favor of the newly declared Jewish state. It said, "The Jewish state has been created; it exists, and the Security Council has every reason to consider the question of its admission to membership favorably."[36] Israel's application was put to a vote on December 17 in the Security Council. Five states voted in favor, one voted against, and five abstained. The five favorable votes were short of the seven required for passage.[37]

This was only a first round, however. A vote of this kind does not doom a membership application for all time. An application may be taken up again. The provisional government assigned Aubrey Eban to take the lead to develop a strategy to get Israel admitted. Eban was asked, as he would relate in his memoir, to "pursue the campaign for Israel's admission to the United Nations."[38]

Prime Minister Ben Gurion did not make it easy for Eban. At Ben Gurion's direction, the IDF took its southern campaign all the way into Egyptian territory. President Truman demanded that Israel withdraw. In a pointed telegram, Truman explained to Ben Gurion, "As first govt to recognize PGI [Provisional Government of Israel] and as a sponsor of Israel's application for admission to UN as a 'peace-loving state' this Govt, with deep concern and as evidence of its consistent friendship for Israel, desires to draw attention of Israeli Govt to grave possibility that by ill-advised action PGI may not only jeopardize peace of Middle East but would also cause reconsideration of its application for membership in UN."[39] The matter was discussed in the UN Security Council, and when it was, Yakov Malik, the Soviet delegate, said that Israel should not be asked to withdraw.[40] Israel, however, shortly withdrew.[41]

Israel's posture at the United Nations was enhanced, however, by a move it made at this time toward regularized governance. Elections were held in January 1949 for a constituent assembly. When the assembly met, it decided to use for itself the Hebrew term for assembly, Knesset. The Knesset replaced the Provisional State Council. Chaim Weizmann became President under this new arrangement, and David Ben Gurion was chosen as Prime Minister. Moshe Shertok was chosen Foreign Minister. The United States, which had recognized the provisional government only *de facto* now recognized this government *de jure*.[42]

Eban would have to find a way around the criticisms over Jerusalem and over repatriation, to convince the world body that Israel was "peace-loving." As for Jerusalem, the provisional government avoided new moves toward claiming the city after it filed for UN membership, seeking to keep the issue off the UN's radar screen. Dov Joseph, who was Military Governor of Jerusalem, would explain that when the General Assembly, by Resolution 194, called again for the internationalization of Jerusalem, the provisional government made no public objection "because we weren't sufficiently strong and we wished to enlarge our presence in Jerusalem." Joseph said that the provisional government wanted to avoid conflict with the United Nations while Israel was asking to be admitted to membership in the United Nations.[43]

Shertok took a soft, if less than candid, approach on Jerusalem in February 1949 when the Conciliation Commission for Palestine quizzed him about Israel's intentions. Shertok said that the Jewish people considered Jerusalem as much a part of their state as any other part of Palestine. He said, however, that he understood the international community's view and was prepared to conform to it so that Jerusalem would be separate. The Conciliation Commission had heard reports that the new constituent assembly might announce the incorporation of the city into Israel. Shertok said that "he, too, had heard rumours that the occasion of the holding of the Constituent Assembly in Jerusalem would be used for the purpose of making an announcement annexing the City to the State of Israel." He affirmed, "The Government of Israel had no such intention."[44]

"HUMILIATION, HUNGER, DEATH"

Israel's conclusion of an armistice with Egypt on February 24, 1949 gave Eban an opening to reinvigorate Israel's admission application in the Security Council.[45] The fact that Israel was concluding an armistice with a major Arab adversary strengthened the argument that Israel was peace-loving. On March 3, the Security Council held a preliminary discussion on Israel's application for admission. Egypt, then a non-permanent member of the Security Council, objected to Israel's admission, saying that a vote in favor of Israel meant "subscribing to terrorism and the continued denial of justice to a whole nation, the Arabs of Palestine."[46] Egypt cited Israel's "disobedience" and "defiance" toward the Security Council, an apparent reference to the fact that Israel was taking territory after the Council forbad any further territorial grabs.[47] Egypt said that "Zionism has extorted most of Palestine from its lawful people," that "it has driven most of them – more than two thirds – from their homes and lands and placed them face-to-face with humiliation, hunger, pestilence and death."[48] Egypt advocated sending the matter to a committee of the Security Council, but most members were prepared to proceed to a vote.[49] The Soviet Union, without referring to any of the problem issues, reiterated its prior view that Israel was peace-loving and should be admitted to membership.[50]

The next day, March 4, the Security Council met with the idea of proceeding to a vote. The refugee question figured prominently in the discussion. Egypt resumed its opposition. It said, with reference to the refugees, that "three-quarters of a whole nation" were being met with "humiliation, hunger, and death." It cited reports from UN observers that homes of displaced Arabs were being demolished so that they would have no homes to which to return.[51] Ominously for Israel, Britain announced that it opposed Israel's admission.[52] Ominously, because Britain held veto power in the Security Council. Sir Terence Shone, as Britain's delegate, said that Israel had not clarified its position on Jerusalem or on repatriation of the displaced Arabs, the two key issues identified by the General Assembly in its December 1948 resolution. Britain's concern was that Israel's position on these issues cast doubt on Israel's peace-loving character.

On Jerusalem, Shone said, "The General Assembly has twice made a definite recommendation in favour of the internationalization of the whole area of Jerusalem, as described in the General Assembly's resolutions of 29 November 1947 *[181 (II)]* and 11 December *1948 [194(III)]*. It is one of the specific tasks of the Conciliation Commission to recommend how this internationalization should be carried out." Shone noted, however, that "we have seen statements by responsible Israeli representatives, including the Prime Minister himself, to the effect that part at least of Jerusalem must be incorporated in the Israeli State and that internationalization, if it is to be applied at all, can only affect that area held by the Arabs."[53] Israel was occupying the western sector of Jerusalem, having fought to a standstill there in 1948 with the Arab Legion of Jordan. The Arab Legion occupied the eastern sector, including the old walled city. The UN position on Jerusalem, as Shone noted, was that Jerusalem should be part of neither a Jewish nor an Arab state.

Shone also challenged Israel's approach on the issue of the displaced Arabs. It is a basic understanding in the international community that when a new sovereignty is established over a piece of territory, the new sovereign is not free to exclude its population. The exclusion of the displaced Arabs from the territory the IDF occupied was a factor working against peace. "This matter of the refugees is one of the most distressing and important questions resulting from events in Palestine," Shone said, "and we believe that Israel's attitude toward it ought to be clarified. In spite of the relief work being carried out by the United Nations – to which the government of the United Kingdom has so far been by far the largest contributor – these refugees are still dying in hundreds and are likely to continue to do so until some further decisive action can be taken to help them. Israel's responsibility with regard to the refugees was recognized by the General Assembly, and we hope that Israel will recognize the obligation imposed by the Assembly resolution. In the opinion of my Government," Shone concluded, "it is insufficiently clear where the Israeli Government stands on this matter. We, for our part, cannot take a definite attitude on the question of Israel's admission to the United Nations until the position of the Israeli Government on this point has been clarified."[54]

"OUTSIDE FORCES" THE CAUSE

The view of Britain that Israel did not qualify as peace-loving could have been fatal to Israel's membership application. By Security Council practice, the veto applied to votes on membership applications. Shone said, however, that even though Israel was unqualified for membership, Britain would not vote in the negative. It would not use its veto. Understanding that a majority on the Security Council were prepared to vote in favor of Israel's admission, it did not regard it as appropriate for a permanent member to vote in the negative and thus defeat a positive recommendation on admission. Britain would instead abstain on the vote.[55] Abstentions by a permanent member, in Security Council practice, were not considered vetoes. It was on this issue of principle, unrelated its view about Israel, that Britain decided not to stop the application.

Warren Austin, the US delegate, offered a resolution the United States had drafted to recommend Israel's admission.[56] Just prior to the vote, the Soviet representative, Yakov Malik, explained why the Soviet Union would vote in favor. Malik lauded Israel, finding none of the faults that Shone had identified. Malik said that Israel was "loyally complying" with "the decisions adopted by the Security Council on the Palestine question." Malik did not mention the fact that Israel was taking territory in Palestine in violation of Resolution 54 of July 15, 1948. Malik then addressed Jerusalem and repatriation, giving the most detailed response of any delegate at the meeting to Shone's criticisms. Jerusalem, Malik said, was a matter to be dealt with by the Conciliation Commission for Palestine, not by the Security Council. "There is no ground," he said, "for linking the question of the status of Jerusalem with that of the admission of Israel to membership in the United Nations."

On repatriation, Malik asked, "Why should the State of Israel be blamed for the existence of that problem?" He said that if peace were established, then the question of the refugees could more readily be resolved. He blamed the refugee problem on "outside forces" who "pursue their own selfish interests for the monopoly exploitation of the oil and wealth of the Near and Middle East and the creation of military strategic bases."[57] This was an apparent reference to the Western powers collaborating with Arab states.

Israel could not have asked for a better defense, and this from a permanent member of the Security Council. The United States never tried in UN debates to justify Israel in relation to the exodus of the Palestine Arabs. The Soviet Union did. For the Soviet Union, there was no reservation to its support for Israel.

The US resolution recommending Israel's admission was put to a vote in the Security Council, and it passed, nine states voting in favor. Britain abstained, and Egypt voted against.[58] In the resolution, the Council recited that it "decides in its judgement Israel is a peace-loving state."[59] The Security Council sent its recommendation to the General Assembly for final action.[60] Eban expressed delight at the outcome in the Security Council, because Israel had escaped relatively unscathed on the issues that could have been used to defeat a favorable recommendation. In a message he sent from New York to the Foreign Ministry, Eban said that Israel had gained this positive vote "without any compromise on a single territorial or political issue." Israel had not given ground on Jerusalem or on repatriation. It had not had to give up territory it had taken in violation of Security Council prescription.[61]

The policy of non-identification that kept Soviet support coming for Israel was given formal status by the government of Israel the next day. On March 8, the government adopted a document titled Basic Principles of the Government Programme. One section dealt with principles to be followed in foreign relations. The first such principle read, "Loyalty to the principles of the United Nations Charter and friendship with all freedom-loving states, and in particular with the United States and the Soviet Union."[62]

A FORTUNATE OMISSION

Even though Israel faced criticism in the Security Council over Jerusalem and repatriation, it dodged a bullet on one other issue that could have been troublesome. From mid-1948, in areas under Israel's control in which Arabs were remaining in place, the IDF was taking Arab males from their villages and putting them into camps where they were holding Arab prisoners of war.[63] The International Committee of the Red Cross (ICRC), whose presence we saw in connection with its Deir Yassin investigation, maintained contact with the provisional government.[64] The ICRC sent delegates to rural areas of Palestine still inhabited by Arabs and was concerned about what it found.

"Arab towns and villages occupied by the Jewish forces are in a critical situation," read a report by an ICRC delegate, recorded November 12, 1948. "All the able-bodied men have been arrested and taken to work camps as prisoners of war. There remain older men, women, and children." The economic situation in these localities was dire, because the IDF was not allowing harvesting of crops planted in Spring 1948. "This population is absolutely on their own, abandoned with no assistance," read the ICRC report. "These poor people don't even have the possibility to go to pick olives or vegetables in the surrounding countryside, because it is forbidden to them to go out of their towns or villages." The IDF was imposing martial law. The Arab population could not engage in normal economic activity. "What a horrible sight to see these unfortunates!," the report continued. "Upon our arrival in Shef-Amr [an Arab town with a population of 5000], women carrying hungry and malnourished children who had not even the strength to cry came to ask us for help." An Arab medical doctor was still living in the town, the report related, but he had no medications to treat anyone.[65]

The ICRC investigated four internment camps into which rural Arabs were being placed. The four camps were in the towns of Djelil, Athlit, Sarafand, and Tel Litvinsky. A total of 6360 persons, it was reported, were detained as of January 28, 1949.[66] Many of these had been combatants, most were not.[67] The IDF put them to work in quarries and kept them on subsistence diets.[68] Conditions during the winter of 1948–49 were harsh. Arabs "who were snatched from their villages and put without reason in a camp" were "obliged to pass the winter under wet tents." As reported by one ICRC delegate, "those who could not survive these conditions died."[69]

Information about these camps was reported to the United Nations by the Arab Higher Committee.[70] This information gained little attention, perhaps because the IDF kept the civilians together with POWs, so the detention of civilians was disguised. Then too, detention of Arab civilians may have seemed less heinous than the expulsions. Jacques de Reynier, one of the ICRC delegates, considered these detainees in a way to be fortunate, since most Arabs were being expelled. The ICRC was only too aware of the policy of expelling Arabs. "Had they been set free," de Reynier wrote, "they would have been immediately expelled, one way or another, and would have had to live as refugees in conditions still worse and more hopeless."[71]

TROUBLE FROM THE WHITE HOUSE

The strong backing Eban was receiving from the Soviet Union for admission to the United Nations was especially important, because the support of the United States was fragile at best. Even though the United States had tabled the resolution in the Security Council to recommend Israel's admission, it shared Britain's reservations. The United States was especially concerned over Israel's refusal to repatriate the Palestine Arabs. Mark Ethridge was President Truman's appointee serving as the US member of the Conciliation Commission for Palestine. In February the Commission had raised the repatriation issue with Shertok. Ethridge reported that Shertok's reply "offended [the] Commission." Ethridge said that Israel was adopting an "inhuman position" on the issue.[72] On March 14, just ten days after the Security Council vote, Ethridge gave Secretary of State Dean Acheson another dire assessment. Ethridge said that "six weeks of effort to get the Israeli government to commit itself on the refugee problem have resulted in not one single statement of position. That is true also of Jerusalem and all other problems with which we have to deal."[73] Acheson met in Washington with Shertok. Shertok told Acheson that "it was out of the question to consider the possibility of repatriation of any substantial number of the refugees. The most logical solution," said Shertok, "was resettlement in the Arab countries, where so much land was available."[74] When Acheson told President Truman what Shertok said, Truman "was disturbed over the uncooperative attitude being taken." He told Acheson, "we must continue to maintain firm pressure."[75]

The issue came up, along with the Jerusalem issue, when President Chaim Weizmann approached the United States with a request for help on Israel's admission to the United Nations. Weizmann, as we have seen, was now serving as President under the recently adopted arrangements. Weizmann wanted the United States not only to vote for Israel's admission when the matter reached the General Assembly, but to rally other states as well. He asked for a meeting with President Truman. Truman agreed to meet. When Weizmann asked Truman to lobby at the UN in favor of Israel's application, Truman responded by pressing Weizmann on Jerusalem and on repatriation. Weizmann got no agreement from Truman.[76]

Following the meeting, Weizmann wrote Truman a letter, thanking Truman for the meeting and summarizing the issues they had discussed.

As for repatriation, Weizmann rejected it flat out, in terms similar to Shertok's. "Except to a limited degree," Weizmann wrote to Truman, "the answer lies, as I stated, not in repatriation but in resettlement." Weizmann explained, "I have long felt that the underpopulated and fertile acres in the river valleys of Iraq constitute both a seductive invitation to neighboring countries and a massive opportunity for development and progress in the Middle East. Similar opportunities exist also in northern Syria and western Transjordan."[77] So the reaction of both Shertok and Weizmann to the UN demand for repatriation was that the Palestine Arabs should go elsewhere. They were not even willing to have the repatriation issue raised if peace treaties were signed with the Arab states, as was being promised at the United Nations.

Truman showed Weizmann's letter to Acheson and told Acheson "that Dr. Weizmann's attitude on refugees was not satisfactory and thought that we were not in a position to bring pressure on other members of the United Nations."[78] Truman sent a message to Ethridge, to let him know that Weizmann was being no more conciliatory than Shertok. "I am rather disgusted with the manner in which the Jews are approaching the refugee problem," Truman wrote to Ethridge. "I told the President of Israel in the presence of his Ambassador just exactly what I thought about it. It may have some effect, I hope so."[79]

That ambassador was Eliahu Elath, Israel's ambassador in Washington. The same day as Weizmann sent his letter to Truman, Elath brought Aubrey Eban to meet Secretary Acheson. The topic of the meeting, as Acheson recorded it, was "Israel's Desire for Admission to the U.N." Eban addressed the issue of Jerusalem. He said that the Israelis had not only supported "the plan for Jerusalem set forth in the resolution of November 29, 1947 but had participated in its drafting."[80] It was true that the Jewish Agency had supported the internationalization plan for Jerusalem, but only because it came as part of a package deal that would recommend a Jewish state. On repatriation, as recorded by Acheson, Eban "thought that emphasis should be on resettlement rather than repatriation, although the Israeli Government had never rejected the idea of repatriation."[81] Eban was stating the same view as Shertok and Weizmann. The Palestine Arabs should find some other country.

Truman's anger did not lead the United States to abandon its support for Israel's admission to the United Nations. But Truman would not ask other states to back Israel's admission.[82] That made all the more crucial the support that Israel getting from the Soviet Union. The Soviet Union showed no reservations about Israel's policies. Soviet support remained solid, even though by this time the Soviet government understood that Israel was in the Western camp. A Soviet Ministry of Foreign Affairs assessment circulated internally just at this time recited that the dominant Mapai Party would likely "continue, as before, the policy of alignment with America." Nonetheless, the assessment continued, "since the State of Israel has a number of unsolved problems (the city of Jerusalem, frontiers etc.) in the solution of which the USSR will play a substantial role, the government of Israel is unlikely at present to take up positions openly hostile to us."[83] The Soviet assessment was that since the Soviet government was helping Israel at the United Nations, Israel was likely to continue on friendly terms with the Soviet Union. But the Soviet government was adjusting its expectations about Israel. It was losing the hope of having Israel as a long-term friend in the region.

12

Joining the World with Fingers Crossed

In its bid for membership in the United Nations, Israel confronted more objections in the General Assembly than it had faced in the Security Council. The Security Council takes war and peace as its main issue of concern, so Israel's conclusion of an armistice with Egypt weighed heavily in its favor. The General Assembly takes a broader frame of reference in thinking about the peace-loving character of an applicant state. The issues of repatriation and Jerusalem would figure more heavily in its deliberations. And the General Assembly included all member states of the United Nations, so Israel would fact more delegates who could ask uncomfortable questions.

During the weeks following the Security Council recommendation, Israel did not help itself to show its peace-loving character. Just after the Security Council vote, Israel took more territory in violation of Security Council Resolution 54. The IDF seized an Arab fishing village called Umm Resh Resh at the northern tip of the Gulf of Aqaba.[1] One fishing village may not seem important in the overall picture in Palestine, but this one was special. It sat at the southern tip of the Negev Desert, on the Gulf of Aqaba. Shertok had said that Israel sought "a foothold on the Gulf of Aqaba" as a "gateway to the Eastern seas."[2] Resolution 181 envisaged this access point to the Gulf of Aqaba as adhering to the prospective Jewish state. By Resolution 54, the Security Council in July 1948 had decided, as we saw, that no more territory should change hands by use of force. Mark Ethridge denounced the action as a violation of Security Council Resolution 54.[3] Umm Resh Resh was renamed Eilat. Israel would open a port facility there in 1952.[4]

Nor did Israel take action on the two hot-button issues – repatriation and Jerusalem – to blunt the objections raised by Britain in the Security Council. During this time, more governmental offices were relocated from

Tel Aviv to Jerusalem.[5] No move was made to repatriate the displaced Arabs. On the contrary, the IDF continued to expel Arabs from rural areas of Palestine. During this time, it intimidated several thousand villagers in the northern Negev into fleeing. In the Galilee, it emptied a number of villages.[6]

The General Assembly took up Israel's application the first week of May, on the basis of the Security Council's recommendation. The application could have gone directly to the plenary, but there was sentiment that the underlying issues required discussion. Aubrey Eban maneuvered to try to keep the General Assembly from sending the application to a committee, as he sought to avoid criticism of Israel.[7] The General Assembly, however, referred the application to its Ad Hoc Political Committee.[8] This was a committee of the whole, each UN member state being represented. It decided to hold hearings.

The Arab states were harsh in their criticism of Israel. As the Ad Hoc Political Committee opened its debate on Israel's application, Charles Malik of Lebanon did not mince words. Malik said that "90 per cent of the Arab population of Israel had been driven outside its boundaries by military operations, had been forced to seek refuge in neighbouring Arab territories, had been reduced to misery and destitution, and had been prevented by Israel from returning to their homes. Their homes and property had been seized and were being used by thousands of European Jewish immigrants."[9] Malik accused Israel of violating Resolution 194 on both repatriation and Jerusalem: "There had been no major developments affecting the situation of the Arab refugees and the establishment of an international regime for Jerusalem since the Assembly had adopted the resolution governing those questions on 11 December 1948," Malik said. "Israel had given no assurances on the acceptance of the principle of repatriation or internationalization."[10] "In no case," Malik concluded, "should the Assembly condone Israel's defiance of United Nations decisions and admit it on the assumption that it might later change its policies."[11]

Israel was given an opportunity to participate by the Ad Hoc Political Committee.[12] Aubrey Eban represented Israel. Eban replied to the criticisms, saying that he "understood that the questions raised in connexion with Israel's application for membership in the United Nations were being discussed in the light of the compliance of Israel with the relevant resolutions of the General Assembly."[13] Eban objected that "Israel was the only State involved in the war which had undertaken to comply with the Security Council's resolution of 16 November 1948, calling upon the Governments concerned to negotiate an armistice as a transition to lasting peace."[14] Eban was referring to Security Council Resolution 62.[15] By the time Eban spoke, however, Egypt, Lebanon, and Jordan had concluded armistice agreements with Israel, and one with Syria was in the works, as he himself later noted.[16] It would be finalized in July. So Israel was not the only state to comply with Resolution 62.

Eban did not mention Security Council Resolution 54 of July 15, 1948, which, as we have seen, forbad further acquisition of territory by force in Palestine. Ralph Bunche, the UN mediator, took the July 15, 1948 resolution to mean that "all recourse to military action to settle the Palestine dispute had been forbidden."[17] Israel continued, as we have also seen, to take territory by force after July 15, 1948.

On Jerusalem, Eban said, "Integration of the Jewish part of Jerusalem into the life of the State of Israel had occurred as a natural historical process arising from the conditions of war, the vacuum of authority created by the termination of the Mandate, and the refusal of the United Nations to assume a direct administrative responsibility on the scene."[18] By this time, Israeli political figures were referring to the area of Jerusalem that Israel controlled as "Jewish" Jerusalem. That designation was intended to give the impression that the western sector, sometimes called the New City, should adhere to Israel because of its predominantly Jewish population.

ARABS WERE NOT EXPELLED

The "Jewish" sector of Jerusalem did, to be sure, have a predominantly Jewish population, but only because, as we saw in Chapter Nine, most Arabs had been run out in 1948. Syria raised this point but never got a response from Eban. What Eban called the "Jewish part" Syria called the "modern city" of Jerusalem. Syria said that the "population of the modern city was half Jewish and half Arab. Now the majority of the Arab population had been expelled. Consequently, if the *status quo* were accepted, the Jews would continue in illegal occupation of the houses and property of the Arabs in the modern city."[19]

Eban gave his analysis of the Arab exodus. "The problem of the Arab refugees," he said, "had been a direct consequence of the launching of a war for the purpose of overthrowing by force the General Assembly's November 1947 resolution on partition. No great movements of population would have occurred if the Arab world would have joined with Israel in an attempt to give peaceful implementation to that resolution." So if the Arab states had acquiesced in a partition that they regarded as skewed against them, all would have been well.

"Such tragic movements," Eban continued, "were a familiar accompaniment of any war, and especially of wars affecting countries of mixed populations and conflicting allegiances. The representative of Lebanon had correctly remarked that it had never been the General Assembly's intention that the Arab population should be driven out of Palestine. But neither had it been its intention that Lebanon and six other States should wage war upon Israel, a war of which the plight of the Arab population of Palestine was a direct sequel." So the exodus of the Arabs of Palestine came about simply because there was a war. Here of course, Eban was covering up the strenuous efforts to drive the Arabs out of Palestine. "The exodus of the Arab population had already assumed large proportions by the time the Government of Israel had been established," he said. "Efforts by that Government to stem the flood of refugees had been unavailing."[20]

This statement was even more counterfactual than those that preceded it. Eban was saying, as was true, that the exodus was substantial prior to May 15, 1948. His implication was that Israel was not responsible for it, because Israel did not exist then. However, it was the same elements that assumed governmental authority after May 15 that were carrying out the expulsions prior to May 15. The IDF, as we saw, was created by merger of the three Zionist militias: Haganah, Irgun Zvei Leumi, and LEHI. It has long been accepted in the international community that when a new state forms, it is responsible for misdeeds of military units that brought it into being.[21]

Eban was also claiming that after May 15, 1948, the provisional government of Israel had tried to "stem" the exodus. Eban cited no specifics to prove what efforts it had made. The provisional government had, under pressure from the major powers, issued an order on the subject, and this may be what Eban had in mind. On July 6, 1948, Ben Gurion told the Chief of Staff to issue an order concerning behavior toward Arab civilians. An order did go out from the Chief of Staff, reading: "Outside the actual time of fighting, it is forbidden to destroy, burn or demolish Arab cities and villages, to expel Arab inhabitants from villages, neighbourhoods and cities, and to uproot inhabitants from their places without special permission or explicit order from the Defence Minister in each specific case."[22]

Eban, wisely, did not cite this directive to the Ad Hoc Committee. It read in part as a limitation, but at the same time as authorization. The implication of the directive was that it was permissible to "destroy, burn or demolish Arab cities and villages" and "to expel Arab inhabitants" so long as it was done during combat operations. And that was how most of the expulsion was being done. Moreover, the directive allowed for destroying or expelling even outside combat operations with the consent of the Defence Minister.

Ben Gurion issued this directive on July 6. As we saw, only one week later he ordered the expulsion of the populations of Lydda and Ramleh. Technically, there was no violation of the directive, because he authorized the expulsion. Practically speaking, there were no restraints on expulsions. Far from "stemming" the exodus, the provisional government was propelling it. As we saw, expulsions accelerated after May 15.

Blaming the Arab exodus on the Arab states, Eban drew what for him was a logical conclusion. The responsibility for "the problem of refugees" rested "with the Arab States which, by virtue of having proclaimed and initiated the war which had rendered those refugees homeless, were under moral obligation to take a full share in the solution of their problem, even apart from their own ties of kinship with the refugee population."[23] Since the Arabs were responsible for the exodus, they had to deal with the consequences. They should take in the Arabs of Palestine. This conclusion, for Eban, was reinforced by the "ties of kinship" between the Arabs of Palestine and the neighboring Arabs. This conclusion, of course, disregarded the rights of the people who were displaced, which was the focus of General Assembly Resolution 194.

The policy of the government of Israel on the refugee question, Eban said, was "that resettlement in neighbouring areas should be considered as the main principle of solution. Israel, however, would be ready to make its own contribution to a solution of the problem. It was not yet ascertainable how many Arabs wished to return under conditions that might be prescribed by the Assembly or how many Arabs Israel could receive in the light of existing political and economic considerations."[24] So Israel might take some, regardless of how many wanted repatriation. The majority should stay where they were.

EBAN ON THE HOT SEAT

In the Ad Hoc Political Committee hearings, some states were more concerned than others over repatriation and Jerusalem as factors in their decision on Israel's admission. El Salvador was one of the states that saw Israel's compliance on these two matters as necessary to its admission. Before Israel could be admitted, said El Salvador, "it is indispensable to remove the doubts which have existed, and perhaps still exist, on the attitude of the government of Israel to the General Assembly recommendations contained in its resolution on the internationalization of the City of Jerusalem and the surrounding area. These doubts emanate from the official statements made by the representative of the government of Israel, and seem to indicate that government's opposition to the proposal to internationalize Jerusalem. The same remarks apply to Israel's attitude to that part of the General Assembly resolution dealing with the repatriation of Arab refugees."[25]

As we saw in Chapter Eleven, Ben Gurion began referring to Jerusalem as Israel's in 1948. And on April 7, 1949 Ben Gurion had told the Conciliation Commission for Palestine flat out that Israel would not acquiesce in an international status for Jerusalem. "For historical, political and religious reasons," Ben Gurion told the Commission, "the State of Israel could not accept the establishment of an international regime for the City of Jerusalem."[26] The internationalization proposal in Resolution 181, said Ben Gurion, had been misguided.[27] Syria cited these statements of Ben Gurion to show that Israel did not plan to comply on Jerusalem, no matter what Eban might say.[28]

On both Jerusalem and repatriation, El Salvador did not understand why Israel should not be able to comply. "Present conditions," it said, "appear to be favourable for the implementation of these resolutions, as the war between Israel and the Arab States has ended, and the belligerents are observing a truce which might almost be called an armistice. The delegation of El Salvador," it went on, "feels that the State of Israel should take advantage of those conditions to implement, in collaboration with the United Nations, the General Assembly resolutions on the internationalization of Jerusalem and the repatriation of the Arab refugees. The delegation of El Salvador would like to have some assurances on these matters from the Israeli Government."[29]

El Salvador then put the issues directly to Eban. "I wish to ask the representative of Israel," said its delegate, "whether he is authorized by his Government to assure the Committee that the State of Israel will do everything in its power to co-operate with the United Nations in order to put into effect: (1) the General Assembly resolution of 29 November 1947 on the internationalization of the City of Jerusalem and the surrounding area, and (2) the General Assembly resolution of 11 December 1948 on the repatriation of refugees."[30]

Eban replied to both parts of the question. On Jerusalem, Eban said that Israel had put forward the idea that internationalization should apply to the holy places only, not to the entirety of Jerusalem.[31] That response led El Salvador's delegate to ask "who, in the view of the Government of Israel, would exercise sovereignty over Jerusalem and the surrounding area."[32]

Eban's reply came as follows. "The question of sovereignty over the area has not yet been finally settled and will be settled, perhaps, at the fourth session of the General Assembly. It will not be for the Government of Israel alone to determine that issue of sovereignty. All we can do – and even then only if we are members of the United Nations – will be to propose formally certain solutions of our own."[33] So Eban was agreeing that Israel did not have the right to determine sovereignty over Jerusalem. Israel would await a solution as yet to be devised by the United Nations. At the same time, Israel had its own idea what the United Nations should say on Jerusalem. Eban said, "We should suggest that the incorporation of the Jewish part of Jerusalem in the State of Israel should receive formal recognition by the General Assembly."[34]

TROUBLE FROM A DUBIOUS DANE

Denmark took a turn posing pointed questions to Eban, focusing on repatriation. Eban replied that "the study of the question of the resettlement of Arab refugees formerly living in Palestine must take account of the changes which have taken place in the structure of the country." That response suggested an unwillingness to implement Resolution 194, because Resolution 194 did not condition repatriation on the "structure of the country." Eban continued. "The Arab part of the country previously had a separate economy which no longer exists. As a result of the war many villages have been either destroyed or evacuated and there has been migration of the population."[35] Resolution 194 similarly did not condition repatriation on the economic picture. And Eban's mention of the destruction and evacuation of villages as a reason to keep the Arabs out was questionable, since it was the IDF that destroyed the villages and forced the evacuation. Eban perhaps thought that the Committee members would not know that the villages were destroyed by the IDF. What Eban was saying was that the Arabs had no right to be repatriated because the government that was denying them repatriation had blown up their houses.

Denmark's delegate, Per Federspiel, was not satisfied with Eban's rationalizations. He asked pointedly, "I take this answer to mean that the Government of Israel will not accept the provision set forth in paragraph 11 of the General Assembly resolution of 11 December 1948, which says that the refugees who might desire to return to their homes and live at peace with their neighbours should be permitted to do so."[36]

Eban objected that he had not so said. He referred to what Ben Gurion had told the Conciliation Commission. "The statement of Mr. Ben-Gurion to the Conciliation Commission makes it quite clear," he said, "that he rejected no principle laid down by the General Assembly, but that the question of return hinged upon two factors: first, the restoration of peace, after which the Arabs would return to their homes in such conditions as would enable them to live at peace with their neighbours; in other words, not a truce or an armistice, but real peace between Arabs and Jews; and, secondly, there is the question of the extent to which the return of the refugees is practicable. This aspect of the problem is acknowledged by the resolution of the General Assembly. Those are the two qualifying references to the right of return to which Mr. Ben-Gurion drew attention, but he certainly did not lay down or encourage a rejection of the principle of repatriation."[37]

Eban here was taking two elements in paragraph 11 of Resolution 194 and distorting them to make them mean the opposite of what was intended. Paragraph 11 said "that the refugees wishing to return to their homes and live at peace with their neighbours should be permitted to do so at the earliest practicable date." So it did call for repatriation only of those willing to live at peace. But the reference was to individuals, not to states. Eban was taking that phrase to mean that the states had to be willing to live at peace, and to show that willingness by concluding treaties with Israel.

Paragraph 11 said that repatriation should be effected "as the earliest practicable date." This was a phrase intended to inject urgency into the situation. In December 1948, hostilities were still a reality in some parts of Palestine. Refugees could not be repatriated if mortars were landing in their village. "Practicable date" referred to the military situation, and to it only. Eban separated the word "practicable" from its context. He distorted the word to make it apply to the practicability of fitting the Arabs into the life of Israel. He took it, per his earlier statement to Denmark, to refer to whether Arabs could be integrated into a Jewish economy.

Federspiel was unimpressed. Again he inquired, "Am I right in understanding that the Government of Israel will neither accept nor reject paragraph 11 of the Assembly resolution of 11 December 1948?"[38]

Now Eban retreated further still from what paragraph 11 required of Israel. "The Government of Israel," Eban said, "considers and has made clear that the return of Arab refugees was one of the methods of settling this problem." But, said Eban, there was one other method. That, he said, was "resettlement of the refugees in neighbouring countries. The balance of those resettled in neighbouring countries, in comparison with the numbers resettled in Israel, is a matter to be settled by mutual consent after negotiations for which we are immediately prepared."[39] Resettlement outside Israel, as we have seen, was the solution truly espoused by the Government of Israel. It wanted no repatriation at all. Here Eban was saying that Israel would negotiate as to how many might return, and how many might stay out. There was no suggestion of such a procedure in paragraph 11 of Resolution 194. That paragraph did not give Israel a veto over repatriation.

Without replying to Eban's assertions, Federspiel posed a question that implied his rejection of what Eban was saying. "I should like to stress," Federspiel said, "that this is a question of principle. The General Assembly resolution of December 11, 1948 treated the Arab refugees as individuals having individual rights of resettlement in their country of origin. We have today heard the representative of Israel stating that the plight of these refugees, and their future, will be the subject of negotiations between the Government of Israel on the one hand and the Governments of neighbouring Arab countries on the other. I should therefore like to ask the representative of Israel a question: Does the Government of Israel consider the rights of the Arab refugees as rights of individuals, or as a subject of negotiations between States?"[40]

Federspiel would not get an answer from Eban. "Again I am less concerned with legal principles than with facts," Eban replied. "The problem can be solved only by negotiations between the Governments concerned."[41] Resolution 194, as Federspiel said, simply placed an obligation on Israel to repatriate. It nowhere said that there was anything to be negotiated with other states.

Federspiel now gave up on getting Eban to say that Israel would comply with Resolution 194. He moved the discussion to the UN Charter, and its mention of self-determination. "If the Government of Israel does not accept the principles of the individual rights of property and of living in their own country of the refugee Arabs," Federspiel said, "and if the latter want to return, how will the Government of Israel reconcile that attitude with the principle laid down in Article 1, paragraph 2 of the Charter, dealing with the principle of equal rights and self-determination of peoples."[42]

Eban acknowledged the self-determination principle and said that Israel respected it. But, he said, "This Article refers to the relations between groups, that is, either nations or peoples, Governments concerned, and does not affect the duty of Government in the rehabilitation of individual refugees." But it was Eban who had rejected the General Assembly's proposition that individual refugees had a right to be repatriated and had moved the discussion to the group level.

A NICE QUESTION OF PRINCIPLE

Belgium posed a question of principle that applied to both Jerusalem and repatriation. Belgium's delegate, Joseph Nisot, asked Eban, "Could the representative of Israel tell us whether, if Israel were admitted to membership in the United Nations, it would agree to co-operate subsequently with the General Assembly in settling the question of Jerusalem and the refugee problem or whether, on the contrary, it would invoke Article 2, paragraph 7, of the Charter which deals with the domestic jurisdiction of States?"

Article 2, paragraph 7 of the UN Charter reserves matters of domestic jurisdiction to member states. The Charter imposes obligations relating only to international matters. Thus, Nisot was asking if Eban regarded the status of Jerusalem as a matter falling wholly under its domestic jurisdiction. Resolution 181 took Jerusalem as an international issue by calling for a UN administration over the city. So the question was more than theoretical.

Eban gave a clear answer. "I do not think," he said, "that Article 2, paragraph 7, of the Charter, which relates to domestic jurisdiction, could possibly affect the Jerusalem problem, since the legal status of Jerusalem is different from that of the territory in which Israel is sovereign."[43] Eban was saying that the status of Jerusalem was an international matter, in other words that Israel could not unilaterally claim Jerusalem as part of its territory, even though it did claim the rest of the territory of Palestine that it had occupied. Eban clarified that "the territory of Jerusalem ... has not the same juridical status as the territory of Israel." This was a response that the members of the Ad Hoc Committee wanted to hear.

Nisot then asked the Charter question to Eban in regard to repatriation of the displaced Palestine Arabs. Did Israel consider repatriation a matter of domestic jurisdiction on which it could do as it pleased? Eban's answer was less clear. Eban said that repatriation was different in this regard from Jerusalem. He invoked sovereignty. "The principle of the sovereignty of Israel," he said, "is more applicable in the case of the refugees, since it affects the territory of Israel itself, than it could be in relation to the territory of Jerusalem, which has not the same juridical status as the territory of Israel. That is, in my opinion, the legal position."

That answer seemed to be a rejection of Resolution 194. The resolution's paragraph on repatriation assumed an obligation on Israel to repatriate the displaced Palestine Arabs. But then Eban, apparently realizing that his answer would not rest well with the Ad Hoc Political Committee, equivocated. He said that he did not know "whether that legal distinction should be allowed to have any practical effect." He went on to say that "it would be a mistake for any of the governments concerned to take refuge, with regard to the refugee problem, in their legal right to exclude people form their territories." Instead, they should "make a constructive effort to expedite the resettlement and rehabilitation of such numbers as are agreed upon amongst themselves, without worrying whether they are legally compelled to accept them or not."[44] This addition to Eban's answer seemed to mean that Israel would not hide behind what he saw as its legal right to invoke sovereignty in regard to the refugees. But he also seemed to be referring to the Arab states, and to be putting the onus on them to figure out what to do with the refugees.

Eban's answer went in two opposite directions. In the first instance, Israel did not have to answer internationally in how it dealt with the refugees. In the second, Israel would make an effort to resolve the issue in agreement with the neighboring states.

MIXED REVIEWS FOR EBAN

As Eban's testimony concluded, some delegates gave their reactions to his answers. Arab-state delegates reacted negatively, indicating they would vote against Israel. Delegates from outside the region reacted more favorably, but a number of them expressed serious doubts about Eban's answers. Quite a few said they would vote for Israel in the hope that it would follow through on the commitments Eban was making.

Iraq was among the harshest in criticizing Eban. It accused him of making "many wrong statements."[45] It noted in regard to Jerusalem that Israel was moving governmental offices into the city. "It was well known that, while the Conciliation Commission was trying to arrive at an equitable solution, Israel was gradually moving the seat of its Government into Jerusalem in order once more to force the hand of the United Nations."[46]

Iraq said that Eban's answers on Jerusalem were evasive, to cover for Israel's real intentions. "The attitude of the Zionist leaders with regard to the internationalization of Jerusalem," it said, "betrayed their utter contempt for the United Nations. Mr. Eban's replies to the questions put to him by the representatives in the Committee were evasive, and must convince the Committee of the bad faith with which the Zionists approached the solution of the problems. They were trying to deceive the United Nations and to persuade the world that all would be well if they were given control of Jerusalem. They had no hesitation in once again solemnly promising to implement the United Nations resolutions and decisions."[47]

Canada was more positive on Eban's answers. Regarding both Jerusalem and repatriation, Canada "welcomed his co-operative and constructive suggestions." "The pledge of the Israeli Government to co-operate fully in solving the important problem of Arab refugees implied, it was hoped, a recognition of the need for a long-term basis of friendly collaboration between all the peoples of the area."[48] Canada announced it would vote for Israel's admission.

Eban had not convinced Yemen. Like Iraq, it accused Eban of "distorting the facts."[49] Eban's stated preference for resettlement of the Palestine Arabs outside Palestine showed that Israel was not prepared to comply with Resolution 194.[50] Yemen did not trust Eban's promises. "The Committee," it said, "should not accept mere Zionist pledges of co-operation as final proof that they would abide by United Nations decisions or comply with the requirements of Article 4 of the Charter. Those pledges had been belied by the facts." Israel did not qualify as "peace-loving."[51]

China was "not satisfied with the policy of Israel" that "the new city of Jerusalem would be incorporated in the State of Israel. However, in view of Israel's pledge to co-operate in the settlement of all questions within the framework of the United Nations and its recognition of the moral authority of Assembly decisions, China was prepared to support the position of Israel with regard to Jerusalem. "The attitude of the Israeli Government on the repatriation of Arab refugees was far more disturbing," China said. "The theory of national homogeneity could not be supported by the United Nations." China concluded from Eban's statements on repatriation that Israel was trying to have a state composed solely of Jews. "In view of the express guarantees of human rights in the Charter," China said, "the United Nations could never sanction the attempt by any Government to force the refugees to leave their ancestral homes."

But even this sharp rebuke to Eban did not lead China to oppose Israel's admission to the United Nations. "The delegation of China," it said, "had been gratified to hear the Israeli representative's assurances that his Government desired to co-operate with and to accept the moral authority of the United Nations." As regarded repatriation, despite its harsh criticism, China "was satisfied with the attitude that Government had adopted on the substance of the matter."[52] China announced it would vote in favor of Israel's admission.

Norway did not think that Eban's statements on repatriation showed compliance with Resolution 194. "With regard to the refugee problem, the delegation of Norway was still not entirely satisfied by the Israeli representative's statement." Norway planned, it said, to vote to admit Israel, but it had doubts. "If the General Assembly were to decide in favour of the admission of Israel," Norway said, "it should do so on the assumption that that State would do its utmost to arrive at a solution of the problem of Arab refugees which would be equitable not only from the political but also from the humanitarian point of view."[53]

Colombia thought, in regard to repatriation, that "none of those refugees who wished to return to their homes should be prevented from doing so." Colombia said it would vote for Israel's admission because of Eban's interventions. "The statements and answers of the representative of Israel," it said, "had cleared up a number of important points."[54]

Cuba said it would vote to admit Israel even though it found that "some of the statements made by the Israeli representative had been hardly satisfactory."[55] Cuba appreciated Eban's answers on domestic jurisdiction, which it took as a commitment to resolve the most serious outstanding issues. "The representative of Israel," it said, "had given an assurance that, if that country were admitted as a Member, such matters as the settlement of frontiers, the internationalization of Jerusalem and the Arab refugee problem would not be regarded as within its domestic jurisdiction and protected from intervention under the terms of Article 2, paragraph 7."[56]

Britain said that Eban's replies on Jerusalem and repatriation had not been reassuring, and therefore Britain advocated deferring Israel's application.[57] Brazil said the same about Eban's replies. It too said the application should be deferred.[58] Any concern Eban might have had about the position the United States would take in the Ad Hoc Political Committee was alleviated when Warren Austin spoke for the United States. In a brief intervention, Austin said that Israel met the criteria for membership under Article 4 of the UN Charter and that the United States would vote in favor of admission. He said nothing about Jerusalem or repatriation.[59]

Eban's answers to the Ad Hoc Political Committee reflected a greater willingness to conform to what the United Nations was asking of Israel than did statements that he and other Israeli officials were making elsewhere. Eban was tailoring his answers. His statements answers to the Ad Hoc Political Committee on the displaced Arabs suggested greater willingness to consider repatriation than Israeli officials were telling US officials or the Conciliation Commission for Palestine. Eban was suggesting to the Committee that repatriation might be possible at some point in time. Before the Conciliation Commission for Palestine and in conversations with US officials, Israeli officials were saying that the displaced Palestine Arabs should look for homes outside Israel. Eban espoused that view to the Ad Hoc Political Committee, but he suggested flexibility on Israel's part.

The United States was not prepared to take Eban on during the hearings in the Ad Hoc Political Committee. But it did not buy what he was saying. As the hearings were concluding, Eliahu Elath, Israel's ambassador Washington, received a telephone call at his home from Dean Rusk of the US Department of State. Rusk warned Elath that unless Israel acted immediately to contribute to solving the refugee problem, it would antagonize the whole world and risk its own security.[60]

Luckily for Eban, no one raised the issue of the detention camps. No one mentioned the taking of Umm Resh Resh. No one mentioned ongoing expulsions. The Ad Hoc Political Committee vote went in Israel's favor. The vote to recommend Israel's admission was 33 to 11, with 13 abstentions.[61] Since the membership of the Ad Hoc Political Committee was the same as the membership of the General Assembly, this vote virtually guaranteed that the General Assembly would admit Israel.

A GREAT MOMENT

Confident of victory on a final vote in the General Assembly, Eban cabled Shertok, who by this time was using "Sharett" as his surname. Eban asked him to fly to New York for the General Assembly meeting. Eban wanted Sharett as Foreign Minister to make the acceptance speech after the vote. Sharett arrived in the General Assembly's hall just as the delegates were approaching the vote on Israel's application.

Warren Austin, the US delegate, announced, as he had in the Ad Hoc Political Committee, that the United States would vote for Israel's admission. Austin referred to the discussions of Israel's application in the Ad Hoc Political Committee. But now Austin did address Jerusalem and repatriation. "The long discussion of Israel's application," Austin said, "was evidence of the general deep-rooted desire for a just solution of questions relating to Palestine, and especially those of Jerusalem and the Arab refugees."[62] So the United States was solid for Israel, even though what Austin was saying about Israel's desire for solutions was directly contrary to what Mark Ethridge was reporting to President Truman.

The discussion in the General Assembly went well for Israel. Cuba explained that it had posed questions to Eban in the Ad Hoc Political Committee. Cuba was complimentary of Eban. It "paid tribute to the ability and diplomacy displayed by the representative of Israel in answering those questions."[63] Belgium, however, had not been won over. In the vote, Belgium abstained. But Israel got an easy majority for admission. General Assembly Resolution 273 was titled Admission of Israel to membership in the United Nations. The vote in favour of Israel was 37 to 12, with 9 abstentions.[64] Eban had done his job well.

While the resolution did what Eban asked, by finding Israel to be peace-loving and on that basis admitting it to membership, it also recited Israel's commitments that formed the basis for the General Assembly's decision to admit Israel, as well as the General Assembly's prior resolutions that imposed obligations on Israel. Resolution 273 read:

> *Having received* the report of the Security Council on the application of Israel for membership in the United Nations,
>
> *Noting* that, in the judgment of the Security Council, Israel is a peace-loving State and is able and willing to carry out the obligations contained in the Charter,
>
> *Noting* that the Security Council has recommended to the General Assembly that it admit Israel to membership in the United Nations,
>
> *Noting* furthermore the declaration by the State of Israel that it "unreservedly accepts the obligations of the United Nations Charter and undertakes to honour them from the day when it becomes a Member of the United Nations",
>
> *Recalling* its resolutions of 29 November 1947 and 11 December 1948 and taking note of the declarations and explanations made by the representative of the Government of Israel before the *ad hoc* Political Committee in respect of the implementation of the said resolutions,
>
> *The General Assembly,*
>
> *Acting* in discharge of its functions under Article 4 of the Charter and rule 125 of its rules of procedure,
>
> 1. *Decides* that Israel is a peace-loving State which accepts the obligations contained in the Charter and is able and willing to carry out those obligations;
>
> 2. *Decides* to admit Israel to membership in the United Nations.[65]

The General Assembly thus was explaining that its decision to admit Israel was premised on the commitments Eban had made to the Ad Hoc Political Committee in regard to repatriation and to Jerusalem. The reference to the resolution of "29 November 1947," the partition resolution, was pointed, because that resolution specified that a Jewish state, were it to be formed, must accord equality without reference to ethnicity. The reference to the resolution of "11 December 1948" similarly meant obligations for Israel, in particular the obligation to repatriate the displaced Arabs.

Resolution 273 was unusual in United Nations practice. General Assembly resolutions admitting a new member typically recite only that the Security Council has recommended membership. They make no mention of dialogue with the applicant state preceding admission, and no mention of commitments the state may have made in order to secure admission. By its references to commitments made by Israel, the General Assembly was indicating that it would not have decided to admit absent those commitments.

As the voting ended, Sharett was invited to the podium. Arab delegates demonstratively walked out of the hall in protest. Sharett was given the floor. "The admission of Israel," he said, "was a great moment for the new State and for the Jewish people throughout the world." Sharett hailed Israel's admission as "the consummation of a people's transition from political anonymity to clear identity, from inferiority to equal status, from mere passive protest to active responsibility, from exclusion to membership in the family of nations."[66]

Sharett did mention, if only briefly and indirectly, the issues that had been raised against Israel. "The Israeli Government," he said, "had taken careful note of the discussions in the *Ad Hoc* Political Committee on certain problems still outstanding between Israel and its neighbours on the one hand and between Israel and the United Nations on the other." The reference to problems with "its neighbours" was a reference to territory and to refugees. The reference to problems with the United Nations was a reference to the status of Jerusalem. Sharett said that Israel "would pursue its steadfast efforts to assist in the earliest possible settlement of those issues by discussions between Israel and the neighbouring States and through the good offices of the United Nations."[67]

This statement was directly contrary to what Sharett was doing in the Conciliation Commission for Palestine. As Ethridge had reported to Truman, Sharett was evading any commitments in his interaction with the Conciliation Commission. By his disingenuous promise to make "steadfast efforts," Sharett was making a commitment Israel would flaunt.

Nonetheless, Eban and Sharett had scored a major gain for Israel. UN membership, said lawyer Shabtai Rosenne, concretized "the acceptance of Israel into the international community."[68] Membership at the United Nations encouraged other states to recognize Israel. The success in gaining both passage of Resolution 181 and admission to the United Nations were widely viewed as major achievements of diplomacy.[69]

Membership had been achieved on the back of obfuscation and exaggerated promises. Israel had dodged a bullet on the Jerusalem issue, and as well on the repatriation issue. A few weeks after the admission vote, the Conciliation Commission for Palestine completed an investigation it had been conducting into the October 1948 killings at Dawayma. The Commission issued a damning report, finding that there had been mass killing of villagers without justification at the hands of the IDF.[70] But Israel was riding high in the wake of its admission to the United Nations. The report attracted little attention.

EBAN HITS HIS STRIDE

Eban's performance in the Ad Hoc Political Committee represented a significant personal achievement. In Israel's formative years, Eban was a powerful weapon. Born Aubrey Solomon Eban in South Africa, he was raised in England, where he trained in classics and oriental languages at the University of Cambridge. There he gained fluency in Hebrew and in Arabic. There he became an active Zionist, editing for a time a publication called *The Young Zionist*.[71] In London he came to work with Chaim Weizmann in the Zionist movement.[72] During World War II, he served as an officer in the British Army in Egypt and in Palestine. While in Palestine he trained fighters for a Jewish military force.[73] Eban's fluency in Arabic was such that he was able to translate from Arabic a novel by a noted Arabic author. Once Israel was admitted to the United Nations in 1949, Eban became its Permanent Representative. In 1950, he would begin using "Abba" (father) as a first name in place of "Aubrey."

Eban was an ideal practitioner of *hasbara*. Eban's success in the persuasive art was facilitated by his breadth of knowledge. His erudition made him seem unassailable as he asserted facts and explained Israel's motives. His command of English impressed his listeners. Eban became renowned for his oratorical skills. In the later years of his career, Eban would interact with the US national security advisor, Henry Kissinger. In his memoir, Kissinger lauded Eban's skill as a diplomat. "I have never encountered anyone," wrote Kissinger, "who matched his command of the English language. Sentences poured forth in mellifluous constructions complicated enough to test the listener's intelligence and simultaneously leave him transfixed by the speaker's virtuosity."

According to Kissinger, an accomplished diplomat himself, Eban's eloquence gave him a great advantage in an argument. "To interrupt seemed almost unthinkable, for one knew that one would have to do so in an idiom that seemed barbaric by comparison." Kissinger waxed eloquent on Eban's ability to persuade others of his views. "Eban's eloquence – unfortunately for those who had to negotiate with him – was allied to a first-class intelligence and fully professional grasp of diplomacy. He was always well prepared; he knew what he wanted. He practiced to the full his maxim that anything less than one hundred percent agreement with Israel's point of view demonstrated lack of objectivity."[74]

Kissinger astutely captured Eban's mindset. Eban's diplomatic efforts were shaped by a view that an opponent's criticism of Israel or Zionism reflected anti-Semitism. "One of the chief tasks of any dialogue with the Gentile world," Eban would say in 1972, "is to prove that the distinction between anti-Semitism and anti-Zionism is not a distinction at all."[75] Eban's phrase "dialogue with the Gentile world" was telling, as an indication of how Eban regarded interaction with other diplomats. It was Israel against everyone else. The imperative was to achieve acceptance for a Jewish state. "Because precisely in the light of Jewish traumatic experience," Eban said, "if Israel were really a kind of leper colony, boycotted, shunned, banished, denied the equality of status in the international enterprise, then the resulting mental and psychological effects would be severe."[76] The diplomats who shepherded Israel to statehood evinced an "us versus them" mentality that had its roots in the Jewish experience in Europe, reinforced by the Nazi atrocities of the Second World War. The goal of protecting Jews took precedence over accuracy in what might need to be said in a particular diplomatic skirmish.

13

Israel: 1, United Nations: 0

Sharett's promise of cooperation to the UN General Assembly was short-lived. On neither the issue of Jerusalem nor the issue of repatriation would Israel conform its policy to what the United Nations deemed necessary. It did admit a small number of refugees through a family reunification program, but at the same time it generated new refugees. In the latter part of 1949 and into 1950, the IDF expelled inhabitants from villages where they had remained during the offensives of 1948 of the Zionist militias.[1] When able to identify Arabs who had reentered clandestinely, it expelled them – in some cases large groups.[2] In the Galilee, it collected Arab males who had been displaced internally, forced them into trucks and drove them across the frontier.[3] The IDF expelled in particular from areas near the armistice lines, rationalizing these expulsions on security grounds.[4] In other instances the stated rationale was to make room for arriving Jewish immigrants.[5] Neither of these explanations would have justified the expulsions. The 1948 expulsions Eban and Sharett had tried to attribute to wartime conditions. But the new expulsions were being carried out in the absence of hostilities.

The United States pressed Israel on repatriation. Truman continued to call Israel out – in private – for its refusal to repatriate. Just two weeks after the admission vote, Truman sent a pointed message to Ben Gurion, threatening repercussions. "If the Govt of Israel continues to reject the basic principles set forth by the res of the GA of Dec 11, 1948," Truman said in a cable to Ben Gurion, "the US Govt will regretfully be forced to the conclusion that a revision of its attitude toward Israel has become unavoidable."[6] Instead of offering concessions, Ben Gurion mounted a counter-attack. In a message to the United States, Ben Gurion said that as long as the Arab states refused to make peace, "refugees are potential enemies of Israel."[7] He characterized the refugees as "members of an aggressor-group defeated in a war of its own making. History," he said, "does not record any case of large-scale repatriation after such experience."[8] This language suggested permanent rejection of repatriation. Ben Gurion convinced James McDonald, the US ambassador, to ask Truman to back off. McDonald did cable Truman, suggesting that "further US views not be expressed in terms of imperatives."[9]

The Department of State, however, kept up the pressure. When the government of Israel pressed its views on Jerusalem and on repatriation in contacts with delegates at the United Nations, the Department of State accused Israel of duplicity in the admission process. In a note to the government of Israel, the Department noted Abba Eban's views on Jerusalem and repatriation from the hearings before the Ad Hoc Political Committee on Israel's admission to UN membership. "The present effort of the Government of Israel to invoke support from the General Assembly for its position on such questions," the Department said, "seems to be at variance with the basis on which it itself sought support for its admission to the United Nations."[10]

The Conciliation Commission for Palestine also continued to press Israel on repatriation after the admission vote, but with no better results. Mark Ethridge seethed over Israel's refusal to make concessions. He held Israel responsible for all the displaced Palestinians but said that it had "particular responsibility for those who have been driven out by terrorism, repression and forcible ejection." He said that "her attitude toward refugees is morally reprehensible and politically short-sighted."[11]

The Conciliation Commission for Palestine told Ben Gurion that repatriation should not await a political settlement. The Commission regarded repatriation as a precondition for a political settlement. Ethridge reported to Washington, "Commission members, particularly USRep, have consistently pointed out to Prime Minister, Foreign Minister, and Israeli delegation that key to peace is some Israeli concession on refugees."[12]

The Commission organized a conference in Lausanne, Switzerland, in Summer 1949, to deal with all outstanding issues relating to Palestine. As for refugees, Israel proposed that it was prepared to accept 100,000 of the displaced Arabs, but with the understanding that they be resettled in areas designated by Israel rather than in their home areas, and on the further understanding that this limited repatriation be part of an overall peace between Israel and the Arab states. The Commission found this proposal "unsatisfactory."[13] Ben Gurion was offering to repatriate only 100,000 of what may have been 750,000. The others would be left exiled. And even these 100,000 were not to be repatriated in the sense of Resolution 194, because the repatriation was not to be to their homes. This was an offer that Ben Gurion knew would be rejected.

A BOND CEMENTED BY BLOOD

Winter 1949 saw a major push by the Conciliation Commission for Palestine on Jerusalem. It drafted a document on governance of the city to implement internationalization. Israel's UN delegation, in a lengthy memorandum, objected. The delegation opposed the Conciliation Commission's view that the United Nations had "full and permanent authority" in Jerusalem. The delegation said that Israel's "legal title in the Jewish area would be destroyed" by that language.[14] So the Government of Israel was asserting "legal title," contrary to Eban's statement to the Ad Hoc Political Committee that Israel had no claim to Jerusalem.

Israel's rejection of the Conciliation Commission's statement on Jerusalem drew the attention of the Ad Hoc Political Committee. Members of that committee, having been responsible for shepherding Israel's admission application, were concerned about the commitments Israel made to gain admission, and whether Israel was keeping them. Israel faced blistering criticism in the Ad Hoc Political Committee. Australia accused it of duplicity. Australia referred to Resolution 273. "It should be pointed out," Australia said, "that in resolution 273 (III), in pursuance of which Israel had been admitted to membership of the United Nations, reference was made to resolution 181(II) of 29 November 1947 and to the statements made by the representative of Israel at that time, which had given grounds for the hope that that State, recognizing all that it owed to the United Nations, would abide by its recommendations with fidelity and good will. Moreover," Australia continued, "the current attitude of the Israel delegation seemed hardly consonant with the attitude it had previously adopted."[15]

Australia was calling Israel out for reneging on Eban's commitments. Sharett appeared for Israel in the Ad Hoc Political Committee. Sharett said that the United Nations may have originally accepted responsibility for Jerusalem, a reference to Resolution 181, but that it had not followed through. Rather, "the Jews had regained not merely their stake in Jerusalem, but the link between it and the State of Israel. That bond had been cemented by the blood shed by the 1,490 Jewish men, women and children who had fallen, as civilians or as soldiers of Israel's Army, in Jerusalem alone," Sharett said. "The sufferings and resistance of those heroes had only reinforced their will and conviction that the State of Israel and the City of Jerusalem should constitute an inseparable whole."[16] This too was a claim to sovereignty over Jerusalem.

The events that Sharett was referencing – the battle between Israeli and Jordanian forces over Jerusalem – took place in 1948, prior to Israel's application for UN membership. If the military confrontation over Jerusalem had the effect Sharett claimed, of cementing the connection with Jerusalem, then Israel could have said so to the Ad Hoc Political Committee in May 1949. Eban had avoided any such statement.

Sharett attributed Australia's view that Israel was reneging to "a misunderstanding on the part of either the Australian or the Israeli delegation."[17] But the Israeli delegation, meaning Eban, had been quite clear on the point. Eban had said that Israel had no claim to Jerusalem. There was no misunderstanding about what Eban had promised. Sharett was trying to paper over Israel's deception.

Sharett voiced a new argument for opposing an international regime for Jerusalem. He said that such a regime would not "derive its authority from the freely expressed will of its inhabitants."[18] The inhabitants of what he was calling "Jewish Jerusalem," Sharett was saying, wanted to be part of Israel. If that was so, it was, of course, only because the Zionist militias had forced the Arabs out of "Jewish Jerusalem."

In an effort to soften his disputation of the UN view on Jerusalem, Sharett told the Ad Hoc Political Committee that "Israel would always be conscious of the debt it owed to the United Nations for the recognition of its right to live as an independent nation in its own country, which was to Israel the main and eternal element of the resolution of 29 November 1947."[19] But Israel's gratitude did not extend to being honest with the United Nations. To make matters worse, Sharett proposed to the United Nations to conclude a treaty with Israel relating to holy sites in "Jewish Jerusalem." The issue of protection of such sites had come up in the Ad Hoc Political Committee. Israel sent to the United Nations a draft resolution that would authorize the Secretary-General to conclude with Israel a treaty to govern the protection of holy sites in "Jewish Jerusalem." Israel attached to the draft resolution a treaty it had composed for this purpose.[20] While the draft treaty did not explicitly address the status of "Jewish Jerusalem," the conclusion by the United Nations of a treaty relating to the holy sites only would implicitly have constituted an acceptance by the United Nations that Israel had sovereignty in Jerusalem. Nothing came of the draft treaty.

ETERNAL CAPITAL

One of the concerns of the Ad Hoc Political Committee in regard to Jerusalem in May 1949 had been that government offices were being transferred from Tel Aviv to Jerusalem. Sharett now defended that transfer unapologetically. He said that what he called "Jewish Jerusalem" had been "integrated in the State" administratively. He said that the transfer to Jerusalem of the main institutions of government was "indispensable."[21]

The Government of Israel was not concealing its claim to Jerusalem. On December 5, 1949, Prime Minister Ben Gurion declared in the Knesset "that Jewish Jerusalem is an organic and inseparable part of the State of Israel." In regard to the UN efforts at internationalization, he said that "it is inconceivable that the UN should attempt to sever Jerusalem from the State of Israel or to infringe the sovereignty of Israel over its eternal capital."[22] The Knesset voted approval of Ben Gurion's statement.[23] This action provoked counteraction from the UN General Assembly. It adopted a resolution reaffirming that Jerusalem must be internationalized.[24]

The Government was undeterred. Two days later, it voted to make Jerusalem the seat of government for Israel.[25] Ben Gurion demonstratively moved his own office from Tel Aviv to Jerusalem.[26] Sharett, as Foreign Minister and a Cabinet member, dissented, because he did not see how Israel could go so directly against what the United Nations was demanding on Jerusalem. Sharett viewed his own position as the voice of Israel's foreign policy as untenable while Israel's government disregarded the United Nations so blatantly. From New York, Sharett cabled Ben Gurion to offer his resignation as Foreign Minister. Ben Gurion kept the letter to himself, and Sharett continued as Foreign Minister.[27] Ben Gurion ignored Sharett's act of protest and proceeded on a course at odds with what had been promised during the admission hearings. Ben Gurion announced in the Knesset that more government offices would move to Jerusalem, even adding a proposal that the Knesset meet there as well.[28] The Knesset agreed and decided that it would hold its sessions in Jerusalem.[29] Ben Gurion also declared that Jerusalem was Israel's capital.[30]

The United Nations continued to press for internationalization of Jerusalem and to insist on the cooperation that had been promised. The UN Trusteeship Council, the body that was to have administered an internationalized Jerusalem under Resolution 181, moved ahead with drafting a statute to govern Jerusalem.[31] Like the Ad Hoc Political Committee, the Trusteeship Council was concerned over the transfer of government offices from Tel Aviv to Jerusalem. It adopted a resolution expressing its concern over those moves, and asking Israel "to revoke these measures."[32] But by the end of 1949, most government offices were functioning in Jerusalem, turning it into the hub of government activity for Israel.[33]

The Trusteeship Council sent Israel the text of its resolution, prompting a letter in reply from Eban. Arguing that the relocation of Israel's governmental offices to Jerusalem was nothing new, Eban wrote "that the highest organs of the State of Israel, the Presidency and the Knesset, were founded and instituted in Jerusalem early in 1949, even before Israel's admission to membership in the United Nations."[34] If government offices were in Jerusalem prior to Israel's admission, Eban's logic ran, the UN knew about it then and didn't object.

It was true that some government offices had been moved to Jerusalem prior to May 1949. As we saw, Iraq complained about these moves in the Ad Hoc Political Committee. But the Knesset had not moved to Jerusalem at that point. It held its first brief session in Jerusalem in February 1949 but thereafter met in Tel Aviv. So it had not been located in Jerusalem prior to the Ad Hoc Political Committee's consideration of Israel's membership application. In mid-January 1950, the Knesset took a step that further solidified Jerusalem as the center of governmental activity for Israel when it decreed that buildings should be constructed in Jerusalem to house both the Knesset and executive branch offices.[35] It also followed Prime Minister Ben Gurion's declaration of a month earlier and declared Jerusalem to be the capital of Israel.[36]

In a statement about Jerusalem to the Trusteeship Council in February 1950, Eban argued against an international regime for Jerusalem. He said that the General Assembly had not set up any machinery to follow through with the Resolution 181 recommendation for an international regime for Jerusalem, hence that that idea had been abandoned.[37] But if that was true, it had been true when Eban testified to the Ad Hoc Political Committee in May 1949. On that occasion, he had said nothing of the sort. He had said that Israel's policy on Jerusalem derived from Resolution 181. Eban's contradiction in February 1950 of his May 1949 testimony could not have been clearer. Eban was reneging on the commitment he had given to the Ad Hoc Political Committee. Eban's parting shot to the Trusteeship Council was that "the sole abiding objective of the United Nations in the Jerusalem question is the protection of the Holy Places."[38] So Eban was telling the United Nations to stop trying to govern Jerusalem.

Foreign governments resisted Israel's claim to Jerusalem. Even after the Foreign Ministry moved its offices to Jerusalem in 1953, they kept their embassies in Tel Aviv, not wanting to acknowledge Israel's claim to

Jerusalem.[39] The United States publicly announced its concern over the move as a repudiation of the status Jerusalem was to enjoy under Resolution 181.[40] Many states refused to attend Ministry functions in Jerusalem. They directed communications not to Ministry headquarters but to a liaison office the Ministry kept in Tel Aviv.[41] They were trying to hold Israel to the commitment Eban had given the Ad Hoc Political Committee. An Israeli claim to Jerusalem was seen as damaging the chances for any negotiated settlement in Palestine.

A CLOSE READING

Repatriation was also raised. The Ad Hoc Political Committee pressed Israel to follow through on the commitment to flexibility that Eban made in May 1949. Eban told the Ad Hoc Political Committee in December 1949 that Israel's "insistence on making the general settlement of the Palestinian problem a preliminary condition to the solution of the problem of refugees" was "solely determined by the fact that the State of Israel had recently emerged from an assault on its very existence and survival."[42] That statement left doubt as to how flexible Israel was willing to be. But Eban made an additional argument that cast doubt on Israel's willingness to repatriate even if there were a peace settlement. Eban said "that the tragic fate of the Arab refugees of the Near East was one of the most serious consequences of the war declared in 1948 by Egypt, Jordan, Lebanon, Saudi Arabia, Syria and Yemen for the purpose of crushing the State of Israel out of existence, in defiance of an international recommendation. Those who had initiated that war were, consequently, responsible for its tragic consequences."[43] That statement repeated earlier Israeli views, as we have seen, that the Arab states were responsible for the exodus from Palestine, hence should provide the solution.

The Conciliation Commission for Palestine also kept pressing Israel on repatriation. Meeting with Ben Gurion on April 7, 1950, the Commission "asked if the Government of Israel accepted the principle established by the General Assembly's resolution, permitting the return to their homes of those refugees who expressed the desire to do so." In reply, Ben Gurion disputed the Commission's reading of the resolution. He referred to the phrase "live at peace with their neighbours." "In Mr. Ben Gurion's view," as reported by the Commission, "this passage made the possibility of a return of the refugees to their homes contingent, so to speak, on the establishment of peace: so long as the Arab States refused to make peace with the State of Israel, it was evident that Israel could not fully rely upon the declaration that Arab refugees might make concerning their intention to live at peace with their neighbours."

Ben Gurion made clear his view, consistent with what Eban was telling the Ad Hoc Political Committee, that the bulk of the displaced Arabs should resettle elsewhere. But he told the Commission that Israel regarded the issue as one of those to be examined during general negotiations for the establishment of peace.[44] There was, of course, little prospect at the time for peace, so the delay Ben Gurion proposed would have put repatriation off to a distant future date.

The one atrocity incident that was related to the Arab exodus that Israeli officials did not deny was the Deir Yassin killings of April 1948. The incident was raised in the Ad Hoc Political Committee in November 1950. These killings continued to be a source of criticism of Israel because of the numbers killed, the absence of any plausible justification, and the impact they had on causing Arab flight from Palestine. Moshe Sharett, speaking for Israel, did not deny that what occurred at Deir Yassin was an atrocity. He called it "terrorism" and said that "the Government of Israel had not failed to state how horrified they had been by the event."[45] We have seen that the Jewish Agency did at the time acknowledge the atrocity and even sent regrets to King Abdullah. But then as now, stress was laid on the fact that the atrocity was perpetrated by the Irgun Zvei Leumi and LEHI. Eban, as we have seen, deflected Israel's responsibility for anything done prior to its declaration of statehood. In any case, the government of Israel did not regard itself as responsible for the Arab exodus and was making no steps toward repatriation of any significant number of displaced Arabs.

A STRANGE VIEW OF THE UNITED NATIONS POSITION

In these same discussions in the Ad Hoc Political Committee, Abba Eban devised a new way of avoiding repatriation. He argued that Israel was not in fact out of line with the United Nations on the repatriation issue. He asserted that the approach that Ben Gurion was advocating before the Conciliation Commission for Palestine, namely, putting off discussion of repatriation until there were political settlements, was in fact the approach of the United Nations. Eban derived this analysis from his reading of the context of the repatriation obligation in General Assembly Resolution 194. "Whatever the nature of resolution 194 (III) adopted 11 December 1948," Eban told the Ad Hoc Political Committee in December 1950, "the United Nations had not then or on any other occasion made any promise with regard to the repatriation or resettlement of the refugees except as part of the general restoration of peace and stability between Israel and the Arab States of the Middle East."[46]

"United Nations policy," Eban claimed, "explicitly recognized the inter-relation between a solution of the refugee question and a restoration of normal relations among the States concerned. That United Nations view," he averred, "had been set forth in resolution 194 (III) adopted 11 December 1948 and in the report of the United Nations Conciliation Commission (A/1367, A/1367/Corr.1). The proposals of Egypt and Pakistan repudiated that view and attempted to separate what were in fact two facets of the same problem."[47]

What Eban characterized as the view of Egypt and Pakistan was in fact the view of the UN General Assembly as a whole. Resolution 194 was, to be sure, a comprehensive resolution that sought an overall settlement to be brokered by the Conciliation Commission for Palestine. But the inclusion of all the major outstanding issues in one resolution did not mean that repatriation depended on an overall settlement. Repatriation was regarded by the General Assembly as a humanitarian issue, separate from other issues. Dean Rusk, it will be recalled, said that the refugees "should not be made pawns in the negotiations for a final settlement."[48] Rusk clearly regarded paragraph 11 of Resolution 194 as calling for repatriation in such a way that it did not depend on peace treaties.

France said that Eban was misreading what the United Nations had done. France said that the fact that the United Nations sought both repatriation and a political settlement did not mean that the former must await the latter. In 1950, a resolution was proposed by France, Turkey, Britain, and the United States to deal with both issues.[49] France said that, although it included both issues in the resolution, it sought a solution on repatriation consistent with Resolution 194.[50] Turkey, a member state of the Conciliation Commission for Palestine, explained, "With regard to the connexion between the question of refugees and other questions still outstanding in Palestine, it was true that all those questions were inter-related. That interdependence could be interpreted in two different ways. It might be said that, if certain questions were interdependent, one question could not be solved before another; it might also be said that, when one of the questions was being solved, an attempt should also be made to solve the others. The joint resolution was based on the latter point of view. It gave priority to the question of refugees, but also provided for the solution of all the other outstanding questions."[51] The joint draft resolution was adopted by the General Assembly.[52]

Britain, too, explained that repatriation was an issue to be resolved separately from that of peace. "There could be no question," it said during the same discussion, "that refugees wishing to return and live at peace with their neighbours had the right to do so. The joint draft resolution contemplated progress both regarding the refugee question and regarding all other outstanding issues. It did not, however, directly link negotiations regarding other outstanding issues with the taking of urgent measures to alleviate the refugee problem."[53] The United States expressed agreement with France and Britain on this approach to repatriation.[54]

Other states did as well, making it clear that Eban was distorting the United Nations position. The Philippines said "that the Arab refugees' right to return to their homes was a basic human right recognized by the General Assembly, which had thus become responsible for seeing that the right was implemented. It should not be made dependent on negotiations between the parties concerned, and, although it was admittedly part of the general problem, its solution could not be made contingent upon the settlement of larger issues."[55]

Eban took still another tack aimed at characterizing Israel's stance on the repatriation issue as consistent with that of the United Nations. In 1952, the issue of Israel's refusal to repatriate the displaced Arabs was again on the agenda of the Ad Hoc Political Committee. The Committee continued to be concerned that Israel was not doing what Eban had promised in May 1949. Eban cited efforts that were being made at that time at the United Nations to encourage Arab states to accept Palestine Arab refugees who might want to settle in their territory permanently. He said that those efforts reflected a view "that repatriation would result in cultural conflict, economic adversity, and a threat to the security of Israel. Resettlement, on the other hand, would be in harmony with a growing international sentiment based on concern for the welfare of the refugees and the economic stability of the Middle East."[56] This assertion by Eban that repatriation would not be in the best interests of the refugees themselves was inconsistent with Resolution 194.

The General Assembly rejected this argument of Eban's as another distortion of its Resolution 194. Each year from then on, the General Assembly would adopt a resolution calling on Israel to implement repatriation, and criticizing it for not having done so already.[57] The fact that the General Assembly was urging Arab states to accept those refugees who wanted to stay there in no way negated the position taken in Resolution 194 that repatriation was required of Israel then and there.

14

A Phantom Attack

By the early 1950s, the Zionist Organization's objectives were largely accomplished. It had taken territory in Palestine, occupying nearly 80 percent of it. Only the Gaza Strip and a sector of east central Palestine remained out of the control of the newly declared state. The Gaza Strip was being held by Egypt. East Central Palestine, now denominated the West Bank of the Jordan River, was being held by Jordan. So with those two exceptions, the aims of the Biltmore program of 1942 were accomplished. The armistice agreements that Egypt, Lebanon, Jordan, and Syria had been forced to conclude with Israel in 1949 were holding. Under each armistice agreement, a mixed commission, made up of representatives of each pair of states, policed the armistice line. Each mixed commission was chaired by an official appointed by the United Nations.[1] Israel still held the seat it had won in the United Nations, without keeping the commitments it made to gain admission. It continued successfully to resist pressure to repatriate the displaced Arabs. It was consolidating its hold on Jerusalem.

A persistent problem remained for Israel, however. The displaced Palestine Arabs were sheltering in the neighboring Arab states, in many instances just across the armistice line from Israeli-held territory. Palestine Arabs who had fled north languished in Lebanon or Syria. Those who had gone east were under Jordan – either in Jordan's earlier-held territory east of the Jordan River, or in the West Bank of the Jordan River. Those who had gone south were in the Gaza Strip. Not content with what was turning into a long-term exile, and seeing that the United Nations was taking no decisive action, Arab refugees sought ways to get back to Palestine on their own.

Some Palestine Arabs hazarded individual ventures back into their home areas, clandestinely crossing into what was now Israel. Some went to collect belongings. Some went to harvest crops they had planted. Since cultivable land was scarce, the pattern of agriculture in Palestine typically involved a village in which the inhabitants lived in proximity to one another, built on less desirable land. The fields would be outside the village, on the better land. In some instances, particularly with Jordan, the armistice line separated farmers from their fields, hence the frequency of line-crossing in the early years after 1949.[2] The Israeli government classified Arabs who crossed the armistice line as infiltrators. In 1954, the Knesset formalized a prohibition on clandestine crossings by adopting a penal law titled "Prevention of Infiltration."[3]

Eventually, groups of displaced Palestine Arabs formed and began to carry out armed raids across the armistice lines with Jordan, Syria, or Egypt, even in the face of the United Nations efforts to police the lines. These raids often resulted in casualties on the Israeli side. Many Israeli civilians were killed. E.L.M. Burns, a retired Canadian general who served as Chief of Staff of the UN Truce Supervision Organization 1954 to 1956, explained the state of mind among the displaced Arabs, specifically those in the Gaza Strip. That sector, General Burns recounted, had grown in population in 1948 from 100,000 to 310,000, with the influx of refugees from other sectors of Palestine. General Burns called Gaza "a vast concentration camp." He said that the refugees in Gaza "can look to the east and see wide fields, once Arab land, cultivated extensively by a few Israelis." He said, "It is not surprising that they look with hatred on those who have dispossessed them."[4] These groups of irregulars – *fedayeen* as they were called – said General Burns, were "Palestinian Arabs who had a burning sense of injustice that they had suffered at the hands of the Israelis."[5]

The government of Israel adopted a policy of reprisal against these raids.[6] In some of these raids, the numbers killed far surpassed the numbers killed in the Arab actions to which they were a response. In a series of incidents, such raids were dealt with by the UN Security Council, which became alarmed at the scope of the reprisals.[7]

General Burns saw repatriation of the displaced Palestine Arabs as a cure for the armistice line violence he was assigned to police. Burns was in close touch with Prime Minister Ben Gurion and discussed repatriation. Burns concluded that Ben Gurion would never allow it. Burns said that a repatriation would, to Ben Gurion, be "inconsistent with the continued existence of the State of Israel."[8] General Burns in fact wrote that he pressed Ben Gurion more than once on the issue of repatriation. He got what he called the "stereotyped Israeli answer," namely, "that the refugees had left Palestine of their own accord, or, rather, on the orders of the Arab Higher Committee and in accordance with its war plan against the new-born State of Israel." General Burns saw little possibility of peace until Israel allowed repatriation.[9] General Burns was in an odd position in regard to the refugees. His task was to keep the armistice line quiet. But the effect of doing that was to keep the refugees from reclaiming what the General Assembly regarded as their right to be repatriated. General Burns had to live with the contradiction inherent in his role. By agreeing to the provisions in the armistice documents calling for monitoring, Israel had managed to enlist the United Nations in keeping the Palestine Arabs out.

"NOT A SINGLE ARMY UNIT"

The downside for Israel of the armistice arrangements was that Israel too was monitored when its forces crossed the lines for reprisal raids. The UN Truce Supervision Organization employed a staff that might intercept them, or at least investigate after the fact. If Israel sent squads of combat-trained soldiers into civilian areas across the line, causing casualties, the monitors might publicize what Israel was doing. The matter could then also be raised against Israel in the UN Security Council.

One of the more visible, and deadly, of such incidents was a raid in 1953 into a town in Jordanian-held territory, in the West Bank of the Jordan River. The village was called Qibya. The attack was launched on the night of October 14, 1953, around 9:30 p.m. The villagers were in their homes at that hour. IDF attackers fired rifles and threw grenades into homes, causing some villagers to flee into the streets, others to hide inside. There was no armed resistance from the side of the villagers.

A military attaché from the US embassy in Amman, Jordan, hurried to the scene the next day and reported on the attack to Talcott Seelye, the US *Chargé d'affaires* in Jordan. Seelye was asked to go to the office of Jordan's foreign minister, who briefed Seelye on the raid. The accounts by the Jordanian foreign minister and by a US military attaché were consistent in concluding that Israeli military personnel estimated at "reinforced battalion strength" shelled the village with mortar and artillery fire for three to four hours. Then demolition parties entered the village and blew up 39 houses. The deaths of 45 villagers could be confirmed. Seelye reported the attack to the US Department of State.[10]

Foreign Minister Moshe Sharett went into damage control mode, understanding that the large number of casualties would not look good for Israel. Sharett called in Francis Russell, the US *Chargé d'affaires* in Israel, on October 17. Sharett did not attempt to justify the raid. But he asked Russell to view it in the context of a "recent rising tide" of "border lawlessness" on the Israel-Jordan frontier. Sharett told Russell that he would say no "word in justification." Oddly, Sharett did not say who carried out the raid, specifically whether it had been the IDF. So Russell asked whether that meant "that Israel disavows the Qibya raid." Sharett did not give a direct answer. Instead he told Russell "that he could not say before tomorrow's Cabinet meeting."[11] Sharett as it happened kept a diary, and he made entries at the time of the Qibya raid.[12] For the date of October 17, Sharett wrote an account of this meeting. Sharett's diary entry is consistent with the account that Russell sent to the US Department of State.[13] Russell had pressed Sharett on reprisal raids. Russell had reminded Sharett of having raised with him, in August of that year, the "question of whether it was Israel's intention to continue [to] pursue reprisals as [an] instrument of national policy." Russell told Sharett that the "first reply from [the] Israeli Government had been [the] Qibya reprisal attack."[14] The United States issued a public statement on the raid, calling it an "attack by Israeli forces." The United States conveyed condolences to the families of those killed in Qibya and said "that those who are responsible should be brought to account."[15]

Attending the Sharett-Russell meeting was Gideon Rafael, formerly of Israel's delegation at the United Nations. At the time Rafael was stationed in Israel, as Counselor on Middle East and United Nations Affairs in the Foreign Ministry. Rafael asked Russell that the United States not press Israel on its reprisal policy, pleading that US pressure "has dangerous effects on [the] Israeli population, whose feeling of isolation and lack of friendship tends to lead to despair."[16]

Israel's Cabinet met in crisis mode. Sharett said that the raid "projected the Israeli leadership" as being "capable of large massacres." He suggested that the government take responsibility and express regret.[17] Ben Gurion insisted that the government deny IDF involvement and attribute the attack to Israeli civilians who took justice into their own hands.[18] A hand grenade had indeed been thrown into a house in an Israeli village called Yahud near the armistice line two days earlier, killing two children and their mother. Blaming the Qibya raid on Israeli civilians angered over this incident would be plausible, Ben Gurion argued, because residents in villages near the armistice line included trained fighters among their number, and many of them kept weapons.[19] Sharett was not convinced. He replied at the Cabinet meeting "that no one in the world will believe such a story and we shall only expose ourselves as liars."[20] Sharett said that the raid had done great harm to Israel's good name.[21]

Prime Minister Ben Gurion's view prevailed. The government had to speak with one voice. Sharett sent a cable to Israeli diplomatic missions, giving the government's account of the Qibya raid as having been committed by "the border settlements," which had "lost their patience."[22] The next day, Ben Gurion broadcast an address by radio to give the government's account. The government deplored the killings, Ben Gurion said, but he placed blame on the Jordanian government, which, he said, "for years has tolerated, and thereby encouraged, acts of murder and pillage against the inhabitants of Israel." Ben Gurion said that the raid was conducted by Israeli villagers from the Israeli side of the armistice line. Ben Gurion claimed to have investigated. "We have carried out a searching investigation and it is clear beyond doubt," he said, "that not a single army unit was absent from its base on the night of the attack on Kibya." Ben Gurion said that "the Government rejects with all vigor the absurd and fantastic allegation that 600 men of the Israel defense forces took part in the action against the village of Kibya village."[23]

The only aspect of Ben Gurion's October 19 statement that was accurate was his denial that the raid was carried out by a force of 600. The number was probably much lower. But the raid had been carried out by the IDF.[24] It was ordered by Pinchas Lavon, Minister of Defense.[25] Within the government, Lavon said the raid was justified to prevent the murder of Israelis in the future.[26] The raid was led by Ariel Sharon, a 25-year-old major who would later become Israel's prime minister. In August 1953, Sharon was asked to take charge of a newly forming unit, called Unit 101.[27] The order setting up Unit 101 described its purpose as being "to carry out special reprisals across the state's borders."[28] Moshe Dayan, head of the Operations Branch of the General Staff, was instrumental in establishing Unit 101. Dayan described Unit 101 as "a volunteer unit which undertook special operations across the border."[29]

The Qibya raid was one of the first operations of Unit 101. Paratroopers were also involved, outnumbering the Unit 101 personnel, but with Major Sharon in overall command.[30] Moshe Dayan, on behalf of the General Staff, oversaw the planning for the raid.[31] Denying IDF involvement, as it turned out, was part of the plan from the beginning. The operational order for the raid from the Operations Branch cautioned participants to avoid leaving traces that they were IDF.[32] The operational order for the raid issued by Central Command defined the objective as "destruction and maximum killing, in order to drive out the inhabitants of the village from their homes."[33] A preoperation order written in hand by Sharon directed his forces to "inflict maximum damage on human life and property."[34]

Explosives were prepared and packed, to take along to blow up buildings in Qibya. Several days after the operation, Sharon was debriefed by Ben Gurion, who, according to Sharon, expressed approval of what Sharon's unit had done.[35]

"COLD-BLOODED MURDER"

UN Truce Supervision Organization personnel visited Qibya the morning after the raid. They reported to the UN Security Council. "Bullet-riddled bodies near the doorways and multiple bullet hits on the doors of the demolished houses indicated that the inhabitants had been forced to remain inside until their homes were blown up over them."[36] "Witnesses were uniform," the report recited, "in describing their experience as a night of horror, during which Israeli soldiers moved about in their village blowing up buildings, firing into doorways and windows with automatic weapons and throwing hand grenades."[37]

It was the task of the Jordan-Israel Mixed Armistice Commission to inquire into incidents of this type. Before the Commission, the Israeli representative said that the raid was not carried out by the armed forces of Israel.[38] The Commission, based on information it had received, rejected this denial. In its report the Commission characterized the incident as "the crossing of the demarcation line by a force approximating one half of a battalion from the Israel regular army, fully equipped, into Qibya village on the night of 14–15 October 1953 to attack the inhabitants by firing from automatic weapons and throwing grenades and using bangalore torpedoes together with TNT explosive, by which forty-one dwelling houses and a school building were completely blown up, resulting in the cold-blooded murder of forty-two lives, including men, women [and] children, and the wounding of fifteen persons."[39] The UN-appointed chair of the Jordan-Israel Mixed Armistice Commission was US Navy Commander E.H. Hutchison, who later wrote a book about his experiences. Commander Hutchison wrote that in a number of houses in Qibya on the morning after the raid, the door was bullet-splintered, and a body found "sprawled across the threshold, indicating that the inhabitants had been forced by heavy fire to stay inside until their homes were blown up over them."[40]

Aware that the critical issue was the identity of the attackers, the Mixed Armistice Commission gave reasons for its conclusion that the attackers were from the IDF. It cited to the Security Council a report from Commander Hutchison in which he described the weaponry and equipment that had been used. The equipment included items that were standard for the IDF. "This raid was well planned," concluded Hutchison, "and carried out by men expertly trained in the fundamentals of sudden and sustained attack. It seems highly improbable that other than active military forces could have carried out this raid without suffering heavy casualties from their own fire, or from the explosions of their demolition charges."[41]

The Mixed Armistice Commission acknowledged the fact that Ben Gurion cited about recent incursions from the Jordanian side of the armistice line. The Commission said, "Public opinion on either side has been inflamed by incidents." It cited in particular the incident of two days earlier. "The hand grenade thrown on the night of 12–13 October into a house in the Israel village of Yahud, which caused the death of two small children and their mother, may have provoked the attack on Qibya forty-eight hours later."[42] Yahud was located on Israel's side of the armistice line, not far from Qibya. The Mixed Armistice Commission did not speculate who might have been responsible for the Yahud raid. However, the Mixed Armistice Commission concluded that the raid into Qibya was of a magnitude that required advance planning. So a spontaneous reaction of villagers was not plausible as an explanation for the Qibya raid.

"ACCURATE IN EVERY RESPECT"

The United Nations could not be avoided. Reaction of UN delegates was sharp. David Hacohen of the Israeli delegation reported to Sharett that he found it "difficult to meet the eyes of persons at the UN who express their astonishment 'at the Nazi actions of my colleagues and myself.' "[43]

Moshe Sharett as Foreign Minister might have been expected to make the defense, given the notoriety of the raid, but he opted to leave the task to Abba Eban.[44] Rafael had wired word of the raid to Eban, eliciting a pained reaction in return. If Rafael's information were accurate, Eban cabled back, Israel had perpetrated "an act it cannot be proud of and that cannot be excused even by Arab crimes that preceded it." Eban anticipated "extremely harsh international reactions."[45]

Moshe Dayan and Gideon Rafael were flown to New York to assist Eban in the presentations he would be making to the Security Council. Sharett sent them less to convey details of the operation than to provide moral support, given that Eban did not relish his task.[46] Rafael agreed with Eban that the raid was indefensible and had said so in a cable he sent on October 18.[47] Rafael suggested that Israel acknowledge the IDF role but argue that Israel was in a continuing state of belligerence with Jordan since

Israel and Jordan had only an armistice but no peace agreement, hence that a military intrusion by the IDF was not unlawful.[48]

Rafael wrote up an account of the Qibya raid for Foreign Minister Sharett the morning after it happened, explaining the extent of the slaughter and bemoaning the "erosion of moral standards" of the IDF. Rafael explained in the memorandum that the raid had been commanded by Ariel Sharon. In this memorandum, Rafael said that he offered his resignation, because he did not think he could defend what the IDF had done.[49]

France, Britain, and the United States jointly put the Qibya raid on the agenda of the UN Security Council. Eban questioned the evidence of IDF involvement. He challenged Commander Hutchison's conclusion that the type of weaponry used at Qibya showed that the attack was carried out by the IDF. He asked Vagn Bennike, who preceded Burns as UNTSO Chief of Staff, whether the types of weapons held by Israeli civilians in villages near the armistice line were different from those used by the IDF.[50] General Bennike responded, citing the Mixed Armistice Commission's experience in examining armistice line incidents. General Bennike said that the torpedoes, mortars, and demolition charges used in the Qibya raid were weaponry that would not be found in the hands of Israeli civilians.[51]

Ben Gurion's explanation, voiced by Eban, did not play well in the Security Council. Britain said that the raid was carried out by a "disciplined, organized, well-armed, Israel military force."[52] The United States said that there was "no doubt concerning the facts of the military action which took place in Qibya." It subscribed to what Britain had said.[53] France also associated itself with the British statement. France called the incident the "Qibya massacre" and said that it had been "undertaken by the armed forces of Israel against the inhabitants of the village of Qibya."[54]

Eban listened to these repudiations of Israel's version but gave no ground. In reply on November 12, Eban said that he believed Ben Gurion's account. Eban expressed Israel's regret for the deaths at Qibya but attributed them to "a most unfortunate explosion of pent-up feeling and a tragic breakdown of restraint after the provocation of brutal attacks such as the cold-blooded murder of a mother and her children in their sleep."[55] As he mounted this defense for Israel, Eban understood that he was fighting a losing battle. In a cable to Foreign Minister Sharett, Eban said that he expected the Security Council to condemn Israel.[56]

Eban's denial did not convince the United States to change its view. It was drafting a resolution that would condemn Israel for the raid. In a message to the US mission at the United Nations, US Secretary of State

John Foster Dulles wrote, "We do not believe we should modify our plan to table in [the] S[ecurity] C[ouncil] [the] Qibya resolution as now drafted because of Eban's speech of November 12." Dulles said that "Bennike's reports demonstrated Israel's culpability for [the] Qibya incident and we believe she should be censured."[57]

France, Britain, and the United States submitted a resolution that recited that the raid was carried out by "armed forces of Israel on 14–15 October 1953."[58] In a meeting with US officials in Washington, Eban tried to convince the United States to withdraw the resolution. He said that the resolution would "make peace impossible for a long time to come."[59] As the Security Council approached a vote on the resolution, Eban told the Security Council "that it is not accurate to describe this retaliatory action as one taken by the armed forces of Israel on 14–15 October 1953." Eban referred again to Ben Gurion's radio address. "The statement of the Prime Minister of Israel on 19 October 1953," Eban affirmed, "is accurate in every respect."[60]

Eban was constrained not only by Ben Gurion's October 19 statement but by a decision of the government. Faced with the draft resolution and knowing it would come up for a vote in the UN Security Council, the Cabinet on November 22 decided that Israel's position on the Qibya raid should be what Ben Gurion said on October 19.[61] Ben Gurion made another radio broadcast, stating again that the IDF was not involved. "We vigorously question the veracity of the report that Gen. Bennike submitted on the Qibya affair, on which the Three Powers based themselves when they attributed responsibility to the armed forces of Israel."[62]

Eban carried out the Cabinet's wishes when the Security Council met on November 24 to vote. In a last-ditch effort to convince the Security Council that the IDF was not involved, Eban told the delegates that "observers" had concluded that the evidence was "in favour of Mr. Ben-Gurion's statement." By "observers," Eban implied that he had eyewitnesses. He had none. What he cited was an analyst who had not been on the scene. And despite his use of the plural, Eban cited only one. "I refer," Eban said, "especially to an article published on 23 October 1953 in the London *Sunday Times* by Lieutenant-General Sir Brian Horrocks who, in discussing this event as a military specialist, concludes that 'it could not possibly have been carried out' – those are his words – 'by the armed forces of Israel.' "[63] General Horrocks had been a well-respected commander of British forces in the Second World War. After the war, he embarked on a career as a publicist. So General Horrocks would have been known to the Security Council as a responsible military specialist.

Eban then referred to his question to General Bennike about the types of weaponry used in the Qibya raid, and those in the possession of Israeli civilian settlers. "For the entire definition of this grievous act as having been carried out by the armed forces of Israel, which would of course mean by its regular military forces under central governmental command, the chief evidence was said to reside in the name and the character of the weapons used. But when I asked the question whether the armaments held in Israel's frontier settlements to withstand the brutal incursions which were so vividly portrayed by the representative of Pakistan at the 640th meeting [of the Security Council] were of a category and type different from those used in the action at Qibya, the answer was virtually "no", and that the Chief of Staff was not in a position to say, never having been able either to inspect or to certify the character of the armaments in Israel's frontier villages." Eban said that what General Bennike said was "military opinion" that did "not constitute any finding that there is any distinction whatever between the armaments of an Israel defence unit and the armaments of an Israel village on the frontier zone; and, in point of fact, there are no such distinctions at all. Therefore," Eban concluded, "our first objection is to a matter of fact: namely, the attribution to the armed forces of Israel of the action which did take place at Qibya, and by such attribution to deny without cause, justification or accuracy the statement to the contrary made by Mr. David Ben-Gurion to which I have referred."[64]

Eban's mention of General Horrocks' opinion omitted details that would have made the opinion seem less compelling. Eban gave an incorrect date for the article. (Eban gave the date as October 23. The correct date was October 25.) But even had they had the correct date, the delegates would not have had time to find the article, since they were planning to vote then and there. Eban referred to General Horrocks as a "military specialist." Eban gave the impression that General Horrocks had undertaken some inquiry into the Qibya raid, or at least had knowledge of the circumstances. And Eban gave the impression that the topic of General Horrocks' article was the Qibya raid.

In fact, the topic of the article was quite different, and General Horrocks claimed no knowledge of what occurred at Qibya. Eban avoided giving the title of the article. It was "Israeli Army Training Soldiers and Citizens: Year on Land: Frontier Tension Background to 'Horror Raids.' " The article was a summary of General Horrocks' recent two-week stay in Israel at the invitation of the IDF. The article was an account of the training techniques employed by the IDF, techniques that had impressed him. On the basis of this favorable account of IDF training, General Horrocks made in the article a one-paragraph reference to the Qibya raid. Without indicating the source of his information, General Horrocks stated that raids were occurring back and forth across the armistice line with Jordan, carried out by civilians living nearby. He then stated, "It is against this sort of background that the last so called 'horror raid,' which occurred after I left, must be viewed. Nothing can possibly condone the killing of innocent Arabs, but I do not believe for one moment that this operation was organised by the Israeli Army."[65] The reference to a "horror raid" was evidently to the Qibya raid.

Eban's quoting of General Horrocks thus was less than accurate. General Horrocks did not say that the raid "could not possibly have been carried out" by the IDF. That formulation suggested that General Horrocks knew something about the circumstances of the raid. What General Horrocks said was based on what he knew about the IDF and its general practice.

Eban did not tell the Security Council that General Horrocks had left Israel before the raid. Nor did he tell the Security Council that General Horrocks had visited Israel as a guest of the IDF. General Horrocks later wrote a highly laudatory analysis of the IDF titled *Report on the Israel Army for 1952; visit of retired General Sir Brian Horrocks to Israel, September-October 1953*.[66] The most that one can draw from General Horrocks' *Sunday Times* article is that he had a high opinion of the IDF. His article hardly constituted "evidence" as Eban was claiming.

The Security Council in any event gave little weight to Eban's denial of IDF involvement in the Qibya raid. The Council adopted the tripartite resolution, which affirmed that it

1. *Finds* that the retaliatory action at Qibya taken by armed forces of Israel on 14–15 October 1953 and all such actions constitute a violation of the cease-fire provisions of Security Council resolution 54 (1948) and are inconsistent with the parties' obligations under the General Armistice Agreement between Israel and Jordan and the Charter of the United Nations;
2. *Expresses the strongest censure* of that action, which can only prejudice the chances of that peaceful settlement which both parties, in accordance with the Charter, are bound to seek, and calls upon Israel to take effective measures to prevent all such actions in the future.[67]

Eban's assessment of the Qibya affair was that the IDF had acted in a way that could not be cured by *hasbara*. In a message to Foreign Minister Sharett after the Security Council vote condemning Israel, Eban said that "sending regular armed forces across an international border, without the intention of triggering a full-scale war, is a step that distinguishes Israel from all other countries." That action "shocked the world."[68] In his own memoir, Eban said of the Qibya raid only that it "was regarded by most Israelis as excessive."[69]

NOT THE FIRST TIME

One factor that may have inclined the government to lie about Qibya is that it had lied successfully about other cross-armistice-line raids. In some instances, it had succeeded by attributing a raid to civilians, as Ben Gurion did here, while in other instances the UN observers had refuted the claim.[70] In operations that were smaller in scale of killing than at Qibya, IDF units had even disguised themselves as civilians, wearing nonmilitary dress and using ammunition and weapons that could in principle be used by civilians.[71] On the night of August 28, 1953, Unit 101 had attacked the Bureij refugee camp in the Gaza Strip. Three small Unit 101 squads were led by Ariel Sharon.[72] The Bureij raid "caused intense alarm and unrest in the whole Strip," reported Leslie Carver, who at the time was acting director of the UN Relief and Works Agency (UNRWA), which oversees relief for Palestine Arab refugees.[73]

The Bureij raid was investigated by the Mixed Armistice Commission that worked the Egypt-Israel armistice line. General Bennike recounted the Commission's investigation of the Bureij raid when he testified before the Security Council on the Qibya raid. As a preface to his Qibya testimony, General Bennike listed several earlier cross-line raids from Israel, including the Bureij raid. Describing the Bureij raid to the Security Council, General Bennike said, "Bombs were thrown through the windows of huts in which refugees were sleeping and, as they fled, they were attacked by small arms and automatic weapons." Twenty Arab refugees were killed and 62 wounded, he said. Then General Bennike described the investigation. "The Mixed Armistice Commission, in an emergency meeting, adopted by a majority vote a resolution according to which the attack was made by a group of armed Israelis. A likely explanation is that it was a ruthless reprisal raid. This seems probable in view of the fact that a quarter of the Israel complaints during the preceding four weeks referred to infiltration in this area."[74] By "armed Israelis," the Mixed Armistice Commission meant civilian Israelis. The Mixed Commission missed the fact that the raid was conducted by Unit 101. In the investigation by the Mixed Commission, the Israeli authorities denied that the IDF was involved.[75] And unlike the

Qibya situation, the types of weapons used – "small arms and automatic weapons" – could have been used by civilian Israelis. The Israeli authorities successfully deceived the Mixed Armistice Commission by denying IDF involvement. Israel's success with prevarication over the Bureij raid may have encouraged Ben Gurion to believe that it would work with the Qibya raid.

A DIFFERENT YARDSTICK

A factor in Israel's lack of success with its Qibya denial was that as of 1953 Israel's support from the major powers was at a low point. The Soviet Union by now was disenchanted with Israel and was no longer giving it the support that had been so critical to it earlier at the United Nations. During the Qibya debate in the Security Council, the Soviet delegate sat silent and abstained on the vote of condemnation.[76]

Of the three Western powers that sat on the Security Council, none saw an advantage in covering for Israel. Britain was still more closely tied to the Arab states than to Israel. France would grow closer to Israel within a short time, as we shall see, but that rapprochement had yet to gel. For the United States, the Truman Administration had been replaced in 1953 by the Eisenhower Administration, and that change had seen the exit of many pro-Israel officials at high levels. Under President Dwight Eisenhower, the Zionist lobby in the United States, while still strong, did not have automatic access when it came to executive branch decisions affecting Israel.

Israel's handling of the Qibya raid reflected a developing operational ethic that falsehood was justifiable in such situations. "Ben-Gurion felt the need to issue a fabrication," wrote an Israeli military analyst in regard to Ben Gurion's explanation for Qibya and other reprisal incidents, "in order to protect the standing and honour of the state, the IDF and the Chief-of-Staff."[77] Ben Gurion may have seen himself protecting subordinates who carried out questionable actions at his direction, but the major motivation for lying was to cover an incident that had brought criticism.[78] Ben Gurion never publicly acknowledged lying about Qibya. But some years later, when asked by a colleague in private, he did. What's more, Ben Gurion explained why he lied.

Ben Gurion's biographer told the story. Ben Gurion asked if his colleague had read the novel *Les Misérables* by the French author Victor Hugo. Ben Gurion recounted a passage in that book in which a police inspector was hunting to arrest a man whose only offense was theft of a loaf of bread. The man, knowing the inspector was after him, sought refuge in a convent and asked a nun to hide him. The police inspector, suspecting the man might be hiding there, entered the convent and asked the nun if she had seen him. The nun promptly answered in the negative. The police inspector, believing the nun would not lie, went away. Ben Gurion said that the nun's lie was designed to save a human life, therefore was no sin. "A lie like that," Ben Gurion said, "is measured by a different yardstick." According to Ben Gurion's biographer, "Ben-Gurion believed that under certain circumstances, it was permissible to lie for the good of the state."[79]

That ethic was not limited to Ben Gurion alone. Israeli political leaders by 1953 had seen that bending the truth can work, so long as the departure from the truth is not so great as to be obvious. They had used questionable methods to draw the UN Special Committee on Palestine to their side in their quest for a Jewish state. They had made questionable commitments to the United Nations to gain membership for Israel in the United Nations. They had resorted to falsehoods and false promises and had made gains for their cause. The diplomats for Zionism, and later for the Israeli state, saw their work as providing protection for a people that had been subjected to discrimination and worse. In their interactions with other diplomats they had to portray themselves as conforming to the rules that applied in the international community, but altering the truth to give the appearance of conformity to the rules could readily be rationalized.

15

Sabras in Sinai: Pardon My French

Cross-line incidents of violence did not diminish in intensity after Qibya. The UN Truce Supervision Organization reported a significant number along the lines with both Egypt and Jordan in the winter months of 1953–54.[1] On March 28, 1954, the IDF again tried to deny a reprisal raid. This incident involved an incursion into the West Bank village of Nahhalin. Houses were attacked, and several village guards were killed.[2] A government spokesperson attributed the raid to civilian Israeli settlers, denying involvement by the Israel Defense Force.[3] The Mixed Armistice Commission investigated and concluded that the raid was carried out by "militarily trained Israelis," who were firing automatic weapons, detonating explosives, throwing hand grenades and incendiary bombs."[4] The raid was indeed the work of an IDF force, a unit of 60 paratroopers under the command of Major Ariel Sharon.[5] The government was caught again lying. The very public exposure of its false denial in the Qibya raid had not deterred it from trying again.

THE EGYPTIANS ATTACKED FIRST

A different defense was claimed for a raid on February 28, 1955 into the Gaza Strip. This time the target was not a village, but a military post and a major one – Egypt's main army encampment in the Gaza Strip. The IDF sent one hundred twenty paratroopers to blow up buildings at the camp. One contingent ambushed a truck carrying 35 soldiers who tried to get to the camp to reinforce the camp's defenders.[6] Overall in the raid, 36 soldiers were killed on the Egyptian side, and eight IDF soldiers. The IDF raiders managed to avoid being observed by UN Truce Supervision personnel who were nearby at the time.[7]

The raid was led, as at Bureij, Qibya, and Nahhalin, by Ariel Sharon. In his memoir, Sharon explained that he confronted a number of obstacles in staging raids of this kind. One "complication," as he called it, "was that teams of UN observers constantly patrolled the border region looking for signs of trouble. If they noticed anything unusual they would report to their own people in Gaza and word would get out immediately to the Egyptians." The risk of detection was particularly great as Sharon planned the February 28, 1955 raid because a Jewish worker had been killed by elements coming from Gaza the previous day. As Sharon explained, the truce observers "knew that whenever a Jew was murdered something was likely to happen. Somehow we would have to camouflage our movements from the observers."[8]

This raid was the most serious incident of violence since the signing of the armistice with Egypt in 1949.[9] It represented a major escalation in Israel's reprisal raids, targeting as it did a military post.[10] Sharon managed to escape detection by the UN observers, a circumstance that opened the possibility of denying IDF involvement. However, given that the target was military in character, this raid could not plausibly be blamed on Israeli civilians. It had involved a clash of military forces on each side, with resulting casualties.

By this time, Moshe Sharett had succeeded David Ben Gurion as Prime Minister. Ben Gurion retained the post of Minister of Defense. Ben Gurion decided that Israel could not afford to admit to the raid. He devised an explanation that an Egyptian unit had ambushed an IDF patrol inside Israel, and that in response the Israeli unit, plus reinforcements, chased the Egyptian soldiers across the armistice line to the Gaza camp.[11] That explanation made the raid appear as a defensive response to an aggressive act by Egypt. On Ben Gurion's order, this account was disseminated by the IDF press corps. A major flaw in this explanation was that Israel had no physical evidence of an Egyptian intrusion, since there had been none. As with the Qibya raid, Sharett was chagrined that Ben Gurion was putting a false version into the public domain. Sharett thought that Ben Gurion's account would not be believed.[12] Another Cabinet member, Trade Minister Peretz Bernstein, agreed with Sharett.[13]

The Israel-Egypt Mixed Armistice Commission investigated and found that the raid had been carried out by the IDF. It found Israel at fault for the raid. The Gaza raid was sufficiently serious that, like the Qibya raid, it drew the attention of the UN Security Council. This time, however, Eban refused to repeat an account he knew to be false. When it came to the

Security Council debate, Eban in his defense of Israel managed to avoid the question of how the raid was initiated. He spoke in general about violations from the Egyptian side, but he did not repeat the IDF press story that an Egyptian force had intruded into Israel to start this incident. In a lengthy statement, Eban recounted prior raids into Israel from the Gaza Strip, portraying Israel as the victim over an extended period of time.[14]

Eban's avoidance of the IDF explanation was not lost on the Security Council delegates. It was a rarity that a country's military would publicly give an account that its UN ambassador would refuse to repeat. France picked up on the discrepancy. It pointed out during the Security Council discussion that Eban was not backing up the IDF story of an initial incursion by Egyptian forces. France said, "No evidence was found in support of Israel assertions that Egyptian armed forces had been the first to penetrate into Israel territory and had attacked an Israel security patrol. Mr. Eban himself refrained from mentioning this alleged incursion in the statement he made before the Council on 23 March [*694th meeting*]."[15]

France was not alone in drawing a conclusion from Eban's silence on the genesis of the IDF raid. The Security Council had no difficulty deciding that the IDF account was false. It adopted a resolution condemning Israel for the raid. The Security Council quoted the conclusion of the Israel-Egypt Mixed Armistice Commission that the raid was "a prearranged and planned attack ordered by Israeli authorities," and "committed by Israel regular army forces."[16]

Three days after the Security Council resolution on the raid, Eban sent a confidential cable to the Foreign Ministry office denouncing the IDF for the raid.[17] The government was putting Eban in an untenable position as Israel's representative in the Security Council by issuing explanations for military raids that were so palpably false.

The IDF raid on the Gaza military encampment had ramifications in the political realm. Egypt drew a lesson from the fact that the IDF was able so easily to penetrate into a major military objective. General Burns, who at the time still served as Chief of Staff of the UN Truce Supervision Organization, thought that this raid convinced Egyptian President Gamal Abdul Nasser to upgrade his army to match the IDF.[18] To that end President Nasser decided to seek armaments from abroad. He approached the Soviet government and was able to secure significant quantities of armaments.[19]

Abba Eban shared General Burns' view that this raid precipitated President Nasser's decision to bolster his military.[20] Beyond arming itself, Egypt also began to promote the activities of the Palestine Arab irregulars – *fedayeen* – in making raids into Israel.[21] Moshe Dayan, who by then was

Chief of Staff of the IDF, advocated a preventive strike against Egypt before it got stronger.[22] In April 1956, Shimon Peres, Director-General of the Ministry of Defense, met in Paris with Abel Thomas, an aide to France's Minister of Defense, to ask for arms for Israel. Peres told Thomas, by the latter's recollection of the meeting, to expect a major military confrontation between Egypt and Israel within six months to a year.[23]

PLANNING UNDER THE TABLE

In Israel, a Jew born in the territory is called a "Sabra." The term in Hebrew means a cactus, or prickly pear. It is a plant with a hard exterior, but sweetness inside. The idea behind the name is that Israelis are tough on the outside, but soft on the inside. By 1956, many of the soldiers in the IDF were Sabras.

On October 29, 1956, the IDF sent its soldiers into the Sinai. This attack was not of the hit-and-run variety like the reprisal raids we have seen. The IDF entered in force, quite openly and did not simply attack and withdraw. The attack was by regular IDF troops, not just General Sharon's Unit 101. The stated rationale was to stop infiltration into Israel once and for all. Egyptian troops responded to defend. Almost immediately, Britain and France called on Egypt and Israel to stop the fighting. Britain and France said the hostilities threatened free passage through the Suez Canal, a vital shipping lane for world commerce. When Egypt refused to stop defending, Britain and France landed troops in Egypt and began bombing around Cairo.

The public appearance was that Israel first invaded Egypt, and that Britain and France intervened to stop the fighting. But this was not the reality. Israel had not taken upon itself to invade Egypt on its own. France and Britain were not responding to an Israeli-Egyptian war in an effort to stop it. The entire scenario had been preplanned by France, Britain, and Israel.

The precipitating circumstance was Egypt's July 1956 nationalization of the Suez Canal, which was owned by British and French interests. Starting in that month, France and Britain began looking for ways to invade Egypt and force it to put the Canal back in the hands of its owners. Finding a way to do that proved difficult. They felt out the United States. President Dwight Eisenhower wanted no part of a military action against Egypt. Shimon Peres happened to be in Paris arranging for French armaments for Israel when Nasser announced nationalization of the Canal. Peres was called in by France's Defense Minister, Maurice Bourgès-Maunoury. The Defense Minister asked how long it would take the IDF to move across the

Sinai. Bourgès-Maunoury asked if Israel might be willing to attack along with France. Peres said Israel would be willing.[24] Israel was already contemplating a military move into Sinai for reasons of its own.[25]

On September 1, Israel's military *attaché* in Paris forwarded a message from the French government to Ben Gurion, repeating Bourgès-Maunoury's query to Peres. But now the suggestion came not from France alone, but from Britain as well.[26] Ben Gurion replied positively.[27] Arrangements were made for General Meir Amit, who served as chief of operations under Chief of Staff Dayan, to visit Paris to discuss details.[28] On September 19, Peres flew to Paris to confer further with Bourgès-Maunoury.[29] At this juncture, France was dealing separately with Britain and with Israel.[30]

In late September, a larger Israeli group flew to Paris to concretize the plan.[31] The French suggested that Israel attack first.[32] They then let Britain know that Israel was on board and floated what would become the final plan. Israel would attack first, then Britain and France would demand that Egypt and Israel cease fire. Expecting Egypt to decline, Britain and France would then attack Egypt. This plan was solidified on October 24.[33]

THREE IS COMPANY

In Britain, confidential government records are made public after a period of thirty years. However, the records are scrutinized to determine if some should remain secret. In 1986, as the thirty-year period from 1956 was about to run, two British officials communicated about how the culling would be done. In preparation for that task, a Minute was recorded that read: "On 24 October 1956 a secret meeting was held in a villa in Sèvres, near Paris, at which the French Foreign Minister, Monsieur Pineau, the Israeli Prime Minister, Mr Ben Gurion, and Sir Patrick Dean and Sir Donald Logan, representing the British government, discussed the plan for Israeli invasion of Egypt and subsequent Anglo-French intervention in the Suez Canal region. The plan of events agreed as a result of this discussion was written down, and the document was signed by the representatives of the three governments, each of which took away a copy."[34]

These British officials had come upon British communications from 1956. The military action against Egypt had, they found, been coordinated by Britain with Israel and France. The document to which the officials referred came to be called the Sèvres Protocol. Ben Gurion had worried that the French and British might not come through, so the agreement was committed to paper. The plot, after all, put Israel at some risk. It was to attack first. If France and Britain failed to follow through, Israel would be fighting Egypt alone.[35] Ben Gurion had reason for doubt, because Britain and France, as we saw in the last chapter, had been calling Israel to account for reprisal raids. Ben Gurion was not sure they were on his side.

The Minute went on to say that the officials could not find a text of the Sèvres Protocol in British files. It had apparently been destroyed, perhaps by Prime Minister Anthony Eden, to erase a written record of what would doubtless be regarded as an act of aggression. Eden had tried, unsuccessfully, to get the French and Israeli copies destroyed.[36]

Copies of the Sèvres Protocol survived and eventually made their way into the hands of researchers. The document was precise in detailing the anticipated military actions. It recited, "The Israeli forces launch in the evening of 29 October 1956 a large scale attack on the Egyptian forces with the aim of reaching the Canal Zone the following day." France and Britain, the document continued, would make a demand of Egypt on October 30 that it withdraw its troops ten miles from the Canal and let an Anglo-French force occupy the Canal. Simultaneously, France and Britain would demand of Israel that it stop fighting and withdraw ten miles from the Canal on the other side. But, the document continued, if Egypt did not comply, Israel would not have to comply either. It was anticipated that Egypt would not comply. The Sèvres Protocol called in that situation for Anglo-French military action against Egypt on the morning of October 31.[37] The trio of states even came up with a code name. Taking their inspiration from Alexander Dumas' novel *The Three Musketeers*, they dubbed themselves the "Musketeers."

A number of Israeli leadership figures would eventually write about the Suez episode, acknowledging their collaboration with France and Britain, and explaining why Israel found the idea attractive. Ariel Sharon, who commanded a paratroop brigade going into Sinai in this operation, recounted that Ben Gurion told him in preparation for the assault, "A deal had been struck by which Israel, France, and Great Britain would each gain their objectives. Ours were in Sinai. We would open the blockaded Strait of Tiran, eliminate the storm of terror from Gaza, and destroy all Nasser's pretensions to leadership, perhaps even bring about his downfall. At the same time the French and British would reestablish their control over the Suez Canal."

Sharon described how the scheme would be carried out. "The campaign was to be initiated by a carefully co-ordinated ploy. Israel would take action against the Egyptians deep in Sinai, dropping a paratroop battalion close enough to the canal to 'threaten' the waterway. At that point

Great Britain and France would give an ultimatum to both sides to move their forces away from the canal zone. Israel would agree. Egypt of course would not, and French and British forces would intervene to insure the canal's continued operation. Once the opening phase was over, we would pursue our own objectives by destroying Egypt's forces in the Sinai."[38]

The IDF concentrated troops near the Jordan frontier to draw attention away from its real target.[39] The United States became suspicious that military action by Israel was in the offing. US Secretary of State John Foster Dulles called in Abba Eban, who was serving as Ambassador to the United States, in addition to his UN post.[40] Dulles asked Eban whether Israel was planning to invade Jordan. Eban said Israel's measures were defensive only.[41]

Israel invaded into Sinai on October 29, saying that it was responding to Egyptian attacks of the previous months.[42] The IDF moved quickly toward the Suez Canal. When that operation kicked off, Eban was in a meeting at the Department of State in Washington with William Rountree, a deputy assistant secretary who dealt with the Middle East. Eban was explaining to Rountree, as he had to Dulles, Israel's "defensive posture."[43] The Arab states were preparing to attack Israel, Eban told Rountree. The Egyptian Navy was moving toward Israeli waters. Egypt, Syria and Jordan had established a joint command. As Eban was listing these hostile moves by the Arab states, a Department of State aide entered the room and handed Rountree press tickers reporting that Israel had just invaded into the Sinai.[44] Rountree turned to Eban and said, "I'm certain, Mr. Ambassador, that you will wish to get back to your embassy to find out exactly what is happening in your country."[45] Eban beat a hasty retreat.

THE CONSPIRATORS "EXPLAIN"

The United States took the lead in trying to stop Israel's invasion into Sinai. It approached the UN Security Council, placing on the agenda an item headed "steps for the immediate cessation of the military action of Israel in Egypt."[46] Dag Hammarskjold, who had succeeded Trygve Lie as UN Secretary-General, recited information from General Burns, who was still serving as Chief of Staff of the UN Truce Supervision Organization. General Burns reported that the Israeli forces were sabotaging UN monitoring operations. He said that the IDF, at the start of the invasion into Sinai, expelled UN military observers and set land mines in their observation post to keep them from using it. He had asked Israel to withdraw from Sinai, telling its government that it was in violation of the 1949 Israel-Egypt armistice agreement.[47]

Britain cast itself in the role of peacemaker. Its delegate, Sir Pierson Dixon, said that Britain was trying to stop the fighting. "As a result of the consultations held in London today," Dixon began, "the Governments of the United Kingdom and France have now addressed urgent communications to the Governments of Egypt and Israel. In these we have called upon both sides to stop all warlike action by land, sea and air forthwith and to withdraw their military forces to a distance of ten miles from the Canal. Further, in order to separate the belligerents and to guarantee freedom of transit through the Canal by the ships of all nations, we have asked the Egyptian Government to agree that Anglo-French forces should move temporarily – I repeat, temporarily – into key positions at Port Said, Ismailia, and Suez. The Governments of Egypt and Israel have been asked to answer this communication within twelve hours. It has been made clear to them that, if at the expiration of that time one or both have not undertaken to comply with these requirements, British and French forces will intervene in whatever strength may be necessary to secure compliance."[48]

Of course, no such "consultations" had been "held in London today." Britain and France had decided at Sèvres, together with Israel, that Israel would invade and that Britain and France would pretend to be peacemakers. Dixon read out the text of a message that the French and British governments had hand-delivered to Israel's *Chargé d'affaires* in London. It read:

"The Governments of the United Kingdom and France have taken note of the outbreak of hostilities between Israel and Egypt. This event threatens to disrupt the freedom of navigation through the Suez Canal, on which the economic life of many nations depends. The Governments of the United Kingdom and France are resolved to do all in their power to bring about the early cessation of hostilities and to safeguard the free passage of the Canal. They accordingly request the Government of Israel: *(a)* to stop all warlike action on land, sea and air forthwith, and *(b)* to withdraw all Israel military forces to a distance of ten miles east of the Canal."[49] This communication was a ruse, designed to disguise the collaboration of Israel with Britain and France. In no way were they in reality asking Israel to cease military operations.

"A communication has been addressed to the Government of Egypt, requesting them to cease hostilities and to withdraw their forces from the neighbourhood of the Canal, and to accept the temporary occupation by Anglo-French forces of key positions at Port Said, Ismailia and Suez. The United Kingdom and French Governments request an answer to this communication within twelve hours. If at the expiration of that time one or both Governments have not undertaken to comply with the above requirements, United Kingdom and French forces will intervene in whatever strength may be necessary to secure compliance."[50]

Dixon then read out the text of a message just sent to Egypt, making the same threat of intervention unless Egypt stopped fighting within twelve hours and moved its forces back from the Suez Canal.[51] The threat to Egypt was, of course, the point of the three-state plan.

To make this demand on Egypt seem credible, Dixon alluded to the Security Council's practice on the earlier Egypt-Israel raids, saying that neither side had heeded the Council's demands for cessation. "Both sides, in different ways," he said, "have shown such repeated disregard for the resolutions of the Security Council that we have felt confident that we should have the general support of the Council, and the United Nations as a whole, for what we are doing – namely, everything in our power to bring about the earliest cessation of hostilities and to safeguard the free passage of the Canal."[52] Bernard Cornut-Gentille, France's delegate, said he concurred in what Dixon said.[53]

THE FIRST MUSKETEER

The United States reacted strongly. It called the British-French ultimatum illegal. It tabled a draft resolution that called Israel's military incursion into Sinai a violation of the 1949 Egypt-Israel armistice agreement and demanded Israel's withdrawal from Egyptian territory.[54] Most Security Council members were unsure what to make of what seemed an odd situation. Yugoslavia, which held a non-permanent seat in the Security Council, reacted, however, to the call on Egypt to stop fighting, and the threat to send forces into Egypt. It realized that the real threat here was against Egypt, not against Israel. Yugoslavia said that "this threat of force is primarily directed against the country which is the victim of aggression. Egypt is being enjoined to waive its inherent right of self-defence."[55] Arkady Sobolev, the Soviet delegate, said the same. He accused Britain and France of aggression for their threat to send troops into Egypt. He called their posture "an attempt to exploit the situation that has arisen in Egypt as a result of Israel's aggression to seize the Suez Canal by force."[56]

Abba Eban, as Israel's Permanent Representative at the United Nations, spoke for Israel. "The object of those operations," he began, referring to Israel's move into Sinai, "is to eliminate the Egyptian *fedayeen* bases from which armed Egyptian units, under the special care and authority of Mr. Nasser, invade Israel's territory for purposes of murder, sabotage and the creation of permanent insecurity to peaceful life."[57] Eban followed up with a list of incursions from the Egyptian side into Israeli territory.[58]

This recitation was Eban's by then standard Security Council speech in justification of a reprisal action. "There is aggression, there is belligerency in the Middle East," said Eban, "but we are its victims and not its authors." In an oblique reference to the Holocaust, Eban characterized the Israelis as "a people which knows that the appeasement of despots yields nothing but an uneasy respite."[59] The despot now was not Hitler, but Nasser.

Eban at this time may not have known that Israel was collaborating with Britain and France. Eban had not been involved in the Sèvres meetings, which were kept quiet even within the higher echelons of the Government of Israel.[60] The day before Israel's invasion into Sinai, Eban had cabled Ben Gurion to complain that Ben Gurion was not telling him what was afoot.[61]

France backed up Eban's justification of Israel's invasion. "Incidents have occurred," Cornut-Gentille said, "to remind the Government and citizens of Israel that they were surrounded by watchful enemies. The Egyptian High Command long ago organized special commando units of *fedayeen* trained to attack property, communications and people in Israel territory."[62]

In a broad brush attack on Egypt, Cornut-Gentille characterized Egypt's aims as "the annihilation of the State of Israel, the expansion of Egyptian imperialism from the Atlantic to the Persian Gulf, open intervention in French internal affairs, direct material assistance to rebellious citizens, and the seizure, in defiance of all treaties and rules of international law, of a water-way which is essential to the life of the nations." From this analysis, France found justification for Israel's invasion of Egypt. "It was inevitable in these circumstances that Israel, faced with a policy so diametrically opposed to the Charter, should at some given moment feel compelled to react."[63]

The British-French aim, said Cornut-Gentille, was only to stop the fighting. "The French and United Kingdom Governments," he continued, "have asked the Governments of Egypt and Israel to withdraw their respective military forces from the Suez Canal zone. In order to ensure that the cease fire is effective, the French and United Kingdom Governments have also asked that they should be allowed to move temporarily into key positions in the Canal zone."[64]

Eban's argument, as supported by France, fell on deaf ears. Security Council delegates said they considered Israel's action to be aggression.

The Soviet Union and United States stood together in denouncing Britain, France, and Israel. This was a far cry from 1948, when the two superpowers had jointly insisted on Israel's admission to the United Nations as a peace-loving state. Now they were together again, but this time speaking against Israel.

The US draft resolution was put to a vote. It gained seven votes in favor, enough for passage, but France and Britain both voted against it. Those two negative votes constituted vetoes. So the draft resolution failed.[65] The next day the discussion continued, with a view to a resolution that might pass. Sobolev by now was accusing Britain, France, and Israel of acting together. "Israel's invasion of Egypt," he said, "was planned to provide a pretext for joint action by the United Kingdom and France to seize the Suez Canal by force of arms."[66] Sobolev did not explain whether the Soviet Union had new information, or whether it had surmised from the unfolding sequence of events that the three states must have been coordinating their actions. Again a resolution calling for a ceasefire was proposed and failed, again because of vetoes cast by France and Britain.[67]

16

Suez Smoke-Screen

Beginning October 31 and continuing the next several days, France and Britain initiated military action against Egypt. They engaged Egyptian fighter aircraft. Paratroopers descended on Egyptian soil. Cairo was bombed.[1] British-French action following so quickly upon Israel's invasion fed suspicion of collusion among the three states. The Soviet Union said that the whole operation was concocted. "Israel's aggression, like the aggression of the United Kingdom and France against Egypt," delegate Arkady Sobolev said, "is being carried out in accordance with a single, previously prepared plan." Sobolev said "that Israel's aggression was planned in order to create conditions favourable for the seizure of the Suez Canal by the armed forces of the United Kingdom and France."[2]

France and Britain held to their script. Dixon said that "the Egyptian Government regrettably has rejected the communication from Her Majesty's Government and from the French Government dated 30 October, and as a consequence Her Majesty's Government and the French Government have intervened in accordance with that communication."[3] Britain described the objectives of the French–British intervention as being "to stop all warlike action on land, sea and air as soon as possible; secondly, to enforce a separation of the belligerents; and thirdly, to protect the Suez Canal for the free passage of ships of all nations."[4]

France, too, continued to play its role, declaring, "We were confronted with an attack by the forces of Israel in the Suez zone heading towards the Canal. We had every reason to believe that the military developments arising out of this action might reach the point where free passage through the Canal would be impeded. The latest news received from Egypt, which reports the position of the Israel troops, shows how well our fears were justified."[5]

The Security Council, unable to adopt a resolution because of the French and British vetoes, voted to convene an emergency special session of the General Assembly. Britain and France voted against convening the Assembly, but on procedure the veto does not apply.[6]

MORE FICTION IN THE GENERAL ASSEMBLY

The General Assembly took up the crisis. It met the next day, November 1. Israeli forces were still in Sinai, and the British-French force was now on the ground near the Suez Canal. For the United States, eager to stop the military action, the advantage of operating in the General Assembly was that each member state has an equal vote. No state holds a veto. The disadvantage was that the General Assembly has only the power of recommendation. It cannot order sanctions that member states would have to observe.

As the emergency special session opened, Egypt repeated its charge of aggression by Israel. "During the night of 29 October 1956, Israel committed the most serious act of unprovoked armed aggression that has taken place since the conclusion of the armistice agreements. This time, it was not a reprisal raid. It was a premeditated, carefully prepared armed attack for the purpose of occupying part of Egyptian territory and provoking war in that area."[7] And Egypt charged that Israel had coordinated its attack with France and Britain. Egypt was "the victim of combined premeditated aggression by Israel, the United Kingdom and France. It is now clear that the aggressors conspired together to commit this act of war."[8]

Britain, as in the Security Council, stuck to the Sèvres script. It invoked Britain's history of involvement in the Middle East to add credibility to its false account. "I do not believe that it has been fully realized by those who may not be as intimately concerned with Middle Eastern affairs as we are," Dixon said, "how explosive the situation in the Middle East was a few days ago, when the United Kingdom and French Governments took the drastic steps which they felt obliged to take. From all the information at our disposal, we had reason to judge that a major clash, whose consequences would have been incalculable, between Israel and its Arab neighbours was more imminent than at any time since the signing of the armistice agreements in 1949. The sudden Israel mobilization and incursion into Egypt made it imperative to take very speedy and effective measures to prevent a war between Israel and Egypt which could only lead to a general conflagration throughout the Middle East and which would, in its train, have involved prolonged disruption of free passage through the Suez Canal, the canal which is of such vital interest to so many nations."[9] All this was fiction.

Britain reacted to the Soviet-Egyptian charge that it was colluding with Israel. "It is absurd to suggest – as it has, I regret, been suggested – that our intervention was part of a long prepared plot concerted with Israel. Such allegations are not only absurd, they are false. It is common knowledge, I think, that, over the past few months, our relations with Israel have been difficult and strained, precisely because of our efforts to restrain Israel from retaliation against its Arab neighbours."[10] This was a clever point for Britain to make, because it was true, as we saw in the Qibya incident, that Britain had been critical of Israel's reprisal raids. Britain and Israel had been at odds from the time of the White Paper in 1939. So collusion with Israel to invade an Arab country did seem out of character for Britain.

The United States sent its Secretary of State to the emergency special session. John Foster Dulles proposed a resolution urging the parties to agree to a ceasefire and a withdrawal of all military forces.[11] In describing the factual situation, Dulles stopped short of accepting the Egyptian and Soviet analysis of collusion. Outlining the factual situation as the United States understood it, Dulles said that there had been "a deep penetration of Egypt by Israel forces. Then, quickly following upon that action, there came action by France and the United Kingdom in subjecting Egypt first to a twelve-hour ultimatum, and then to an armed attack, which is now going on from the air with the declared purpose of gaining temporary control of the Suez Canal, presumably to make it more secure."[12]

The Soviet Union repeated the charge of collusion. "Israel aggression was planned," Sobolev said, "with the purpose of creating a pretext for the seizure of the Suez Canal by British and French armed forces."[13] Eban defended Israel with the same argument he made in the Security Council. "On Monday, 29 October 1956, the Israel defence forces took security measures in the Sinai peninsula in the exercise of Israel's inherent right of self-defense. The object of these operations is to eliminate the bases from which armed Egyptian units under the special care and authority of Mr. Nasser invade Israel's territory for purposes of murder, sabotage and the creation of permanent insecurity to peaceful life. These are the only military activities for which the Government of Israel is responsible."[14]

Eban was choosing his words carefully. The last sentence was peculiar. States are responsible internationally not only for what they themselves do. They can also be responsible for aiding and abetting another state to act unlawfully. The sentence makes sense only as a response to the charge of collusion with Britain and France. By saying that Israel's incursion constituted "the only military activities for which the Government of Israel is responsible," Eban was indirectly saying that Israel had nothing to do with the attack by Britain and France.

In his justification of Israel, Eban was at his most eloquent. "Surrounded by hostile armies on all its land frontiers," he intoned, "subjected to savage and relentless hostility, exposed to penetrations, raids and assaults by day and by night, suffering constant toll of life amongst its citizenry, bombarded by threats of neighbouring Governments to accomplish its extinction by armed force, overshadowed by a new menace of irresponsible rearmament, embattled, blockaded, besieged, Israel alone amongst the nations faces a battle for its security anew with every rising dawn and with every approaching nightfall. In a country of small area and intricate configuration, the proximity of enemy guns is a constant and haunting theme."[15] Eban was so proud of this speech that he inserted it verbatim into his memoir, commenting that newspaper reports had called this passage his "punchline."[16]

Some UN member states were taken in by Eban's denial of complicity. Ecuador was one of them. "We have before us two cases of aggression, of a very clear aggression, which does not need to be defined in order to be immediately understood and judged morally: first, that of Israel against Egypt, and secondly, that of the United Kingdom and France against Egypt." But then Ecuador posed the question about a link between the two actions. "Are the two related? Was one the historical antecedent of the other?" Ecuador answered in the negative. It said it "does not believe that Israel has lent itself to a manoeuvre of this kind, not even on the pretext of defending its vital interests." Ecuador found "inconceivable the idea that they can have lent themselves to such trickery."

Ecuador did not accept the British–French plea that they were acting as peacemakers. But it did not see their invasion as part and parcel of Israel's. Britain and France had simply seen an opportunity. "The second act of aggression, that of the United Kingdom and France against Egypt, followed upon the invasion of Egypt by the Israel armed forces; was it deliberately linked to the Israel invasion?" Answering its own question, Ecuador said that "the United Kingdom and France merely took advantage of the political, economic and social circumstances to carry out a plan which had been maturing for many months."[17]

Britain, France, and Israel kept denying coordination. Yugoslavia thought that the circumstances bespoke coordination. "Can there be any doubt," it said, "that what is now unfolding before our very eyes is a single pattern of aggression? The planning, the timing and the only too apparent ulterior motives are surely conclusive in this regard."[18]

France defended, saying, "The Franco-British intervention in the Suez Canal zone is designed, in the first place, to call an immediate halt to hostilities between Egyptian and Israel armed forces by setting a screen, as it were, between the belligerent forces, and, in the second place, to protect the Suez Canal and establish lasting peace in the Middle East."[19] Romania did not accept that explanation. It said "that, in order to achieve their designs, the two Western Governments found a docile and willing cat's-paw in the Israel Government, which furnished a pretext for their joint intervention."[20]

Still conferring after midnight, the General Assembly passed the resolution drafted by the United States that called for cessation of hostilities and withdrawal of forces.[21] The General Assembly did not address by resolution the issue of aggression. It made no finding on the question of collaboration.

A FRENCH CONFESSION

Even though the France-Britain-Israel front in the Security Council and General Assembly seemed solid, France was cracking. On October 30, Allen Dulles, Director of the Central Intelligence Agency (and brother of the Secretary of State), visited France's ambassador in Washington and told him that he suspected that it was all coordinated.[22] The United States had been following the military situation closely and did suspect that the three states were acting in concert.[23] It may well have known the truth.[24]

In any event, on November 1, C. Douglas Dillon, the US ambassador in France, sent the Department of State a message relaying a conversation with Christian Pineau, France's foreign minister. Pineau had disclosed to Dillon that the three states were working together. Pineau told Dillon that the invasions had been planned jointly by France, Israel, and Britain.[25] So France was reneging on the vow of silence about the collaboration. The apparent reason was the pressure the United States was exerting at the United Nations. US delegate Henry Cabot Lodge reported from UN headquarters in New York that the French and British delegates at one point were "next door in a very emotional condition."[26] Pineau explained to Dillon that the decision to invade had been made at a meeting in Paris, an apparent reference to the Sèvres encounters, and that the three agreed not to inform the United States.

Asked about the aim of France and Britain, Pineau said it was to occupy the Canal zone. As for the aim of Israel, Pineau said that it was to destroy or capture all Egyptian forces east of Suez. Pineau was at pains to stress that the action would be short-lived, thus creating the impression that the reason he was being frank with Dillon was that France was concerned about the vehemence of US efforts against France in the Security Council and General Assembly. Pineau apparently hoped that if the United States understood that the military action would soon end, it might back off.[27]

Pineau's "confession" was communicated to President Eisenhower, as evidenced by a remarkable letter Eisenhower wrote at the time to a high school friend. Eisenhower told his friend that the three states had not done their planning well. He thought that "the Israeli mobilized pretty rapidly and apparently got ready to attack before the others were immediately ready to follow up, using the Israeli attack as an excuse to 'protect' the Canal." Eisenhower wrote that he had gotten information prior to the events that Israel was planning to attack Egypt, and that he had "demanded pledges from Ben-Gurion that he would keep the peace." Eisenhower thought that Ben Gurion was counting on the fact that Eisenhower was facing reelection, with the election set for early November, and that Eisenhower would not want to antagonize Jewish voters by criticizing Israel. "We realized that he [Ben Gurion] might think he could take advantage of this country because of the approaching election and because of the importance that so many politicians in the past have attached to our Jewish vote." "I gave strict orders to the State Department," Eisenhower wrote in the letter, "that they should inform Israel that we would handle our affairs exactly as though we didn't have a Jew in America."[28]

Just as Dillon's message about Pineau's revelation was arriving at the Department of State, Secretary of State Dulles was closeted with Eban. Dulles had called Eban in to let him know that the United States was considering cutting aid to Israel in light of its invasion of Egypt. Dulles wanted to know if Eban had anything to say, in particular as to Israel's intentions in Sinai.[29] Eban had just received word of the successes of the IDF in Sinai. "Our forces had come within ten miles of the Suez Canal; most of Sinai and the Gaza Strip were in our hands," Eban would record in his memoir.[30] So Eban, as he records, "decided to go on the offensive."[31] Instead of defending Israel as Eban normally did for reprisal raids, he highlighted for Dulles how well the IDF was doing militarily. Nasser's government was collapsing, Eban predicted. The change about to occur in Middle East politics as result of that impending collapse was "equivalent to the defeat of Soviet

Communism in East Europe." Eban invited Dulles to get the United States on board, rather than ask Israel to withdraw from Sinai.

Not knowing that Pineau had just acknowledged collusion, Eban maintained the pretense that Israel acted alone in invading Sinai. Israel, he said, had responded to the threat that Egypt posed. He said that Israel might withdraw if the threat from Egypt, including from *fedayeen* raids, were eliminated, but that Israel would need to confer with Britain and France. Eban explained that Israel had become "linked" with Britain and France because of their own military action, giving the impression that the "linking" occurred only after Israel invaded.[32]

At the General Assembly's emergency special session, Eban spoke at length about Israel's tortured relationship with Egypt, and about incursions from the Gaza Strip into Israel. Syria, reacting to Eban, called his recitation "a monologue replete with lies and distortion of facts such as has been inflicted on our ears for many years by the representative of Israel."[33] Yemen said, "Everyone has now realized that aggression against Egypt was planned and synchronized by Israel, the United Kingdom and France."[34]

Delegates from outside the Arab world were still unsure what to believe. Some accepted Eban's denial of collusion. Others did not. The United States kept Pineau's confession to itself, never letting on in the General Assembly that it knew. Bolivia perceived pre-planning. "There is only one fitting description of this stupendous *grand guignol* performance of colonial diplomacy: deceit and retrogression," it said, with this reference to a theatrical genre featuring horror themes. "Why deceit?", Bolivia continued. "Because an attempt was made to convince us that Paris and London had no knowledge whatsoever of Israel's invasion of Egyptian territory, and this in spite of the fact that the land, sea and air expedition with which France and the United Kingdom expect to seize the Suez Canal again had been prepared weeks ago."[35] Czechoslovakia denounced Britain and France for using Israel as "their tool."[36]

Leaving the coordination issue unresolved, the General Assembly turned its attention to devising a mechanism to protect against future strikes between Egypt and Israel. It set up a military force to be stationed on the armistice line, to forestall military incursions in either direction.[37] It was to be called the United Nations Emergency Force (UNEF), and it would replace the Mixed Armistice Commission. Israel was not willing to have the Force stationed on its side of the armistice line.[38] Egypt was willing, and that was where it was placed. It would be headed by General Burns. The military action ended within a few days.

Even with Pineau's confession, Secretary Dulles asked an intelligence officer of the US Department of State, once the major military action ended, to analyze what had occurred and to report to him on "collusion" on the part of France, Israel, and Britain in their attacks on Egypt and on "deception" directed against the United States. The report came back to Secretary Dulles concluding "that collusion and deception did exist," and that the deception was directed against both Egypt and the United States.[39]

A SUBSTANTIAL PAYOFF

The 1956 troop insertion into Egypt was one of the most devious international invasions of modern times. It is not uncommon that a state committing aggression invents a story that, if true, would justify its action. But it is far from common that not one, not two, but three states combine to invent a story. The Suez war yielded little gain for France or Britain. They did not remove Nasser from power. They did not reverse Egypt's nationalization of the Suez Canal. Israel, however, came out well. Abba Eban wrote on November 7, 1956, that Israel had achieved "enormous benefits."[40] Ben Gurion would list two objectives as "the aims for which the campaign had been fought." They were "neutralization of the fedayun bases in the Gaza Strip and Sinai" and "freedom of passage through the Gulf of Aqaba." Ben Gurion said that only when these aims were achieved did he "give the order for our forces to withdraw."[41] Ben Gurion in fact had hoped for more. He wanted to wrest from Egypt the Sinai territory on the western side of the Gulf of Aqaba. He also had his eyes on oil reserves in the Sinai and hoped to keep Sinai to get access to them.[42] Furthermore, Ben Gurion hoped to keep the Gaza Strip for Israel. Golda Meir, who at the time was Foreign Minister, made a formal claim of sovereignty over the Gaza Strip, calling it an "integral part" of Israel. Meir said that Israel would not return to the 1949 Israel-Egypt armistice line that left the Gaza Strip on Egypt's side.[43]

Here President Eisenhower stepped in. Eisenhower said it would damage Israeli–US relations if Israel were to keep these territories.[44] Ben Gurion tried an alternative route to keep from returning the Gaza Strip to Egyptian control. He proposed to UN Secretary-General Hammarskjold that Israel take over the administration of the Gaza Strip from Egypt. This would not have involved sovereignty for Israel over the Gaza Strip. But Hammarskjold refused to promote the idea, and it was dropped.[45] The General Assembly called on Israel to withdraw immediately from Sinai and Gaza.[46] Israel stalled. The General Assembly adopted more resolutions calling on Israel to withdraw.[47] The United States threatened to cut off economic aid to Israel, and finally it withdrew from the Sinai Peninsula and the Gaza Strip in March 1957.[48]

"When we were finally forced to leave," Ariel Sharon recalled in his memoir, "I took it very hard. Most of all I could not understand why we withdrew from Gaza."[49] But the IDF had destroyed *fedayeen* bases in Gaza and Sinai. Shimon Peres identified one Israeli objective in the war as being "to destroy or capture" the weaponry that Egypt had gotten from the Soviet Union in the arms buildup that began in 1955. In Peres' view, Israel succeeded, collecting "vast quantities" of weapons as the IDF swept through Sinai.[50] Dayan gives a long list that includes 4300 rifles, 1170 sub-machine guns, 52 Sherman tanks, millions of rounds of ammunition, and one naval destroyer.[51] The IDF had routed the army of the strongest Arab state.[52] No other Arab state had come to Egypt's aid, despite Egypt's request.[53] As for passage through the Gulf of Aqaba to the Israeli port of Eilat, even though Israel withdrew from Sinai territory commanding the entrance to the Gulf, the introduction there of the UN Emergency Force ensured passage.[54] Moshe Dayan could exult that the Sinai campaign brought Israel freedom of navigation and "cessation of terrorism."[55] The deception had paid off. The 1949 armistice agreements had given Israel a UN monitoring force to keep the Palestine Arabs out. Now Israel got a full-blown military force on the armistice line with Egypt. For the following years, Israel experienced no raids from the Gaza Strip.

WHITHER ISRAEL AND THE UNITED NATIONS?

Israel's payoff came at some cost to its relationship with the United Nations. Israel's credibility was already fragile after its failure to keep the commitments it made when it was admitted to the Organization. As we saw, it lied about reprisal raids in the early 1950s, further damaging its credibility. Now it carried out a major invasion of a neighboring country and concealed the circumstances.

The United Nations' response, however, to Israel and its collaborators left Israel's leaders of a mind that the United Nations was not a forum that would do any good for Israel. The Security Council had been pressuring Israel through the early 1950s about armistice line raids into Jordan and Egypt. The United Nations was interfering with Israel in operations it regarded as necessary for defense. Now it had pressured Israel to withdraw from one of the territories that made Israel's life as a nation difficult.

A difference among Israel's leaders could now be discerned in how to deal with the United Nations. Moshe Sharett and Abba Eban were cast in the role of justifying to the outside world what Israel did. They were sensitive to the international dimensions of actions Israel might take. David Ben Gurion, Golda Meir, Moshe Dayan, and Shimon Peres were inclined to advocate whatever action they thought Israel should take without giving consideration to the possible international reaction.[56] This dynamic was especially visible between Ben Gurion and Sharett during Israel's early years. Sharett described himself as being concerned about the external consequences of actions the Government might take, whereas he described Ben Gurion as indifferent. Sharett and Eban were often in the position of putting the best face on an action taken without careful consideration of the fallout, or how it could be rationalized. Not infrequently, the approach they found open to them involved distorting the facts or making commitments that Israel was not likely to honor.

The government of Israel publicized Eban's UN speeches, viewing them as vehicles to promote Israel's image. Israel's Office of Information in New York distributed copies to the press and to the public.[57] Eban even included some of his UN speeches in a collection of addresses that he published as a book in 1957. Eban titled the collection *Voice of Israel*.[58]

ROSENNE'S DANGEROUS THEORY

Outside the United Nations, Israel's denial of collaboration with France and Britain was carried effectively by Shabtai Rosenne, the Legal Adviser of the Foreign Ministry. Writing five years after the events, in 1961, Rosenne explained Israel's invasion into Gaza and Sinai as Eban had done in the Security Council and General Assembly, as an action by Israel entirely on its own.

Rosenne was doubtless in the loop in the run-up to Israel's incursion into Egypt. But Rosenne did not disclose coordination with Britain and France. He referred to these two powers only in passing, in an almost casual remark that France and Britain "for reasons of their own, and in connection with the Suez Canal, had also undertaken military operations against Egypt."[59]

Rosenne found justification for the invasion along the same lines as Eban, saying that it had been "provoked by an activist Egyptian policy of sending bands of armed and trained *Fedayeen* into Israel. Israel was compelled to take up arms in self-defence.... The strengthening under Egyptian leadership of direct military ties between the Arab States, and particularly between Egypt and Syria (prior to the establishment, in 1958, of the United Arab Republic), presented a direct and urgent military threat to Israel's national security which was sought to be forestalled by full-scale military operations undertaken in October of 1956 in the Sinai Peninsula."[60]

In putting forward this analysis, Rosenne was projecting an extended form of self-defense. The increase in Egypt's armaments Rosenne took as creating an "urgent" threat, justifying immediate military action by Israel. A doctrine that allows for defensive action when anticipated aggression is still some distance off lends itself to pretextual use. If military force can be used when the target state has done nothing but may do something in future, the path is open to inventing scenarios to justify military force. President Eisenhower, perceptively, identified an extended concept of defense in Israel's invasion of Suez. In his November 2 letter to his friend, Eisenhower addressed the evident aim of Britain, France, and Israel to remove Nasser as leader of the Egyptian Government. "Britain, France and Israel had come to believe – probably correctly – that Nasser was their worst enemy in the Mid East and that until he was removed or deflated, they would have no peace. I do not quarrel with the idea that there is justification for such fears, but I have insisted long and earnestly that you cannot resort to force in international relationships because of your fear of what might happen in the future."[61]

A POTENT LEGAL WEAPON

Shabtai Rosenne was the ideal complement to Eban as Israel sought to deceive the international community about the Suez invasion. Eban covered the diplomatic front, while Rosenne made legal arguments to back him up. As Legal Adviser to the Minister of Foreign Affairs, Rosenne was the leading lawyer for Israel on international matters in early years of its existence. Rosenne plotted strategy with Israel's UN delegation as it maneuvered to gain acceptance for Israeli statehood.[62]

Like Eban, Rosenne enjoyed credibility with Western governments and audiences. Rosenne's biography mirrored Eban's. Rosenne was reared in England by parents who had moved there from tsarist Russia. His name at birth was Sefton Wilfred David Rowson. He served in the Royal Air Force in World War II and completed a law degree in London in 1944. He worked as a lawyer for the Jewish Agency, first in London, and from 1947 in Palestine. Like Eban, he hebraicized his name, altering his surname "Rowson" to "Rosenne" and adopting as a given name "Shabtai," common as a Hebrew given name, thought to derive from Shabbat (Sabbath).

As a lawyer for the Jewish Agency, Rosenne was at the center of activity when the National Council declared statehood in 1948. When a foreign ministry was set up for Israel, Rosenne became Legal Adviser. In that capacity he was part of Israel's delegation in Rhodes in 1949 when the armistice agreements were concluded with the Arab states. Rosenne held the Legal Adviser position until 1967. Rosenne then moved into diplomatic work as Israel's deputy permanent representative at the United Nations, serving until 1971. Rosenne was a central figure in framing Israel's policy positions in the international arena. He formed part of what one historian of Israel's Foreign Ministry called a "brain trust" working under Moshe Sharett in Israel's formative years.[63]

Rosenne's utility as a legal advisor and diplomat went far beyond that of the legal advisors and diplomats one finds in most countries. Prolific as a scholar in international law, Rosenne became the leading authority on the court that was set up under the United Nations, the International Court of Justice. Rosenne conducted meticulous research on the Court and in 1965 published a book on it. Titled *The Law and Practice of the International Court*, it became a standard reference work for lawyers arguing cases in the International Court of Justice.[64] Rosenne became prominent representing states around the world in their international disputes. At Rosenne's death in 2010, an obituary writer could say with justification that Rosenne was "arguably the foremost international lawyer of the second half of the 20th century."[65]

Much of the argumentation necessary to put Israel on the map and keep it there revolved around treaties and the international rules on war. Rosenne was a master at these topics. He knew not only the rules, but the background of the rules as they were developed in Europe. Rosenne occupied a space comparable to Eban's in the sense that when he spoke, anyone with a contrary view would think twice before objecting. Rosenne's prominence made him effective in securing acceptance for Israel's version of events in the world legal community, whether that Arabs had not been expelled in 1948, or that Israel had not collaborated in 1956 with Britain and France.

Rosenne's attempt to cover for Israel's 1956 action would eventually be unmasked, but only after some years. In 1959, Christian Pineau, the French foreign minister, was asked about the coordination with Britain and Israel by reporters who had gotten wind of it. Pineau did not acknowledge it.[66] In a 1964 book, British political scientist Herman Finer wrote about the coordination in convincing detail.[67] The first official directly involved to give a public revelation was Anthony Nutting, a British Foreign Officer who was involved in the talks at Sèvres. Nutting, who thought the project was ill conceived, resigned his post over it. In 1967, Nutting wrote a book in which he detailed the tripartite coordination.[68] In a 1970 interview about the Suez war, Abba Eban said that "we should have avoided the Franco-British collusion," thereby acknowledging what he had concealed from the General Assembly.[69] In a book he wrote in 1965 on the Suez war, *Diary of the Sinai Campaign*, Moshe Dayan did not mention the coordination, even though he himself had been at the center of the negotiations.[70] But in his 1976 memoir he gave a full account of the agreement reached at Sèvres.[71]

Israel's 1956 deception had not become general knowledge by the time of its next major confrontation with the Arab world. And in that confrontation, Rosenne's concept of extended self-defense would prove useful to cover for what Israel was to do.

17

Mr. Nasser, Please Attack

The United Nations Emergency Force set up by the United Nations in 1957 remained in place on the Egyptian side of the Egypt-Israel armistice line for a decade. Then in May 1967, the situation in the region changed. Israel and Syria nearly came to blows over guerrilla raids from Syria and Israeli intrusions into a demilitarized zone that had been set up in the 1949 Syria-Israel armistice agreement.[1] Israel charged Syria with provoking violence and filed a complaint with the United Nations in which it said it would retaliate in force if the violence continued.[2] Syria in turn filed a complaint of its own at the United Nations about this threat.[3] Egypt drew troops up to armistice line with Israel. Egypt asked the United Nations to remove the Emergency Force. U Thant, who became UN Secretary-General in 1961, ordered the Force to begin withdrawal. Egypt imposed restrictions on shipping entering the Gulf of Aqaba en route to the Israeli port of Eilat. Israel complained of these moves. It said that the shipping restrictions were illegal and that the troop movement, plus the request for removal of the Emergency Force, bespoke an Egyptian intent to invade Israel.

COAXING EGYPT TO INVADE

In late May 1967, as these events unfolded, the Government of Israel tentatively decided to attack the Egyptian troops and to invade Egypt. Egypt's forces were not well supplied, stationed far from central Egypt. Egypt had brought these troops up near the armistice line as a show of force, but they were ill prepared for battle. The IDF made a calculation, one that would turn out to be correct, that the Egyptian troops could not withstand an assault by the IDF. Crushing this huge contingent of Egyptian troops would diminish Egypt's warmaking capability for some time.

By now Abba Eban was Foreign Minister in a government led by Levi Eshkol as prime minister. Eshkol asked Eban to go to Washington to convince the United States that Egypt was about to invade Israel. The Government of Israel did not know how the United States might react if it invaded Egypt. Eban initiated the contact, in an effort to get the US imprimatur on an Israeli attack on Egypt. It worried that it might encounter the same reaction as it got from President Eisenhower when it carried out roughly the same invasion in 1956. The Government reasoned that if the United States could be convinced that Egypt was going to invade Israel, it might find a preemptive invasion by Israel to be warranted.

In Washington, Eban asked the United States to declare that an attack by Egypt on Israel would be tantamount to an attack on the United States. President Lyndon Johnson refused to make such a statement. With that possibility off the table, Eban used all his persuasive powers to convince the United States at least to indicate, off the record, that it would support Israel if it invaded Egypt. By so saying, Eban was letting the United States know that Israel planned to initiate hostilities. In a May 25 meeting, Eban came up empty.[4]

The United States was following the situation on the ground closely through its own sources. The Central Intelligence Agency was reporting to President Johnson almost daily. It told Johnson that Eban's claim that Egypt was about to attack had no basis. Johnson told Eban in no uncertain terms not to invade Egypt. The CIA acknowledged that "Nasser shows increasing willingness to pursue a policy of high risk in challenging Israeli interests, such as free access to the port of Elath [Eilat]." But the CIA did not believe that Nasser would take on the IDF. "Nasser still probably estimates that he does not have – even with the support of the other Arabs – the capability to destroy Israel by a military attack." Nasser's purpose in the moves he was making, the report said, was "to put pressure on Israel short of attack on Israeli soil."[5] The CIA saw Egypt acting to deter Israel from attacking Syria.[6] Egypt's forces, moreover, were said by the CIA to be arrayed for defense, not for attack.[7] The IDF, for its part, was not digging in on its side of the line as if it were expecting to have to defend against an invasion from Egypt.[8]

With Eban's mission to Washington a failure, the Government of Israel, decided on a different tack. It agreed to postpone invading Egypt, but it sent to Washington the head of the Mossad, Israel's intelligence agency, to put the matter differently. Meir Amit did not try to convince Washington of an imminent Egyptian attack on Israel. In contradiction of what Eban had been telling official Washington, Amit conceded that Egypt was not about to attack Israel. In a meeting with US Secretary of Defense Robert McNamara, Amit is recorded as "inform[ing] the Secretary that there were no differences between the U.S. and the Israelis on the military intelligence picture or its interpretation."[9] Amit knew full well that the US assessment was that Egypt would not attack.

Amit simply informed US officials that Israel was going to invade and asked what the United States would do.[10] Would it respond as Eisenhower had in 1956? Would it try to stop Israel in the UN Security Council? Would it tell the world that Israel started the fighting? Amit was able to satisfy himself that the United States would hold its tongue. It would not make public its estimation that Egypt was not going to invade Israel. It would not disclose the fact that it had been trying to keep Israel from attacking Egypt. It would not condemn Israel before the world. It would not seek UN Security Council action against Israel.

As of 1967, Yitzhak Rabin had risen to the post of Chief of Staff of the IDF. Rabin was asked by Prime Minister Eshkol whether Egypt, having drawn troops up to the Israeli border, was going to invade. Rabin was concerned about the possibility that Egypt might launch an air attack, and he did advocate attacking Egypt, but at the same time he, like the Americans, said that Egypt's ground troops were set up for defense, not for attack.[11] Rabin's assessment about Egyptian intentions was identical to Washington's.

An episode that was playing out in East Africa suggests that the assessment that Egypt would not attack was the prevailing view among Israel's leaders. A scheme was afoot to draw Egypt into war. At the Government's instruction, the Israeli Zim shipping line had purchased a Greek cargo ship and sailed it to the Red Sea port of Massawa in east Africa. On May 25, a crew of sixty Israeli seamen was flown to Nairobi, Kenya.[12] From Nairobi, the seamen were flown to Massawa. There they became the new crew of the Greek ship. They painted a new name, the *Dolphin*, on its side. The crew was instructed to prepare the *Dolphin* to sail across the Red Sea into the Straits of Tiran, which commands the entrance into the Gulf of Aqaba, where they should be prepared to take fire from Egyptian shore batteries.[13] The IDF would take the Egyptian firing as the occasion to launch an invasion into Sinai. The firing by the shore batteries would let the IDF say that Egypt struck first.

The government went so far as to run the *Dolphin* plan past the US government, in the hope of getting its blessing. President Johnson had been telling Israel not to fire the first shot. Would it satisfy President Johnson if

Israel could manage to get Egypt to fire first? Raising this scheme with the United States carried some risk, because it gave the United States proof that Israel did not expect Egypt to attack on its own. On June 2, Ephraim Evron, Israel's ambassador in Washington, met with Walter Rostow, who was Special Assistant to President Lyndon Johnson. Knowing that President Johnson did not want Israel to initiate hostilities, Evron asked Rostow if an Egyptian firing on the *Dolphin* followed by an Israeli invasion would be acceptable to Washington as a way of starting a war against Egypt. Rostow said he would ask President Johnson. If the *Dolphin* pretext were to succeed, it obviously had to be kept quiet. Evron worried about a leak of information. He asked Rostow to keep the *Dolphin* plan "within our [US] government in the narrowest possible circle."[14]

Before Evron got a response, however, the government decided, on June 3, to scrap its *Dolphin* plan. The concern was that if the *Dolphin* drew fire, Egypt would know that an Israeli attack was coming and could prepare accordingly.[15] Moshe Dayan feared that Egypt might not limit itself to firing on the *Dolphin*, but might start a wider war. That would deprive Israel of the advantage of striking first.[16] Or Egypt might understand that it was being tricked when the *Dolphin* approached and refuse to take the bait.

A second ruse was considered around June 1 by Chief of Staff Rabin and other top generals. A mock shelling of an Israel settlement town was to be arranged that would then have been attributed to Egypt, making it appear that Egypt had attacked Israel. This scheme too was abandoned.[17]

On June 4, the Israeli Cabinet met. The plans to coax Egypt into firing now off the table, the Cabinet simply authorized the IDF to attack.[18] H-hour was set by Dayan for 7:45 A.M. the next day.[19] The IDF plan was for an initial aerial attack on Egypt's airfields followed almost immediately by a tank assault into Sinai.[20]

The Cabinet had no plan for how to portray this invasion to the world. That too was left to for the Prime Minister and the IDF to determine, and it had to be determined quickly. There were no ideal options. The Government could not say that it was invading Egypt because it saw a chance to destroy Egypt's army. The Government had been saying that Egypt's restrictions on Israeli shipping through the Straits of Tiran constituted an act of war on Egypt's part. However, the waters of the Straits of Tiran are quite narrow, and within Egypt's territorial sea. A full-scale invasion of Egypt over the shipping restrictions would seem disproportionate. Another possibility was to say that Egypt was about to invade Israel, hence Israel attacked first. But that story might not be believed. And even if Egypt were planning to attack, there was scant historical precedent for invoking an anticipated attack as justification for starting a war.

The only solid basis for attacking Egypt would be as a response to an actual attack by Egypt. So it was decided to put out a story that Egypt had attacked first.[21] The United States would know that the story was false, but it was expected not to tell.[22] Little time remained to come up with a credible story that would make it appear that Egypt struck first. One Cabinet member, Housing Minister Mordecai Bentov, said they needed what he called an "alibi."[23] Dayan imposed military censorship over information about what was to happen and ordered that whatever was issued "for the first twenty-four hours" must show Israel as, in his words, "the victim."[24]

On the morning of June 5, at 7:45 A.M., precisely on Dayan's schedule, Israel's Air Force launched jet fighters in the direction of Egypt.[25] Entering Egyptian air space, they found most of Egypt's fighter aircraft on the ground at an airfield and destroyed them. A few minutes after 7:45 A.M., IDF ground troops crossed the line into Sinai and engaged the Egyptian troops drawn up there.[26]

EBAN ON THE CASE

At 8:05 A.M., the Government gave its first public information about what was occurring. This information indeed portrayed Israel as the victim. Voice of Israel radio broadcast an announcement from an IDF spokesperson: "Since the early hours of this morning, heavy fighting has been taking place on the southern front between Egyptian armoured and aerial forces which moved against Israel, and our forces which went into action in order to check them."[27] At 8:45 A.M., a second broadcast had it that Egyptian forces began to advance that morning in the direction of the Negev and that IDF forces went out to meet and stop them. This announcement went on to say that Egyptian jet aircraft were detected on radar screens moving toward the Israel coast and towards the Negev, and further, that Israel Air Force aircraft had gone up and intercepted them and that air combat had begun.[28]

By 1967 Abba Eban was Foreign Minister of Israel. As this military confrontation broke out, he was at the center of diplomatic activity. By an account he wrote some years later for his memoir, Eban went to the Prime Minister's office in Tel Aviv around 8:00 A.M. on the morning of June 5. "When I reached the Prime Minister's room, I learned that Egyptian planes advancing toward us had been sighted on the radar screens. In accordance with our decision of the previous day, our own aircraft had gone out to meet the advancing force."[29] Eban's reference to "our decision of the previous day" was to the June 4 decision the Cabinet had taken to attack Egypt. "Shortly afterward," Eban continued, "the Egyptian ground forces in the Gaza Strip had bombarded Israeli settlements. Our armored forces were instructed to make a total response."[30]

Eban asked the American, French, British, and Soviet ambassadors, each separately, to his office in Tel Aviv to inform them what was happening.[31] By the account of Walworth Barbour, the US ambassador, in a confidential telegram to Washington that day, "Eban said that early this morning Israelis observed Egyptian units moving in large numbers toward Israel and in fact [a] considerable force penetrated Israeli territory and clashed with Israeli ground forces. Consequently, GOI [Government of Israel] gave order to attack." Eban also told Barbour that Israel's "attack on Egyptian airfields has been a success." And further, "Eban thinks [the] Egyptian ground movement from Gaza [has] probably stopped."[32]

Via Ambassador Barbour, Prime Minister Eshkol sent an urgent message to President Lyndon Johnson in the United States, explaining Israel's military action as a response to hostile acts by Egypt over the previous weeks, including Egyptian fighter aircraft in the air that morning, and an attack by Egypt that morning on three villages in Israel.[33] In Washington at the White House, Eshkol's message landed on the desk of Walter Rostow. Rostow passed it on to President Johnson, adding a cover note to give his opinion of the message. Rostow explained in the note that Eshkol "builds his case mainly on the general environment, but refers to bombardment of three Israeli towns as the trigger." As a comment on that part of Eshkol's message, Rostow added, "At least that's his story."[34]

At 10:40 A.M., Moshe Dayan as Defense Minister broadcast a message over Voice of Israel radio, saying "Our land forces have gone out to silence the Egyptian artillery which is heavily bombarding our villages opposite the Gaza Strip, and to halt the Egyptian armoured forces which are trying in the first stage to cut off the southern part of the Negev." Dayan continued, "We have no organization for conquest. Our own aim is to frustrate the attempt of the Arab armies to conquer our country, and to sever and crush the ring of blockade and aggression which had been created round us."[35]

To make the claim of an Egyptian attack seem credible, the Government put its own population on emergency footing. Deceiving the world required deceiving Israel's citizenry. The IDF announcement at 8:00 A.M. led the Israeli public to think that Egypt was attacking.[36] Israelis descended on retail stores, buying up basic commodities. They scurried to air raid shelters. The impression was created that Egypt might overrun Israel then and there.[37] At 12:00 noon Levi Eshkol as Prime Minister broadcast a message intended for the public. "Egypt has forced a military campaign upon us." He said, "we shall not attack any state as long as it does not wage war against us. But anyone attacking us will meet with our full power of self-defense."[38]

Prime Minister Eshkol also sent a message to the Soviet Prime Minister, Alexei Kosygin, that was nearly identical to his message to President Johnson. Again Eshkol claimed Egypt fighter aircraft in the air and an Egyptian attack on three Israeli villages. In his message to President Johnson, Eshkol named the three villages as Kissufim, Nahal Oz, and Tsur Maon. In his message to Prime Minister Kosygin, he named them as Kissufim, Nahal Oz, and Ein Hashelosha.[39] So the two messages varied as to the name of a third village. Tsur Maon and Ein Hashelosha are a considerable distance apart from each other, so the discrepancy could not have been confusion over where the shells landed. Eban would write in his memoir that he drafted both messages.[40] Eban did not explain the discrepancy.

These messages to Johnson and Kosygin were at odds with Eban's statement to Barbour. Eban had claimed movement of Egyptian ground troops and a confrontation between them and the IDF. The messages to Johnson and Eshkol mentioned no contact between Israeli and Egyptian ground forces. The messages did add the claim that three villages had been attacked by Egypt. These villages were within the range of Egyptian artillery, and prior to the 1956 war, they had been the object of attack, so a claim of this sort might have been thought to be plausible.[41]

United States intelligence services were following the situation closely. Within hours of Prime Minister Eshkol's message to President Johnson, they concluded that the explanations emanating from the government of Israel were false. "An analysis of presently available information," wrote the CIA that same day, "suggests that Israel fired the first shots today."[42] The conclusion in Washington was that "the Israelis had launched a pre-emptive strike, pure and simple."[43] The CIA could detect no military action by Egypt prior to the massive Israeli air and ground invasion of Egypt.[44]

The other major powers reached the same conclusion. Prime Minister Kosygin sent Prime Minister Eshkol a blistering reply, and the Soviet Government issued a statement naming Israel as the aggressor for having opened the hostilities.[45] In the House of Commons that morning in London, members asked the Government what was happening. George Brown, Britain's Secretary of State for Foreign Affairs, replied that Egypt's position about the start of hostilities "is a case which has not only plausibility, but legality and force."[46] The French Government said nothing at the time, but two weeks later issued a press statement saying that it "condemns the opening of hostilities by Israel."[47] In an interview with Kosygin made public some years later, General Charles de Gaulle called Israel the aggressor. "We told the Arabs as well as the Israelis, in a formal way: whoever attacks first we will consider at fault. Israel attacked first and we thought that it was at fault."[48]

CONFUSION IN THE SECURITY COUNCIL

The real test for maintaining the fiction that Egypt started the war would come in New York at the United Nations. As soon as it launched its invasion of Egypt, Israel sent notice to the President of the UN Security Council. It said that hostilities had been initiated by Egypt. A few minutes later, the Egyptian Government sent a message of its own. Egypt said that the hostilities had been initiated by Israel.[49] Egypt and Israel were each basing a claim of aggression on what happened in the morning hours of June 5.

The Security Council would provide the diplomatic battlefield for international acceptance, just as it had in 1956. The Security Council met within hours. Neither Israel nor Egypt was a Council member, but as the states involved, they were invited to participate. Israel's posture as the meeting began was complicated by a report that Secretary-General U Thant conveyed from General Indar Jit Rikhye, Commander of the UN Emergency Force. The Emergency Force was in process of evacuating its positions, in line with Egypt's request. It was no longer conducting any monitoring. When the IDF went into Sinai in 1956, it will be recalled, the IDF sabotaged the monitoring activity of the Mixed Armistice Commission. Now General Rikhye was reporting that an Israel Air Force fighter jet, on a run to Egypt, had strafed vehicles in a convoy of Emergency Force troops, and that three soldiers from India were killed. General Rikhye indicated that the vehicles, like all Emergency Force vehicles, were painted white, hence should have been observable as belonging to the Emergency Force. General Rikhye reported as well that at 12:45 p.m., IDF artillery opened fire on two camps of India's contingent of the Emergency Force.[50] India happened to be a non-permanent member of the Security Council in 1967. Its delegate called the strafing an "irresponsible and brutal action" on Israel's part.[51]

Gideon Rafael was now Israel's UN representative, having replaced Abba Eban. Rafael spoke immediately after the Indian delegate but did not mention either of the two incidents or provide an explanation. Instead, he addressed the overall hostilities. Rafael claimed aggression by Egypt. "I wish to draw the Council's attention," Rafael began, "to the grave news that fighting has erupted on Israel's frontiers and that the Israel Defense Forces are now repelling the Egyptian Army and Air Force. I have so far received only first reports about the developments. From these it is evident that in the early hours of this morning Egyptian armored columns moved in an offensive thrust against Israel's borders. At the same time Egyptian planes took off from airfields in Sinai and struck out towards Israel. Egyptian artillery in the Gaza Strip shelled the Israel villages of Kissufim, Nahal-Oz and Ein Hashelosha. Netania and Kefar Yavetz have also been bombed. Israel forces engaged the Egyptians in the air and on land, and fighting is still going on." Rafael depicted Israel's military action as a reaction to these moves by Egypt. "The Egyptian forces," he said, "met with the immediate response of the Israel Defense Forces, acting in self-defense. In accordance with Article 51 of the Charter, I bring this development to the immediate attention of the Security Council."[52] Article 51 allows a state to defend itself if attacked.

Egypt's representative, Awad el-Kony, replied. El-Kony flatly denied that Egypt started the fighting. Rafael's statement, he said, was false through and through. "At this moment while I am addressing the Security Council, and for several hours now," el-Kony began, "the Israel Armed Forces and the Israel Air Force have again committed a cowardly and treacherous aggression against my country." El-Kony knew he needed do more than simply deny. He argued from the circumstances that it was obvious that Israel was the initiator. "The dimensions of the Israel attack are so wide that no one can doubt the premeditated nature of this aggression. Israelis are attacking, all of a sudden and simultaneously, the Gaza strip, Sinai, Cairo airports, and Sharm el Sheikh, together with other places. And yet we have just been told that the Israelis did not initiate any action and that they were in fact attacked by us." El-Kony's point was that all of this could not have been done by the IDF on the spur of the moment.

To bolster his case, el-Kony built on past Israeli attacks and past questionable explanations. "These Israel manoeuvres are not new. The happenings of the early hours of the day indicate beyond doubt that the Israelis have, as usual, engineered and planned this aggression of today." El-Kony reminded the delegates about 1956. "We cannot but recall history," he said, "which is in fact repeating itself today. The world has indeed not forgotten the black days of 1956 when Israel, in defiance of all norms of law and decency and in flagrant contravention of the United

Nations Charter, planned and engineered the treacherous aggression of those evil days against my country." El-Kony noted that then too Israel claimed self-defense. "At that time also they said that they were the victims in essence, the same story. But who is not aware of the facts, the real and staggering story?"

El-Kony adduced another circumstance to show that Egypt was not the aggressor. He pointed out that Egypt's vice president "was scheduled to arrive in Washington the day after tomorrow for talks on the subject. This amply proves our peaceful intention and goodwill." Indeed, Egypt had a high level delegation set to meet in Washington to discuss the Israel-Egypt standoff. El-Kony's reasoning was that Egypt was seeking a peaceful way out. El-Kony, like Rafael, relied on the UN Charter and claimed self-defense. "In view of this treacherous aggression, my country has no other choice," he said, "than to defend itself by all means at its disposal, in accordance with Article 51 of the Charter of the United Nations. We will most certainly continue to do so. This aggression should be vigorously condemned by the Security Council."[53]

A FORTUITOUS DELAY

Following el-Kony's statement, the Security Council adjourned for consultations. It met briefly in the evening, but only to set a time to meet the following day.[54] Hans Tabor, who as Denmark's representative was Security Council President that month, set 11:30 A.M.of June 6 as the meeting time.[55] But Rafael lobbied to delay, using the fact that Abba Eban was traveling to New York to state Israel's case.[56] Tabor acquiesced. The Security Council meeting did not start until 6:30 pm on June 6. The delay gave the IDF time to inflict major casualties on the Egyptian forces and to advance well into Sinai before the Security Council had a chance to call for a ceasefire. Rafael, in his memoir, was self-congratulatory for gaining the delay. Between the time of the June 5 morning meeting and the June 6 evening meeting, Rafael explained, "an entirely new situation was created in the Middle East."[57] By 6:30 P.M. on June 6, the IDF had broken through Egypt's defensive lines and was chasing the Egyptian army towards the Suez Canal.

Rafael would explain in his memoir what his marching orders were in the Security Council. Foreign Minister Eban was trying at all costs to delay any ceasefire resolution from being adopted by the Security Council.[58] "From the crisp instructions which I received from home," Rafael recorded, "I understood that they expected me to carry out a diplomatic holding-action. The strategic outcome of the fighting was a race between time and space. Our armoured divisions would cover the space as fast as they could and our diplomatic corps was to provide the time for them to reach their objectives."[59]

As the Security Council's evening session of June 6 began, with Eban at the table, a ceasefire was indeed at the top of the agenda. A resolution calling for an immediate ceasefire was quickly passed on a unanimous vote.[60] As is the Security Council's custom, member states were given a chance to explain their votes. Several bemoaned the fact that it took until evening of the second day of the conflict to call for a ceasefire.

Some said Israel was the aggressor. The Soviet Union read out a statement. "Israel commenced hostilities against the United Arab Republic, thereby committing an aggression. The armed forces of the United Arab Republic are engaged in battle against the Israel troops which have invaded the territory of that State."[61] Bulgaria, Mali, and India, all of which held non-permanent seats on the Security Council that year, followed up, backing the Soviet condemnation of Israel. So four member states out of the fifteen quickly went on record charging Israel with aggression.[62]

India said it would have preferred a resolution that called not only for a ceasefire but for a troop withdrawal. "My delegation, among others, would have preferred a resolution which called upon the Governments concerned for a withdrawal of armed forces to positions held by them prior to the outbreak of hostilities, that is as on 4 June 1967, along with the cease-fire," India explained. "Such a linking of the cease-fire with a withdrawal would be in accordance with the practice which this Council has evolved in the past. This practice is obviously based upon the sound principle that the aggressor should not be permitted by the international community to enjoy the fruits of aggression. This is also a most important tenet of international law and practice indeed, and is the only basis on which lasting peace can be built in the troubled area of the Middle East."[63]

18

Abba Eban's Finest Hour

Abba Eban, freshly arrived in New York, took over from Gideon Rafael to make Israel's case. "I have just come from Jerusalem," Eban announced, thanking the chair for recognizing him to speak, "to tell the Security Council that Israel, by its independent effort and sacrifice, has passed from serious danger to successful resistance." Like Rafael, Eban claimed that Egypt started the war. Eban recounted the events of the previous weeks that reflected the tension between Egypt and Israel. He put the onus on Egypt for those events and said that Israel had tried to calm matters through diplomatic channels. Eban related Egypt's request to the United Nations to remove the UN Emergency Force. He related the restrictions that Egypt had imposed on Israel's shipping through the Straits of Tiran. He related Egypt's drawing of troops up to the armistice line. "These acts taken together – the blockade, the dismissal of the United Nations Emergency Force, and the heavy concentration in Sinai – effectively disrupted the *status quo* which had ensured a relative stability on the Egyptian-Israel frontier for ten years."

Eban thus characterized these three acts of Egypt not as aggression but as a change in the *status quo*. He cited them as prelude and context for the acts he would charge against Egypt as aggression. "As time went on," Eban continued, "there was no doubt that our margin of general security was becoming smaller and smaller. Thus, on the morning of 5 June, when Egyptian forces engaged us by air and land, bombarding the villages of Kissufim, Nahal-Oz and Ein Hashelosha we knew that our limit of safety had been reached, and perhaps passed. In accordance with its inherent right of self-defense as formulated in Article 51 of the United Nations Charter. Israel responded defensively in full strength. Never in the history of nations has armed force been used in a more righteous or compelling cause." Eban claimed as well that Egypt had fighter jets in the air, on their way to Israel. "When the approaching Egyptian aircraft appeared on our radar screens, soon to be followed by artillery attacks on our villages near the Gaza Strip, I instructed Mr. Rafael to inform the Security Council, in accordance with the provisions of Article 51 of the Charter."[1]

Eban did not show physical evidence for any of his claims, nor did he promise physical evidence that he would show later. In repeating Prime Minister Eshkol's claim about the shelling of three Israeli villages, Eban gave their names as in Eshkol's message to Prime Minister Kosygin, not as in Eshkol's message to President Johnson. Curiously, Eban did not mention what had been recited in the initial IDF announcement about Egyptian troops approaching Israel on the ground.

At that Security Council meeting, no member state endorsed Eban's claims. No member state accused Egypt of aggression. Eban had sown enough doubt, however, that most Security Council members were unsure what to believe. Eban was not seriously pressed for evidence, or even for detail. Eban was not asked about the Egyptian aircraft that were supposedly detected. Did Eban have any documentation of the radar sightings? And what had become of these aircraft? Had they been shot down over the Mediterranean? Had they been shot down over Israel? Had the pilots bailed out and been captured? Had the pilots been killed? And the shells that landed in the three settlements. Were there casualties among Israeli civilians? Did Israel have photographs of damage to structures? None of this was raised.

The reticence to quiz Eban was the more startling in light of the facts that were known. Israel launched a coordinated land and air assault on Egypt, using massive force. And it did so almost immediately after Egypt's supposed attacks on Israel's three villages. Even for an Army and an Air Force on high alert, a prompt launch on such a scale seemed unlikely. Egypt denied having sent aircraft. It denied shelling Israeli settlements. But Egypt had nothing physical to show to substantiate its denials. The evidence, were there any, was in Israeli hands.

Eban was implying that the decision to invade Egypt was made in the morning of June 5, when the IDF became aware of the hostile moves that Eban was attributing to Egypt. But the secret decision to invade Egypt had, as we saw, been made the day before, at a meeting of the Cabinet. Eban concealed the Cabinet decision from the Security Council. Had the Security Council members known that the Cabinet voted on June 4 for an immediate invasion, that 7:45 A.M. had been set as H-hour, and that the IDF executed at that hour, Eban's story about an attack by Egypt would have seemed even less credible, and the Security Council might have tried to force an immediate Israeli withdrawal.

As Abba Eban spun his tale in the Security Council, Arthur Goldberg, the US representative, uttered no word of disagreement. Goldberg had been on the telephone to Washington that day, speaking to Secretary of State Dean Rusk.[2] Goldberg must have been informed that the Department of State gave little credibility to Israel's claim of an early morning attack by Egypt.

The United States was honoring its gentleman's agreement with Mossad Director Amit. It would not play the role President Eisenhower had played in 1956. By now Egypt was more or less allied with the Soviet Union as result of arms shipments. Israel's victory over Egypt was at once a defeat for Egypt and a black eye for the Soviet Union. A loss for the Soviet Union, in the Cold War calculus, was a victory for the United States.

Gideon Rafael would write in his memoir that as the war broke out he was approached by Goldberg, asking what the United States might do to help Israel in the Security Council. According to Rafael, he gave Goldberg a one-word response: "Time."[3] Israel needed time to destroy Egypt's army. Israel needed to deflect attention from the question of who started the hostilities. In Tel Aviv, the United States got a similar request from Israel's Foreign Ministry. Harry McPherson, who served as Special Counsel to President Johnson, visited Tel Aviv at Johnson's request to size up the situation. McPherson met with Moshe Bitan, an official in the Foreign Ministry. As McPherson recounts the conversation, Bitan initiated a request for US assistance. Bitan asked the United States to give Israel "two or three days to finish the job."[4]

A STELLAR PERFORMANCE

Eban was at his rhetorical best as he painted a picture of an Israel on the brink of disaster. To add poignancy to his account, he invoked the Holocaust, calling Israel "the last sanctuary of people which had seen six million of its sons exterminated by a more powerful dictator two decades before."[5] "There was peril for Israel wherever it looked," he intoned after describing the movements of the forces of the neighboring Arab states. Israel's "manpower had been hastily mobilized. Its economy and commerce were beating with feeble pulses. Its streets were dark and empty. There was an apocalyptic air of approaching peril."

Israel's allies were leaving it to its fate, even as the world understood its dire situation. "Israel faced this danger alone," he said. "We were buoyed up by an unforgettable surge of public sympathy across the world. The friendly Governments expressed the rather ominous hope that Israel would manage to live, but the dominant theme of our condition was danger and solitude."[6] In fact, Israel's allies were telling Israel that Egypt was unlikely to attack, and that if it did, it would lose badly.

Eban was delighted with how his address in the Security Council was received. He may not have convinced anyone that Egypt was the aggressor, but he had sown enough doubt to stem any movement for a withdrawal of Israeli troops. Eban's address had resonated well beyond the confines of UN headquarters. It was carried on television and radio in the United States, quite unusual for a Security Council meeting. In his memoir, Eban would relate that when he reached his hotel after the late night session on June 6, he was deluged with congratulatory telephone calls and cables. "My speech had reached a massive audience and had apparently evoked strong reactions." Eban quoted the *New York Times* coverage of his address. The *Times* wrote, "Abba Eban, the Oxford-educated Foreign Minister of Israel, took honors for mastery of phrase-making and drew applause from the gallery." Eban was also impressive to the television audience, said the *Times*. "To the viewer, a primary feature was Mr. Eban's composure compared with the indignation of Arab representatives over a ceasefire that would cost them the territory already won by the Israelis." The *Times* heaped high praise on the television networks for carrying the debate. "The telecast constituted one of television's finest moments."[7]

Eban savored the moment.[8] He basked in praise from "a chain of thirty major newspapers in the Midwest," as he described in his memoir, that wrote that "Americans who listened to Israel's Foreign Minister Abba Eban's address at the historic session of the Security Council on Tuesday night heard one of the great diplomatic speeches of all time. Eloquent in its phrasing, brilliantly devastating in its array of facts against the Arab enemy, Eban's speech at the same time avoided any semblance of boasting over Israel's sensational military triumphs."[9]

The *Chicago Tribune* went further in lauding Eban, using superlatives that took Eban's address beyond the realm of diplomacy. In an editorial article, the *Chicago Tribune* said that Eban's address "deserves to be recorded as one of the great speeches of history."[10] The *Chicago Tribune* re-printed the text of key sections.[11] A widely read syndicated columnist, Ralph McGill, used a Biblical turn of phrase to describe Egypt's ambassador el-Kony after Eban took him on in the Security Council debate. "Rarely," wrote McGill, "has one diplomat been so badly cut up by the sword of truth."[12]

Eban was appropriately proud. Speeches made in the Security Council were rarely reviewed. The accolades were the more remarkable because the crux of Eban's argument was based on a false premise. The opinion makers in the major American media were taken in by his recitation of Egyptian aggression. No one pointed out that Eban offered no proof for his claims of what Egypt did on the morning of June 5. The Egyptian ambassador was depicted as the one who was telling tall tales.

More importantly for Israel, Eban had neutralized the United Nations. He used an invented story about the outbreak of hostilities to keep the Security Council in the dark. When a Soviet draft resolution to condemn Israel for aggression was put to a vote in the Security Council on June 14, no state voted against it, but eleven of the fifteen members abstained. Only four states voted in favor. So the draft failed.[13] Eban got not a single Security Council delegate to express acceptance of his claim of an Egyptian attack. But Eban did not need acceptance. The eleven abstentions were testament to Eban's success.

EBAN'S REPRISE

The Soviet Union, unable to get the Security Council to denounce Israel for aggression, asked for an emergency special session of the UN General Assembly, and one was called.[14] Just as in 1956, the action at the United Nations moved from the Security Council to the General Assembly. The Soviet Union hoped that the General Assembly would pin blame on Israel and call for a withdrawal of Israel's forces, which by then occupied not only Egypt's Sinai Peninsula, but Syria's Golan Heights, plus the Gaza Strip and the West Bank of the Jordan River. In 1956, the General Assembly had pressured Israel to withdraw, so Israel had reason for concern over what might happen at this emergency special session.

All the principals attended the session, which began on June 19. Egypt denounced Israel for aggression, again denying that it had begun military action against Israel on June 5. Israel, again represented by Eban, repeated its claim of aggression by Egypt. Eban was at his most dramatic as he spoke in the emergency special session. He compared the Arab states to Nazi Germany going after the Jews. "June 1967 was to be the month of decision. The 'final solution' was at hand," he declared.[15] Eban recited the measures taken by Egypt that, by Israel's account, meant Egypt was preparing to attack. Then "on the fateful morning of 5 June," he charged, "Egyptian forces moved by air and land against Israel's western coast and southern territory." For Israel, Eban declared dramatically, "the choice was to live or perish, to defend the national existence or to forfeit it for all time."[16]

So Israel had been attacked and had to use military force to defend itself. By this time, however, the claim of an initial attack by Egypt was becoming more difficult to sustain. It was two full weeks after the event, and Israel had presented no evidence. At the emergency special session, Eban presented none. He simply re-stated his claim of what Egypt supposedly did on the morning of June 5. Again kudos greeted Eban in the press. James Reston, lead columnist of the *New York Times*, extolled Eban's style. Eban "talks like a Cambridge Don," Reston wrote. He "comes through like a tank commander." He "went through Kosygin's arguments with all the gentility of Maj. General Moshe Dayan's tanks in the desert."[17]

New York Post columnist James Wechsler called Eban's speech at the emergency special session "one of the most impressive rhetorical performances in the annals of the UN or any other major parliament." Wechsler provided a brief biography of Eban from his childhood in South Africa to his University accomplishments, then concluded, "All of this heritage seemed blended yesterday in the lyrical, Churchillian cadences that Eban brought to the finest hour (and 25 minutes) of his life. The case and the cause of a lonely, encircled nation, born of centuries of travail, achieved new dignity and drama in the UN hall and on millions of TV screens." And then, "Listening to him one had the sense that almost every day of his life had been a preparation for this interlude when he would summon all his resources to articulate so majestically the anguish and the glory of a people so long under siege." Wechsler wrote that Eban "with mingled power and grace, challenged the proposition that this little state for which he spoke had intimidated its larger neighbors."[18] Wechsler's praise found its way into Eban's autobiography.[19]

EBAN'S MEMORY LAPSE

But even Wechsler, enthralled as he was with Eban's performance, could not avoid mentioning one point Eban made that Wechsler thought "a misfortune." During his speech at the emergency special session, Eban criticized UN Secretary-General Thant for complying with Egypt's request to withdraw the UN Emergency Force from the Egypt-Israel line. "On 18 May," Eban had told the emergency special session, "Egypt called for the total removal of the United Nations Emergency Force. The Secretary-General of the United Nations acceded to this request and moved to carry it out, without reference to the Security Council or the General Assembly."[20]

What Eban stated was accurate. Egypt had asked for withdrawal on May 18. Thant had ordered the withdrawal without reference to the Security Council or the General Assembly. Thant's view was that once Egypt's consent was withdrawn, he had no basis for keeping it on Egyptian soil. Thant saw no need to consult the Security Council or General Assembly.

Eban's implication was that Egypt asked for the removal of the Emergency Force so that it could attack Israel unimpeded, and that the withdrawal set the stage for the attack that Eban claimed Egypt made on June 5. "What is the use of a fire brigade," Eban asked, with reference to the Emergency Force, "which vanishes from the scene as soon as the first smoke and flames appear?"[21] Egypt's position, as we saw in Chapter Seventeen, was that Israel was threatening Syria, and that Egypt needed to be able to move against Israel were Israel to invade Syria.

Eban made one additional claim, and this is what caught Wechsler's attention. Eban said that Thant had made the decision to withdraw the UN Emergency Force "without consulting Israel on the consequent prejudice to its military security."[22] In fact, however, Thant had contacted Israel before making his decision to order the withdrawal of the Emergency Force. Thant responded at the emergency special session the next day.[23] He referred to Eban's statement about Thant's withdrawal of the Emergency Force. "The Foreign Minister of Israel," Thant began, "made no mention in his critical analysis of my decision of certain decisive facts and factors with which he is certainly very well acquainted." Thant recited that the Emergency Force had been in Egypt with Egypt's consent and that Israel, despite being asked back in 1957, had refused to allow it on its side of the armistice line.

Importantly, and here Thant disputed Eban's veracity, he said "that prior to receiving the United Arab Republic [Egypt] request for withdrawal and prior to giving my reply to it, I had raised with the Permanent Representative of Israel to the United Nations the possibility of stationing elements of the United Nations Emergency Force on the Israel side of the line. I was told that the idea was completely unacceptable to Israel."[24] This was a reference to a conversation Thant had with Gideon Rafael. Thant would recount that conversation, including Rafael's reply, in a report he filed the next week with the United Nations.[25] Thant also said he had discussed the matter with Eban himself.[26]

That Eban would claim that Israel had not been contacted was the stranger, because Thant's plea to Israel to take the Emergency Force on its side once Egypt asked for withdrawal was well known to the diplomats of the major powers. Moving the Force across the frontier would have given Israel protection if Israel was truly concerned about being attacked by Egypt. Both the British and American governments had made similar pleas to Israel. British Prime Minister Harold Wilson had approached Prime Minister Eshkol on the subject, asking that Israel allow the Force to be stationed on its side of the line.[27] US Ambassador Walworth Barbour had raised the matter with Eban and reported Eban's reaction as "strongly negative." The same plea had been made by the US State Department in Washington to Israel's ambassador, Avraham Harman.[28] There was no way Eban could credibly claim that Israel had not been consulted about the withdrawal of the Emergency Force.

"During the last five and a half years," Thant said, referring to his time as Secretary-General, "I have never had reason to comment upon a statement made to this Assembly by a representative of any Government." But now Thant called Eban out for lying. Eban's accusation was more than the normally understated Thant could stomach. Thant's criticism required Eban to respond. Eban did so at the next meeting of the emergency special session. Eban described Egypt's request to withdraw the Emergency Force and how Thant responded to it. He gave his view on how such situations should be handled within the United Nations. But he avoided responding to Thant's charge that he had falsely claimed that Israel was not consulted.[29] Eban never explained why he chose to make the charge. Eban's choice to make the charge is the stranger because the issue of the stationing of the Emergency Force bore heavily on the issue of who started the war. If Israel was, as Eban claimed, expecting an Egyptian attack, why should Israel object to a UN monitoring force that might keep Egypt at bay? The only logical answer is that Israel did not anticipate an attack from Egypt, and that Israel preferred having no monitoring force so that it could itself attack Egypt.

GOOD ENOUGH

Eban was not the whole show that Israel put on at the emergency special session of the General Assembly. In the Security Council, Eban had invoked the Holocaust. At the emergency special session, it did so in more dramatic fashion. It included Gideon Hausner as a member of its team at the emergency special session. Hausner had no experience as a diplomat and no particular knowledge of the recent hostilities. In 1961, Hausner had been Attorney-General of Israel and in that capacity had conducted the prosecution in Jerusalem of the German Nazi leader Adolf Eichmann for crimes against Jews during the Second World War. Hausner spoke at the emergency special session. He said nothing about the issue at hand. Instead he recounted his prosecution of Eichmann, reminding the delegates of what had been done to the Jews of Europe. Hausner's appearance was condemned as a gimmick by Arab-state delegates, who said it was designed to divert attention from Israel's aggression.[30]

At the emergency special session, as had been the case in the Security Council, no state spoke up to support Israel's claim of an Egyptian attack. Even the United States, as Israel's main ally, skirted the issue. The United States was willing to cover for Israel to the extent of holding its tongue about how the war started. But it was not willing to endorse a story it knew to be false.

On June 26, Eban spoke again at the emergency special session. He repeated his claim of an Egyptian attack on the morning of June 5, as the culmination of Egypt's other hostile measures. Eban spoke dramatically, asking his fellow delegates to put themselves in Israel's shoes. "I invite every State here represented to ask itself how it would have acted in the following conditions," he began, "a group of neighbouring States encircle you with infantry and armoured divisions; issue detailed orders to their commanders on how to bomb your airfields and capture your territory; announce their intention to wage a war of annihilation against you; proclaim and establish a blockade of your coasts; announce that the object of the blockade is to precipitate a war, and then, with the Security Council ignoring your peril, send their aircraft moving towards you and shell your frontier villages. How would you react? What would you do?[31]

Again, as in the Security Council, the Soviet Union proposed a resolution to condemn Israel as the aggressor. A vote was taken on July 4. Thirty-six states voted in favor, fifty-seven voted against, and twenty-three abstained. Those voting in favor considered Israel the aggressor. But curiously, among the states that voted against or abstained, none defended Israel's version of events or called Egypt an aggressor. Some said they could not figure out who was in the right. Others said it was more helpful to seek resolution of the overall Middle East conflict than to focus on aggression. Cyprus, which abstained, nonetheless pointed a finger at Israel. It characterized Israel's actions as "aggression: co-ordinated armed attack by air and land."[32] Spain, which also abstained, said that the United Nations made a "grave mistake" by failing to investigate Israel's claim of an Egyptian attack. Like Cyprus, it pointed to the rapid massive attack by Israel as a circumstance inconsistent with Israel's claim.[33] Eban again had failed to convince delegates of Israel's innocence, but he had created enough uncertainty to avoid action against Israel.

THE FICTION IS ABANDONED

On July 7, three days after the vote in the General Assembly's emergency special session, an Israeli newspaper carried an interview with Prime Minister Eshkol about the war. Eshkol was asked by a *Yediot aharonot* reporter to explain how the war with Egypt came about. Incredibly, Eshkol answered without mentioning Eban's insistent claim of an attack by Egypt on the morning of June 5. Eshkol said nothing about Egyptian fighter planes supposedly in the air en route to Israel. He did not mention three villages having been shelled, even though, as we saw, he himself had mentioned them in his communications to President Johnson and Prime Minister Kosygin. Instead, Eshkol depicted the Israeli invasion as a reaction to Egypt's concentration of troops near the frontier and to its restrictions on shipping in the Gulf of Aqaba. Egypt had created a state of war, said Eshkol, by bringing troops up to the frontier and by restricting Israeli shipping in the Gulf of Aqaba.[34] These were circumstances that, as we saw, Eban had mentioned as context but had not identified as circumstances to justify an Israeli attack.

Eshkol had, to be sure, made a radio broadcast on May 28 in which he called Egypt's restrictions on Israeli shipping an act of aggression. "The blockade of the Straits of Tiran," Eshkol said on that occasion, "is equivalent to aggression against Israel. We shall oppose it at the proper time, in accordance with the right to self-defence vested in every State."[35] A blockade can in principle be an act of war giving rise to a right of self-defense. But whether Egypt's shipping restrictions constituted a blockade was not obvious. Eban, as we saw, did not push this line of argument at the United Nations.

Eshkol's July 7 interview was a bombshell. It drew comment from world media. The *Times* of London and Paris' *Le Monde* newspaper both took the interview as a complete repudiation of Eban's claims at the United Nations. The *Times* wrote that Eshkol had "buried the often-repeated statement that Egyptian [air] and land forces attacked Israel before she launched her devastating lightning offensive on June 5."[36] *Le Monde* wrote, "The fiction of the prior land or air attack by the Egyptian forces thus seems definitively abandoned in favor of the thesis asserted already many times that a state of war dates from the day Colonel Nasser imposed a blockade of the Straits of Tiran."[37]

The judgment of the *Times* and of *Le Monde* that Israel was abandoning Eban's claim would be borne out. From that time, Israeli officials avoided referring to any Egyptian military action on the morning of June 5 preceding Israel's assault on Egypt. They never publicly disavowed those claims. They simply acted as if those claims had never been made. Israel had survived condemnation motions in both the Security Council and General Assembly. Its story about an actual Egyptian attack on the morning of June 5 had served its purpose. To be sure, the issue of the 1967 war was still on the Security Council's radar screen, likely to be taken up again within a few months. One might have thought that Israel would need a new justification to use in the Security Council, but the politics of the matter saved Israel. When the Security Council began work again on the 1967 war in the Autumn of 1967, the Soviet Union gave up on getting Israel condemned.

It was clear to the major powers in Autumn 1967 that the only way the Security Council could come to agreement on any resolution aimed at a peaceful resolution would be to sidestep the question of responsibility for the war. That had been the approach of the United States at the emergency special session, and many other states took the same view. Some did so because they viewed it as more productive to find a solution than to affix blame. Others did so because they could not figure out who was to blame. So Eban was saved the embarrassment of having to explain to the Security Council why his prime minister did not back him up on the story he had used with such flair, and with such success, in New York.

The upshot in the Security Council was a resolution that seemed almost unrelated to the war that it was addressing. Security Council Resolution 242, adopted in November 1967, spoke, in a preamble clause, about the "inadmissibility" of acquiring territory by force. But that statement related not to who started the war, but to whether Israel should be able to retain the territory. Israel, Resolution 242 recited, should withdraw. But at the same time, Resolution 242 called on the Arab states to make peace with Israel. Without expressly saying that the two items were related, Resolution 242 was open to the reading that they were, hence that Israel was required to withdraw only at such time as the Arab states might recognize it.[38] Israel read Resolution 242 that way.

This watered-down resolution was a product of the fact that Israel was able to fend off charges of aggression by inventing a version of the war that did not accord with the facts. Israel's great success in 1967 was that it was able to attack its neighbors, take territory from them, and avoid being castigated for doing so.

One other aspect of the 1967 war must be mentioned. On June 5, by mid-morning Jordan's army began lobbing shells into Israel, hoping to defend Egypt. The IDF attacked in response and drove through the West Bank of the Jordan River, occupying it within three days and taking the old city of Jerusalem in the process. The capture of Jerusalem would bring a new confrontation for Abba Eban at the United Nations.

19

Old Issues, New Lies

In the wake of the 1967 war, the two issues that saw Eban bobbing and weaving when Israel was being admitted to the United Nations in 1949 rose again to the top of the international agenda. On the issue of Jerusalem and the issue of the Palestine Arab refugees, Israel took its confrontation with the United Nations to a new level. Israel claimed more territory in Jerusalem. It generated thousands of new refugees. On both issues, it would justify its actions by making claims that raised eyebrows.

A DENIAL ON JERUSALEM

In the 1967 war, the Israel Defense Force was able to accomplish an aim that had eluded it in 1948 when it took the old city and eastern sectors of the city of Jerusalem. Israel's capture of those sectors immediately raised concern that it would consider its tenure there permanent and that if it did, the chances for peace would recede even further. As the General Assembly's emergency special session opened, a speech was given in which that concern was pointedly stated. British Foreign Secretary George Brown attended the session and spoke for Britain. Brown spoke about finding a solution for the war. "I now want to set out certain principles," Brown began, "which I think should guide us in striving collectively for a lasting settlement. Clearly such principles must derive from the United Nations Charter. Article 2 of the Charter," Brown reminded his audience, "provides that 'All members shall refrain in their international relations from the threat or use of force against the territorial integrity or political independence of any state.' "

Then Brown applied these principles to the war just ended. "Here the words 'territorial integrity' have a direct bearing on the question of withdrawal, on which much has been said in earlier speeches. I see no two ways about this," Brown continued. "And I state this very clearly. In my view war should not lead to territorial aggrandizement." Then Brown came to the situation of Jerusalem. "Reports suggest that one particular point may be of special urgency. This concerns Jerusalem. I call upon the Government of Israel not to take any steps in relation to Jerusalem that would conflict with this principle. I say very solemnly to that Government that, if they purport to annex the Old City or legislate for its annexation, they will be taking a step which will isolate them not only from world opinion but will lose them the support that they have."[1] Brown's warning was the more problematic for Israel because, as Israeli officials knew, Brown viewed Israel as the aggressor in the recent war.

Eban, who was present when Brown spoke, took his statement as a call "for the withholding of international recognition from Israel's unification of the city."[2] Israel had "unified" Jerusalem by taking control of the entirety of its territory. Brown had understood, correctly, that the Government of Israel sought permanent control of the old city and surrounding areas.

Brown's address led some members of the Israeli cabinet to seek to act fast on Jerusalem, to make clear that it intended to keep it all. As Eban describes the sentiment within the Cabinet, the ministers were "divided about whether we should immediately give this [unification] any formal juridical expression." There was no disagreement about keeping all of Jerusalem permanently. The only issue on which the Cabinet members differed was timing. The Cabinet knew that if Israel asserted a claim then and there, the General Assembly might take a tougher stance against Israel. The General Assembly might exert pressure on Israel to withdraw immediately from the territory it had taken in the June war.

That consideration did not prevail. The Cabinet members who advocating acting fast won the day. Brown's address, as Eban reported, had an effect precisely the opposite of what Brown sought. "It strengthened the feeling of Israeli ministers," Eban would write, "that it was urgent to affirm our position on Jerusalem's unity before it became too late."[3]

Prime Minister Levi Eshkol, Eban wrote, sided with the group that favored making an immediate claim. For Eshkol, as Eban explained, Brown's address "raised the specter of preventive international action. In other words, the longer we waited, the stronger would become the international pressure against giving full effect to Jerusalem's union."[4] So the Cabinet decided that legal measures should be taken on Jerusalem.[5] That decision, Eban knew, would not play well at the emergency special session.

He sent urgent cables to the Government, warning that the United Nations might call for action against Israel.[6]

Eban's cables were ignored. The matter was taken to the Knesset. On June 27, the Knesset decreed that "the law, jurisdiction and administration of the state" of Israel "shall extend to any area of Eretz Israel [the Land of Israel] designated by the Government by order."[7] Using this statute, the Cabinet declared Israeli law applicable to east Jerusalem and expanded its boundaries to include substantial tracts in adjacent West Bank territory. The Cabinet then merged this newly enlarged east Jerusalem with west Jerusalem, making Jerusalem a single juridical entity under Israeli law.[8]

News of this legislation hit the emergency special session like a bombshell.[9] Delegates could not believe that Israel would dare tighten its grip on Jerusalem just as the General Assembly was sitting to figure out what to do about the whole situation. Any territory Israel took during the hostilities was under its belligerent occupation only, hence a claim of sovereignty would be invalid under accepted international principles. Israel was saying that its laws would apply. A state's laws apply only in its own territory. The General Assembly saw a repetition of what Prime Minister Ben Gurion had done in 1948 when he decreed that the laws of Israel would apply in the sector of Jerusalem that Israel controlled at that time. The Knesset's new action looked like a claim of sovereignty. And to make matters worse, Israel was enlarging the boundaries of Jerusalem, claiming additional West Bank territory as being within Jerusalem's boundaries.

Peru expressed the outrage of many delegates at the emergency special session of the General Assembly. Peru said that the "unilateral measures by the Government of Israel to annex the whole of the city of Jerusalem, as announced in the Press yesterday" showed "a complete disregard of the purposes for which this Assembly is meeting."[10] Cyprus called the measures "annexation." "The news today of the annexation of Jerusalem by Israel is a matter of the gravest concern to the United Nations," it said. "First, this action clearly denotes an expansionist policy by Israel in violation of the Charter. It therefore goes to the very root of the problem before us, most prejudicially affecting the prospects for a settlement and for peace in the area. Second, it is a concrete action taken by a Member State in utter contempt of the very resolutions of the United Nations under which its establishment as a State was brought about."[11]

Eban had to respond. He denied any annexation. He told his fellow delegates, "There seems to me to be a basic misunderstanding about the import of yesterday's administrative legislation. This, as the General Assembly will be aware, contained no new political statement, and concerned itself exclusively with the urgent necessities of repairing the ravages and dislocations arising from the division of the city's life and from the hostilities which Jordan inflicted upon it."[12] So the measures were aimed solely at efficient administration. The measures did not mean that Israel was claiming the entirety of Jerusalem. Moreover, Eban was deflecting blame from Israel and placing it on Jordan.

Eban got more specific. "The import of the recent legislation is to assure for the inhabitants of all parts of the city social, municipal and fiscal services, on a basis of equality and non-discrimination. This was the purport, this is the effect, of that legislation."[13] So the measures were aimed at benefiting the inhabitants, by ensuring them equal services. But they portended no claim of sovereignty. In a press encounter the same day, Eban was asked whether the Knesset was annexing the eastern sector of Jerusalem. He replied that "that word has not occurred in the legislation introduced by the Knesset or in anything I have said."[14]

The delegates were not convinced. "All Israel's efforts to misrepresent the annexation of Arab Jerusalem as bureaucratic or technical steps," one historian has written, "were doomed to failure."[15] The delegates understood that the Knesset was claiming sovereignty. As the emergency special session ended, they adopted a resolution they titled "Measures Taken by Israel to Change the Status of the City of Jerusalem." The title showed how the General Assembly understood what Israel was doing. The resolution stated that the Knesset's measures did purport to change the city's status. The resolution found the measures invalid and called for their rescission. Not a single state voted against the resolution. The resolution further asked the Secretary-General to report back to it within one week on how Israel was implementing the resolution.[16]

To carry out that follow-through, Secretary-General Thant sent a letter the next day to Eban, advising Israel of the General Assembly's stance. On July 10, Eban responded by letter. Again Eban claimed that Israel was not asserting sovereignty. "The term 'annexation' used by supporters of the resolution is out of place," he wrote. "The measures adopted relate to the integration of Jerusalem in the administrative and municipal spheres, and furnish a legal basis for the protection of the Holy Places in Jerusalem." Thant included the text of Eban's letter in his report to the General Assembly.[17] The members of the General Assembly found Eban's explanation to be fraudulent in its claim that Israel were merely providing for smooth administration. Upon receiving this report, the General Assembly adopted another resolution, "deploring" Israel's failure to comply with the first resolution, and calling on Israel again to rescind the measures and to take no additional measures aimed at changing the status of Jerusalem. Again, no state voted against the resolution. The members of the General Assembly were adamant. They wanted to verify Israel's compliance, so in the same resolution they asked Thant to follow up and report back to it again.[18]

As result of that request, Thant sent a special envoy to Jerusalem to make inquiries. Ernesto Thalmann, a Swiss diplomat, visited Jerusalem in August and met with officials. He filed a report that Thant made public on September 12. Thalmann related that he discussed the Knesset legislation on Jerusalem with a range of Israeli officials, including Foreign Minister Eban and Prime Minister Eshkol, and that they "made clear beyond any doubt that Israel was taking every step to place under its sovereignty those parts of the city which were not controlled by Israel before June 1967," and further that "the statutory bases for this had already been created, and the administrative authorities had started to apply Israel laws and regulations in those parts of the city."[19] If Thalmann was accurate, and there is no reason to think he was not, Israeli officials, including Eban himself, were telling him precisely the opposite of what Eban wrote in his letter of July 10. Eban had said that the legislation did not portend a claim of sovereignty. Now the sovereignty claim was being admitted.

In his memoir published ten years later, Eban confirmed that the legislation on Jerusalem had indeed been a claim of sovereignty. There Eban wrote, "On June 27 [1967] the Israeli Parliament voted in favor of adding Jerusalem to the area of Israeli sovereignty."[20] In the memoir, Eban did not relate that he had written the opposite to the United Nations on July 10, 1967. In 1980, the Knesset would further belie Eban's July 10, 1967 letter when it adopted a statute titled Basic Law on Jerusalem, declaring that Jerusalem "united" was the capital of Israel.[21]

REFUGEE CAMPS STRAFED

As the IDF moved through the West Bank of the Jordan River, occupying it, it did something similar to what the Zionist militias had done in 1948 in the territory of Palestine taken at that time. It drove out population. And again, as in 1948, it denied doing so. After initial opposition from the Jordanian army, the IDF met only modest resistance as it swept through the West Bank to its eastern border at the Jordan River. The Jordanian army fled east ahead of the IDF. So in many of the towns and villages it entered, the IDF was unopposed. Palestine Arabs in large numbers were streaming across the Jordan River. Almost immediately, allegations were made of population expulsion. On June 14, the Security Council adopted Resolution 237, calling for humane treatment of the Palestine Arabs of the West Bank, and in particular urging Israel to "facilitate the return of those inhabitants who have fled the areas since the outbreak of hostilities."[22] That resolution asked Secretary-General Thant to follow up and to report back to the Security Council. Thant did so on June 29. Thant said that he needed to send a representative to carry out investigations.

Thant also reported that he had received a letter from Israel's permanent UN representative, Gideon Rafael, about Israel's treatment of the civilian populations. Regarding population flight, Rafael acknowledged, "During and after the hostilities, there were movements of population in several parts of the areas." Rafael was not specific as to locations. But he addressed reports of expulsions, saying, "Any allegation that Israel has been expelling residents from their homes and thus creating a new refugee problem is untrue and inconsistent with the facts."[23]

The General Assembly, as its emergency special session was ending on July 4, adopted a resolution calling on Israel, as the Security Council had done in Resolution 237, to repatriate Palestine Arabs who had been displaced during the fighting.[24] Thant appointed a representative, who collected information that Thant compiled into a report that he delivered to the Security Council on September 15. This report gave figures separately for West Bank Palestine Arabs who were registered with the United Nations as being refugees from other parts of Palestine, and West Bank Palestine Arabs who were not so registered. According to this report, 95,000 registered Palestine Arabs had gone from the West Bank across the Jordan River into what was called Jordan's East Bank. Another 105,000, who were not registered, moved across the Jordan River as well.[25]

The displacement generated by the IDF was more intense in some localities than in others. The largest number of those fleeing across the Jordan River were from Jericho, numbering 65,000.[26] These were UN-registered Palestine Arabs residing in UN-operated refugee camps. Their camps had been strafed by IDF aircraft using flammable weaponry during the IDF assault on the West Bank. This strafing of civilians was a major atrocity that made international headlines. "There seems to be little doubt that the 60,000 inhabitants of the three United Nations camps around Jericho were attacked by planes on the second day of the fighting," the *New York Times* reported shortly after the fighting ended. "They are now the biggest single group among the refugees who have arrived."[27] The number in the *Times* article turned out to be exaggerated. The number who fled from the three camps was closer to 35,000. In other respects, the story was accurate.

Inhabitants who fled from these camps reported napalm being dropped on the camps from IDF aircraft. These refugees also reported that IDF aircraft dropped additional napalm on them as they were in transit towards the Jordan River.[28]

Rafael's blanket denial of expulsions was simply not true. Beyond what occurred at the camps near Jericho, the IDF put inhabitants onto trucks in some areas of the West Bank and drove them to points near the border, instructing them to leave.[29] Many inhabitants fled after the IDF occupied a town or village, reporting not that they had been forced out, but that they fled out of fear of the IDF, after seeing houses blown up, or seeing others arrested.[30] IDF aircraft caused extreme panic. Even in situations in which inhabitants were not directly fired upon from the air, many took it upon themselves to flee after seeing the sky filled with military aircraft. In localities in the Latrun area to the west of Jerusalem, the IDF demolished entire villages and used loudspeakers to instruct the inhabitants to leave, even providing buses that drove them to the Jordan River.[31]

In a number of these towns and villages, the IDF acted as we saw during reprisal raids of the early 1950s, blowing up buildings. After occupying Qalqilya, one of the West Bank's major towns, IDF soldiers forced residents to leave.[32] The residents were later allowed to return, but when they did they found that the IDF had destroyed 850 dwellings, nearly half of the dwellings in Qalqilya.[33]

Pressure was put on Israel by the United Nations to allow Palestine Arabs who fled out of the West Bank to return. During the summer months of 1967, Israel agreed in principle, but negotiations broke down over procedures to be followed, resulting in only about 14,000 returning.[34] Beyond those who fled during and immediately after the hostilities, Israel refused admission to Palestine Arab residents of the West Bank who happened to be abroad at the time of the hostilities.[35] This new Arab flight caused by direct expulsion or intimidation constituted a new chapter in Israel's refusal to comply with the commitments Abba Eban made to the Ad Hoc Political Committee in 1949.

A NEW OFFICIAL VERSION

Once the Security Council adopted Resolution 242, the question of which side was responsible for starting the 1967 war was off the UN radar screen. Neither the Security Council nor the General Assembly held more proceedings dealing with the genesis of the war. Israel would not be called on to justify itself in any formal setting. Israel continued to occupy territory it took in the 1967 war and needed to have some explanation to justify how it got there. A statement in justification of Israel's role in the 1967 war came within a few months, from an authoritative Israeli source. In 1968, Shabtai Rosenne, writing in a legal journal, offered a justification for Israel for the 1967 war. At the time, Rosenne had left the post of Legal Adviser to the Foreign Ministry. Instead, he was serving as Israel's Deputy Permanent Representative at the United Nations. Rosenne inserted in the article a note to explain whose views he was expressing. The note read, "Insofar as a person holding an official and representative position can maintain personal views, the opinions expressed in this article are not necessarily those of the government which the author has the honor to represent." It is common for government officials who write in such publications to disclaim any intent of representing official views. Rosenne's coyly phrased note all but says that he was writing a view of the Government.

Rosenne's argument was that Israel was forced to defend itself in June 1967 because of "the real and urgent threat posed to Israel's very existence by the massed armies of her immediate neighbors, backed by all the other Arab states." Rosenne characterized the 1967 hostilities as "the Arabs' war on Israel."[36] In another article a few years later, Rosenne spoke of "Arab aggressions which had led to the Six Day War" as a way of characterizing that war.[37] Rosenne did not go into detail, but his argument was based, from a factual standpoint, on an assertion that Egypt and other Arab states were going to attack Israel. Rosenne's argument was that in such a situation it is permissible to attack to prevent the other side from attacking first.

Tellingly, Rosenne did not mention Eban's claim of an attack by Egypt on the morning of June 5. That omission in Rosenne's article was remarkable. A Government lawyer, analyzing a war just ended, did not even mention the rationale that the Government, through its Foreign Minister, had given at the time. The rather obvious reason for the omission was that the Government had abandoned the claim of an Egyptian attack.

WHISTLE-BLOWING ON THE 1967 WAR

Rosenne's explanation would soon be shattered by press statements made by a number of Israeli military and civilian officials about how the war really started. Officials who had been involved in Israeli decision-making in the 1967 war, one after another, would say that Israel did not expect Egypt to attack. In 1968, Yitzhak Rabin, Chief of Staff of the IDF in 1967, gave an interview to the French journalist Eric Rouleau. Rouleau asked

Rabin about the troops Egypt had drawn up to the Israeli line. Rouleau was asking essentially the same question Eshkol had asked Rabin in 1967. Rabin told Rouleau that those troops "would not have been enough to unleash an offensive against Israel." Referring to Egyptian President Nasser, Rabin said, "He knew it and we knew it."[38] So Rabin, even as he oversaw the invasion of Egypt in 1967, did not think Israel was in danger of being overrun by Egyptian forces.

Abba Eban, still serving as Foreign Minister, kept his silence on the 1967 war and how it started. He did take the occasion of having delivered speeches at the United Nations in connection with the 1967 war for a new edition of his *Voice of Israel* book. Eban included in this new edition, published in 1969, his June 6, 1967 address to the Security Council, even though the Government was no longer backing what he said there about how the war started.[39]

In 1972, Mordecai Bentov, who, as we saw, was Housing Minister in 1967, wrote a newspaper piece in which he discussed the 1967 war. As a member of the Cabinet, Bentov attended the June 4, 1967, meeting at which the decision was taken to invade Egypt. Bentov voted in favor of invading. Bentov wrote that when he voted to invade Egypt, he did not labor under any apprehension that Egypt was about to invade Israel. A "story," as he called it, was "invented" after the fact about a danger of extermination in order to provide a public rationale for attacking Egypt. Bentov himself apparently voted in favor of invading because the IDF has drawn its own troops up to the armistice line, facing the Egyptians, and could not conveniently be kept there longer without attacking.[40]

Several high-ranking military officers who had been close to the events in 1967 said that Egypt had not been intended to attack Israel. A public discussion ensued, with the Government, then led by Golda Meir as Prime Minister, mounting a counter effort to establish that Israel attacked in 1967 because Egypt indeed was itself about to attack. Taking the fifth anniversary of the 1967 war as the occasion, Meir read out for the press the text of the Cabinet decision adopted on June 4, 1967. The decision took the form of a resolution, with preamble clauses and operative clauses. The key operative clause recited, "The Government authorizes the Prime Minister and the Defence Minister to confirm to the General Staff of the IDF the time for action." The key preamble clause recited that the cabinet believed that Egypt was going to attack. This preamble clause made the point Meir wanted the public to see. The preamble clause affirmed that the Cabinet thought Egypt was going to attack. "After hearing a report on the military and political situation from the Prime Minister, the Foreign

Minister, the Defense Minister, the Chief of Staff and the head of military intelligence, the Government ascertained that the armies of Egypt, Syria and Jordan are deployed for immediate multi-front aggression, threatening the very existence of the state."[41]

Asher Wallfish, a writer for the *Jerusalem Post*, successor to the *Palestine Post*, wrote that Prime Minister Meir was reacting to "the current debate among military experts and politicians, as to whether Israel's existence was threatened in June 1967." He wrote that Meir was hoping to "put an end to that debate."[42] The French daily *Le Monde* said that Meir acted because "a minister and several generals who were on the general staff of the Israeli army at the time" had said "in recent months that there was no danger on the eve of the six-day war threatening the existence of Israel or possibly leading to its extermination."[43]

The Cabinet decision, however, was significant as well for what it meant about the justification that Israel asserted in 1967 at the United Nations. As we saw, Foreign Minister Eban had not mentioned there that the Cabinet decided on June 4, 1967 to attack Egypt. The *Washington Post* commented on the import of Meir's announcement. It wrote that her revelation was that the 1967 hostilities began "as the result of a formal resolution adopted by the Israeli government. Until now, Israel had never disclosed when and where the decision to go to war was taken." The precise time at which to attack Egypt, the *Post* reported accurately, was left to Prime Minister Eshkol and Defense Minister Dayan.[44]

The *Post* captured the significance of Meir's statement. She was saying that Israel started the 1967 war, something the government of Israel had never acknowledged in so many words. Meir was criticized in some quarters in Israel for that admission.[45] Meir's acknowledgment that Israel struck first contradicted what Eban had told the Security Council and General Assembly about Egyptian military moves toward Israel on the morning of June 5, 1967. After Prime Minister Eshkol's interview of July 7, 1967, to be sure, the government did not repeat Eban's false account of an attack by Egypt. Meir was saying out loud what the Government had already more or less acknowledged.[46]

The Cabinet decision was of importance as well for the preamble clause that recited that the government had been briefed on the military situation at the June 4, 1967 meeting, and that the briefing led the Cabinet to conclude that Egypt was going to attack. The preamble clause listed five high officials as having provided the briefing – the Prime Minister, the Foreign Minister, the Defense Minister, the Chief of Staff, and the head of military intelligence.

Neither the Prime Minister, Levi Eshkol, nor the Foreign Minister, Abba Eban, would have had independent information about the military posture. The Defense Minister, Moshe Dayan, would later write that during the pre-invasion discussion, he did say that Egypt would attack, but perhaps not right away.[47] The Chief of Staff, Yitzhak Rabin, as we saw, had declined when asked to say that Egypt was going to attack Israel. The head of military intelligence was Aharon Yariv. Yariv had assessed the Egyptian troops as being short on provisions, hence ripe for being overrun. Yariv was also saying at the time that Egypt would strike Israel.[48]

Against this evidence of a possible Egyptian attack stood the later statement we saw from Housing Minister Bentov, who said that at the June 4, 1967, meeting, his understanding was that Egypt was not going to invade Israel. The Cabinet on June 4, 1967, also had the benefit of the assessment of Meir Amit, head of Mossad. As we saw, Amit had just told Secretary McNamara in Washington that Israeli intelligence on the Egypt deployment was the same as that of the CIA. Moreover, the top generals in the IDF were involved in the *Dolphin* plan. The fact that the top generals were looking for a way to provoke Egypt shows that they did not expect it to attack on its own.

Another operative clause in the Cabinet decision suggested that the Cabinet understood it would have trouble getting the major powers to accept what Israel might say to justify an invasion of Egypt. "The Government charges the Foreign Minister," the clause read, "with the task of exhausting all possibilities of political action in order to explain Israel's stand to obtain the support of the powers." The concern was that the United States needed to be kept from opposing Israel if it attacked Egypt. As well, France was threatening to cut off armaments to Israel were it to attack Egypt.

WAR STORIES IN SHREDS

In the years that followed, the account that Foreign Minister Eban gave in 1967 of the war of that year would experience further repudiation. In 1976, Moshe Dayan published his memoir. Dayan gave a detailed account of the start of the June 1967 war. Dayan mentioned no hostile moves by Egypt on the morning of June 5. He mentioned no radar blips showing Egyptian aircraft en route to Israel. He mentioned no advance by Egyptian troops, He mentioned no shelling by Egypt of Israeli villages.[49] All these allegations had, as we saw, been included in his Ministry's press announcements on the morning of June 5, 1967. By this omission, Dayan was contradicting the stories he had authorized to be broadcast. He was also contradicting Eban's repetition of those stories.

A year later, in 1977, Eban published his own memoir. Now, like Dayan, retired from public life, Eban wrote an extended account of his diplomatic work from the earliest years. Eban included a substantial section on his major triumph, his defense of Israel in the 1967 war. By 1977, public discussion in Israel about the June 1967 war pitted those who said that Egypt had been on the verge of attacking against those who said it had not. The Government no longer espoused Eban's claim at the United Nations of an attack by Egypt on the morning of June 5, 1967. Nevertheless, in his memoir Eban repeated what he told the Security Council and General Assembly in 1967 about hostile moves by Egypt on the morning of June 5 as the precipitating factor in the war.[50] This mention by Eban of his earlier statements caught the attention of Israeli scholar Avi Raz, who commented that Eban's memoir was published "long after it had become clear that Israel initiated the hostilities," but that "Eban astonishingly reiterates the lie about Egyptian planes advancing toward Israel on the morning of 5 June."[51]

In 1982, Eban's factual recitation from 1967 took yet another blow. Menachem Begin, whom we saw earlier as leader of the Irgun, had joined the Government in 1967, just days before the hostilities with Egypt. As a Cabinet member, Begin attended the June 4, 1967, meeting and voted to invade Egypt. By 1982, Begin was prime minister, and Israel was embarking on an invasion of Lebanon. Israel had not been attacked by Lebanon, so the reason for invading Lebanon required explanation. In an address at Israel's National Defense College, Begin acknowledged both that there had been no invasion from Lebanon, and that none was expected. Yet militant groups hostile to Israel had formed in Lebanon. Begin said he decided to invade Lebanon, to prevent attacks that might be mounted against Israel in the future.

Begin's rationale for invading Lebanon took its inspiration from Shabtai Rosenne's theory of extended self-defense. Israel was not about to be invaded by Lebanon, but such an invasion might come in the future. To bolster his rationale that invading Lebanon was appropriate in order to prevent possible future attacks, Begin drew an analogy to the 1967 war. Since the 1967 action had been broadly supported by the Israeli public, it provided a solid point of reference for Begin if he could equate the Lebanon action with it. "In June 1967, we again had a choice," Begin told his audience, using "again" to indicate that the 1982 Lebanon situation was like the 1967 Egypt situation. "The Egyptian Army concentrations in the Sinai approaches do not prove that Nasser was really about to attack us. We must be honest with ourselves. We decided to attack him." In Begin's mind, Israel's 1982 invasion of Lebanon action was as fully justified as its 1967 invasion of Egypt. In neither instance did Israel face an imminent attack. In each instance, the reason for invading was to forestall attacks that might come in the future. Begin further explained, with regard to the 1967 action, that Israel had decided to "take the initiative and attack the enemy, drive him back, and thus assure the security of Israel and the future of the nation." The 1967 war, he said, was "a war of self-defense in the noblest sense of the term." So Begin was acknowledging that when he voted on June 4, 1967, to invade Egypt, he understood that Egypt was not about to invade Israel.

Prime Minister Begin was repudiating the rationale that Israel through Foreign Minister Eban had given the United Nations for the June 1967 war. He was also repudiating the rationale recited in the June 4, 1967, Cabinet decision. The Cabinet had recited that the Arab armies were "deployed for immediate multi-front aggression" against Israel. But Begin said that from Israel's standpoint the June 1967 was a war of choice. He said, "We could have sent the army home. Who knows if there would have been an attack against us. There is no proof of it."[52]

These statements from authoritative voices notwithstanding, the analysis Rosenne gave in his 1968 article – that Israel was under a threat to its existence in 1967 – became the official analysis projected by the Israeli Government. Prime Minister Begin's more candid account has been ignored. The website of Israel's Ministry of Foreign Affairs provides brief analysis of major events in Israel's history, including its wars. The website in recent years has given an explanation of how Israel came to control the Gaza Strip and West Bank in 1967. A 2012 posting recited, echoing Rosenne, "It is important to remember that Israel's control of the territories was the result of a war of self-defense, fought after Israel's very existence was threatened."[53]

A REVERSAL ON DEIR YASSIN

Other instances of Israel's diplomatic prevarication have had equally curious after-lives. The prevarication in 1948 about the exodus of the Palestine Arabs has not been acknowledged. The Deir Yassin killings of April 1948 proved a particular source of continuing embarrassment for Israel, because of the impact they had on Arabs all over Palestine. The Deir Yassin incident was continually thrown up at Israel in public dialogue as a serious atrocity, and as a reason it needed to implement repatriation. At the time, it will be recalled, the Jewish Agency and Ben Gurion personally apologized for what the Irgun and LEHI did at Deir Yassin, in a letter to King Abdullah. In 1961, US President John Kennedy ramped up pressure on Israel to repatriate the displaced Palestine Arabs.[54] Ben Gurion decided to shore up Israel's story about the exodus in order to blunt this effort at forcing Israel to repatriate. Ben Gurion called a meeting of top officials in his Tel Aviv office. The result of the meeting was the organization of a coterie of researchers at an Israeli think tank to undertake what Ben Gurion called "a serious operation, both in written form and in oral hasbara," to show that the Arabs were not forced out.[55]

One product of that effort was the publication in 1969 of a pamphlet, issued by the Foreign Ministry, then headed by Abba Eban as Foreign Minister. The pamphlet addressed the Deir Yassin incident. The pamphlet sought to justify the Irgun and LEHI. It asserted that the civilians who perished at Deir Yassin were killed inside houses into which the Irgun and LEHI soldiers were shooting while combat to take the village was still in progress. The presence of civilians in these houses was not known to the Irgun and LEHI soldiers, it was stated.[56]

The 1969 pamphlet's version of the Deir Yassin incident contradicted not only Ben Gurion's apology, but contemporary accounts and later scholarship. The only major discrepancy noted in later scholarship concerns the number of deaths. The original claim of the International Committee of the Red Cross that 250 were killed was evidently too high. However, the villagers do seem to have been killed after hostilities ended, not in the manner claimed in the 1969 pamphlet. Moreover, when Israel was denounced at the United Nations for the Deir Yassin incident, Moshe Sharett did not deny that it was an atrocity. He called it "terrorism" and said that "the Government of Israel had not failed to state how horrified they had been by the event."[57]

In 1979, the Government of Israel took another action to cover up its role in the 1948 Arab exodus. Second only to the Deir Yassin killings, the incident that gained the most notoriety from the 1948 events was the expulsion of the Arab populations of Lydda and Ramleh. By 1979, Yitzhak Rabin had served a term as prime minister of Israel and was writing a memoir. In the memoir, Rabin described his activity during 1948, including what he did as a commander at Lydda and Ramleh in July 1948. In that description, Rabin explained how he had implemented Ben Gurion's order to expel the Lydda and Ramleh Arabs.

A Government censorship board vetted Rabin's draft and made him delete his account of expelling the Lydda and Ramleh Arabs. The deleted sections were obtained by the media. The *New York Times* published a summary of them. In these sections, Rabin portrayed himself as having been personally troubled by what he had done at Ben Gurion's order. Some of his soldiers refused his order to expel the Lydda residents. Others complied. "We took them on foot towards the Bet Horon Road," Rabin wrote. "The population of Lod did not leave willingly." The Provisional Government re-named Lydda as "Lod." Force, Rabin explained, had been required to get the inhabitants to leave. "There was no way of avoiding the use of force and warning shots in order to make the inhabitants march the 10 to 15 miles to the point where they met up with the [Arab] legion."[58] The deleted sections gave, in sum, an accurate account of the expulsions from the two Arab towns. These sections did not appear in Rabin's memoir as published. The military operation of July 1948 during which the Lydda-Ramleh expulsions occurred is explained, but nothing about what occurred at Lydda or Ramleh.[59]

20

An Organization Turned Sinister

It was only after Israel had taken Palestine that the United Nations turned to being critical of Israel. Israel's honeymoon period with the United Nations ended as the United Nations came to be populated by formerly colonial territories. The newly independent states had an instinctive feel for the situation of the Palestine Arabs, viewing Israel as a European implant. Like the older Third World governments at the United Nations, they were skeptical of Israeli factual claims. After the 1967 war, Israel would increasingly find itself at odds with the United Nations. Israel's occupation of the Gaza Strip and West Bank was regarded in a negative light, even if the Security Council in Resolution 242 seemed to accept Israel's tenure there at least temporarily. It was Israel's practices in the Gaza Strip and West Bank that created the divide between Israel and the United Nations. Israel was criticized repeatedly by the United Nations Commission on Human Rights. The General Assembly set up an investigate body to examine Israel's treatment of the Arab populations of the Gaza Strip and West Bank. It was called the Special Committee to Investigate Israeli Practices Affecting the Human Rights of the Population of the Occupied Territories.[1] That committee castigated Israel for civilian settlements, interrogation practices, deportations, and house demolitions, under the rubric of the body of law that requires a belligerent occupant to give fair treatment to a population under its control.

"ANTI-ISRAELISM"

Beyond focusing on occupation practices, the UN General Assembly set up a committee to explore ways to effectuate Palestine Arab sovereignty. It was called the Committee on the Exercise of the Inalienable Rights of the Palestinian People.[2] A Division for Palestinian Rights was set up to publicize UN activities in support of self-determination for the Palestine Arabs.[3] When the Palestine Liberation Organization was formed, it was accepted at the United Nations in an observer capacity. As various UN bodies scrutinized Israel's conduct, Israel reacted to protect itself. When the Special Committee to Investigate Israeli Practices Affecting the Human Rights of the Population of the Occupied Territories tried to visit Israel to collect information, Israel refused.

In 1984, Shabtai Rosenne cited positions adopted at the United Nations adverse to Israel and declared that "the United Nations is today one of the principal propagators of naked anti-Semitism in the world."[4] That perception by Rosenne, doubtless shared by other Israeli government figures, did not enhance Israel's inclination to be forthright in UN discussions. Rosenne did not see the UN's anti-Semitism as limited to its own activities. He said that the United Nations was propagating anti-Semitism around the world. "Since 1975 the UN has developed into a very sinister organization as regards the encouragement to all antisemitic elements throughout the world, and to anti-Zionism and anti-Israelism."[5]

Rosenne mentioned 1975, because in that year Israel and the United Nations hit a low point. The General Assembly adopted a resolution about Zionism, affirming that that concept was "a form of racism and racial discrimination."[6] Because Zionism provides the rationale for Israel as a state, a condemnation of Zionism was tantamount to saying that the basis for the Jewish Agency's claim to territory was illegitimate.

Efforts, ultimately unsuccessful, were made to expel Israel from the United Nations. In 1982, the UN General Assembly did adopt a resolution that called into question the basis on which Israel had been admitted as a member state in 1949. The resolution followed upon Israel's imposition of its own laws on the Syrian territory known as the Golan Heights that it occupied in the 1967 war. In the resolution, the General Assembly declared that Israel "is not a peace-loving Member State," and that "it has carried out neither its obligations under the Charter nor its commitment under General Assembly Resolution 273 (III) of 11 May 1949."[7]

Later in 1982, fifty East Bloc, African, and Islamic states asked Javier Perez de Cuellar, who then served as UN Secretary-General, to reject the credentials of Israel's delegates for that year's session of the General Assembly. Their letter recited, "Israel has continued systematically to refuse the implementation of the resolutions of the United Nations relating to the inalienable legitimate rights of the Palestinian people to self-determination and to the establishment of their own independent State in Palestine, and has continued its illegal occupation of the

Palestinian territories, including the Holy City of Jerusalem."[8] Israel's credentials were nonetheless accepted.

The United Nations reacted favorably in 1988, when the Palestine National Council affirmed Palestine statehood.[9] The General Assembly adopted a resolution acknowledging the affirmation of Palestine as a state and deciding that it would use the name "Palestine" in place of "Palestine Liberation Organization" for the observer mission.[10] In the vote on that resolution the only negatives were cast by Israel and the United States.[11] Israel was becoming an outlier at the United Nations.

In 1991, the 1975 resolution on Zionism as racism was reversed by the General Assembly.[12] However, Israel continued to be criticized for rights violations for actions in the occupied territories of Palestine. In 1993 the UN Commission on Human Rights appointed a special rapporteur "to investigate Israel's violations of the principles and bases of international law, international humanitarian law and the Geneva Convention relative to the Protection of Civilian Persons in Time of War, of 12 August 1949, in the Palestinian territories occupied by Israel since 1967."[13] Israel declined cooperation with the special rapporteur.

Israel also declined to deal with allegations of its violations in the West Bank of rights assured by human rights treaties. Each human rights treaty is serviced by a committee to which the state must report periodically. Israel, as party to several such treaties, reports on what the Government does in its own territory but declines to report on what it does in the West Bank. The technical reason Israel gives to these committees is that the West Bank is not part of its territory. The monitoring committees read the treaties as applying in territory under belligerent occupation and have pressed Israel to provide information on how Israel was treating the Palestine Arabs in the West Bank. A standoff continues.

The Security Council and General Assembly have viewed Israel's status in the West Bank as that of a belligerent occupant, a status that precludes any claim to sovereignty. Israel's Foreign Affairs Ministry, however, characterizes the West Bank as "disputed" territory. That characterization implies that Israel might have a claim to it.

When the government began building a barrier in the West Bank, in the vicinity of the armistice line between the West Bank and Israel, the General Assembly adopted a resolution declaring it unlawful and asked the International Court of Justice for an opinion about the consequences of that illegality.[14] The UN's court, the International Court of Justice, determined that the barrier should be torn down.[15] Israel remains at odds with the United Nations on Jerusalem and on repatriation of the Palestine Arabs displaced in 1948. UN member states continue to decline to accept Israel's claim to sovereignty in any part of Jerusalem.[16] The General Assembly continues to adopt resolutions re-affirming its Resolution 194 of 1948 as requiring Israel to repatriate the Palestine Arabs.[17]

"A PLACE OF DARKNESS"

Israel has not been quiet about the actions the General Assembly and the UN human rights organs have taken against it. In 2011, Benjamin Netanyahu, as prime minister of Israel, made a speech at the United Nations that reflected Israel's alienation from the world body. Speaking in distinctly undiplomatic language, Netanyahu castigated the United Nations for its stance on Israel. The world often condemns Israel in an irrational way, he said. It addresses actions that Israel undertakes properly and characterizes them negatively. Standing at the dais before the General Assembly of the United Nations in New York, Netanyahu excoriated the world body for being less than truthful in challenges to Israel. Netanyahu called the United Nations "the theater of the absurd." Netanyahu said that the United Nations "doesn't only cast Israel as the villain; it often casts real villains in leading roles."

Netanyahu criticized votes taken at the United Nations on issues relating to Israel: "Here in the UN, automatic majorities can decide anything. They can decide that the sun rises in the west." He recited statistics to show how many resolutions had been adopted at the United Nations criticizing Israel for one action or another, selecting Israel for condemnation when others merited it more.

Netanyahu declared that he had come to New York to provide a corrective, if only temporarily. "Today I hope that the light of truth will shine, if only for a few minutes, in a hall that for too long has been a place of darkness for my country. As Israel's prime minister, I did not come here to win applause. I came here to speak the truth."[18] When Israel was criticized by a UN Human Rights Council panel over its 2014 military action in the Gaza Strip, Ron Prosor, Israel's ambassador to the United Nations, said that "the UN has been taken hostage by terrorist organizations."[19]

21

Prevarication Pays

In its early years, the Zionist Organization advanced its cause by making promises to governments, coupled with predictions of benefits that would accrue if it were given a foothold in Palestine. Those promises and predictions involved considerable speculation, as the addressees of the promises sometimes realized. If a Jewish state were given by the Turkish empire, Turkey would be freed of its debts to Europe, and Arab nationalism would be curbed. If a Jewish state were given by Britain, the Turkish empire along with Germany would be defeated. If the League of Nations endorsed a Jewish state, Jewish settlement would not cause any detriment to the Palestine Arabs, who to the contrary would see their lives improve. The same plea was made by the Zionist Organization's new international wing, the Jewish Agency for Palestine, to the League's Permanent Mandates Commission. If the Commission would press Britain to allow more migration to Palestine, prosperity for all would prevail, and peace would reign.

By the time the British government informed the Permanent Mandates Commission that the promises and predictions made by the Jewish Agency could not be realized, and that large-scale Jewish migration to Palestine could not continue, the Zionist Organization had a critical mass of population in place that could not be displaced. As disaster loomed for the Jewish population of Europe, Palestine was projected as the only solution, even as the Zionist Organization maneuvered to keep Jews from being admitted elsewhere.

When the USSR and United States came into the role of power brokers, attention was turned to them. To the United States, electoral assistance was projected. To the Soviet Union, influence in the Middle East. A Jewish state would ally with the Soviet Union against the neo-feudal Arab states aligned with Britain and the West.

By the time hearings were called before the UN Special Committee on Palestine, the Zionist Organization and Jewish Agency were accustomed to fashioning outlandish promises and unlikely predictions to make a case for their cause. Facts could be turned when needed to back an argument. Harmony in Palestine was promised to a panel that was not well positioned to dispute what it was being told.

When the Special Committee reported to the UN General Assembly, the Jewish Agency reaped the rewards of its approaches to the United States and the Soviet Union. In a remarkable set of discussions in the Ad Hoc Committee on the Palestinian Question, delegate after delegate said that partition was unlikely to bring peace to Palestine, but that they could see no better way out. The Soviet Union, alone among the major powers, extolled the virtues of partition as a principled solution that promised a rosy future.

The Jewish Agency enjoyed near unquestioning support from the Soviet Government as it navigated the politics of the new United Nations. When the Arab states charged the Jewish Agency with expelling Palestine Arabs, the Soviet Union came to its defense. When the United States abandoned partition in favor of a trusteeship, the Soviet Union backed the Jewish Agency in its quest for unilateral control of territory. The result was the expulsion of Palestine Arabs from the bulk of the territory of Palestine. When the Jewish Agency sought recognition of Israel at the United Nations, the Soviet Union used parliamentary tactics to give Israel a voice. When the newly declared state applied for UN membership, the Soviet Union was its first and strongest backer. When other states pointed to negative conduct by Israel that meant it was not qualified for membership, the Soviet Union dismissed the objections.

In neither Israel nor the Soviet Union did one find, for quite a few years, any mention of the Jewish Agency's overtures to the Soviet Union. For the Soviet Union, its support for the Jewish Agency became an embarrassment, after Israel and the Soviet Union parted ways and the Soviet Union switched to backing the Arab states. For Israel, the thrust in writings on diplomacy has been to portray the acceptance of a Jewish state as recognition of the rights of the Jewish people. Attributing the success, even in part, to what turned out to be a miscalculation by the Soviet Union is less appealing. Only after the demise of the Soviet Union was a collection of documents relating to that interaction published, under the auspices of the Israeli and Russian governments.[1] The level of support from the Soviet Union was, however, quite remarkable. That support was critical in getting Israel on its feet as a state.

After being admitted to the United Nations, Israel flaunted its commitments to the United Nations on the status of Jerusalem, and on repatriation of the refugees. In the 1950s, when it battled refugees across the armistice lines, it lied to UN monitors and to the Security Council to cover up the high level of violence it employed against Arab civilians. It gained advantage for itself in 1956 by invading Egypt, again by deceiving the United Nations as to what it was doing.

Then in 1967 Israel was able to take the Gaza Strip and West Bank sectors of Palestine by making a false assertion in the United Nations that it had been attacked. At that time Israel extended its control over Jerusalem and tried to cover up what it was doing there. At that time as well, Israel expelled more Palestine Arabs and similarly tried to cover up these expulsions. On both counts – Jerusalem and the new expulsions – Israel succeeded in avoiding more than verbal condemnation by the United Nations.

Blame should perhaps be laid at the doorstep of the United Nations for gullibility in accepting Israel's portrayal of facts and for believing commitments that were not likely to be kept. As Ari Shavit has astutely observed, the destruction of Arab villages in 1948 and the accompanying expulsion of Arabs from Palestine virtually assured long-term enmity against Israel from the Arab world.[2] Israel's diplomats covered up those atrocities when challenged on them at the United Nations. Had the United Nations dealt with them at the time, the history of the Middle East might not have turned into the perpetual tragedy it has become.

The acceptance by the United Nations of Israel's prevarication in the early years of the United Nations had secondary effects that could not have been foreseen at the time. The enmity that Shavit identifies affects not only the peoples of Palestine and Israel but the peoples of the entire Middle East region. The continuing hostility became a source of anger against the Western world, which was seen as collaborating with Israel in its refusal to accommodate the Arabs of Palestine.

DÉJÀ VU: JERUSALEM AND THE PALESTINE ARABS

The significance of the prevarication of Zionist diplomats came into sharp focus in 2000, when US President Bill Clinton called the leaders of Palestine and Israel together at the presidential retreat at Camp David, Maryland. On the agenda were all the issues outstanding between two. Of the issues that turned out to be most problematic were the same two that troubled the Ad Hoc Political Committee in 1949: Jerusalem and the repatriation of the displaced Palestine Arabs. In both instances, Israel's negotiators relied on Israel's past prevarication to espouse positions that were so distant from the positions of Palestine as to make it all but impossible to reach a peace agreement.

In those negotiations, Israel's negotiators demanded Israeli sovereignty over all of Jerusalem, plus another 10 percent of the West Bank.[3] The Palestinian negotiators hinged their position in regard to territory on UN Security Council Resolution 242. They were prepared to concede to Israel the territory it had held from 1948, so long as Palestine would have the Gaza Strip and the West Bank of the Jordan River.[4] That meant the sector of Jerusalem that was part of the West Bank, prominently the Old City of Jerusalem, would fall to the Palestine state. The Israeli negotiators, supported by President Clinton regarded this demand by the Palestinian negotiators as excessive.[5]

Prime Minister Ehud Barak used his reading of the 1967 war to back Israel's claim. His reasoning was that the Arab side committed aggression in 1967, therefore that Palestine should not get the territory of the West Bank. Barak relied on the post-1967 official Israeli version of the 1967 war, the version that, it will be recalled, had been skewered by Prime Minister Menachem Begin in 1982. "In 1967," he said in his written account of the Camp David talks, "although we were the ones to fire the first shot, the world saw us as trying to free ourselves of strangulation by our neighbors. The international community had failed to meet the commitments it had undertaken in 1967, and our war enjoyed broad legitimacy."[6]

Barak's reference to the international community's 1967 commitments was apparently to its inability to reverse Egypt's restrictions on shipping in the Gulf of Aqaba. By conceding that Israel fired the first shot, Barak was espousing the view that Shabtai Rosenne espoused in 1968, and Prime Minister Golda Meir espoused in 1972, that Israel was justified to fire because if it hadn't done so Egypt would have fired. This view had been accepted by "the world," said Barak, and as a result "our war enjoyed broad legitimacy." Barak was probably correct that Israeli *hasbara* had been successful in deceiving "the world." Now that "the world" thought that Israel was in the clear on the June 1967 war, Barak would deny the Palestinians a state in the territory Israel then occupied. "As I told Clinton and Arafat many times, both before and at Camp David," Barak wrote, "we will never apologize for our victory in 1967."[7] Barak's perspective on the June 1967 war was not challenged by President Clinton.

On repatriation, Israel's negotiators at Camp David acted on what Shertok and Eban told the United Nations in 1948 about the reasons for the

Arab exodus. Israel would assume no responsibility for creating the "refugee problem."[8] By the year 2000, that analysis was so solidly engrained in Zionist diplomacy that it did not need to be said out loud. They brushed off Palestinian demands for repatriation as baseless.

The Ministry of Foreign Affairs, on its website in recent years, has repeated what Shertok and Eban told the United Nations in 1948. The website, as of 2015, stated with regard to the exodus of Palestine Arabs in 1948, "Many Palestinian Arabs who lived in areas where the fighting took place abandoned their homes, either at the request, of Arab leaders, or due to fear of the fighting and the uncertainty of living under Jewish rule." "Israel does not bear any culpability for the creation or the perpetuation of the Palestinian refugee problem," the Foreign Ministry website stated. "Thus it cannot declare, even as a gesture, responsibility for the problem."[9]

The cover-up carried out in 1948 at the United Nations of the expulsions of that year was, as we saw, followed by a commitment during Israel's UN admission in 1949 to consider repatriation, at least when and if peace were made with the Arab states. In the discussions of repatriation in the Conciliation Commission for Palestine, Shertok had said, as did Ben Gurion, that repatriation should be on the agenda once peace came with the Arab world. In 1979, Israel signed a peace treaty with Egypt in 1979, but did not agree to repatriate the Palestine Arabs from the territory Egypt had held, the Gaza Strip. In 1994, Israel signed a peace treaty with Jordan, but did not agree to repatriate the Palestine Arabs from the West Bank, or from Jordan itself. Now at Camp David, the Zionist diplomats were negotiating over a peace treaty with Palestine that would have resolved the conflict that began with Britain's sponsorship of Zionism at the time of World War I. Ben Gurion had proclaimed that this would be the time to deal with the refugee issue. Palestine negotiators tried to inject the repatriation question into the negotiations. They insisted on implementation of the General Assembly's Resolution 194 of 1948 that called for repatriation of the displaced Palestine Arabs. Prime Minister Barak's refusal at Camp David to give repatriation any serious consideration meant that Israel was not keeping Ben Gurion's commitment to deal with repatriation in the context of peace with the Arab world.

Putting a further nail in the coffin of possible negotiation over repatriation, the government of Israel began to argue that repatriation would be rejected by Israel on grounds of practicality and preserving the character of Israel. This argument was made on the Foreign Ministry website. "Under present conditions," read a passage on the website, "the influx of a large number of descendants of refugees into Israel is not a viable option. Given that the present population of Israel is approximately 7 million (of whom about one-fifth are Arab-Israelis), the influx of millions of Palestinians into the State of Israel would threaten the existence of Israel as a Jewish state, obliterating its basic identity as the homeland of the Jewish people and a refuge for persecuted Jews worldwide. Consequently, the demand to 'return' to Israel is nothing more than a euphemism for the demographic destruction of the Jewish state."[10] This consideration was not stated early on, when Israel sought admission to the United Nations. As we saw, however, Shertok was clear, in private, as early as June 1948 in rejecting repatriation at any time in the future. The argument appearing on the website was consistent with Shertok's privately stated June 1948 view that repatriation was off the table for all time.

THE IMPACT OF PREVARICATION

Israel is far from the only country to invent facts to advance its interests in international diplomacy. The tongue-in-cheek definition of a diplomat as one who is willing to lie for his country is founded on reality. All nations seek to appear in a favorable light, even when their actions are on the dark side. Their leaders may regard lying as justifiable.[11] We saw Britain and France lying at the United Nations when their forces landed at the Suez Canal in 1956. What is remarkable about Israel is that it was able to put itself on the map – literally – by dubious assertion of facts.

It was only after 1967 that *hasbara* ceased to work well for Israel in international diplomacy. *Hasbara* worked well for Israel in its formative years. It played an essential role in helping the Jewish Agency succeed in taking territory in Palestine. Had the United Nations seen through the prevarication and the disingenuous commitments, it might have taken a radically different approach to Palestine.

The impact of the obfuscation over the time period from Zionism's founding is hard to assess. An argument could be made that it yielded little benefit. This argument would run that it made no difference in the eventual disposition in Palestine. The promises made by Herzl, the first Zionist diplomat to the Sultan gained no territory. Britain acted for reasons of its own self-interest and would have promoted Zionism in any event. The Permanent Mandates Commission may have been deceived, but it held little real power. The United Nations was unlikely in any event to stop the Jewish Agency and Zionist Organization from taking the bulk of Palestine's territory in 1948. The backing Israel got from the Soviet Union would have come about even without the lobbying of Maiskii, because the

Soviet Union's aim was to keep Britain out of the Middle East. And in 1967 Israel had the United States on its side in the aftermath of attacking Egypt, so there was little chance of international action against Israel, regardless of what anyone believed about the genesis of the 1967 war. In the final analysis, the Zionists took the territory of Palestine militarily. It was not given to them, despite the recommendations that came out of the United Nations. So perhaps the favorable reception the Zionists got at the United Nations was of only marginal importance.

Furthermore, the Zionist diplomats were not always believed. One long-time Israeli diplomat, Yohanan Meroz, coined the term "hasbarable." By this term, Meroz meant that some actions that cannot otherwise be justified can be mitigated by *hasbara*. For other acts, nothing one might try by way of *hasbara* will work.[12] On Qibya, the Security Council did not accept Eban and Ben Gurion's story that the raid was carried out by civilians.

On the other hand, the case is strong for the proposition that much was gained for the Zionist cause through prevarication in diplomacy. Zionist diplomats might not have gained territory had their lies not been believed. Their testimony before the Paris Peace Conference came at a time when it was far from clear that the League of Nations would implement the Balfour Declaration. The Zionist diplomats gained what was by international practice a rare and odd measure – international support for the insertion of an outside population into a territory whose inhabitants were bitterly opposed. Had the Council of Ten understood the weakness of support for Zionism, it might have been less inclined to lead the League to write Zionism into the Palestine Mandate. Had it understood that the Zionists were taking over land in a way that was displacing locals, the League might not have given Palestine to Britain with an instruction to promote Jewish migration.

The strong support that the Zionist diplomats received from the Permanent Mandates Commission might not have been forthcoming without the skewed analysis the Commission got. Had the Permanent Mandates Commission understood that both Britain and the Zionists were lying when they said, as they did over most of the years of the Palestine Mandate, that Jewish migration and Arab well-being were compatible, it might have raised an alarm that would have kept the Jewish segment of population from growing, as it did under the Mandate, from 10 percent to nearly one-third of Palestine's population. In the event, the Permanent Mandates Commission did virtually nothing while the situation in Palestine deteriorated to a point of no return.

The UN Special Committee on Palestine accepted the bulk of the falsehoods perpetrated by the Jewish Agency spokespersons who testified at the Jerusalem hearings. Those falsehoods led the Special Committee, at least its majority group of eight who proposed partition of Palestine, to overestimate the attachment of Jews through history to migrate to Palestine. They led them to think that substantial Jewish migration to Palestine could be accomplished without damaging the status of Palestine's majority Arab population. They led them to believe that a partition proposal would, in the long run, be accepted by the Arab population.

The disingenuous commitments made in the Ad Hoc Political Committee in 1949 were instrumental in gaining Israel's admission to the United Nations. The Committee was desperate to gain Israel's assurances on Jerusalem and on repatriation, because absent Israel's acquiescence on these issues, it was hard to make a case that Israel was peace-loving. Israel was pursuing policies that would only inflame the situation and preclude peaceful resolution. The importance the Committee attached to Israel's assurances is seen in the text of the UN General Assembly's resolution of admission to membership, in which the General Assembly recites the commitments regarding Jerusalem and repatriation.

The deception perpetrated in the invasion of Egypt in 1956, through the covert collaboration with France and Britain, gained for Israel a UN force on the Egypt-Israel line that kept Palestine Arab refugees from engaging in self-help as a way of regaining their homeland. The deception perpetrated in the invasion of Egypt in 1967 kept the UN Security Council from calling for a withdrawal of Israeli forces, thereby allowing the long-term occupation by Israel of the Gaza Strip and the West Bank. The fact that most Security Council members were unsure what to believe about the onset of the hostilities did appear in the Security Council discussions to incline them away from taking a position against Israel.

One can assess the Zionist prevarication in line with one's view of the Zionist project. To some, and as we saw this was Ben Gurion's philosophy, prevarication was a tool that could be used by a people in great need. The goal of providing them protection overrode considerations of accuracy in explaining one's action. To others, the Zionist prevarication has created and perpetuated a situation of injustice and instability that has had hugely negative consequences in Palestine and beyond.

Notes

1 A PUBLIC RELATIONS IMPERATIVE

1 Abba Eban, Our Place in the Human Scheme: A Presentation, *Congress Bi-Weekly*, vol. 40, no. 6, at 6 (March 30, 1973).
2 Gideon Levy, Israeli propaganda isn't fooling anyone – except Israelis, *Ha'aretz*, June 4, 2015.
3 Jodi Rudoren, Netanyahu calls international criticism an effort to "delegitimize Israel," *New York Times*, June 1, 2015, at A9.
4 Id. at A9.
5 Eban, Our Place in the Human Scheme, at 6.
6 Jerusalem Programme Defines Aim and Tasks of Zionism, *Jerusalem Post*, July 23, 1951, at 1.
7 Aharon Klieman, *Statecraft in the Dark: Israel's Practice of Quiet Diplomacy* (Boulder CO: Westview Press, 1988) (Tel Aviv University, Jaffe Center for Strategic Studies), at 39.
8 Id. at 41.
9 International Covenant on Civil and Political Rights, art. 9, UN Treaty Series, vol. 999, at 171.
10 Id., art. 4.
11 Law and Administration Ordinance, art. 9(a), *Laws of the State of Israel*, vol. 1, at 7 (1948).
12 Declaration, filed October 3, 1991. *Multilateral Treaties Deposited with the Secretary-General*, accessible at www.un.org.
13 Joanna Paraszczuk, High court upholds state of emergency, *Jerusalem Post*, May 8, 2012.

2 PROMISES, PROMISES

1 Raphael Patai (ed.), *The Complete Diaries of Theodor Herzl* (New York: Herzl Press, 1960), vol. 2, at 445–446.
2 Raphael Patai (ed.), *The Complete Diaries of Theodor Herzl* (New York: Herzl Press, 1960), vol. 1, at 375–377.
3 Id. at 367.

4 Isaiah Friedman, *Germany, Turkey, and Zionism 1897–1918* (Oxford: Clarendon Press, 1977), at 93–94.
5 Hannah Arendt, Zionism Reconsidered, in Hannah Arendt, *The Jew as Pariah: Jewish Identity and Politics in the Modern Age* (New York: Random House, 1978), at 152. Walter Laqueur, *A History of Zionism* (New York: Schocken Books, 1976), at 114–119.
6 Friedman, *Germany, Turkey, and Zionism 1897–1918*, at 94.
7 William Langer, *The Diplomacy of Imperialism 1890–1902* (New York: Alfred A. Knopf, 1935), vol. 2, at 645.
8 Patai, *The Complete Diaries of Theodor Herzl*, vol. 2, at 670–1.
9 Langer, *The Diplomacy of Imperialism 1890–1902*, vol. 2, at 629–47.
10 Patai, *The Complete Diaries of Theodor Herzl*, vol. 2, at 720.
11 Raphael Patai (ed.), *The Complete Diaries of Theodor Herzl* (New York: Herzl Press, 1960), vol. 3, at 1114.
12 Achad Ha-am, Pinsker and Political Zionism (To the memory of Dr. Pinsker, on the tenth anniversary of his death) (1902), in Achad Ha-am, *Ten Essays on Zionism and Judaism* (London: George Routledge and Sons, 1922), 56, at 87.
13 Patai, *The Complete Diaries of Theodor Herzl*, vol. 3, at 1115.
14 Dan Cohn-Sherbok, *Introduction to Zionism and Israel: From Ideology to History* (London: Continuum, 2012), at 57.
15 Nevill Barbour, *Palestine: Star or Crescent* (New York: Odyssey Press, 1947), at 55.
16 Id. at 56.
17 Id. at 56.
18 Id. at 57.
19 Chaim Weizmann, *Trial and Error: The Autobiography of Chaim Weizmann* (New York: Schocken Books, 1966), at 149.
20 Geoffrey Lewis, *Balfour and Weizmann: The Zionist, the Zealot and the Emergence of Israel* (London: Continuum, 2009), at 115–16.
21 Id. at 119–20.
22 Id. at 35.
23 Nahum Sokolow, *History of Zionism 1600–1918* (New York: Ktav Publishing House, 1969), vol. 2, at 56.
24 Norman Rose, *Chaim Weizmann: A Biography* (New York: Viking Penguin, 1986), at 175.
25 Arnold Toynbee, *Acquaintances* (London: Oxford University Press, 1967), at 153.
26 Isaiah Friedman, *The Question of Palestine: British-Jewish-Arab Relations: 1914–1918* (London: Transaction Books, 1992), at 161.
27 Id. at 194.
28 Lewis, *Balfour and Weizmann*, at 143.
29 David Lloyd George, *The Truth about the Peace Treaties* (London: Gallancz, 1938), vol. 2, at 1139.
30 Doreen Ingrams, *Palestine Papers 1917–1922* (London: John Murray, 1972), at 16.
31 Friedman, *The Question of Palestine*, at 294.
32 Ingrams, *Palestine Papers 1917–1922*, at 19.
33 Friedman, *The Question of Palestine*, at 292.

34 To Israel Rosov, Petrograd, November 23–26, 1917, in Dvorah Barzilay and Barnet Litvinoff (eds.), *The Letters and Papers of Chaim Weizmann* (New Brunswick, NJ: Transaction Books, 1977), vol. 8: Series A Letters November 1917–October 1918, at 11–12.

35 Peace Treaty between Russia and Germany, Austria-Hungary, Bulgaria and Turkey, Brest-Litovsk, March 3, 1918, art. 1, in J.A.S. Grenville and Bernard Wasserstein (eds.), *The Major International Treaties of the Twentieth Century: A History and Guide with Texts* (London: Routledge, 2001), vol. 1, at 83.

36 Chaim Weizmann, Reminiscences at a Banquet at Czernowitz, December 12, 1927, in Paul Goodman (ed.), *Chaim Weizmann: A Tribute on His Seventieth Birthday* (London: Victor Gollancz, 1945), 196, at 199.

37 To Louis D. Brandeis, Washington, January 14, 1918, in Barzilay and Litvinoff, *The Letters and Papers of Chaim Weizmann*, vol. 8, 45, at 50.

38 Tom Segev, *One Palestine, Complete: Jews and Arabs under the British Mandate* (New York: Henry Holt, 2000), at 114.

39 Achad Ha-am, Summa Summarum (1912), in Achad Ha-am, *Ten Essays on Zionism and Judaism* (London: George Routledge and Sons, 1922), 130, at 140.

40 Jehuda Reinharz, *Chaim Weizmann: The Making of a Statesman* (New York: Oxford University Press, 1993), at 232.

41 A. Granott, *The Land System in Palestine: History and Structure* (London: Eyre and Spottiswoode, 1952), at 305.

42 Kenneth Stein, *The Land Question in Palestine, 1917–1939* (Chapel Hill, NC: University of North Carolina Press, 1984), at 39–40.

43 Reinharz, *Chaim Weizmann*, at 222.

44 Id. at 223.

45 Segev, *One Palestine, Complete*, at 109–10.

46 To Arthur J. Balfour, London, May 30, 1918, in Barzilay and Litvinoff, *The Letters and Papers of Chaim Weizmann*, vol. 8, 197, at 198.

47 Segev, *One Palestine, Complete*, at 110.

48 To Vera Weizmann, London, April 30, 1918, in Barzilay and Litvinoff, *The Letters and Papers of Chaim Weizmann*, vol. 8, 170, at 171.

49 Ahad Ha'am, A Truth from Eretz Yisrael, in Tony Kushner and Alisa Solomon, *Wrestling with Zion: Progressive Jewish-American Responses to the Israeli-Palestinian Conflict* (New York: Grove Press, 2003), 14, at 15.

3 PRANKS IN PARIS AND GENEVA

1 Muhammad Muslih, *The Origins of Palestinian Nationalism* (New York: Columbia University Press, 1988), at 178–190.

2 Secretary's Notes of a Conversation Held in M. Pichon's Room at the Quai d'Orsay, Paris, on Thursday, 27th February, 1919, at 3 p.m., *FRUS Paris Peace Conference 1919*, vol. 4, 159, at 161–162.

3 Id. at 161.

4 Tom Segev, *One Palestine, Complete: Jews and Arabs under the British Mandate* (New York: Henry Holt, 2000), at 16.

5 Herbert Adams Gibbons, Zionism and the World Peace, *The Century*, vol. 97, 368, at 374 (1919).
6 Chaim Weizmann, *Trial and Error: The Autobiography of Chaim Weizmann* (New York: Schocken Books, 1966), at 125–126.
7 Secretary's Notes of a Conversation Held in M. Pichon's Room, at 162.
8 Simcha Kling, *The Mighty Warrior: The Life Story of Menahem Ussishkin* (New York: Jonathan David, 1965).
9 Secretary's Notes of a Conversation Held in M. Pichon's Room, at 165.
10 Joseph Klausner, *Menahem Ussishkin: His Life and Work* (New York: Scopus, 1942), at 108.
11 Nahum Sokolow, *History of Zionism 1600–1918* (New York: Ktav Publishing House, 1969), vol. 2, at 38–39.
12 Salo Baron, *The Russian Jew Under Tsars and Soviets* (New York: Macmillan, 1976), at 182.
13 Leon Shapiro, Outline of the History of Russian and Soviet Jewry 1912–1974, in S.M. Dubnow, *History of the Jews in Russia and Poland from the Earliest Times until the Present Day* (New York: Ktav Publishing House, 1975), vol. 3, 413, at 419.
14 Isaiah Friedman, *The Question of Palestine: British-Jewish-Arab Relations: 1914-1918* (London: Transaction Books, 1992), at 294. Joseph Schechtman, *Zionism and Zionists in Soviet Russia: Greatness and Drama* (New York: Zionist Organization of America, 1966), at 18.
15 Secretary's Notes of a Conversation Held in M. Pichon's Room, at 170.
16 Id. at 164.
17 Id. at 169.
18 Id. at 164–165.
19 Segev, *One Palestine, Complete*, at 116.
20 Chaim Weizmann, Report on March 5th, 1919, to the International Zionist Conference held in London, in Paul Goodman (ed.), *Chaim Weizmann: A Tribute on His Seventieth Birthday* (London: Victor Gollancz, 1945), 155, at 158.
21 Geoffrey Lewis, *Balfour and Weizmann: The Zionist, the Zealot and the Emergence of Israel* (London: Continuum, 2009), at 166.
22 League of Nations, Covenant, art. 22.
23 Report of the American Section of the International Commission on Mandates in Turkey (King-Crane), August 28, 1919, in *FRUS Paris Peace Conference 1919*, vol. 12, 751, at 854–856.
24 Harry Sacher, *A Jewish Palestine: The Jewish Case for a British Trusteeship* (London: Zionist Organization, 1919), at 17.
25 Mandate for Palestine, Preamble and art. 2, in League of Nations, *Official Journal*, vol. 3, no. 8, at 1007 (1922).
26 See, e.g., League of Nations, Permanent Mandates Commission, *Minutes of the Thirty-Fourth Session Held at Geneva from June 8th to 23rd, 1938*, League of Nations Document C.216-M.119.1938.VI.
27 Mandate for Palestine, art. 4.
28 M. Anina Gannon, *The Influence of the Permanent Mandates Commission in the Administration of the Class A Mandate* (New York: St. John's University dissertation, 1968), at 57.

29 Quincy Wright, *Mandates under the League of Nations* (Chicago: University of Chicago Press, 1930), at 140–141.

30 William Rappard, *International Relations as Viewed from Geneva* (New York: Arno Press, 1972 – reprint of 1925 edition), at 34.

31 Pierre Rondot, L'Expérience du mandat français en Syrie et au Liban (1918–1945), *Revue générale de droit international public*, vol. 52, 387, at 407 (July-December 1948).

32 Farid Zeineddine, *Le régime du contrôle des mandats de la Société des Nations* (Paris: Presses Universitaires de France, 1932), at 242–245.

33 D.F.W. Van Rees, *Les mandats internationaux: Le Contrôle International de l'Administration Mandataire* (Paris: Rousseau & Co., 1927), at 133–135.

34 H. Duncan Hall, *Mandates, Dependencies and Trusteeship* (London: Stevens & Sons, 1948), at 204. Zeineddine, *Le régime du contrôle des mandats de la Société des Nations*, at 248.

35 Norman Rose, *The Gentile Zionists: A Study in Anglo-Zionist Diplomacy, 1929–1939* (London: Frank Cass, 1973), at 211.

36 Susan Pedersen, Settler Colonialism at the Bar of the League of Nations, in Caroline Elkins and Susan Pedersen (eds.), *Settler Colonialism in the Twentieth Century: Projects, Practices, Legacies* (New York: Routledge, 2005), 113, at 126.

37 To Vera Weizmann, Paris, October 19, 1925, in Barnet Litvinoff (ed.), *The Letters and Papers of Chaim Weizmann* (New Brunswick, NJ: Transaction Books, 1977), vol. 12: Series A August 1923-March 1926, at 427.

38 Weizmann, *Trial and Error*, at 376.

39 William Rappard, Practical Working of the Mandate System, *Journal of the British Institute of International Affairs*, vol. 4, at 205 (September 1925).

40 Aaron Margalith, *The International Mandates* (Baltimore: Johns Hopkins Press, 1930), at 78.

41 Zeineddine, *Le régime du contrôle des mandats de la Société des Nations*, Annex, at 327: Réglement intérieur de la Commission, arts. 4, 7.

42 Van Rees, *Les mandats internationaux*, at 76. Campbell Upthegrove, *Empire by Mandate: A History of the Relations of Great Britain with the Permanent Mandates Commission of the League of Nations* (New York: Bookman Associates, 1954), at 27–28.

43 Weizmann, *Trial and Error*, at 376.

44 To Josef Cohn, Zurich, July 10, 1947, in Barnet Litvinoff (ed.), *The Letters and Papers of Chaim Weizmann* (New Brunswick NJ: Transaction Books, 1979), vol. 22: Series A May 1945-July 1947, at 360.

45 League of Nations, Permanent Mandates Commission, *Minutes of the Seventeenth (Extraordinary) Session Held at Geneva from June 3rd to 21st, 1930*, Fourth Meeting, June 4, 1930, at 4 p.m., at 28, League of Nations Document C.355.M.147.1930.VI.

46 Sally Morphet, The Palestinians and Their Right to Self-Determination, in R.J. Vincent (ed.), *Foreign Policy and Human Rights: Issues and Responses* (1986), at 85, 89. Kenneth Stein, *The Land Question in Palestine, 1917–1939* (Chapel Hill, NC: University of North Carolina Press, 1984), at 36.

47 Quoted in *Palestine: Report on Immigration, Land Settlement and Development* (Sir John Hope Simpson), October 1930, Cmd. 3686, at 128.

48 Shabtai Teveth, *Ben-Gurion and the Palestinian Arabs: From Peace to War* (Oxford: Oxford University Press, 1985), at 44.
49 Constitution of the Jewish Agency, Zurich, August 14, 1929, art. 3(e), quoted in *Report on Immigration, Land Settlement and Development* (Sir John Hope Simpson), October 1930, Cmd. 3686, at 53.
50 Report of the Palestine Royal Commission (Peel Commission), July 1937, Cmd. 5479, at 241.
51 Conclusions of a Meeting of the Cabinet held at 10, Downing Street, S.W., on Thursday, 18th August, 1921, at 11.30 a.m., at 8, Cabinet 70(21), Secret, August 18, 1921, CAB/23/26.
52 Palestine: Memorandum by the Secretary of State for the Colonies (Devonshire), at 13, C.P. 106 (23), February 17, 1923, Secret, CAB/24/159.
53 Id. at 12.
54 Report of the Palestine Royal Commission (Peel Commission), July 1937, Cmd. 5479, at 225.
55 Susan Pedersen, The Impact of League Oversight on British Policy in Palestine, in Rory Miller (ed.), *Britain, Palestine, and Empire: The Mandate Years* (Farnham, Surrey: Ashgate, 2010), 39, at 41.
56 League of Nations, Permanent Mandates Commission, *Minutes of the Ninth Session Held at Geneva from June 8th to 25th, 1926*, 202, at 203–204: Annex 7: *Petition from the Executive Committee of the Palestine Arab Congress: Letter to the Chairman of the Permanent Mandates Commission*, May 9, 1926, League of Nations Document C.405.M.144. 1926. VI
57 Stein, *The Land Question in Palestine, 1917–1939*, at 175.
58 Report of the Palestine Royal Commission (Peel Commission), July 1937, Cmd. 5479.

4 COURTING THE COMMISSAR

1 *Palestine: Statement of Policy* (White Paper on Palestine), May 1939, Cmd. 6019.
2 Gabriel Sheffer, *Moshe Sharett: Biography of a Political Moderate* (Oxford: Clarendon Press, 1996), at 111.
3 Guido Goldman, *Zionism under Soviet Rule (1917–1928)* (New York: Herzl Press, 1960), at 19.
4 Ziva Galili and Boris Morozov, *Exiled to Palestine: The Emigration of Zionist Convicts from the Soviet Union, 1924–1934* (London: Routledge, 2006), at 15.
5 J.B. Schechtman, The U.S.S.R., Zionism, and Israel, in Lionel Kochan (ed.), *The Jews in Soviet Russia since 1917* (London: Oxford University Press, 1972), 99, at 112.
6 Meeting: I.M. Maiskii – Ch. Weizmann (London, February 3, 1941), in *Documents on Israeli-Soviet Relations 1941–1953: Part I: 1941-May 1949* (London: Frank Cass, 2000), at 3–5 (meeting held January 30, 1941).
7 Meeting of the Jewish Agency Executive (London, January 30, 1941), id. at 1–3.
8 Ilan Halevi, *A History of the Jews: Ancient and Modern* (London: Zed Press, 1987), at 186–188. Michael Palumbo, *The Palestinian Catastrophe: The 1948*

Expulsion of a People from Their Homeland (London: Faber and Faber, 1987), at 23, 32.

9 Chaim Simons, *International Proposals to Transfer Arabs from Palestine 1895–1946: A Historical Survey* (Hoboken NJ: Ktav Publishing House, 1988), at 167–169. Nur Masalha, *Expulsion of the Palestinians: The Concept of "Transfer" in Zionist Political Thought 1882–1948* (Washington: Institute for Palestine Studies, 1992), at 130–141. Palumbo, *The Palestinian Catastrophe*, at 4.

10 Kenneth Stein, *The Land Question in Palestine, 1917–1939* (Chapel Hill, NC: University of North Carolina Press, 1984), at 91; David Gilmour, *The Dispossessed: The Ordeal of the Palestinians* (London: Sphere Books, 1980), at 40–41. Simha Flapan, *Zionism and the Palestinians* (London: Croom Helm, 1979), at 69, 246.

11 Joseph Weitz, A Solution to the Refugee Problem, *Davar*, September 29, 1967 (quoting his own statement from 1940), as cited in Uri Davis and Norton Mezvinsky (eds.), *Documents from Israel, 1967–1973: Readings for a Critique of Zionism* (London: Ithaca Press, 1975), at 21.

12 *Policy in Palestine: Despatch dated 23rd December, 1937, from the Secretary of State for Colonies to High Commissioner for Palestine*, Cmd. 5634, at 2. *Report: Palestine Partition Commission*, November 9, 1938, Cmd. 5854, at 52. Simons, *International Proposals to Transfer Arabs from Palestine 1895–1946*, at 180–181.

13 Meeting: E. Neumann and M.L. Perlzweig – K. Umanskii, Washington, July 17, 1941, in *Documents on Israeli-Soviet Relations 1941–1953: Part I: 1941-May 1949* (London: Frank Cass, 2000), at 5–7.

14 Meeting: D. Ben-Gurion – I.M. Maiskii, London, October 9, 1941, id. at 11–12.

15 Ch. Weizmann to I.M. Maiskii (London), Appendix: Memorandum on the USSR and Zionist Aims, March 2, 1942, id. 25, at 28.

16 Ch. Weizmann to I.M. Maiskii (London), March 2, 1942, id. at 25.

17 Norman Rose, *Chaim Weizmann: A Biography* (New York: Viking Penguin, 1986), at 374.

18 Ch. Weizmann to I.M. Maiskii (London), March 2, 1942, in *Documents on Israeli-Soviet Relations*, at 25 (altered per Russian original).

19 Meeting: M.M. Litvinov – Ch. Weizmann (Washington), May 6, 1942, id. at 29.

20 Excerpts from the Diary of Y. Ben-Zvi, id. 35, at 37.

21 Id. at 42.

22 Sasson Sofer, *Zionism and the Foundations of Israeli Diplomacy* (Cambridge: Cambridge University Press, 1998), at 127.

23 D. Ben Gurion's Report to the Meeting of the Jewish Agency Executive (Jerusalem, 4 October 1943): Meeting with Maiskii, in *Documents on Israeli-Soviet Relations*, at 70–72.

24 Schechtman, The U.S.S.R., Zionism, and Israel, at 114–115.

25 S.I. Kavtaradze to V.I. Molotov (Moscow), March 31, 1945, in *Documents on Israeli-Soviet Relations*, at 95, 96.

26 Memorandum of the Commission for Preparation of Peace Agreements and Postwar Settlement (M. Litvinov, Chairman): The Palestine Question, July 27, 1945, id., 100, at 105.

27 Iurii Strizhov, The Soviet Position on the Establishment of the State of Israel, in Yaakov Ro'i, *Jews and Jewish Life in Russia and the Soviet Union* (Ilford, Essex: Frank Cass, 1995), 303, at 304–305.
28 Memorandum by M.A. Maksimov: The Palestine Question, May 15, 1946, in *Documents on Israeli-Soviet Relations*, 126, at 128.
29 Raphael Patai, *Nahum Goldmann: His Missions to the Gentiles* (University AL: University of Alabama Press, 1987), at 92–93.

5 SAVING EUROPE'S JEWS – OUR WAY

1 *Proceedings of the Intergovernmental Committee*, Evian, July 6th to 15th, 1938, Verbatim Record of the Plenary Meetings of the Committee, Resolutions, and Reports (London, 1938), at 12. See also Barbara McDonald Stewart, *United States Government Policy on Refugees from Nazism, 1933–1940* (New York: Garland, 1982), 267. A.J. Sherman, *Island Refuge: Britain and Refugees from the Third Reich 1933–1939* (Berkeley: University of California Press, 1973), 112.
2 Sherman, *Island Refuge*, at 116.
3 *Proceedings of the Intergovernmental Committee*, Evian, July 6th to 15th, 1938, at 42.
4 More immigration is Zionist demand, *New York Times*, September 3, 1938, at 15 (quoting Weizmann's address to World Conference for Palestine, sponsored by the Palestine Foundation Fund).
5 Arie Bober (ed.), *The Other Israel: The Radical Case against Zionism* (Garden City, NY: Doubleday, 1972), at 171.
6 Richard Breitman, Barbara McDonald Stewart, and Severin Hochberg (eds.), *Refugees and Rescue: The Diaries and Papers of James G. McDonald 1935–1945* (Bloomington: Indiana University Press, 2009), at 176. John Judis, *Genesis: Truman, American Jews, and the Origins of the Arab-Israeli Conflict* (New York: Farrar, Straus and Giroux, 2014), at 173.
7 Aaron Berman, *Nazism, the Jews and American Zionism 1933–1948* (Detroit: Wayne State University Press, 1990) at 96.
8 Aaron Berman, Abba Hillel Silver, Zionism and the Rescue of the European Jews, in Paula Hyman (ed.), Center for Israel and Jewish Studies: *Working Papers*, II (New York: Columbia University, 1979), at 8.
9 Morris Ernst, *So Far So Good* (New York: Harper, 1948), at 170–177.
10 Moshe Menuhin, *The Decadence of Judaism in Our Time* (New York: Exposition Press, 1965), at 95–96.
11 Berman, *Nazism, the Jews and American Zionism 1933–1948*, at 131–132.
12 Report of the Executive of the Jewish Agency for Palestine, in *Reports of the Executives submitted to the Twenty-Second Zionist Congress at Basle, Kislev 5707/December 1946* (Jerusalem: Executives of the Zionist Organization and of the Jewish Agency for Palestine, 1946), at 75.
13 Political Resolutions Adopted by the World Zionist Conference held in London, August 1st to 13th, 1945: Political Declaration, para. 6, as Appendix A to *Political Report of the London Office of the Executive of the Jewish Agency submitted to the World Zionist Congress at Basle, December 1946* (London: Executive of the Jewish Agency for Palestine, 1946), at 78.

14 Report of Earl G. Harrison, *Department of State Bulletin*, vol. 13, 456, at 458 (September 30, 1945). Text also as: Earl Harrison, Report to the President of the United States, *New York Times*, September 30, 1945, at 38.
15 Truman statement on displaced persons, *New York Times*, December 23, 1945, at 9.
16 Maurice R. Davie, Refugee Aid, *American Jewish Year Book*, vol. 49, 212, at 213 (1947–1948).
17 Situation of Jews in Europe: Statement by the President, *Department of State Bulletin*, vol. 13, at 790 (November 18, 1945).
18 Judis, *Genesis*, at 209.
19 Yehoshua Freundlich (ed.), *Political Documents of the Jewish Agency*, vol. 1, May 1945-December 1946 (Jerusalem: Hassifriya Haziyonit, Publishing House of the World Zionist Organization, 1996), at 225.
20 Dean Acheson, The Acting Secretary of State to the Ambassador to the United Kingdom (Harriman), at Paris, August 15, 1946, *FRUS 1946*, vol. 7, 684, at 685.
21 Memorandum by the Acting Secretary of State to President Truman, September 12, 1946, *FRUS 1946*, vol. 7, at 693.
22 Memorandum by the Deputy Director of the Office of Near Eastern and African Affairs (Villard) to the Under Secretary of State for Economic Affairs (Clayton), September 27, 1946, *FRUS 1946*, vol. 7, at 699.
23 President Truman to the British Prime Minister (Attlee), October 3, 1946, *FRUS 1946*, vol. 7, at 701.
24 Dean Acheson, Memorandum of Conversation, by the Acting Secretary of State, November 22, 1946, *FRUS 1946*, vol. 7, at 723.
25 Memorandum by Mr. Fraser Wilkins of the Division of Near Eastern Affairs, December 27, 1946, *FRUS 1946*, vol. 7, at 735.

6 SMOKE AND MIRRORS AT THE YMCA

1 *House of Commons Debates (Hansard), February 25, 1947, vol. 433 c1901.*
2 *Question of Palestine: United Kingdom Delegation to the United Nations*, New York, April 3, 1947, UN Document A/286.
3 UN Charter, art. 18.
4 David Horowitz, *State in the Making* (New York: Alfred A. Knopf, 1953), at 143.
5 To Selig Brodetsky, London, February 19, 1947, in Barnet Litvinoff (ed.), *The Letters and Papers of Chaim Weizmann* (New Brunswick NJ: Transaction Books, 1979), vol.22: Series A May 1945-July 1947, 245, at 246.
6 Clayton Knowles, U.S. would allow Zionists U.N. voice: Flushing Delegation Shifts Its View After Protests to Washington by Groups, *New York Times*, May 2, 1947, at 1.
7 UN General Assembly, 1st special session, Resolution 104, May 5, 1947.
8 Memorandum by the Middle East Department of the USSR Ministry of Foreign Affairs, April 15, 1947, in *Documents on Israeli-Soviet Relations 1941–1953: Part I: 1941-May 1949* (London: Frank Cass, 2000), at 176–180. Translation varies slightly from the cited source to conform more closely to the Russian original.

9 UN General Assembly, 1st special session, *Plenary Meetings Verbatim Record 28 April – 15 May 1947*, 77th meeting, May 14, 1947, at 134, UN Document A/PV.77.

10 Thomas Hamilton, Russia urges U.N. to split Palestine failing dual state, *New York Times*, May 15, 1947, at 1; Clifton Daniel, Palestine excited over Soviet stand: pure Zionism says one Jew of Gromyko speech, Arabs conceal disappointment, *New York Times*, May 16, 1947, at 3.

11 Horowitz, *State in the Making*, at 157.

12 Gabriel Sheffer, *Moshe Sharett: Biography of a Political Moderate* (Oxford: Clarendon Press, 1996), at 232.

13 Id. at 111.

14 Arnold Krammer, *The Forgotten Friendship: Israel and the Soviet Bloc, 1947–53* (Urbana IL: University of Illinois Press, 1974), at 34.

15 UN General Assembly, Resolution 106 (S-1), May 15, 1947.

16 UN General Assembly, 2nd session, Supplement No. 11, United Nations Special Committee on Palestine, *Report to the General Assembly*, September 3, 1947, vol. 2, Annexes, Appendix and Maps, at 5, UN Document A/364, Add.1.

17 Elad Ben-Dror, The Arab Struggle against Partition: The International Arena of Summer 1947, *Middle Eastern Studies*, vol. 43, issue 2, 259 at 268 (2007).

18 Sheffer, *Moshe Sharett*, at 234.

19 Id. at 232.

20 Letters of June 29 and July 15, 1947, in Brian Urquhart, *Ralph Bunche: An American Life* (New York: W.W. Norton, 1993), at 140.

21 Ben-Dror, The Arab Struggle against Partition, at 286.

22 Ilan Pappé, *A History of Modern Palestine* (Cambridge: Cambridge University Press, 2006), at 122.

23 Ronen Bergman, A state is born in Palestine, *New York Times*, October 7, 2011.

24 UN General Assembly, 2nd session, Supplement No. 11, United Nations Special Committee on Palestine, *Report to the General Assembly*, September 3, 1947, vol. 3, Annex A: Oral Evidence presented at public meetings, June 17, 1947, at 22–23, UN Document A/364, Add.2.

25 Id. at 62.

26 Id. at 1.

27 Hugh Trevor-Roper, Jewish and Other Nationalisms, *Commentary*, January 1963, at 16–17.

28 UN General Assembly, 2nd session, Supplement No. 11, United Nations Special Committee on Palestine, *Report to the General Assembly*, September 3, 1947, vol. 3, Annex A: Oral Evidence presented at public meetings, June 17, 1947, at 1, UN Document A/364, Add.2.

29 Trevor-Roper, Jewish and Other Nationalisms, at 16–17.

30 The Line of Least Injustice, Jerusalem, March 8, 1946, Testimony to Anglo-American Committee, in Barnet Litvinoff (ed.), *The Letters and Papers of Chaim Weizmann* (New Brunswick NJ: Transaction Books, 1984), vol. 2: Series B December 1931 – April 1952, 576, at 577. Also published as *The Jewish Case Before the Anglo-American Committee of Inquiry on Palestine as presented by the Jewish Agency for Palestine: Statements & Memoranda* (Jerusalem: Jewish Agency for Palestine, 1947), at 4.

31 Gur Alroey, *An Unpromising Land: Jewish Migration to Palestine in the Early Twentieth Century* (Stanford: Stanford University Press, 2014), at 110.
32 Mark Wischnitzer, *To Dwell in Safety: The Story of Jewish Migration since 1800* (Philadelphia: Jewish Publication Society of America, 1948), at 289.
33 Ben Halpern, *The Idea of the Jewish State*, (Cambridge MA: Harvard University Press, 1969), 120. Alroey, *An Unpromising Land*, at 110.
34 Jacob Metzer, *The Divided Economy of Mandatory Palestine* (Cambridge: Cambridge University Press, 1998), at 60.
35 Alroey, *An Unpromising Land*, at 223–224.
36 Id. at 230.
37 Id. at 17.
38 UN General Assembly, 2nd session, Supplement No. 11, United Nations Special Committee on Palestine, *Report to the General Assembly*, September 3, 1947, vol. 3, Annex A: Oral Evidence presented at public meetings, June 17, 1947, at 1, UN Document A/364, Add.2.
39 Sheffer, *Moshe Sharett*, at 235.
40 Kenneth Stein, *The Land Question in Palestine, 1917–1939* (Chapel Hill NC: University of North Carolina Press, 1984), at 77.
41 Walter Lehn and Uri Davis, *The Jewish National Fund* (London: Routledge, 1988), at 59.
42 *Report on Immigration, Land Settlement and Development* (Hope Simpson Commission), October 1930, Cmd. 3686, at 54.
43 Anglo-American Committee of Inquiry, *Report to the United States Government and His Majesty's Government in the United Kingdom*, Lausanne, April 20, 1946, Cmd. 6808, at 39 (para. 3).
44 Arnold Toynbee, The Present Situation in Palestine, *International Affairs: Journal of the Royal Institute of International Affairs*, vol. 10, no. 1, 38, at 53 (January 1931).
45 UN General Assembly, 2nd session, Supplement No. 11, United Nations Special Committee on Palestine, *Report to the General Assembly*, September 3, 1947, vol. 3, Annex A: Oral Evidence presented at public meetings, June 17, 1947, at 5, UN Document A/364, Add.2.
46 Jorge García-Granados, *The Birth of Israel: The Drama as I Saw It* (New York: Alfred A. Knopf, 1948), at 48.
47 UN General Assembly, 2nd session, Supplement No. 11, United Nations Special Committee on Palestine, *Report to the General Assembly*, September 3, 1947, vol. 3, Annex A: Oral Evidence presented at public meetings, June 17, 1947, at 6, UN Document A/364, Add.2.
48 Metzer, *The Divided Economy of Mandatory Palestine*, at 185–186.
49 Id. at 108.
50 UN General Assembly, 2nd session, Supplement No. 11, United Nations Special Committee on Palestine, *Report to the General Assembly*, September 3, 1947, vol. 3, Annex A: Oral Evidence presented at public meetings, June 17, 1947, at 10, UN Document A/364, Add.2.
51 Id. at 11. Report of the Palestine Royal Commission (Peel Commission), July 1937, Cmd. 5479, at 380.

52 *Palestine: Statement of Policy* (White Paper on Palestine), May 1939, Cmd. 6019, para. 4.

53 UN General Assembly, 2nd session, Supplement No. 11, United Nations Special Committee on Palestine, *Report to the General Assembly*, September 3, 1947, vol. 3, Annex A: Oral Evidence presented at public meetings, at 13, UN Document A/364, Add.2.

54 League of Nations, Permanent Mandates Commission, *Minutes of the Thirty-Sixth Session Held at Geneva from June 8th to 29th*, 1939, 273, at 275 (para. 11): Annex 14: *Report to the Council on the Work of the Thirty-Sixth Session of the Permanent Mandates Commission*, League of Nations Document No. C.170 M.100, 1939, VI.

55 League of Nations, Permanent Mandates Commission, *Minutes of the Thirty-Sixth Session Held at Geneva from June 8th to 29th*, 1939, Twenty-Second Meeting, June 21, 1939, at 3.30 p.m., at 196–205; and Twenty-Third Meeting, June 22, 1939, at 3.30 p.m., at 205–208, League of Nations Document No. C.170 M.100, 1939, VI.

56 League of Nations, Permanent Mandates Commission, *Minutes of the Thirty-Sixth Session Held at Geneva from June 8th to 29th*, 1939, 273, at 275 (paras. 13–15): Annex 14: *Report to the Council on the Work of the Thirty-Sixth Session of the Permanent Mandates Commission*, League of Nations Document No. C.170 M.100, 1939, VI.

57 UN General Assembly, 2nd session, Supplement No. 11, United Nations Special Committee on Palestine, *Report to the General Assembly*, September 3, 1947, vol. 1, at 23, UN Document A/364.

58 UN General Assembly, 2nd session, Supplement No. 11, United Nations Special Committee on Palestine, *Report to the General Assembly*, September 3, 1947, vol. 3, Annex A: Oral Evidence presented at public meetings, July 8, 1947, at 89, UN Document A/364, Add.2.

59 Martin Gilbert, *In Ishmael's House: A History of Jews in Muslim Lands* (New Haven: Yale University Press, 2010), at 59.

60 UN General Assembly, 2nd session, Supplement No. 11, United Nations Special Committee on Palestine, *Report to the General Assembly*, vol. 3, Annex A: Oral Evidence presented at public meetings, July 8, 1947, at 89, UN Document A/364, Add.2.

61 Id. at 89.

62 Ilan Halevi, *A History of the Jews: Ancient and Modern* (London: Zed Press, 1987), at 31. Sabatino Moscati, *The Semites in Ancient History* (Cardiff: University of Wales Press, 1959), at 80–85.

63 UN General Assembly, 2nd session, Supplement No. 11, United Nations Special Committee on Palestine, *Report to the General Assembly*, vol. 3, Annex A: Oral Evidence presented at public meetings, July 7, 1947, at 48, UN Document A/364, Add.2.

64 Benny Morris, *The Birth of the Palestinian Refugee Problem, 1947–1949* (Cambridge: Cambridge University Press, 1989), at 27–28.

65 Id. at 27.

66 UN General Assembly, 2nd session, Supplement No. 11, United Nations Special Committee on Palestine, *Report to the General Assembly*, vol. 3, Annex A: Oral

Evidence presented at public meetings, July 8, 1947, at 82, UN Document A/364, Add.2.

67 Eliahu Elath, *Israel and Elath: The Political Struggle for the Inclusion of Elath in the Jewish State* (London: Weidenfeld and Nicolson, 1966), at 5.

7 THE SHIP THAT LAUNCHED A NATION

1 UN General Assembly, 2nd session, Supplement No. 11, United Nations Special Committee on Palestine, *Report to the General Assembly*, September 3, 1947, vol. 1, at 4, UN Document A/364.

2 Abba Eban, *Abba Eban: An Autobiography* (New York: Random House, 1977), at 78.

3 Robert St. John, *Eban* (Garden City NY: Doubleday, 1972), at 167.

4 Brian Urquhart, *Ralph Bunche: An American Life* (New York: W.W. Norton, 1993), at 144–145.

5 Thomas Kolsky, *Jews Against Zionism: The American Council for Judaism, 1942–1948* (Philadelphia: Temple University Press, 2010), at 165.

6 Ada Sereni, *I clandestini del mare: L'emigrazione ebraica in terra d'Israele dal 1945 al 1948* (Milan: U. Mursia, 1973), at 172.

7 Ruth Gruber, *Exodus 1947: The Ship that Launched a Nation* (New York: Random House, 1999), at 73–74. Idith Zertal, *From Catastrophe to Power: Holocaust Survivors and the Emergence of Israel* (Berkeley: University of California Press, 1998), at 68.

8 Zertal, *From Catastrophe to Power*, at 60, 67, 71.

9 Id. at 54, 56.

10 David Hirst, *The Gun and the Olive Branch: The Roots of Violence in the Middle East* (London: Faber and Faber, 1977), at 115.

11 Zertal, *From Catastrophe to Power*, at 74.

12 Id. at 56.

13 John Grauel, *Grauel: Reverend John Stanley Grauel: An Autobiography as Told to Eleanor Elfenbein* (Freehold NJ: Ivory House, 1983), at 44.

14 Id. at 84.

15 Benny Morris, *Righteous Victims: A History of the Zionist-Arab Conflict, 1881–1999* (New York: Alfred A. Knopf, 1999), at 183.

16 Michael J. Cohen, *Palestine and the Great Powers 1945–1948* (Princeton: Princeton University Press, 1982) at 254.

17 Zertal, *From Catastrophe to Power*, at 83.

18 Abba Eban, *Abba Eban: An Autobiography* (New York: Random House, 1977), at 79.

19 United Nations Special Committee on Palestine, Summary Record of the Thirty-Seventh Meeting (Private), Held at the Y.M.C.A. Building, Jerusalem, Saturday, July 19, 1947, at 12.30 p.m., at 1, UN Document A/AC.13/SR.37. This document was not included in the UNSCOP Report but is referenced in UN General Assembly, 2nd session, Supplement No. 11, United Nations Special Committee on Palestine, *Report to the General Assembly*, September 3, 1947, vol. 1, at 28, UN Document A/364.

20 UN Document A/AC.13.SR.37, at 1–2.

21 Jorge García-Granados, *The Birth of Israel: The Drama as I Saw It* (New York: Alfred A. Knopf, 1948), at 172–173.
22 Gruber, *Exodus 1947*, at 92.
23 Eban, *Abba Eban*, at 79.
24 Grauel, *Grauel*, at x, and at 95.
25 García-Granados, *The Birth of Israel*, at 173–182. Grauel, *Grauel*, at 97–98.
26 Zertal, *From Catastrophe to Power*, at 244.
27 Elad Ben-Dror, the Arab Struggle against Partition: The International Arena of Summer 1947, *Middle Eastern Studies*, vol. 43, issue 2, 259 at 272 (2007).
28 Eban, *Abba Eban*, at 80.
29 García-Granados, *The Birth of Israel*, at 4.
30 John Judis, *Genesis: Truman, American Jews, and the Origins of the Arab-Israeli Conflict* (New York: Farrar, Straus and Giroux, 2014), at 260.
31 Grauel, *Grauel*, at 97–98.
32 Rev. J. S. Grauel, 68, A supporter of Israel, *New York Times*, September 10, 1986.
33 Zertal, *From Catastrophe to Power*, at 251.
34 Bartley Crum, Introduction, in Gruber, *Exodus 1947*, at xvii.
35 Teddy Kollek, Introduction, at x, in Grauel, *Grauel.*
36 Leon Uris, *Exodus* (Garden City, NY: Doubleday, 1958).
37 Lazaron asks toleration, *Baltimore Sun*, September 15, 1947, at 8.
38 UN General Assembly, 2nd session, Supplement No. 11, United Nations Special Committee on Palestine, *Report to the General Assembly*, September 3, 1947, vol. 3, Annex A: Oral Evidence presented at public meetings, July 22, 1947, at 240–245, UN Document A/364, Add.2. UN General Assembly, 2nd session, Supplement No. 11, United Nations Special Committee on Palestine, *Report to the General Assembly*, September 3, 1947, vol. 4, Annex B: Oral Evidence presented at private meetings, July 23, 1947, at 32–56, UN Document A/364, Add.3.
39 García-Granados, *The Birth of Israel*, at 93.
40 Eban, *Abba Eban*, at 79.
41 Sheffer, *Moshe Sharett*, at 237–238.
42 UN General Assembly, 2nd session, Supplement No. 11, United Nations Special Committee on Palestine, *Report to the General Assembly*, September 3, 1947, vol. 1, at 7–8, UN Document A/364.
43 Jacob Robinson, *Palestine and the United Nations* (Washington, DC: Public Affairs Press, 1947), at 171–175.
44 UN General Assembly, Resolution 106 (S-1), May 15, 1947.
45 Aviva Halamish, *The Exodus Affair: Holocaust Survivors and the Struggle for Palestine* (Syracuse NY: Syracuse University Press, 1998), at 12–13.
46 UN General Assembly, 2nd session, Supplement No. 11, United Nations Special Committee on Palestine, *Report to the General Assembly*, September 3, 1947, vol. 2, at 14: Annex 18, Report of Sub-Committee 3 on its visit to certain assembly centres for Jewish refugees and displaced persons in Germany and Austria, UN Document A/364, Add.1.
47 Halamish, *The Exodus Affair*, at 12.
48 Zertal, *From Catastrophe to Power*, at 218.

49 Id. at 227.
50 Id. at 231–232.
51 Anglo-American Committee of Inquiry, *Report to the United States Government and His Majesty's Government in the United Kingdom*, Lausanne, Switzerland, April 20, 1946, Cmd. 6808, Chapter I, Recommendations and Comments: The European Problem, Recommendation No. 2. And see Appendix II: European Jewry: Position in Various Countries.
52 UN General Assembly, 2nd session, Supplement No. 11, United Nations Special Committee on Palestine, *Report to the General Assembly*, September 3, 1947, vol. 2, at 14: Annex 18, Report of Sub-Committee 3 on its visit to certain assembly centres for Jewish refugees and displaced persons in Germany and Austria, UN Document A/364, Add.1.
53 UN General Assembly, 2nd session, Supplement No. 11, United Nations Special Committee on Palestine, *Report to the General Assembly*, September 3, 1947, vol. 1, at 13–16, UN Document A/364.
54 Urquhart, *Ralph Bunche*, at 148–149.
55 UN General Assembly, 2nd session, Supplement No. 11, United Nations Special Committee on Palestine, *Report to the General Assembly*, September 3, 1947, vol. 1, at 47, 59, UN Document A/364.
56 Judis, *Genesis*, at 262–263.
57 García-Granados, *The Birth of Israel*, at 84–89.
58 Sheffer, *Moshe Sharett*, at 238.
59 UN General Assembly, 2nd session, Supplement No. 11, United Nations Special Committee on Palestine, *Report to the General Assembly*, September 3, 1947, vol. 1, at 54, UN Document A/364.

8 COCKTAILS AT THE CONSULATE

1 Palestine report held Agency gain, *New York Times*, September 4, 1947, at 8.
2 The Arab Higher Committee to the Consul General at Jerusalem (Macatee), October 3, 1947, *FRUS 1947*, vol. 5, at 1170.
3 Clifton Daniel, Palestine is quiet in strike by Arabs, *New York Times*, October 4, 1947, at 5.
4 Palestine report held Agency gain, *New York Times*, September 4, 1947, at 8.
5 UN General Assembly, 2nd session, *Plenary Meetings 16 September – 29 November 1947*, vol. 1, 90th meeting, September 23, 1947, at 275, UN Document A/PV.90.
6 UN General Assembly, 2nd session, Ad Hoc Committee on the Palestinian Question, *Summary Records of Meetings 25 September – 25 November 1947*, 1st meeting, September 25, 1947, at 1, UN Document A/AC.14/SR.1
7 UN General Assembly, 2nd session, Ad Hoc Committee on the Palestinian Question, *Summary Records of Meetings 25 September – 25 November 1947*, 10th meeting, October 10, 1947, at 57, UN Document A/AC.14/SR.10.
8 Id. at 56.
9 Id. at 58.
10 UN General Assembly, 2nd session, Ad Hoc Committee on the Palestinian Question, *Summary Records of Meetings 25 September – 25 November*

1947, 11th meeting, October 11, 1947, at 61–62, UN Document A/AC.14/SR.11.

11 Id. at 65–66.

12 Excerpts From the Minutes of the Sixth Meeting of the United States Delegation to the Second Session of the General Assembly, New York, September 15, 1947, at 10 a.m., *FRUS 1947*, vol. 5, 1147, at 1149–1150.

13 Memorandum Prepared in the Department of State: United States Position With Respect to the Question of Palestine, Washington, September 30, 1947, *FRUS 1947*, vol. 5, 1166, at 1169.

14 Id. at 1167.

15 UN General Assembly, 2nd session, Ad Hoc Committee on the Palestinian Question, *Summary Records of Meetings 25 September – 25 November* 1947, 11th meeting, October 11, 1947, at 63, UN Document A/AC.14/SR.11.

16 UN General Assembly, 2nd session, Ad Hoc Committee on the Palestinian Question, *Summary Records of Meetings 25 September – 25 November 1947*, 13th meeting, October 14, 1947, at 78, UN Document A/AC.14/SR.13.

17 Id. at 83–84.

18 UN General Assembly, 2nd session, Ad Hoc Committee on the Palestinian Question, *Summary Records of Meetings 25 September – 25 November 1947*, 15th meeting, October 16, 1947, at 95, UN Document A/AC.14/SR.15.

19 Id. at 95.

20 Id. at 96.

21 Id. at 100.

22 Shabtai Teveth, *Ben-Gurion and the Palestinian Arabs: From Peace to War* (Oxford: Oxford University Press, 1985), at 187–188.

23 UN General Assembly, 2nd session, Ad Hoc Committee on the Palestinian Question, *Summary Records of Meetings 25 September – 25 November* 1947, 17th meeting, October 17, 1947, at 115, UN Document A/AC.14/SR.17.

24 UN General Assembly, 2nd session, Ad Hoc Committee on the Palestinian Question, *Summary Records of Meetings 25 September – 25 November* 1947, 18th meeting, October 18, 1947, at 123, UN Document A/AC.14/SR.18.

25 Id. at 125.

26 Ilan Pappé, *The Ethnic Cleansing of Palestine* (Oxford: Oneworld, 2006), at 49.

27 UN General Assembly, 2nd session, Ad Hoc Committee on the Palestinian Question, *Summary Records of Meetings 25 September – 25 November* 1947, 25th meeting, November 20, 1947, at 153, UN Document A/AC.14/SR.25.

28 Memorandum Prepared in the Department of State: United States Position With Respect to the Question of Palestine, September 30, 1947, *FRUS 1947*, vol. 5, 1166, at 1167.

29 UN General Assembly, 2nd session, Ad Hoc Committee on the Palestinian Question, *Summary Records of Meetings 25 September – 25 November 1947*, 33rd meeting, November 25, 1947 at 215–216, UN Document A/AC.14/SR.33.

30 UN General Assembly, 2nd session, Ad Hoc Committee on the Palestinian Question, *Summary Records of Meetings 25 September – 25 November 1947*, 27th meeting, November 22, 1947, at 165, UN Document A/AC.14/SR.27.

31 UN General Assembly, 2nd session, Ad Hoc Committee on the Palestinian Question, *Summary Records of Meetings 25 September – 25 November 1947*, 29th meeting, November 22, 1947, at 180, UN Document A/AC.14/SR.29.
32 Memorandum Prepared in the Department of State: United States Position With Respect to the Question of Palestine, September 30, 1947, *FRUS 1947*, vol. 5, 1166, at 1169.
33 UN General Assembly, 2nd session, Ad Hoc Committee on the Palestinian Question, *Summary Records of Meetings 25 September – 25 November* 1947, 12th meeting, October 13, 1947, at 70, UN Document A/AC.14/SR.12.
34 UN General Assembly, 2nd session, Ad Hoc Committee on the Palestinian Question, *Summary Records of Meetings 25 September – 25 November 1947*, 30th meeting, November 24, 1947, at 184–185, UN Document A/AC.14/SR.30.
35 Yaakov Ro'i, *Soviet Decision Making in Practice: The USSR and Israel 1947–1954* (New Brunswick NJ: Transaction Books, 1980), at 86–88. David Horowitz, *State in the Making* (New York: Alfred A. Knopf, 1953), at 270–272.
36 Horowitz, *State in the Making*, at 266.
37 UN General Assembly, 2nd session, Ad Hoc Committee on the Palestinian Question, *Summary Records of Meetings 25 September – 25 November 1947*, 28th meeting, November 22, 1947, at 173, UN Document A/AC.14/SR.28.
38 UN General Assembly, 2nd session, Ad Hoc Committee on the Palestinian Question, *Summary Records of Meetings 25 September – 25 November 1947*, 31st meeting, November 24, 1947, at 199, UN Document A/AC.14/SR.31.
39 UN General Assembly, 2nd session, Ad Hoc Committee on the Palestinian Question, *Summary Records of Meetings 25 September – 25 November 1947*, 34th meeting, November 25, 1947, at 222–223, UN Document A/AC.14/SR.34.
40 UN General Assembly, 2nd session, *Plenary Meetings Verbatim Record 16 September – 29 November 1947 Vol. 2 110th – 128th Meetings 13 November – 29 November 1947*, 128th meeting, November 29, 1947, at 1424–1425, UN Document A/PV.128.
41 *Future Government of Palestine*, UN General Assembly, Resolution 181, November 29, 1947, Annex: Plan of Partition with Economic Union.
42 David H. Oden, *Israel's Foreign Policy in the United Nations 1948–1967: Security Aspects*, Ph.D. dissertation, University of Pennsylvania (1970) (microfilm), at 1.
43 Gabriel Sheffer, *Moshe Sharett: Biography of a Political Moderate* (Oxford: Clarendon Press, 1996), at 268.
44 Review and Appraisal of Israeli-Arab Relations (1951), in Charles Henry (ed.), *Ralph Bunche: Selected Speeches and Writings* (Ann Arbor: University of Michigan Press, 1995), at 179.
45 Horowitz, *State in the Making*, at 272.
46 The Ambassador in the Soviet Union (Smith) to the Secretary of State, November 14, 1947, *FRUS 1947*, vol. 5, at 1263–1264.

9 CAUSING CHAOS

1 Sam Pope Brewer, Palestine's Arabs kill seven Jews, call 3-day strike, *New York Times*, December 1, 1947, at 1. Sam Pope Brewer, Jerusalem torn by rioting; Arabs use knives, set fires; Jews reply, Haganah in open, *New York Times*,

December 3, 1947, at 1. Sam Pope Brewer, Palestine strife widens, grips Jaffa-Tel Aviv area; Arabs rebuff peace plan, *New York Times*, December 4, 1947, at 1. Sam Pope Brewer, Arabs make roads new battlefields; rake bus convoys, *New York Times*, December 5, 1947, at 1.

2 Ilan Pappé, *The Ethnic Cleansing of Palestine* (Oxford: Oneworld, 2006), at 55.

3 Sam Pope Brewer, Jews carry fight to Arabs, Palestine adds 28 to dead, *New York Times*, December 13, 1947, at 1.

4 Sam Pope Brewer, Irgun attacks in Palestine; 21 Arabs, 3 Jews are slain, *New York Times*, December 14, 1947, at 1.

5 UN General Assembly, 3rd session, Palestine Commission, 15th meeting January 21, 1948, UN Document A/AC.21/SR.15. Also quoted in David Horowitz, *State in the Making* (New York: Alfred A. Knopf, 1953), at 326.

6 UN General Assembly, 3rd session, Palestine Commission, 16th meeting, January 21, 1948, UN Document A/AC.21/SR.16. Also quoted in Horowitz, *State in the Making*, at 326.

7 Netanel Lorch, *The Edge of the Sword: Israel's War of Independence, 1947–1949* (Jerusalem: Massada Press, 1968), at 48. Michael Palumbo, *The Palestinian Catastrophe: The 1948 Expulsion of a People from Their Homeland* (London: Faber and Faber, 1987), at 35.

8 Sam Pope Brewer, Arab Legion force kills 14 Jews in convoy, *New York Times*, December 15, 1947, at 1.

9 Menachem Begin, *The Revolt* (New York: Henry Schuman, 1951), at 337–338.

10 Sam Pope Brewer, Arabs make roads new battlefields; rake bus convoys, *New York Times*, December 5, 1947, at 1.

11 Shooting in Jerusalem, *Times* (London), December 22, 1947, at 4.

12 Sam Pope Brewer, Irgun shoots down 2 British soldiers, Arabs get warning, *New York Times*, December 22, 1947, at 1. Benny Morris, *The Birth of the Palestinian Refugee Problem Revisited* (Cambridge: Cambridge University Press, 2004), at 79.

13 Sam Pope Brewer, Haganah kills 10 in raid on Arabs, *New York Times*, December 20, 1947, at 8. Jon and David Kimche, *Both Sides of the Hill: Britain and the Palestine War* (London: Secker and Warburg, 1960), at 83.

14 Sam Pope Brewer, Haganah attacks a 2d Arab village, *New York Times*, December 21, 1947, at 1.

15 Sam Pope Brewer, Irgun shoots down 2 British soldiers, Arabs get warning, *New York Times*, December 22, 1947, at 1.

16 Benny Morris, *The Birth of the Palestinian Refugee Problem, 1947–1949* (New York: Cambridge University Press, 1989), at 34.

17 Pappé, *The Ethnic Cleansing of Palestine*, at 61–64.

18 Morris, *The Birth of the Palestinian Refugee Problem Revisited*, at 66.

19 Sam Pope Brewer, Palestine blasts rip Arab offices, kill at least 34, *New York Times*, January 5, 1948, at 1. 14 more Arabs die in Haganah blasts; Zionist militia dynamites 3 houses around Safad, says it blew up Jerusalem hotel, *New York Times*, January 6, 1948, at 6.

20 Palumbo, *The Palestinian Catastrophe*, at 83–84. Morris, *The Birth of the Palestinian Refugee Problem, 1947–1949*, at 46. Lorch, *The Edge of the Sword*, at 50–51.

21 Morris, *The Birth of the Palestinian Refugee Problem, 1947–1949*, at 50. Sam Pope Brewer, British condemn Haganah 'murders', *New York Times*, January 7, 1948, at 1.
22 Morris, *The Birth of the Palestinian Refugee Problem, 1947–1949*, at 50–52.
23 Id. at 50.
24 Id. at 52. Morris, *The Birth of the Palestinian Refugee Problem Revisited*, at 69–70.
25 The Consul General at Jerusalem (Macatee) to the Secretary of State, February 9, 1948, *FRUS 1948*, vol. 5, 607, at 608.
26 Morris, *The Birth of the Palestinian Refugee Problem, 1947–1949*, at 52.
27 Pappé, *The Ethnic Cleansing of Palestine*, at 78.
28 Report by the Central Intelligence Agency: Secret: Possible Developments in Palestine, February 28, 1948, *FRUS 1948*, vol. 5, 666, at 672.
29 Morris, *The Birth of the Palestinian Refugee Problem, 1947–1949*, at 63.
30 Pappé, *The Ethnic Cleansing of Palestine*, at 86–126.
31 UN Security Council, 3rd year, 253rd meeting, February 24, 1948, at 258–259, UN Document S/PV.253.
32 UN Security Council, 3rd year, 271st meeting, March 19, 1948, at 31, UN Document S/PV.271. See also The Acting Secretary of State to Certain Diplomatic and Consular Offices, April 6, 1948, *FRUS 1948*, vol. 5, at 801.
33 James Gelvin, *The Israel-Palestine Conflict: One Hundred Years of War* (Cambridge: Cambridge University Press, 2007), at 124–125.
34 UN Security Council, 3rd year, 275th meeting, March 30, 1948, at 248–252, UN Document S/PV.275.
35 UN Security Council, Resolution 44, April 1, 1948.
36 Pappé, *The Ethnic Cleansing of Palestine*, at 88.
37 Morris, *The Birth of the Palestinian Refugee Problem, 1947–1949*, at 41, 52, 59.
38 David Ben Gurion, *Rebirth and Destiny of Israel* (New York: Philosophical Library, 1954), at 237.
39 Dana Adams Schmidt, 200 Arabs killed, stronghold taken, *New York Times*, April 10, 1948, at 6. Harry Levin, *I Saw the Battle of Jerusalem* (New York: Schocken Books, 1950), at 57.
40 I.Z.L.-Stern units take village, *Palestine Post*, April 11, 1948, at 1.
41 Levin, *I Saw the Battle of Jerusalem*, at 57. Palumbo, *The Palestinian Catastrophe*, at 52. Morris, *The Birth of the Palestinian Refugee Problem Revisited*, at 238.
42 Tom Segev, *1949: The First Israelis* (New York: Free Press, 1986), at 25.
43 *Seventeenth International Red Cross Conference: Report* (Stockholm: ICRC, 1948), at 15. Dominique-D. Junod, *The Imperiled Red Cross and the Palestine-Eretz-Yisrael Conflict 1945–1952: The Influence of Institutional Concerns on a Humanitarian Operation* (London: Kegan Paul International, 1996), at 69, 128.
44 Jacques de Reynier, *1948 à Jérusalem* (Neuchatel, Editions de la Baconnière, 1969), at 74. Junod, *The Imperiled Red Cross and the Palestine-Eretz-Yisrael Conflict 1945–1952*, at 131.

45 Agency berates massacre, *Palestine Post*, April 12, 1948, at 1.
46 Avi Shlaim, *The Politics of Partition: King Abdullah, the Zionists and Palestine 1921–1951* (New York: Columbia University Press, 1990), at 136. Robert St. John, *Ben-Gurion: A Biography* (Garden City, NY: Doubleday, 1971), at 133.
47 Leo Heiman, All's Fair…, *Marine Corps Gazette*, June 1964, 37, at 39.
48 *Rosemarie Esber, Under the Cover of War: The Zionist expulsion of the Palestinians* (Alexandria, VA: Arabicus Books, 2008), at 213–214. Palumbo, *The Palestinian Catastrophe*, at 107.
49 Arab exodus from Tiberias, *Palestine Post*, April 19, 1948, at 1.
50 UN Security Council, Resolution 46, April 17, 1948.
51 UN General Assembly, 2nd special session, First Committee, vol. 2, *Main Committees, Summary Records of Meetings 16 April – 14 May 1948*, 118th meeting, April 20, 1948, at 7–8, UN Document A/C.1/SR.118.
52 UN General Assembly, Draft Trusteeship Agreement for Palestine: Working Paper Circulated by the United States Delegation, art. 2, April 20, 1948, UN Document A/C.1/277.
53 Id., art. 47(1).
54 UN General Assembly, 2nd special session, First Committee, vol. 2, *Main Committees, Summary Records of Meetings 16 April – 14 May 1948*, 118th meeting, April 20, 1948, at 7, UN Document A/C.1/SR.118.
55 IDF, Intelligence Branch, The Emigration of the Arabs of Palestine in the Period 1/12/1947-1/6/1948, June 30, 1948, in Benny Morris, The Causes and Character of the Arab Exodus from Palestine: the Israel Defence Forces Intelligence Branch Analysis of June 1948, *Middle Eastern Studies*, vol. 22, 5, at 6 (1986).
56 Haifa's pivotal points fall to Haganah after 30-hour battle, *Palestine Post*, Apr. 23, 1948, at 1.
57 Lynne Reid Banks, *Torn Country: An Oral History of the Israeli War of Independence* (New York: Franklin Watts, 1982), at 116.
58 UN Security Council, 3rd year, 287th meeting, April 23, 1948, at 26, UN Document S/PV.287.
59 Esber, *Under the Cover of War*, at 249–252.
60 UN General Assembly, 2nd special session, First Committee, vol. 2, *Main Committees, Summary Records of Meetings 16 April – 14 May 1948*, 123rd meeting, April 23, 1948, at 71–72, UN Document A/C.1/SR.123.
61 UN General Assembly, 2nd special session, First Committee, vol. 2, *Main Committees Summary Records of Meetings 16 April – 14 May 1948*, 126th meeting, April 26, 1948, at 97, UN Document A/C.1/SR.126.
62 UN General Assembly, 2nd special session, First Committee, vol. 2, *Main Committees Summary Records of Meetings 16 April – 14 May 1948*, 127th meeting, April 27, 1948, at 108, UN Document A/C.1/SR.127.
63 Id. at 111.
64 John Mearsheimer, *Why Leaders Lie: The Truth about Lying in International Politics* (Oxford: Oxford University Press, 2010), at 74.
65 Morris, *The Birth of the Palestinian Refugee Problem Revisited*, at 212.

66 Gene Currivan, Jews split Jaffa, reach sea; RAF planes strafe Zionists; Irgunists press assault on port as Haganah captures 2 villages to isolate defense – Spitfires strafe at near-by colony, *New York Times*, April 29, 1948, at 1. Palumbo, *The Palestinian Catastrophe*, at 93.
67 Morris, *The Birth of the Palestinian Refugee Problem Revisited*, at 213.
68 Flight psychosis among Arabs, *Palestine Post*, May 4, 1948, at 1.
69 Pappé, *The Ethnic Cleansing of Palestine*, at 103.
70 Jaffa capitulates; an open city, *Palestine Post*, May 11, 1948, at 1.
71 Begin, *The Revolt*, at 363.
72 Mr. John C. Ross to the Secretary of State, May 6, 1948, *FRUS 1948*, vol. 5, 917, at 918.
73 Morris, *The Birth of the Palestinian Refugee Problem, 1947–1949*, at 96–97.
74 UN General Assembly, 2nd special session, First Committee, vol. 2, *Main Committees Summary Records of Meetings 16 April – 14 May 1948*, 134th meeting, May 1, 1948, at 197, UN Document A/C.1/SR.134.
75 Arabs flee Safad, *Palestine Post*, May 3, 1948, at 1. Haganah wrests Safad from Iraqis and Syrians in bitter fighting, *Palestine Post*, May 11, 1948, at 1. Palumbo, *The Palestinian Catastrophe*, at 113. Morris, *The Birth of the Palestinian Refugee Problem, 1947–1949*, at 107–108.
76 Uri Avnery, *My Friend, the Enemy* (Westport, CT: Lawrence Hill, 1986), at 264.
77 Morris, *The Birth of the Palestinian Refugee Problem, 1947–1949*, at 116.
78 Ben Gurion on third phase in Arab war: first session of National Council, *Palestine Post*, May 6, 1948, at 1.
79 Jerusalem 'cease fire' exacted by British from foreign Arab chieftains, *Palestine Post*, May 9, 1948, at 1.
80 Charter of the International Military Tribunal, August 8, 1945, art. 6(c).
81 Benny Morris, The Causes and Character of the Arab Exodus from Palestine: the Israel Defence Forces Intelligence Branch Analysis of June 1948, *Middle Eastern Studies*, vol. 22, 5, at 6–7 (1986).
82 Levin, *I Saw the Battle of Jerusalem*, at 160.
83 Memorandum of Conversation, by Secretary of State, May 12, 1948, *FRUS 1948*, vol. 5, 972, at 975.
84 Declaration of the Establishment of the State of Israel, *Laws of the State of Israel*, vol. 1, at 3 (1948).
85 Zionists proclaim new state of Israel; Truman recognizes it and hopes for peace; Tel Aviv is bombed, Egypt orders invasion, *New York Times*, May 15, 1948, at 1. Memorandum of Conversations, by the Under Secretary of State (Lovett), May 17, 1948, *FRUS 1948*, vol. 5, 1005, at 1007. Philip Marshall Brown, The Recognition of Israel, *American Journal of International Law*, vol. 42, at 620 (1948).
86 UN General Assembly, Resolution 186 (S-2), May 14, 1948.
87 Uri Avnery, Les réfugiés arabes, obstacle à la paix, *Le Monde*, May 9, 1964, 1, at 2.
88 IDF, Intelligence Branch, The Emigration of the Arabs of Palestine in the Period 1/12/1947-1/6/1948, June 30, 1948, in Morris, The Causes and Character of the Arab Exodus from Palestine, at 9.

10 DENYING THE UNDENIABLE

1 Egypt, Foreign Minister, Cablegram, UN Document S/743, read aloud in UN Security Council, 3rd year, 292nd meeting, May 15, 1948, at 2–3, UN Document S/PV.292.
2 Tsiang Tingfu, China, in UN Security Council, 3rd year, 292nd meeting, May 15, 1948, at 15, UN Document S/PV.292.
3 Shabtai Rosenne, Basic Elements of Israel's Foreign Policy, *India Quarterly*, vol. 17, 328, at 355 (1961).
4 UN Security Council, 3rd year, 292nd meeting, May 15, 1948, at 8–9, UN Document S/PV.292.
5 Declaration of the Establishment of the State of Israel, *Laws of the State of Israel*, vol. 1, at 3 (1948).
6 Statement by President Truman, May 14, 1948, *Department of State Bulletin*, vol. 18, at 673 (May 23, 1948). George Marshall, The Secretary of State to Mr. Eliahu Epstein, at Washington, Washington, May 14, 1948, *FRUS 1948*, vol. 5, at 992. E. Epstein to M. Shertok, Washington, May 14, 1948, in Yehoshua Freundlich (ed.), *Documents on the Foreign Policy of Israel*, vol. 1, 14 May – 30 September 1948 (Jerusalem: Israel State Archives, 1981), at 3.
7 Philip Marshall Brown, The Recognition of Israel, *American Journal of International Law*, vol. 42, 620, at 622 (1948).
8 U.S. asks U.N. to order end of fighting in Palestine; Soviet recognizes Israel, *New York Times*, May 18, 1948, at 1.
9 V. Molotov to M. Shertok, Moscow, May 18, 1948, in Yehoshua Freundlich (ed.), *Documents on the Foreign Policy of Israel*, vol. 1, 14 May – 30 September 1948 (Jerusalem: Israel State Archives, 1981), at 22–23.
10 Brown, The Recognition of Israel, at 622.
11 Rosenne, Basic Elements of Israel's Foreign Policy, at 341.
12 Cablegram dated 15 May 1948 from the Foreign Secretary of the Provisional Government of Israel to the Secretary-General, May 15, 1948, UN Document S/747. Thomas Hamilton, Israel asks for U.N. membership, *New York Times*, May 17, 1948, at 6.
13 A. Lourie to M. Shertok, New York, May 20, 1948, in Yehoshua Freundlich (ed.), *Documents on the Foreign Policy of Israel*, vol. 1, 14 May – 30 September 1948 (Jerusalem: Israel State Archives, 1981), at 37.
14 UN Security Council, 3rd year, *Letter dated 18 May 1948 from the Assistant Secretary-General for Security Council Affairs addressed to the Jewish Agency for Palestine, and reply dated 22 May 1948 addressed to the Secretary-General concerning the questions submitted by the Security Council*, May 22, 1948, at 4, UN Document S/766.
15 IDF, Intelligence Branch, The Emigration of the Arabs of Palestine in the Period 1/12/1947 – 1/6/1948, June 30, 1948, in Benny Morris, The Causes and Character of the Arab Exodus from Palestine: the Israel Defence Forces Intelligence Branch Analysis of June 1948, *Middle Eastern Studies*, vol. 22, 5, at 9–10 (1986).
16 Benny Morris, *The Birth of the Palestinian Refugee Problem Revisited* (Cambridge: Cambridge University Press, 2004), at 317–318.

17 M. Shertok to N. Goldmann (London), Tel Aviv, June 15, 1948, in Yehoshua Freundlich (ed.), *Documents on the Foreign Policy of Israel*, vol. 1, 14 May – 30 September 1948 (Jerusalem: Israel State Archives, 1981), 162, at 163.
18 A. Eban to M. Shertok, New York, May 21, 1948, id., 56, at 58.
19 A. Eban to M. Shertok, New York, May 25, 1948, id. at 75.
20 *Letter dated 10 June from the acting representative of the Provisional Government of Israel addressed to the Secretary-General transmitting the reply of the Provisional Government of Israel to the cease-fire and truce proposals of the United Nations mediator*, UN Document S/834.
21 Shabtai Rosenne, Recognition of Israel by the Security Council in 1948, *Israel Yearbook on Human Rights*, vol. 13, 295, at 305 (1983).
22 A. Eban to M. Shertok, New York, June 18, 1948, in Yehoshua Freundlich (ed.), *Documents on the Foreign Policy of Israel*, vol. 1, 14 May – 30 September 1948 (Jerusalem: Israel State Archives, 1981), at 187.
23 Robert St. John, *Eban* (Garden City, NY: Doubleday, 1972), at 208. Rosenne, Recognition of Israel by the Security Council in 1948, at 318.
24 A. Eban to P. Jessup (New York), New York, July 1, 1948, in Yehoshua Freundlich (ed.), *Documents on the Foreign Policy of Israel*, vol. 1, 14 May – 30 September 1948 (Jerusalem: Israel State Archives, 1981), at 248.
25 The Secretary of State to the Acting United States Representative at the United Nations (Jessup), June 30, 1948, *FRUS 1948*, vol. 5, at 1160.
26 UN Security Council, 3rd year, 330th meeting, July 7, 1948, at 2, UN Document S/PV.330.
27 Id. at 2–3.
28 Id. at 8.
29 Id. at 8–9.
30 Id. at 9.
31 Id. at 10.
32 Count Bernadotte to M. Shertok, Rhodes, June 27, 1948, in Yehoshua Freundlich (ed.), *Documents on the Foreign Policy of Israel*, vol. 1, 14 May – 30 September 1948 (Jerusalem: Israel State Archives, 1981), 230, at 234.
33 Meeting: M. Sharett – A. Vyshinsky (Paris, December 12, 1948), in Yehoshua Freundlich (ed.), *Documents on the Foreign Policy of Israel*, vol. 2 companion, October 1948 – April 1949 (Jerusalem: Israel State Archives, 1984), 59, at 61.
34 Benny Morris, *The Birth of the Palestinian Refugee Problem Revisited*, at 426.
35 Id. at 429. Benny Morris, Operation Dani and the Palestinian Exodus from Lydda and Ramle in 1948, *Middle East Journal*, vol. 40, 82, at 96 (1986). Reja-e Busailah, The Fall of Lydda, 1948: Impressions and Reminiscences, *Arab Studies Quarterly*, vol. 3, 123, at 128 (1981).
36 Edgar O'Ballance, *The Arab-Israeli War, 1948* (London: Faber and Faber, 1956) at 147.
37 Benny Morris, *The Birth of the Palestinian Refugee Problem, 1947–1949* (Cambridge: Cambridge University Press, 1989), at 210.
38 Ari Shavit, *My Promised Land: The Triumph and Tragedy of Israel* (New York: Spiegel and Grau, 2013), at 108.
39 UN Security Council, Resolution 54, July 15, 1948.

40 UN Charter, arts. 39–43.
41 Nafez Nazzal, The Zionist Occupation of Western Galilee, 1948, *Journal of Palestine Studies*, vol. 3, no. 3, at 58–76 (1974).
42 Morris, *The Birth of the Palestinian Refugee Problem, 1947–1949*, at 200.
43 Nazzal, The Zionist Occupation of Western Galilee, 1948, at 75.
44 M. Shertok to C. Weizmann (Montreux), Tel Aviv, July 20/August 22, 1948, in Yehoshua Freundlich (ed.), *Documents on the Foreign Policy of Israel*, vol. 1, 14 May – 30 September 1948 (Jerusalem: Israel State Archives, 1981), 363, at 364 (in the section of the letter written July 20).
45 A. Eban to M. Shertok, New York, July 23, 1948, id. at 385.
46 Meeting: M. Shertok – Count Bernadotte and Assistants, Tel Aviv, July 26, 1948, id., 409, at 412.
47 Morris, *The Birth of the Palestinian Refugee Problem, 1947–1949*, at 148.
48 The Special Representative of the United States in Israel (McDonald) to the Secretary of State, August 20, 1948, *FRUS 1948*, vol. 5, at 1334. Morris, *The Birth of the Palestinian Refugee Problem, 1947–1949*, at 150.
49 Morris, *The Birth of the Palestinian Refugee Problem, 1947–1949*, at 148–149.
50 M. Shertok to C. Weizmann (Montreux), Tel Aviv, July 20/August 22, 1948, in Yehoshua Freundlich (ed.), *Documents on the Foreign Policy of Israel*, vol. 1, 14 May – 30 September 1948 (Jerusalem: Israel State Archives, 1981), 363, at 369 (in the section of the letter written August 22).
51 Morris, *The Birth of the Palestinian Refugee Problem, 1947–1949*, at 149. Ilan Pappé, *The Ethnic Cleansing of Palestine* (Oxford: Oneworld, 2006), at 188.
52 UN General Assembly, 3rd session, Supplement No. 11, *Progress Report of the United Nations Mediator on Palestine*, September 16, 1948, at 14, UN Document A/648.
53 Id. at 47.
54 Walter Schwarz, *The Arabs in Israel* (1959), at 158. Palumbo, *The Palestinian Catastrophe*, at 173.
55 Morris, *The Birth of the Palestinian Refugee Problem Revisited*, at 466–467.
56 UN Security Council, 3rd session, Supplement for November 1948, *Cablegram dated 3 November 1948 from the Secretary-General of the League of Arab States to the Secretary-General concerning alleged truce violations by Jewish forces in Galilee*, at 6, UN Document S/1068. The spelling of the name of this town in English varies: Dawaymeh, Dawayma, Dawayima.
57 UN Security Council, 3rd year, 377th meeting, November 4, 1948, at 51, UN Document S/PV.377.
58 Id. at 56.
59 UN Security Council, 3rd session, Supplement for November 1948, *Letter dated 8 November 1948 from the representative of the Provisional Government of Israel to the President of the Security Council concerning a letter from the Secretary-General of the League of Arab States (S/1068)*, at 11, UN Document S/1073.
60 UN Security Council, 3rd session, Supplement for November 1948, *Cabled corrigendum to the cablegram dated 3 November 1948 from the Secretary-General of the League of Arab States to the Secretary-General concerning alleged truce*

violations by Jewish forces in Galilee, correcting mistake as to location of village, November 10, 1948, at 6, UN Document S/1068/Corr.1.

61 St. John, *Eban*, at 100.

62 Walid Khalidi, *All That Remains: The Palestinian Villages Occupied and Depopulated by Israel in 1948* (Washington, DC: Institute for Palestine Studies, 1992), at 213–215.

63 Benny Morris, *1948: A History of the First Arab-Israeli War* (New Haven, CT: Yale University Press, 2008), at 333.

64 UN General Assembly, Conciliation Commission for Palestine, Technical Committee, The Dawaymeh Massacre, June 14, 1949, UN Document A/AC.25/Com.Tech/W.3.

65 Pappé, *The Ethnic Cleansing of Palestine*, at 196. Morris, *The Birth of the Palestinian Refugee Problem Revisited*, at 469.

66 Morris, *The Birth of the Palestinian Refugee Problem, 1947–1949*, at 223.

67 Palumbo, *The Palestinian Catastrophe*, at xii-xiv. Morris, *The Birth of the Palestinian Refugee Problem, 1947–1949*, at 222.

68 UN Security Council, 3rd year, 381st meeting, November 16, 1948, at 37, UN Document S/PV.381.

69 UN General Assembly, 3rd session, Part I, First Committee, *Summary Records of Meetings 21 September-8 December 1948*, 200th meeting, November 15, 1948, at 646, UN Document A/C.1/SR.208.

70 Shabtai Rosenne, The Israeli Nationality Law 5712–1952 and the Law of Return 5710–1950, *Journal du droit international*, vol. 81, 4, at 8–9 (1954).

71 UN General Assembly, 3rd session, Part I, First Committee, *Summary Records of Meetings 21 September-8 December 1948*, 200th meeting, November 15, 1948, at 646, UN Document A/C.1/SR.208.

72 UN General Assembly, 3rd session, Part I, First Committee, *Summary Records of Meetings 21 September-8 December 1948*, 207th meeting, November 22, 1948, at 698, UN Document A/C.1/SR.207.

73 Id. at 697.

74 UN General Assembly, 3rd session, Part I, First Committee, *Summary Records of Meetings 21 September-8 December 1948*, 208th meeting, November 23, 1948, at 715, UN Document A/C.1/SR.208.

75 UN General Assembly, 3rd session, Part I, First Committee, *Summary Records of Meetings 21 September-8 December 1948*, 200th meeting, November 15, 1948, at 646, UN Document A/C.1/SR.208.

11 A PEACE-LOVING STATE?

1 M. Shertok (Tel Aviv) to Members of the Provisional Government, September 10, 1948, in Yehoshua Freundlich (ed.), *Documents on the Foreign Policy of Israel*, vol. 1 companion, 14 May – 30 September 1948 (Jerusalem: Israel State Archives, 1981), at 20.

2 Meeting of the Israeli Delegation to the United Nations General Assembly (Paris, October 18, 1948), in Yehoshua Freundlich (ed.), *Documents on the Foreign Policy of Israel*, vol. 2 companion, October 1948 – April 1949 (Jerusalem: Israel State Archives, 1984), 22, at 23.

3 UN Security Council, 3rd year, Supplement for December 1948, *Letter dated 29 November 1948 from the Israeli Minister for Foreign Affairs to the Secretary-General concerning Israel's application for membership in the United Nations and declaration accepting the obligations contained in the Charter*, at 118, UN Document S/1093.
4 UN Security Council, Resolution 61, November 4, 1948.
5 Walter Eytan, *The First Ten Years: A diplomatic history of Israel* (London: Weidenfeld and Nicolson, 1958), at 14.
6 To Emil Sandström, Jerusalem, July 14, 1947, in Barnet Litvinoff (ed.), *The Letters and Papers of Chaim Weizmann* (New Brunswick NJ: Transaction Books, 1979), vol. 22: Series A May 1945-July 1947, 367, at 368.
7 Id. at 370.
8 UN Security Council, 3rd year, Supplement for December 1948, *Letter dated 7 December 1948 from the Chairman of the Commission the Admission of New Members to the President of the Security Council concerning Israel's application for membership in the United Nations*, at 119, UN Document S/1110.
9 Michael Brecher, *The Foreign Policy System of Israel: Setting, Images, Process* (London: Oxford University Press, 1972), at 39. *Israel and the United Nations* (Report of a Study Group set up by the Hebrew University of Jerusalem) (New York: Manhattan Publishing, 1956), at 184.
10 Meeting: M. Sharett – A. Vyshinsky (Paris, December 12, 1948), in Yehoshua Freundlich (ed.), *Documents on the Foreign Policy of Israel*, vol. 2 companion, October 1948 – April 1949 (Jerusalem: Israel State Archives, 1984), at 59.
11 UN General Assembly, Resolution 194, December 11, 1948, para. 8.
12 Shabtai Rosenne, Israel and the United Nations: Changed Perspectives, 1945–1976, *American Jewish Year Book*, vol. 78, 3, at 22 (1978).
13 Proclamation No. 1 of the Israel Defense Forces in Jerusalem, August 2, 1948, in Ruth Lapidoth and Moshe Hirsch (eds.), *The Jerusalem Question and Its Resolution: Selected Documents* (Dordrecht: Martinus Nijhoff Publishers, 1994), at 27.
14 Meeting of the Israeli Delegation to the United Nations General Assembly (Paris, October 3, 1948), in Yehoshua Freundlich (ed.), *Documents on the Foreign Policy of Israel*, vol. 2 companion, October 1948 – April 1949 (Jerusalem: Israel State Archives, 1984), 3, at 5.
15 Israel swears in a supreme court, *New York Times*, September 15, 1948, at 16.
16 Israel Claims Jerusalem, Address by President Weizmann in Jerusalem, 1 December 1948, *Israel's Foreign Relations: Selected Documents 1947–1974* (Jerusalem: Ministry of Foreign Affairs, 1976), vol. 1, 220, at 222.
17 UN General Assembly, Resolution 194, December 11, 1948, para. 11.
18 Review and Appraisal of Israeli-Arab Relations (1951), in Charles P. Henry (ed.), *Ralph Bunche: Selected Speeches and Writings* (Ann Arbor: University of Michigan Press, 1995), at 185.
19 Janet Abu-Lughod, The Demographic Transformation of Palestine, in Ibrahim Abu-Lughod (ed.), *The Transformation of Palestine: Essays on the Origin and Development of the Arab-Israeli Conflict* (Evanston IL: Northwestern University Press, 1971), 139, at 161.

20 M. Sharett [Tel Aviv] to G. Meyerson (Moscow), November 5, 1948, in Yehoshua Freundlich (ed.), *Documents on the Foreign Policy of Israel*, vol. 2 companion, October 1948 – April 1949 (Jerusalem: Israel State Archives, 1984), 31, at 33.
21 UN General Assembly, 3rd session, Part I, *Summary Records of Meetings 21 September – 12 December 1948*, 184th meeting, December 11, 1948, at 945–946, UN Document A/PV.184.
22 Y. Shimoni [Tel Aviv] to E. Sasson (Paris), September 16, 1948, in Yehoshua Freundlich (ed.), *Documents on the Foreign Policy of Israel*, vol. 1 companion, 14 May – 30 September 1948 (Jerusalem: Israel State Archives, 1981), at 24.
23 UN General Assembly, 3rd session, Part I, *Annexes to the Summary Records of Meetings*, at 69, UN Document A/C.1/398.Rev.2 (1948).
24 UN General Assembly, 3rd session, Part II, First Committee, *Summary Records of Meetings 21 September – 8 December 1948*, 226th meeting, December 3, 1948, at 906, UN Document A/C.1/SR.226.
25 Id. at 904.
26 Id. at 909.
27 Id. at 912.
28 David Horowitz, *State in the Making* (New York: Alfred A. Knopf, 1953), at 296–297.
29 UN General Assembly, 3rd session, Part I, First Committee, *Summary Records of Meetings 21 September-8 December 1948*, 200th meeting, November 15, 1948, at 645, UN Document A/C.1/SR.200.
30 UN General Assembly, 3rd session, Part I, First Committee, *Summary Records of Meetings 21 September – 8 December 1948*, 220th meeting, December 1, 1948, at 841, UN Document A/C.1/SR.220.
31 Id. at 841.
32 UN Security Council, 3rd year, 384th meeting, December 15, 1948, at 5, UN Document S/PV.384.
33 UN Security Council, 3rd year, 385th meeting, December 17, 1948, at 4, UN Document S/PV.385.
34 Id. at 8.
35 UN Security Council, 3rd year, 384th meeting, December 15, 1948, at 16, UN Document S/PV.384.
36 UN Security Council, 3rd year, 386th meeting, December 17, 1948, at 32, UN Document S/PV.386.
37 Id. at 37.
38 Abba Eban, *Abba Eban: An Autobiography* (New York: Random House, 1977), at 136.
39 Robert Lovett, The Acting Secretary of State to the Special Representative of the United States in Israel (McDonald), Washington, December 30, 1948, *FRUS 1948*, vol. 5, at 1704.
40 UN Security Council, 3rd year, 396th meeting, December 29, 1948, at 5, UN Document S/PV.396.
41 Bertram Hulen, Israel informs U.S., troops left Egypt; scores British acts, *New York Times*, January 5, 1949, at 1.

42 De jure recognition extended to Israel, January 31, 1949 *Department of State Bulletin*, vol. 20, at 205 (February 6, 1949).
43 Michael Brecher, *Decisions in Israel's Foreign Policy* (New Haven, CT: Yale University Press, 1975), at 24.
44 UN General Assembly, Conciliation Commission for Palestine, *Summary record of a meeting between the conciliation commission and his excellency Mr. Shertok, Minister for Foreign Affairs of Israel*, February 7, 1949, UN Document A/AC.25/SR/G/1.
45 Eban, *Abba Eban*, at 138.
46 UN Security Council, 4th year, 413th meeting, March 3, 1949, at 15, UN Document S/PV.413.
47 Id. at 10.
48 Id. at 14.
49 Id. at 15.
50 Id. at 11.
51 UN Security Council, 4th year, 414th meeting, March 4, 1949, at 5–6, UN Document S/PV.414.
52 Id. at 3.
53 Id. at 2.
54 Id. at 2.
55 Id. at 3.
56 Id. at 8.
57 Id. at 11.
58 Id. at 14.
59 UN Security Council, Resolution 69, March 4, 1949.
60 *Application of Israel for Membership in the United Nations: Letter from the President of the Security Council to the President of the General Assembly*, March 7, 1949, UN Document A/818.
61 A. Eban to W. Eytan, New York, March 7, 1949, in Yehoshua Freundlich (ed.), *Documents on the Foreign Policy of Israel*, vol. 2, October 1948 – April 1949 (Jerusalem: Israel State Archives, 1984), 471, at 473.
62 State of Israel, *Government Year-Book 5711 (1950)* (Jerusalem: Government Printer, 1950), at 50.
63 Jacques de Reynier, *1948 à Jérusalem* (Neuchatel, Editions de la Baconnière, 1969), at 157.
64 P. Rugger to M. Shertok, Geneva, May 20, 1948, in Yehoshua Freundlich (ed.), *Documents on the Foreign Policy of Israel*, vol. 1, 14 May – 30 September 1948 (Jerusalem: Israel State Archives, 1981), at 38.
65 Comité International de la Croix-Rouge, Délégation en Palestine, Rapport No. 21: Visites à Shef'Amr, Iblin, Acre, faites le 10.11.48 par Dr. Moeri et R. Troyon, délégués du CICR, Tel Aviv, le 12 Novembre 1948.
66 Comité International de la Croix-Rouge, Délégation en Palestine, Note à l'attention de M. de Reynold, Délégué du C.I.C.R. à Tel-Aviv. Rapport sur la situation des PG's en mains juives. Tel-Aviv, le 6 Février 1949.
67 Salman Abu Sitta and Terry Rempel, The ICRC and the Detention of Palestinian Civilians in Israel's 1948 POW/Labor Camps, *Journal of Palestine Studies*, vol. 43, no. 4, 11, at 21 (Summer 2014).

68 Ilan Pappé, *The Ethnic Cleansing of Palestine* (Oxford: Oneworld, 2006), at 199–203.

69 International Committee of the Red Cross, Report No. 20, Visit of Ijlil [Djelil] camp 9 November 1948, November 12, 1948, ICRC archives G59/I/GC G/82, at 3, as quoted in Abu Sitta and Rempel, The ICRC and the Detention of Palestinian Civilians in Israel's 1948 POW/Labor Camps, at 18.

70 UN Security Council, 3rd year, *Letter dated 26 July 1948 from the representative of the Arab Higher Committee for Palestine to the Secretary-General enclosing memorandum on "Jewish Atrocities in the Holy Land,"* UN Document S/925.

71 de Reynier, *1948 à Jérusalem*, at 157.

72 The Consul at Jerusalem (Burdett) to the Secretary of State, February 8, 1949, FRUS *1949*, vol. 6, 735, at 738.

73 The Secretary of State to the Consulate General at Jerusalem, March 9, 1949, *FRUS 1949*, vol. 6, 805, at 806.

74 Memorandum of Conversation, by the Secretary of State, March 22, 1949, *FRUS 1949*, vol. 6, 853, at 855.

75 Memorandum by the Secretary of State: Conversation With the President, March 24, 1949, *FRUS 1949*, vol. 6, at 863.

76 Memorandum of Conversation, by the Secretary of State: Item No. 3 – President Weizmann's Visit, April 25, 1949, *FRUS 1949*, vol. 6, at 943.

77 The President of Israel (Weizmann) to President Truman, April 26, 1949, *FRUS 1949*, vol. 6, 947, at 948.

78 Memorandum of Conversation With the President, by the Secretary of State, April 28, 1949: Item No. 2 – Letter from Dr. Weizmann, *FRUS 1949*, vol. 6, at 954.

79 The President to Mr. Mark F. Ethridge, at Jerusalem, April 29, 1949, *FRUS 1949*, vol. 6, at 957.

80 Memorandum of Conversation, by the Secretary of State, April 26, 1949, *FRUS 1949*, vol. 6, at 944.

81 Id. at 945.

82 A. Eban to M. Sharett, New York, April 27, 1949, in Yehoshua Freundlich (ed.), *Documents on the Foreign Policy of Israel*, vol. 2, October 1948 – April 1949 (Jerusalem: Israel State Archives, 1984), at 595.

83 I.N. Bakulin to A.Ia. Vyshinskii, The New Government of the State of Israel (Brief memorandum), March 15, 1949, in *Documents on Israeli-Soviet Relations 1941–1953: Part I: 1941-May 1949* (London: Frank Cass, 2000), 452, at 454.

12 JOINING THE WORLD WITH FINGERS CROSSED

1 A. Eban to W. Eytan, New York, March 14, 1949, in Yehoshua Freundlich (ed.), *Documents on the Foreign Policy of Israel*, vol. 2, October 1948 – April 1949 (Jerusalem: Israel State Archives, 1984), at 498. Trans-Jordan, Israel Ready for Armistice, *Washington Post*, March 17, 1949, at 3.

2 UN General Assembly, 3rd session, Part I, First Committee, *Summary Records of Meetings 21 September-8 December 1948*, 200th meeting, November 15, 1948, at 643, UN Document A/C.1/SR.200.

3 The Consul at Jerusalem (Burdett) to the Secretary of State, Jerusalem, March 14, 1949, *FRUS 1949*, vol. 6, at 825 (relaying message from Mark Ethridge).
4 L. M. Bloomfield, *Egypt, Israel and the Gulf of Aqaba in International Law* (Toronto: Carswell, 1957), at 4.
5 Shabtai Rosenne, Israel and the United Nations: Changed Perspectives, 1945–1976, *American Jewish Year Book*, vol. 78, 3, at 22 (1978).
6 Benny Morris, *The Birth of the Palestinian Refugee Problem, 1947–1949* (Cambridge: Cambridge University Press, 1989), at 242–245.
7 A. Eban to W. Eytan, New York, April 1, 1949, in Yehoshua Freundlich (ed.), *Documents on the Foreign Policy of Israel*, vol. 2, October 1948 – April 1949 (Jerusalem: Israel State Archives, 1984), at 540.
8 UN General Assembly, 3rd session, Part II, *Summary Records of Meetings 5 April – 18 May 1949*, 205th meeting, May 2, 1949, at 293, UN Document A/PV.205.
9 UN General Assembly, 3rd session, Part II, Ad Hoc Political Committee, *Summary Records of Meetings 6 April – 10 May 1949*, 45th meeting, May 5, 1949, at 220, UN Document A/AC.24/SR.45.
10 Id. at 225.
11 Id. at 226.
12 Id. At 226.
13 Id. at 227.
14 Id. at 228.
15 UN Security Council, Resolution 62, November 16, 1948.
16 UN General Assembly, 3rd session, Part II, Ad Hoc Political Committee, *Summary Records of Meetings 6 April – 10 May 1949*, 45th meeting, May 5, 1949, at 229, UN Document A/AC.24/SR.45.
17 UN General Assembly, 3rd session, Part I, First Committee, *Summary Records of Meetings 21 September-8 December 1948*, 161st meeting, October 15, 1948, at 162, UN Document A/C.1/SR.161.
18 UN General Assembly, 3rd session, Part II, Ad Hoc Political Committee, *Summary Records of Meetings 6 April – 10 May 1949*, 45th meeting, May 5, 1949, at 236, UN Document A/AC.24/SR.45.
19 UN General Assembly, 3rd session, Part II, Ad Hoc Political Committee, *Summary Records of Meetings 6 April – 10 May* 1949, 49th meeting, May 7, 1949, at 314, UN Document A/AC.24/SR.49.
20 UN General Assembly, 3rd session, Part II, Ad Hoc Political Committee, *Summary Records of Meetings 6 April – 10 May* 1949, 45th meeting, May 5, 1949, at 237, UN Document A/AC.24/SR.45.
21 UN General Assembly, Resolution 46/83, December 12, 2001, Annex: *Responsibility of States for Internationally Wrongful Acts*, Chapter 2 (Attribution of conduct to a state), art. 10 (Conduct of an insurrectional or other movement).
22 Benny Morris, *The Birth of the Palestinian Refugee Problem, 1947–1949* (Cambridge: Cambridge University Press, 1989), at 197–198.
23 UN General Assembly, 3rd session, Part II, Ad Hoc Political Committee, *Summary Records of Meetings 6 April – 10 May* 1949, 45th meeting, May 5, 1949, at 238, UN Document A/AC.24/SR.45.

24 Id. at 240.
25 UN General Assembly, 3rd session, Part II, Ad Hoc Political Committee, *Summary Records of Meetings 6 April – 10 May* 1949, 47th meeting, May 6, 1949, at 272–273, UN Document A/AC.24/SR.47.
26 UN General Assembly, Conciliation Commission for Palestine, *Second Progress Report*, April 19, 1949, para. 28, UN Document A/838.
27 Meeting of the Conciliation Commission with the Prime Minister and Ministry for Foreign Affairs Staff (Tel Aviv, April 7, 1949), in Yehoshua Freundlich (ed.), *Documents on the Foreign Policy of Israel*, vol. 2 companion, October 1948 – April 1949 (Jerusalem: Israel State Archives, 1984), 92, at 93.
28 UN General Assembly, 3rd session, Part II, Ad Hoc Political Committee, *Summary Records of Meetings 6 April – 10 May* 1949, 49th meeting, May 7, 1949, at 313–314, UN Document A/AC.24/SR.49.
29 UN General Assembly, 3rd session, Part II, Ad Hoc Political Committee, *Summary Records of Meetings 6 April – 10 May 1949*, 47th meeting, May 6, 1949, at 273, UN Document A/AC.24/SR.47.
30 Id. at 273.
31 Id. at 275.
32 Id. at 277.
33 Id. at 278.
34 Id. at 278.
35 Id. at 281.
36 Id. at 281–282.
37 Id. at 282.
38 Id. at 282.
39 Id. at 282.
40 Id. at 282.
41 Id. at 283.
42 Id. at 283.
43 Id. at 286.
44 Id. at 286–287.
45 Id. at 290.
46 Id. at 292.
47 Id. at 296.
48 UN General Assembly, 3rd session, Part II, Ad Hoc Political Committee, *Summary Records of Meetings 6 April – 10 May 1949*, 48th meeting, May 7, 1949, at 305, UN Document A/AC.24/SR.48.
49 Id. at 305.
50 Id. at 306.
51 Id. at 306–307.
52 Id. at 307–308.
53 UN General Assembly, 3rd session, Part II, Ad Hoc Political Committee, *Summary Records of Meetings 6 April – 10 May 1949*, 51st meeting, May 9, 1949, at 342, UN Document A/AC.24/SR.51.
54 Id. at 343–344.
55 Id. at 350.

56 Id. at 351.
57 Id. at 355.
58 Id. at 357–358.
59 UN General Assembly, 3rd session, Part II, Ad Hoc Political Committee, *Summary Records of Meetings 6 April – 10 May* 1949, 47th meeting, May 6, 1949, at 293, UN Document A/AC.24/SR.47.
60 E. Elath to M. Sharett, New York, May 9, 1949, in Yemima Rosenthal (ed.), *Documents on the Foreign Policy of Israel*, vol. 4, May – December 1949 (Jerusalem: Israel State Archives, 1986), at 33.
61 UN General Assembly, 3rd session, Part II, Ad Hoc Political Committee, *Summary Records of Meetings 6 April – 10 May 1949*, 51st meeting, May 9, 1949, at 360, UN Document A/AC.24/SR.51.
62 UN General Assembly, 3rd session, Part II, *Summary Records of Meetings 5 April – 18 May 1949*, 207th meeting, May 11, 1949, at 313, UN Document A/PV.207.
63 Id. at 328.
64 Id. at 331.
65 UN General Assembly, Resolution 273, May 11, 1949.
66 UN General Assembly, 3rd session, Part II, *Summary Records of Meetings 5 April – 18 May 1949*, 207th meeting, May 11, 1949, at 332, UN Document A/PV.207.
67 Id. at 334.
68 Israel and International Organizations: Lecture by Shabtai Rosenne, February 13, 1984, *Bracton Law Journal*, vol. 17, 22, at 26 (1984).
69 Michael Brecher, *The Foreign Policy System of Israel: Setting, Images, Process* (London: Oxford University Press, 1972), at 387.
70 UN General Assembly, Conciliation Commission for Palestine, Technical Committee, The Dawaymeh Massacre, June 14, 1949, UN Document A/AC.25/Com.Tech/W.3.
71 Robert St. John, *Eban* (Garden City, NY: Doubleday, 1972), at 31.
72 Id. at 60.
73 Id. at 106.
74 Henry Kissinger, *White House Years* (Boston: Little, Brown, 1979), at 358–359.
75 Abba Eban, Our Place in the Human Scheme: A Presentation, *Congress Bi-Weekly* (American Jewish Congress), vol. 40, no. 6, at 7 (March 30, 1973).
76 Id. at 6.

13 ISRAEL: 1, UNITED NATIONS: 0

1 Charles Kamen, The Arab Population in Palestine and Israel, 1946–1951, *New Outlook*, vol. 27–28, 36, at 38 (October-November 1984).
2 Tom Segev, *1949: The First Israelis* (New York: Free Press, 1986), at 61.
3 Rosemary Sayigh, *Palestinians: From Peasants to Revolutionaries* (London: Zed Press, 1979), at 85, 88–89.
4 Benny Morris, *The Birth of the Palestinian Refugee Problem, 1947–1949* (Cambridge: Cambridge University Press, 1989), at 245.

5 Segev, *1949*, at 52.
6 The Acting Secretary of State to the Embassy in Israel, May 28, 1949, *FRUS 1949*, vol. 6, 1072, at 1074.
7 The Ambassador in Israel (McDonald) to the Secretary of State, May 29, 1949, *FRUS 1949*, vol. 6, 1074, at 1075.
8 M. Sharett to J.G. McDonald, Tel Aviv, June 8 1949, in Yemima Rosenthal (ed.), *Documents on the Foreign Policy of Israel*, vol. 4, May – December 1949 (Jerusalem: Israel State Archives, 1986), 107, at 109.
9 Editorial Note, *FRUS 1949*, vol. 6, at 1115, quoting Telegram 445 from Tel Aviv, June 11, 1949.
10 Dean Acheson, the Secretary of State to the Embassy in Israel (*Aide-Mémoire* delivered to Israeli Chargé by Deputy Under Secretary Rusk), *FRUS 1949*, vol. 6, 1174, and1176. And see *Aide-Mémoire* by the Government of the United States, Washington, June 24, 1949: Secret, in Yemima Rosenthal (ed.), *Documents on the Foreign Policy of Israel*, vol. 4, May – December 1949 (Jerusalem: Israel State Archives, 1986), 173, at 175.
11 The Ambassador in France (Bruce) to the Secretary of State, Paris, June 12, 1949, *FRUS 1949*, vol. 6, 1124, at 1125 (conveying message from Mark Ethridge).
12 Id. at 1124.
13 UN General Assembly, 5th session, Supplement No. 18, *General Progress Report and Supplementary Report of the United Nations Conciliation Commission for Palestine covering the period from 11 December 1949 to 23 October 1950*, at 14, UN Document A/1367/Rev.1.
14 Memorandum on the Future of Jerusalem: An Analysis of the Palestine Conciliation Commission's Draft Instrument, submitted to the General Assembly of the United Nations by the Delegation of Israel to the United Nations, November 15, 1949, in Ruth Lapidoth and Moshe Hirsch (eds.), *The Jerusalem Question and Its Resolution: Selected Documents* (Dordrecht: Martinus Nijhoff Publishers, 1994), 49, at 69.
15 UN General Assembly, 4th session, Ad Hoc Political Committee, *Summary Records of Meetings 27 September – 7 December 1949*, 43rd meeting, November 24, 1949, at 254, UN Document A/AC.31/SR.43.
16 UN General Assembly, 4th session, Ad Hoc Political Committee, *Summary Records of Meetings 27 September–7 December, 1949*, 44th meeting, November 25, 1949, at 261, UN Document A/AC.31/SR.44.
17 Id. at 262.
18 Id. at 262.
19 Id. at 262.
20 UN General Assembly, 4th session, Ad Hoc Political Committee, Israel: draft resolution, November 25, 1949, UN Document A/AC.31/L.42.
21 UN General Assembly, 4th session, Ad Hoc Political Committee, *Summary Records of Meetings 27 September – 7 December 1949*, 44th meeting, November 25, 1949, at 261–262, UN Document A/AC.31/SR.44.
22 Statement by the Prime Minister concerning Jerusalem and the Holy Places, December 5, 1949, *Divrei Haknesset* (Records of Knesset Proceedings), vol. 4 (2nd session), at 81–82, translated in Lapidoth and Hirsch, *The Jerusalem Question and Its Resolution*, at 81–82.

23 Israel defies U.N. over rule of Jerusalem, *Chicago Daily Tribune*, December 6, 1949, at 7. Premier holds decision void, *New York Times*, December 6, 1949, at 23.
24 UN General Assembly, Resolution 303, December 9, 1949.
25 Michael Brecher, *Decisions in Israel's Foreign Policy* (New Haven, CT: Yale University Press, 1975), at 12, 28–29.
26 Israel defies U.N. in Jerusalem move, *Los Angeles Times*, December 15, 1949, at 25.
27 Brecher, *Decisions in Israel's Foreign Policy*, at 30.
28 Transfer of the Knesset and the Government to Jerusalem, December 13, 1949, Divrei Haknesset (Records of Knesset Proceedings), vol. 4 (2nd session), at 82–83, translated in Lapidoth and Hirsch, *The Jerusalem Question and Its Resolution*, at 83–84.
29 Israel defies U.N. in Jerusalem move, *Los Angeles Times*, December 15, 1949, at 25.
30 Israel to move capital back into Jerusalem, *Chicago Daily Tribune*, December 14, 1949, at A2.
31 UN Trusteeship Council, 2nd special session, Preparation of the Statute for the City of Jerusalem, December 20, 1949, UN Document T/RES/426.
32 UN Trusteeship Council, 2nd special session, Resolution 427, December 21, 1949.
33 Brecher, *Decisions in Israel's Foreign Policy*, at 31–32. Walter Eytan, *The First Ten Years: A Diplomatic History of Israel* (London: Weidenfeld and Nicolson, 1958), at 69.
34 UN Trusteeship Council, 6th session, *Letter dated 30 December 1949 from the Permanent Representative of Israel to the United Nations to the President of the Trusteeship Council*, in Exchange of correspondence between the President of the Trusteeship Council and the Government of Israel, January 5, 1950, UN Document T/431.
35 Declaration of the Knesset regarding Jerusalem, January 23, 1950, Divrei Haknesset (Records of Knesset Proceedings), vol. 4 (2nd session), at 603, in Lapidoth and Hirsch, *The Jerusalem Question and Its Resolution*, at 105.
36 Emergency Regulations (Land Requisition-Accommodation of State Institutions in Jerusalem) (Continuance in Force of Orders) Law, *Laws of the State of Israel*, vol. 4, at 106 (1950); Jerusalem Named Capital of Israel, *New York Times*, January 24, 1950, at 1.
37 Statement by Ambassador Abba Eban to the United Nations Trusteeship Council, February 20, 1950, in Lapidoth and Hirsch, *The Jerusalem Question and Its Resolution*, 106, at 107. UN Trusteeship Council, 4th year, 6th session, 19 January – 4 April 1950, 28th meeting, February 20, 1950, at 202–203. (Quotations are from the Lapidoth and Hirsch rather than the UN Trusteeship Council, because Lapidoth and Hirsch gave actual text rather than a reporter's rendition.)
38 Statement by Ambassador Abba Eban to the United Nations Trusteeship Council, February 20, 1950, in Lapidoth and Hirsch, *The Jerusalem Question and Its Resolution*, 106, at 113. UN Trusteeship Council, 4th year, 6th session, 19 January – 4 April 1950, 28th meeting, February 20, 1950, at 206.
39 Eytan, at 78.

40 U.S. Position on Transfer of Israeli Foreign Office: Press Conference Remarks by Secretary Dulles, July 28, 1953, *Department of State Bulletin*, vol. 29, at 177 (August 10, 1953).
41 Brecher, *Decisions in Israel's Foreign Policy*, at 34.
42 UN General Assembly, 4th session, Ad Hoc Political Committee, *Summary Records of Meetings 27 September – 7 December 1949*, 55th meeting, December 2, 1949, at 330, UN Document A/AC.31/SR.55.
43 Id. at 322.
44 UN General Assembly, 5th session, Supplement No. 18, *General Progress Report and Supplementary Report of the United Nations Conciliation Commission for Palestine covering the period from 11 December 1949 to 23 October 1950*, at 13, UN Document A/1367/Rev.1.
45 UN General Assembly, 5th session, Ad Hoc Political Committee, 64th meeting, November 30, 1950, at 411, UN Document A/AC.38/SR.64.
46 UN General Assembly, 5th session, Ad Hoc Political Committee, *Summary Records of Meetings 30 September to 14 December 1950*, 66th meeting, December 1, 1950, at 427, UN Document A/AC.38/SR.66.
47 UN General Assembly, 5th session, Ad Hoc Political Committee, *Summary Records of Meetings 30 September to 14 December 1950*, 68th meeting, December 4, 1950, at 437, UN Document A/AC.38/SR.68.
48 UN General Assembly, 3rd session, Part I, First Committee, *Summary Records of Meetings 21 September – 8 December 1948*, 226th meeting, December 3, 1948, at 909, UN Document A/C.1/SR.226.
49 UN General Assembly, 5th session, *Annexes*, at 36, UN Document A/AC.38/L.57.
50 UN General Assembly, 5th session, Ad Hoc Political Committee, *Summary Records of Meetings 30 September to 14 December 1950*, 66th meeting, December 1, 1950, at 423, UN Document A/AC.38/SR.66.
51 Id. at 423.
52 UN General Assembly, Resolution 394, December 14, 1950.
53 UN General Assembly, 5th session, Ad Hoc Political Committee, *Summary Records of Meetings 30 September to 14 December 1950*, 66th meeting, December 1, 1950, at 423–424, UN Document A/AC.38/SR.66.
54 Id. at 424.
55 UN General Assembly, 5th session, Ad Hoc Political Committee, *Summary Records of Meetings 30 September to 14 December 1950*, 72nd meeting, December 6, 1950, at 464, UN Document A/AC.38/SR.72.
56 UN General Assembly, 7th session, Ad Hoc Political Committee, *Summary Records of Meetings 14 October to 19 December 1952*, 7th meeting, October 30, 1952, at 32, UN Document A/AC.61/SR.7.
57 See, e.g., UN General Assembly, Resolution 2341(A), art. 1, December 19, 1967.

14 A PHANTOM ATTACK

1 Shabtai Rosenne, *Israel's Armistice Agreements with the Arab States: A Juridical Interpretation* (Tel Aviv: Blumstein's, 1951), at 65.
2 Walter Eytan, *The First Ten Years: A Diplomatic History of Israel* (London: Weidenfeld and Nicolson, 1958), at 39–40.

3 Prevention of Infiltration (Offences and Jurisdiction) Law, *Laws of the State of Israel*, vol. 8, at 133 (1954).
4 E.L.M. Burns, *Between Arab and Israeli* (New York: Ivan Obolensky, 1962), at 70.
5 Id. at 89.
6 Benny Morris, *Israel's Border Wars, 1949–1956: Arab Infiltration, Israeli Retaliation, and the Countdown to the Suez War* (Oxford: Oxford University Press, 1993). Ze'ev Drory, *Israel's Reprisal Policy 1953–1956: The Dynamics of Military Retaliation* (London: Frank Cass, 2005).
7 Derek Bowett, Reprisals Involving Recourse to Armed Force, *American Journal of International Law*, vol. 66, 1, at 7 (1972).
8 Burns, *Between Arab and Israeli*, at 64, 104.
9 Id. at 104.
10 The Chargé in Jordan (Seelye) to the Department of State, October 15, 1953, *FRUS 1952–1954*, vol. 9, at 1358.
11 The Chargé in Israel (Russell) to the Department of State, October 17, 1953, *FRUS 1952–1954*, vol. 9, 1364, at 1365.
12 Drory, *Israel's Reprisal Policy 1953–1956*, at 118–121.
13 Livia Rokach, *Israel's Sacred Terrorism: A Study Based on Moshe Sharett's Personal Diary and Other Documents* (Belmont, MA: Association of Arab-American University Graduates Press, 1986), at 14.
14 The Chargé in Israel (Russell) to the Department of State, October 17, 1953, *FRUS 1952–1954*, vol. 9, 1364, at 1366.
15 Department of State Press Release, October 18, 1953, *FRUS 1952–1954*, vol. 9, at 1367. Attack by Israeli Forces, *Department of State Bulletin*, vol. 9, at 552 (October 26, 1953).
16 The Chargé in Israel (Russell) to the Department of State, October 17, 1953, *FRUS 1952–1954*, vol. 9, 1364, at 1366.
17 Gabriel Sheffer, *Moshe Sharett: Biography of a Political Moderate* (Oxford: Clarendon Press, 1996), at 687–688.
18 Id. at 686.
19 Government Debate on Suspension of Work near the Benot-Yaaqov Bridge and the Qibya Operation, October 18, 1953, in Yemima Rosenthal (ed.), *Documents on the Foreign Policy of Israel*, vol. 8 companion, 1953 (Jerusalem: Israel State Archives, 1995), 368, at 369.
20 Rokach, *Israel's Sacred Terrorism*, at 14.
21 Government Debate on Suspension of Work near the Benot-Yaaqov Bridge and the Qibya Operation, October 18, 1953, in Rosenthal, *Documents on the Foreign Policy of Israel*, vol. 8 companion, 1953, 368, at 371.
22 M. Sharett (Jerusalem) to the Israel Missions Abroad, October 18, 1953, id. at 373.
23 The Prime Minister's Statement on the Qibya Action, Broadcast over the Radio on 19 October 1953, in Rosenthal, *Documents on the Foreign Policy of Israel*, vol. 8 companion, 1953, at 374–375. Ben-Gurion charges Jordan provoked raid by villagers, *New York Times*, October 20, 1953, at 1.
24 Ze'ev Schiff, *A History of the Israeli Army 1874 to the Present* (New York: Macmillan, 1985), at 75.

25 Gideon Rafael, *Destination Peace: Three Decades of Israeli Foreign Policy – A personal Memoir* (New York: Stein and Day, 1981), at 33.
26 Government Debate on Suspension of Work near the Benot-Yaaqov Bridge and the Qibya Operation, October 18, 1953, in Rosenthal, *Documents on the Foreign Policy of Israel*, vol. 8 companion, 1953, 368, at 370.
27 Ariel Sharon, *Warrior: The Autobiography of Ariel Sharon* (New York: Simon and Schuster, 1989), at 83.
28 Morris, *Israel's Border Wars 1949–1956*, at 239.
29 Moshe Dayan, *Story of My Life* (London: Weidenfeld and Nicolson, 1976), at 140–141.
30 Sharon, *Warrior*, at 83–84.
31 Michael Bar-Zohar, *Ben-Gurion: A Biography* (New York: Delacorte Press, 1978), at 204. Sharon, *Warrior*, at 88. Shabtai Teveth, *Moshe Dayan: The Soldier, the Man, the Legend* (Boston: Houghton Mifflin, 1973), at 211.
32 Drory, *Israel's Reprisal Policy 1953–1956*, at 110.
33 Morris, *Israel's Border Wars 1949–1956*, at 245.
34 Drory, *Israel's Reprisal Policy 1953–1956*, at 110.
35 Sharon, *Warrior*, at 90–91.
36 UN Security Council, 8th year, 630th meeting, October 27, 1953, at 4, UN Document S/PV.630.
37 Id. at 5.
38 Drory, *Israel's Reprisal Policy 1953–1956*, at 115.
39 UN Security Council, 8th year, 630th meeting, October 27, 1953, at 5, UN Document S/PV.630.
40 E.H. Hutchison, *Violent Truce: A Military Observer Looks at the Arab-Israeli Conflict 1951–1955* (New York: Devin-Adair, 1956), at 44.
41 UN Security Council, 8th year, 630th meeting, October 27, 1953, at 5–7. UN Document S/PV.630.
42 Id. at 11.
43 D. Hacohen (New York) to M. Sharett, October 16, 1953, in Rosenthal, *Documents on the Foreign Policy of Israel*, vol. 8 companion, 1953, at 362.
44 Sheffer, *Moshe Sharett*, at 687.
45 A. Eban (New York) to G. Rafael, October 15, 1953, in Rosenthal, *Documents on the Foreign Policy of Israel*, vol. 8 companion, 1953, at 361.
46 Robert St. John, *Eban* (Garden City, NY: Doubleday, 1972), at 276.
47 A. Eban (New York) to G. Rafael, October 15, 1953, in Rosenthal, *Documents on the Foreign Policy of Israel*, vol. 8 companion, 1953, at 361, note 3 (noting cable from Rafael October 18, 1953).
48 Rafael, *Destination Peace*, at 34.
49 Id. at 33.
50 UN Security Council, 8th year, 632nd meeting, October 29, 1953, at 6, UN Document S/PV.632.
51 UN Security Council, 8th year, 635th meeting, November 9, 1953, at 35, UN Document S/PV.635.
52 Id. at 9.
53 Id. at 12–13.
54 Id. at 13.

55 UN Security Council, 8th year, 637th meeting, November 12, 1953, at 19, UN Document S/PV.637.
56 A. Eban (New York) to M. Sharett, November 11, 1953, in Rosenthal, *Documents on the Foreign Policy of Israel*, vol. 8 companion, 1953, at 414.
57 The Secretary of State to the United States Mission at the United Nations, November 14, 1953, *FRUS 1952–1954*, vol. 9, at 1412.
58 UN Security Council, France, United Kingdom and United States: draft resolution, November 18, 1953, UN Document S/3139.
59 Memorandum of Conversation, by the Officer in Charge of Palestine-Israel-Jordan Affairs (Waller), November 20, 1953, *FRUS 1952–1954*, vol. 9, 1426, at 1430.
60 UN Security Council, 8th year, 642nd meeting, November 24, 1953, at 10, UN Document S/PV.642.
61 Drory, *Israel's Reprisal Policy 1953–1956*, at 123–124.
62 Government Meeting on the Qibya Operation and Ben-Gurion's Statement Broadcast on Israel radio, 22 November 1953, in Rosenthal, *Documents on the Foreign Policy of Israel*, vol. 8 companion, 1953, at 439.
63 UN Security Council, 8th year, 642nd meeting, November 24, 1953, at 11, UN Document S/PV.642.
64 Id. at 11.
65 Israeli Army Training Soldiers and Citizens: Year on Land: Frontier Tension Background to "Horror Raids," *Sunday Times* (London), October 25, 1953, at 7.
66 United Kingdom, Foreign Office Document FO 371/104806, February 1954.
67 UN Security Council, Resolution 101, November 24, 1953, para. A.
68 A. Eban (New York) to M. Sharett, November 26, 1953, in Rosenthal, *Documents on the Foreign Policy of Israel*, vol. 8 companion, 1953, at 451.
69 Abba Eban, *Abba Eban: An Autobiography* (New York: Random House, 1977). at 173.
70 Hutchison, *Violent Truce*, at 116.
71 Drory, *Israel's Reprisal Policy 1953–1956*, at 107.
72 Morris, *Israel's Border Wars 1949–1956*, at 242.
73 Id. at 243.
74 UN Security Council, 8th year, 630th meeting, October 27, 1953, at 11–12, UN Document S/PV.630.
75 Morris, *Israel's Border Wars 1949–1956*, at 243.
76 UN Security Council, 8th year, 642nd meeting, November 24, 1953, at 24, UN Document S/PV.642.
77 Drory, *Israel's Reprisal Policy 1953–1956*, at 116.
78 John Mearsheimer, *Why Leaders Lie: The Truth about Lying in International Politics* (Oxford: Oxford University Press, 2010), at 65.
79 Bar-Zohar, *Ben-Gurion*, at 205–206.

15 SABRAS IN SINAI: PARDON MY FRENCH

1 UN Security Council, *Report by the Chief of Staff of the Truce Supervision Organization to the Security Council pursuant to the Council's resolution of 24 November 1953 (S/3139/Rev.2)*, March 1, 1954, UN Document S/3183.

2 Ze'ev Drory, *Israel's Reprisal Policy 1953–1956: The Dynamics of Military Retaliation* (London: Frank Cass, 2005), at 127–8.
3 Benny Morris, *Israel's Border Wars, 1949–1956: Arab Infiltration, Israeli Retaliation, and the Countdown to the Suez War* (Oxford: Oxford University Press, 1993), at 302.
4 UN Security Council, *Report dated 15 June 1954 by the Chief of Staff of the United Nations Truce Supervision Organization in Palestine to the Secretary-General concerning the Nahhalin incident*, UN Document S/3251.
5 Morris, *Israel's Border Wars 1949–1956*, at 301.
6 E.L.M. Burns, *Between Arab and Israeli* (New York: Ivan Obolensky, 1962), at 17.
7 Drory, *Israel's Reprisal Policy 1953–1956*, at 133–139.
8 Ariel Sharon, *Warrior: The Autobiography of Ariel Sharon* (New York: Simon and Schuster, 1989), at 103.
9 Burns, *Between Arab and Israeli*, at 17.
10 Michael Oren, Escalation to Suez: The Egypt-Israel Border War, 1949–56, in Ian Lustick (ed.), *From War to War: Israel vs. the Arabs 1948–1967* (New York: Garland Publishing, 1994), 175, at 185.
11 Morris, *Israel's Border Wars 1949–1956*, at 327. Drory, *Israel's Reprisal Policy 1953–1956*, at 133–139.
12 Livia Rokach, *Israel's Sacred Terrorism: A Study Based on Moshe Sharett's Personal Diary and Other Documents* (Belmont, MA: Association of Arab-American University Graduates Press, 1986), at 39.
13 Drory, *Israel's Reprisal Policy 1953–1956*, at 137.
14 UN Security Council, 10th year, 694th meeting, March 23, 1955, at 2–19, UN Document S/PV.694.
15 UN Security Council, 10th year, 695th meeting, March 29, 1955, at 5, UN Document S/PV.695.
16 UN Security Council, Resolution 106, March 29, 1955.
17 Robert St. John, *Eban* (Garden City, NY: Doubleday, 1972), at 286.
18 Burns, *Between Arab and Israeli*, at 18.
19 Michael Brecher, *Decisions in Israel's Foreign Policy* (New Haven, CT: Yale University Press, 1975), at 230–231.
20 St. John, *Eban*, at 286.
21 Burns, *Between Arab and Israeli*, at 58, 85–88. Moshe Dayan, *Diary of the Sinai Campaign* (Jerusalem: Steimatzky's, 1966), at 5.
22 Drory, *Israel's Reprisal Policy 1953–1956*, at 143. Shabtai Teveth, *Moshe Dayan: The soldier, the Man, the Legend* (Boston: Houghton Mifflin, 1973), at 249.
23 Abel Thomas, *Comment Israël fût sauvé: les secrets de l'expédition de Suez* (Paris: Albin Michel, 1978), at 91.
24 Shimon Peres, *Battling for Peace: A Memoir* (New York: Random House, 1995) at 106.
25 Id. at 106. Donald Neff, *Warriors at Suez: Eisenhower Takes America into the Middle East* (New York: Simon and Schuster, 1981), at 295. Dayan, *Diary of the Sinai Campaign*, at 15–19. Michael Oren, *Origins of the Second Arab-Israel*

War: Egypt, Israel and the Great Powers 1952–56 (London: Frank Cass, 1992), at 129.

26 Moshe Dayan, *Story of My Life* (London: Weidenfeld and Nicolson, 1976), at 151.

27 Motti Golani, *Israel in Search of a War: The Sinai Campaign, 1955–1956* (Brighton, UK: Sussex Academic Press, 1998), at 73.

28 Dayan, *Story of My Life*, at 151.

29 Neff, *Warriors at Suez*, at 309. Peres, *Battling for Peace*, at 109.

30 Neff, *Warriors at Suez*, at 321.

31 Ze'ev Schiff, *A History of the Israeli Army 1874 to the Present* (New York: Macmillan, 1985), at 90. Dayan, *Story of My Life*, at 157.

32 Schiff, *A History of the Israeli Army 1874 to the Present*, at 91. Neff, *Warriors at Suez*, at 325. Dayan, *Story of My Life*, at 176.

33 Neff, *Warriors at Suez*, at 336. Dayan, *Story of My Life*, at 189–190.

34 The Question of Reviewing the Suez Papers: Mr Wicks, from Robert Armstrong, UK, PREM 19/1, Ref. A/086/1917, June 30, 1986.

35 Gideon Rafael, *Destination Peace: Three Decades of Israeli Foreign Policy – A Personal Memoir* (New York: Stein and Day, 1981), at 58.

36 Patrick Dean, Assistant Under Secretary, Dean Memorandum, at 7 (1978), U.K., FCO Document 73/205.

37 Avi Shlaim, The Protocol of Sèvres, 1956: Anatomy of a War Plot, *International Affairs*, vol. 73, no. 2, 509 at 530 (1997) (text of Protocol in English translation from the French original).

38 Sharon, *Warrior*, at 141.

39 Burns, *Between Arab and Israeli*, at 177.

40 Israel Embassy in Washington to G. Meir and J. Herzog, October 28, 1956, in Nana Sagi (ed.), *Documents on the Foreign Policy of Israel*, vol. 12 companion, The Sinai Campaign: The Political Struggle October 1956 – March 1957 (Jerusalem: Israel State Archives, 2009), at 9.

41 Abba Eban, *Abba Eban: An Autobiography* (New York: Random House, 1977), at 211.

42 Dayan, *Story of My Life*, at 195.

43 Eban, *Abba Eban*, at 211.

44 Memorandum of a Conversation, Department of State, Washington, October 29, 1956, *FRUS 1955–1957*, vol. 16, 821, at 825.

45 Eban, *Abba Eban*, at 211.

46 UN Security Council, 11th year, 748th meeting, October 29, 1956, at 1–2, UN Document S/PV.748.

47 Id. at 3–4. Burns, *Between Arab and Israeli*, at 179–180.

48 UN Security Council, 11th year, 749th meeting, October 29, 1956, at 2–3, UN Document S/PV.749.

49 Id. at 3.

50 Id. at 3.

51 Id. at 3–4.

52 Id. at 4.

53 Id. at 5.

54 Id. at 6–7.

55 Id. at 7.
56 Id. at 8.
57 Id. at 8.
58 Id. at 12–14.
59 Id. at 18.
60 Brecher, *Decisions in Israel's Foreign Policy*, at 278–279. Eban, *Abba Eban*, at 214.
61 A. Eban (Washington) to D. Ben-Gurion, October 28, 1956, in Sagi, *Documents on the Foreign Policy of Israel*, vol. 12 companion, The Sinai Campaign: The Political Struggle October 1956 – March 1957, at 10. And see Editorial Note: The Security Council Convenes. Veto and Deadlock, transfer of Deliberations to an Emergency Session of the U.N. General Assembly (30 October – 1 November 1956), id., 13, at 14.
62 UN Security Council, 11th year, 749th meeting, October 29, 1956, at 26, UN Document S/PV.749.
63 Id. at 29.
64 Id. at 29.
65 Id. at 31.
66 UN Security Council, 11th year, 750th meeting, October 30, 1956, at 7, UN Document S/PV.750.
67 Id. at 5.

16 SUEZ SMOKE-SCREEN

1 Cairo raided; British, French hit Suez zone; warship sunk in fight, *Los Angeles Times*, November 1, 1956, at 1. Henry Wales, Troops mass; invasion of Suez near: France; Egyptians' naval and air force shattered, *Chicago Daily Tribune*, November 3, 1956, at 1. Drop chutists on Egypt! Anglo-French force lands in Suez zone; ships rush other troops to area, *Chicago Daily Tribune*, November 5, 1956, at 1.
2 UN Security Council, 11th year, 751st meeting, October 31, 1956, at 3, UN Document S/PV.751.
3 Id. at 6–7.
4 Id. at 8.
5 Id. at 10.
6 Id. at 22.
7 UN General Assembly, 1st emergency special session, *Plenary Meetings 1–10 November 1956*, 561st meeting, November 1, 1956, at 2–3, UN Document A/PV.561.
8 Id. at 3.
9 Id. at 5.
10 Id. at 7.
11 Id. at 11–12.
12 Id. at 10.
13 UN General Assembly, 1st emergency special session, *Plenary Meetings 1–10 November 1956*, 562nd meeting, November 1, 1956, at 17, UN Document A/PV.562.

14 Id. at 20.
15 Id. at 21.
16 Abba Eban, *Abba Eban: An Autobiography* (New York: Random House, 1977), at 223.
17 UN General Assembly, 1st emergency special session, *Plenary Meetings 1–10 November 1956*, 562nd meeting, November 1, 1956, at 25, UN Document A/PV.562.
18 Id. at 28.
19 Id. at 30.
20 Id. at 41.
21 Id. at 34–35. UN General Assembly, Resolution 997, November 2, 1956.
22 M. Alphand, Ambassadeur de France à Washington, au Ministère des Affaires étrangères, October 30, 1956, *Documents diplomatiques français 1956*, vol. 3, at 94 (1956).
23 John Foster Dulles, Telegram From the Department of State to the Embassy in France, October 29, 1956, *FRUS 1955–1957*, vol. 16, at 815.
24 Michael Brecher, *Decisions in Israel's Foreign Policy* (New Haven, CT: Yale University Press, 1975), at 280.
25 Telegram From the Embassy in France to the Department of State, November 1, 1956, *FRUS 1955–1957*, vol. 16, at 900–901.
26 Memorandum of a Telephone Conversation Between the Secretary of State in Washington and the Representative at the United Nations (Lodge) in New York, November 2, 1956, 4:11 p.m., *FRUS 1955–1957*, vol. 16, at 938.
27 Telegram From the Embassy in France to the Department of State, November 1, 1956, *FRUS 1955–1957*, vol. 16, 919, at 920–921.
28 Letter From President Eisenhower to Swede Hazlett, November 2, 1956, *FRUS 1955–1957*, vol. 16, 943, at 944–945.
29 Memorandum of a Conversation, Department of State, November 1, 1956, *FRUS 1955–1957*, vol. 16, at 925.
30 Eban, *Abba Eban*, at 219.
31 Id. at 220.
32 Memorandum of a Conversation, Department of State, November 1, 1956, *FRUS 1955–1957*, vol. 16, 925, at 926.
33 UN General Assembly, 1st emergency special session, *Plenary Meetings 1–10 November 1956*, 563rd meeting, November 3, 1956, at 52, UN Document A/PV.563.
34 Id. at 57.
35 Id. at 60.
36 Id. at 77.
37 UN General Assembly, Resolution 1000, November 5, 1956.
38 Brecher, *Decisions in Israel's Foreign Policy*, at 238.
39 Memorandum From the Secretary of State's Special Assistant for Intelligence (Armstrong) to the Secretary of State, December 5, 1956, *FRUS 1955–1957*, vol. 16, 249, at 250.
40 A. Eban (New York) to D. Ben-Gurion and G. Meir, November 7, 1956, in Nana Sagi (ed.), *Documents on the Foreign Policy of Israel*, vol. 12 companion,

The Sinai Campaign: The Political Struggle October 1956 – March 1957 (Jerusalem: Israel State Archives, 2009), at 61.

41 David Ben Gurion, *Ben Gurion Looks Back In Talks with Moshe Pearlman* (New York: Schocken Books, 1970), at 146–147.

42 Avi Shlaim, The Protocol of Sèvres, 1956: Anatomy of a War Plot, *International Affairs*, vol. 73, no. 2, 509, at 521, 523 (1997).

43 Homer Bigart, Israel terms Gaza Strip an integral part of nation, *New York Times*, November 11, 1956, at 1.

44 Donald Neff, *Warriors at Suez: Eisenhower Takes America into the Middle East* (New York: Simon and Schuster, 1981), at 416.

45 UN General Assembly, 11th session, Secretary-General, *Aide mémoire on the Israeli Position on the Sharm-el-Sheikh Area and the Gaza Strip*, January 24, 1957, at 5, UN Document 3511. UN General Assembly, 11th session, *Report by the Secretary-General in Pursuance of the Resolution of the General Assembly of 19 January 1957 (A/RES/453)*, January 24, 1957, part 2, para. 5(a), UN Document A/3512.

46 UN General Assembly, Resolution 1120, November 24, 1956.

47 UN General Assembly, Resolution 1123, January 19, 1957; Resolution 1124, February 2, 1957.

48 Brecher, *Decisions in Israel's Foreign Policy*, at 291–303. Aide-mémoire to Ambassador Abba Eban by Secretary John Foster Dulles, February 11, 1957, *Department of State Bulletin*, vol. 36, at 392 (March 11, 1957). Cheryl Rubenberg, *Israel and the American National Interest* (Urbana: University of Illinois Press, 1986), at 80–87. Richard Locke and Antony Stewart, *Bantustan Gaza* (London: Zed Press, 1985), at 6.

49 Ariel Sharon, *Warrior: The Autobiography of Ariel Sharon* (New York: Simon and Schuster, 1989), at 155.

50 Shimon Peres, *Battling for Peace: A Memoir* (New York: Random House, 1995), 114.

51 Dayan, *Diary of the Sinai Campaign*, at 227.-229.

52 Brecher, *Decisions in Israel's Foreign Policy*, at 275.

53 Moshe Dayan, *Diary of the Sinai Campaign* (Jerusalem: Steimatzky's, 1966), at 109.

54 Peres, *Battling for Peace*, at 114.

55 Dayan, *Diary of the Sinai Campaign*, at 206.

56 Brecher, *Decisions in Israel's Foreign Policy*, at 238.

57 Michael Brecher, *The Foreign Policy System of Israel: Setting, Images, Process* (London: Oxford University Press, 1972), at 330.

58 Abba Eban, *Voice of Israel* (New York: Horizon Press, 1957).

59 Shabtai Rosenne, Basic Elements of Israel's Foreign Policy, *India Quarterly*, vol. 17, 328, at 344 (1961).

60 Id. at 344.

61 Letter From President Eisenhower to Swede Hazlett, November 2, 1956, *FRUS 1955–1957*, vol. 16, 943, at 944.

62 Meeting of the Israeli Delegation to the United Nations General Assembly (Paris, December 5, 1948), in Yehoshua Freundlich (ed.), *Documents on*

the Foreign Policy of Israel, vol. 2 companion, October 1948 – April 1949 (Jerusalem: Israel State Archives, 1984), 55, at 56.

63 Brecher, *The Foreign Policy System of Israel*, at 386.

64 Shabtai Rosenne, *The Law and Practice of the International Court* (Leyden: A.W. Sijthoff, 1965).

65 Malcolm Shaw, Shabtai Rosenne Obituary: Eminent international lawyer, teacher and Israeli diplomat, *Guardian*, October 12, 2010.

66 Christian Pineau, *1956/Suez* (Paris: Robert Laffont, 1976), at 126.

67 Herman Finer, *Dulles over Suez: The Theory and Practice of His Diplomacy* (Chicago: Quadrangle Books, 1964), at 324–366.

68 Anthony Nutting, *No End of a Lesson: The Story of Suez* (New York: Clarkson N. Potter, 1967), at 104.

69 Robert St. John, *Eban* (Garden City, NY: Doubleday, 1972), at 313.

70 Dayan, *Diary of the Sinai Campaign* (Hebrew edition published 1965).

71 Moshe Dayan, *Story of My Life* (London: Weidenfeld and Nicolson, 1976), at 151–194.

17 MR. NASSER, PLEASE ATTACK

1 Arthur Lall, *The UN and the Middle East Crisis, 1967* (New York: Columbia University Press, 1970), at 1–3.

2 UN Security Council, 22nd year, Supplement for April, May and June 1967, *Letter dated 11 May 1967 from the representative of Israel to the President of the Security Council*, at 82, UN Document S/7880.

3 UN Security Council, 22nd year, Supplement for April, May and June 1967, *Letter dated 15 May 1967 from the representative of Syria to the President of the Security Council*, at 90, UN Document S/7885.

4 Memorandum of Conversation, Washington, May 25, 1967, *FRUS 1964–1968*, vol. 19, at 109.

5 Memorandum From the President's Special Assistant (Rostow) to President Johnson, Washington, May 25, 1967, *FRUS 1964–1968*, vol. 19, at 103 (forwarding to Johnson the CIA assessment).

6 Briefing Notes for Director of Central Intelligence Helms for Use at a White House Meeting, Washington, May 23, 1967, *FRUS 1964–1968*, vol. 19, 74, at 75.

7 Harold Saunders, Memorandum for the Record, Washington, May 26, 1967, *FRUS 1964–1968*, vol. 19, at 127. Intelligence Memorandum Prepared in the Central Intelligence Agency, Military Capabilities of Israel and the Arab States, Washington, May 26, 1967, *FRUS 1964–1968*, vol. 19, at 138.

8 Shabtai Teveth, *The Tanks of Tammuz* (London: Sphere Books, 1970), at 112.

9 Rufus Taylor, Memorandum for the Record, Washington, June 1, 1967, *FRUS 1964–1968*, vol. 19, at 223.

10 Richard Parker (ed.), *The Six-Day War: A Retrospective* (Gainesville: University Press of Florida, 1996), at 139 (statement of Meir Amit).

11 Tom Segev, *1967: Israel, the War, and the Year that Transformed the Middle East* (New York: Henry Holt, 2007), at 258, 323–324. Ami Gluska, *The Israeli*

Military and the Origins of the 1967 War: Government, Armed Forces and Defence Policy 1963–1967 (London: Routledge, 2007), at 177.

12 Michael Bar-Zohar, *Histoire secrète de la guerre d'Israël* (Paris: Fayard, 1968), at 137, 147.

13 Id. at 157.

14 Walter Rostow, Memorandum From the President's Special Assistant (Rostow) to President Johnson, Washington, June 2, 1967, *FRUS 1964–1968*, vol. 19, at 244.

15 Gluska, *The Israeli Military and the Origins of the 1967 War*, at 209.

16 Michael Oren, *Six Days of War: June 1967 and the Making of the Modern Middle East* (Oxford: Oxford University Press, 2002), at 156.

17 Avi Raz, *The Bride and the Dowry: Israel, Jordan, and the Palestinians in the Aftermath of the June 1967 War* (New Haven: Yale University Press, 2012), at 22.

18 Government of Israel, Ministerial Committee for Security Affairs, Resolution B/51, June 4, 1967. See also Government of Israel Decision, 4 June 1967, *Israel's Foreign Relations: Selected Documents 1947–1974* (Jerusalem: Ministry of Foreign Affairs, 1976), vol. 2, at 777–778; Asher Wallfish, Meir reveals text of cabinet decision, *Jerusalem Post*, June 5, 1972, at 1.

19 Moshe Dayan, *Story of My Life* (London: Weidenfeld and Nicolson, 1976), at 278. Janice Gross Stein and Raymond Tanter, *Rational Decision-Making: Israel's Security Choices, 1967* (Columbus: Ohio State University Press, 1980), at 241.

20 Ariel Sharon, *Warrior: The Autobiography of Ariel Sharon* (New York: Simon and Schuster, 1989), at 187.

21 Segev, *1967*, at 255.

22 Ezer Weizman, *On Eagles' Wings: The Personal Story of the Leading Commander of the Israeli Air Force* (New York: Macmillan, 1976), at 215.

23 Segev, *1967*, at 336.

24 Id. at 342.

25 Gluska, *The Israeli Military and the Origins of the 1967 War*, at 256.

26 U Thant, *View from the UN* (Garden City, NY: Doubleday, 1978), at 253–254.

27 As the News Broke, *Jerusalem Post*, June 6, 1967, at 6.

28 Daniel Dishon (ed.), *Middle East Record Volume Three 1967* (Jerusalem: Israel Universities Press, 1971), at 207.

29 Abba Eban, *Abba Eban: An Autobiography* (New York: Random House, 1977), at 403.

30 Id. at 403.

31 Id. at 404.

32 Telegram Secret Tel Aviv 3928 From AmEmbassy Tel Aviv to SecState WashDC Flash, June 5, 1967, in Subject Numeric File, Time Segment 1967–1969 POL 127, ARAB-ISR, National Archives, College Park, Maryland, USA.

33 Walworth Barbour, Telegram From the Embassy in Israel to the Department of State, Tel Aviv, June 5, 1967, *FRUS 1964–1968*, vol. 19, at 302.

34 Id. at 302, note 1.

35 Moshe Dayan, 'We are a small people, but a brave one,' *Jerusalem Post*, June 6, 1967, at 3. See also Dishon, *Middle East Record Volume Three 1967*, at 207.
36 Segev, *1967*, at 287.
37 Teveth, *The Tanks of Tammuz*, at 40.
38 Dishon, *Middle East Record Volume Three 1967*, at 207.
39 Prime Minister Eshkol's Note to Premier Kosygin, June 5, 1967, *Israel's Foreign Relations: Selected Documents 1947–1974* (Jerusalem: Ministry of Foreign Affairs, 1976), vol. 2, at 780.
40 Eban, *Abba Eban*, at 404.
41 E.L.M. Burns, *Between Arab and Israeli* (New York: Ivan Obolensky, 1962), at 78.
42 Memorandum Prepared in the Central Intelligence Agency's Office of Current Intelligence, Washington, June 5, 1967, *FRUS 1964–1968*, vol. 19, at 318.
43 Harold Saunders, Memorandum for the Record, Washington, November 17, 1968, *FRUS 1964–1968*, vol. 19, 287, at 289, note 7.
44 Memorandum Prepared in the Central Intelligence Agency's Office of Current Intelligence, Washington, June 5, 1967, *FRUS 1964–1968*, vol. 19, at 318.
45 Zaiavlenie sovetskogo pravitel'stva [Statement of the Soviet Government], *Pravda*, June 6, 1967, at 1.
46 *House of Commons Debates* (Hansard), June 5, 1967, vol. 747, cc640-641.
47 Déclaration officielle du gouvernement français sur le Moyen-Orient, June 21, 1967, *La Politique Étrangère de la France: Textes et Documents*, 1er semestre 1967, at 130–131.
48 Entretien entre le général de Gaulle et M. Kossyguine 16 juin 1967, *Documents Diplomatiques Français*, vol. 1, at 728 (1967).
49 UN Security Council, 22nd year, 1347th meeting, June 5, 1967, at 1–2, UN Document S/PV.1347.
50 Id. at 2. Indar Jit Rikhye, *The Sinai Blunder: Withdrawal of the United Nations Emergency Force leading to the Six-Day War of June 1967* (London: Frank Cass, 1980), at 102–105.
51 UN Security Council, 22nd year, 1347th meeting, June 5, 1967, at 3, UN Document S/PV.1347.
52 Id. at 3–4.
53 Id. at 4–5.
54 Lall, *The UN and the Middle East Crisis, 1967*, at 110.
55 UN Security Council, 22nd year, 1347th meeting, June 5, 1967, at 5, UN Document S/PV.1347.
56 Gideon Rafael, *Destination Peace: Three Decades of Israeli Foreign Policy – A Personal Memoir* (New York: Stein and Day, 1981), at 158.
57 Id. at 157.
58 Eban, *Abba Eban*, at 410–411.
59 Rafael, *Destination Peace*, at 157.
60 UN Security Council, 22nd year, 1348th meeting, June 6, 1967, at 1–2, UN Document S/PV.1348.
61 Id. at 5.
62 Id. at 8–9.
63 Id. at 9.

18 ABBA EBAN'S FINEST HOUR

1 UN Security Council, 22nd year, 1348th meeting, June 6, 1967, at 14–15, UN Document S/PV.1348.
2 Memorandum of Telephone Conversation Between the Representative to the United Nations (Goldberg) and Secretary of State Rusk, June 5, 1967, *FRUS 1964–1968*, vol. 19, at 316.
3 Rafael, *Destination Peace: Three Decades of Israeli Foreign Policy – A Personal Memoir* (New York: Stein and Day, 1981), at 157.
4 Harry C. McPherson, Jr., Memorandum From the President's Special Counsel (McPherson) to President Johnson, Washington, June 11, 1967, *FRUS 1964–1968*, vol. 19, at 433.
5 UN Security Council, 22nd year, 1348th meeting, June 6, 1967, at 15, UN Document S/PV.1348.
6 UN Security Council, 22nd year, 1348th meeting, June 6, 1967, at 15, UN Document S/PV.1348.
7 Jack Gould, TV: Spotlight on Crisis, *New York Times*, June 7, 1967, at 95.
8 Robert St. John, *Eban* (Garden City, NY: Doubleday, 1972), at 458–459.
9 Abba Eban, *Abba Eban: An Autobiography* (New York: Random House, 1977), at 417.
10 Observations on a Crisis, *Chicago Tribune*, June 9, 1967, at 20.
11 Eban to U.N.: Israel Out of Worst Peril, *Chicago Tribune*, June 7, 1967, at 8.
12 Eban, *Abba Eban*, at 418. Ralph McGill, Cut by Sword of Truth, *Daily Reporter* (Dover, Ohio), June 15, 1967, at 4.
13 UN Security Council, 22nd year, 1360th meeting, June 14, 1967, at 18–19, UN Document S/PV.1360.
14 *Year Book of the United Nations 1967* (New York: United Nations Office of Public Information, 1969), at 191.
15 UN General Assembly, 5th emergency special session, *Plenary Meetings Verbatim Records of Meetings 17 June–18 September 1967*, 1526th meeting, June 19, 1967, at 9, UN Document A/PV.1526.
16 Id. at 12.
17 Eban, *Abba Eban*, at 434. James Reston, Few Signs of Hope: First Day's Debate on the Mideast Is Mostly Some Harsh Exchanges, *New York Times*, June 20, 1967, at 19.
18 James Wechsler, Eban's triumph, *New York Post*, June 20, 1967, at 49. And see Eban, *Abba Eban*, at 434.
19 Eban, *Abba Eban*, at 434–435.
20 UN General Assembly, 5th emergency special session, *Plenary Meetings Verbatim Records of Meetings 17 June – 18 September 1967*, 1526th meeting, June 19, 1967, at 9–10, UN Document A/PV.1526.
21 Id. at 10.
22 Id. at 10.
23 U Thant, *View from the UN* (Garden City, NY: Doubleday, 1978), at 268–269.
24 UN General Assembly, 5th emergency special session, *Plenary Meetings Verbatim Records of Meetings 17 June–18 September 1967*, 1527th meeting, June 20, 1967, at 1, UN Document A/PV.1527.

25 *Report of the Secretary-General on the Withdrawal of the UNEF*, June 26, 1967, para. 21, UN Document A/6730/Add.3.

26 UN General Assembly, 5th emergency special session, *Plenary Meetings Verbatim Records of Meetings 17 June–18 September* 1967, 1527th meeting, at 1, June 20, 1967, UN Document A/PV.1527.

27 Dean Rusk, Telegram From the Department of State to the Embassy in the United Kingdom, Washington, May 21, 1967, *FRUS 1964–1968*, vol. 19, 43, at 44.

28 Dean Rusk, Telegram From the Department of State to the Embassy in Israel, Washington, May 21, 1967, *FRUS 1964–1968*, vol. 19, 46, at 47, note 6.

29 UN General Assembly, 5th emergency special session, *Plenary Meetings Verbatim Records of Meetings 17 June–18 September 1967*, 1528th meeting, June 20, 1967, at 6–8, UN Document A/PV.1528.

30 UN General Assembly, 5th emergency special session, *Plenary Meetings Verbatim Records of Meetings 17 June–18 September* 1967, 1538th meeting, June 27, 1967, at 10, UN Document A/PV.1538.

31 UN General Assembly, 5th emergency special session, *Plenary Meetings Verbatim Records of Meetings 17 June–18 September 1967*, 1536th meeting, June 26, 1967, at 9, UN Document A/PV.1536.

32 UN General Assembly, 5th emergency special session, *Plenary Meetings Verbatim Records of Meetings 17 June–18 September 1967*, 1541st meeting, June 29, 1967, at 7–8, UN Document A/PV.1541.

33 UN General Assembly, 5th emergency special session, *Plenary Meetings Verbatim Records of Meetings 17 June–18 September* 1967, 1539th meeting, June 28, 1967, at 9, UN Document A/PV.1539.

34 Ariyeh Tzimuki, We will let the Vatican have some control over the holy places in Jerusalem, *Yediot aharonot*, July 7, 1967, at 1.

35 Broadcast to the Nation by Prime Minister Eshkol, May 28, 1967, *Israel's Foreign Relations: Selected Documents 1947–1974* (Jerusalem: Ministry of Foreign Affairs, 1976), vol. 2, at 773–774.

36 Admission on Attack, *Times* (London), June 8, 1967, at 3.

37 Une nouvelle interview de M. Eshkol fait apparaître l'existence de divergences entre le général Dayan et lui: Le premier ministre admet que les Israëliens ont tiré les premiers, *Le Monde*, July 9–10, 1967, at 2.

38 David Rodman, *Defense and Diplomacy in Israel's National Security Experience: Tactics, Partnerships, and Motives* (Brighton, UK: Sussex Academic Press, 2005), at 69.

19 OLD ISSUES, NEW LIES

1 UN General Assembly, 5th emergency special session, *Plenary Meetings Verbatim Records of Meetings 17 June–18 September* 1967, 1529th meeting, June 21, 1967, at 2, UN Document A/PV.1529.

2 Abba Eban, *Abba Eban: An Autobiography* (New York: Random House, 1977, at 437.

3 Id. at 437.

4 Id. at 438.

5 Michael Brecher, *Decisions in Israel's Foreign Policy* (New Haven, CT: Yale University Press, 1975), at 37. Ian Lustick, Has Israel Annexed East Jerusalem? *Middle East Policy*, vol. 5, issue 1, 34, at 36–37 (1997).
6 Brecher, *Decisions in Israel's Foreign Policy*, at 39.
7 Law and Administration Ordinance (Amendment No. 11) Law, *Laws of the State of Israel*, vol. 21, at 75 (1967).
8 Municipalities Ordinance (Declaration on the Enlargement of Jerusalem's City Limits, Kovetz Ha-Takanot (Official Gazette), No. 2065, June 28, 1967, at 2694, reprinted as Order Unites Holy City, *Jerusalem Post*, June 29, 1967, at 1. For summary, see Daniel Dishon (ed.), *Middle East Record Volume Three 1967* (Jerusalem, Israel Universities Press, 1971), at 290.
9 U Thant, *View from the UN* (Garden City, NY: Doubleday, 1978), at 275.
10 UN General Assembly, 5th emergency special session, *Plenary Meetings Verbatim Records of Meetings 17 June–18 September 1967*, 1541th meeting, June 29, 1967, at 2, UN Document A/PV.1541.
11 Id. at 9.
12 Id. at 9–10.
13 Id. at 10.
14 Thant, *View from the UN*, at 275, citing UN Office of Public Information Minutes, June 29, 1967.
15 Avi Raz, *The Bride and the Dowry: Israel, Jordan, and the Palestinians in the Aftermath of the June 1967 War* (New Haven: Yale University Press, 2012), at 55.
16 UN General Assembly, Resolution 2253, July 4, 1967.
17 Measures taken by Israel to change the status of the City of Jerusalem: Report of the Secretary-General, July 10, 1967, at 3, UN Document A/6753, S/8052.
18 UN General Assembly, Resolution 2254, July 14, 1967.
19 *Report of the Secretary-General under General Assembly Resolution 2254 (ES-V) relating to Jerusalem*, at 7, September 12, 1967, UN Document A/6793, S/8146. See also Dishon, *Middle East Record Volume Three 1967*, at 292.
20 Eban, *Abba Eban*, at 438.
21 Basic Law: Jerusalem, Capital of Israel, *Laws of the State of Israel*, vol. 34, at 209 (1980).
22 UN Security Council, Resolution 237, June 14, 1967.
23 UN Security Council, 22nd year, Supplement for April, May, June 1967, *Report by the Secretary-General to the Security Council in pursuance of operative paragraph 3 of the Council's resolution 237 (1967)*, June 29, 1967, Annex 1: "Note verbale" dated 22 June 1967, addressed to the Secretary-General by the Representative of Israel, at 301, UN Document S/8021.
24 UN General Assembly, Resolution 2252, July 4, 1967.
25 UN General Assembly, 5th emergency special session, *Report of the Secretary-General under General Assembly Resolution 2252 (ES-V) and Security Council Resolution 237*, para. 159, September 15, 1967, UN Document A/6797, S/8158.
26 UN General Assembly, 22nd session, Supplement No. 13, *Report of the Commissioner-General of the United Nations Relief and Works Agency for*

Palestine Refugees in the Near East, 1 July 1966–30 June 1967, June 30, 1967, para. 30, UN Document A/6713.

27 Dana Adams Schmidt, 100,000 in Jordan said to have fled across river: UN relief officials believe the Israelis have expelled at least some forcibly, *New York Times*, June 12, 1967, at 19.

28 Peter Dodd and Halim Barakat, *River without Bridges* (Beirut: Institute for Palestine Studies, 1969), at 40–43.

29 Id. at 40.

30 Id. at 43.

31 Id. at 47. John Richardson, *The West Bank: A Portrait* (Washington, DC: Middle East Institute, 1984), at 66. David Pryce-Jones, *The Face of Defeat: Palestinian Refugees and Guerrillas* (London: Weidenfeld and Nicolson, 1972), at 6–7.

32 Raz, *The Bride and the Dowry*, at 105.

33 UN General Assembly, 5th emergency special session, *Report of the Secretary-General under General Assembly Resolution 2252 (ES-V) and Security Council Resolution 237*, September 15, 1967, para. 54, UN Document A/6797, S/8158. UN General Assembly, 22nd session, Supplement No. 13, *Report of the Commissioner-General of the United Nations Relief and Works Agency for Palestine Refugees in the Near East, 1 July 1966–30 June 1967*, June 30, 1967, at 11, UN Document A/6713. Donald Neff, *Warriors for Jerusalem: The Six Days that Changed the Middle East* (New York: Simon and Schuster, 1984), at 292.

34 UN General Assembly, 22nd session, Supplement No. 13, *Report of the Commissioner-General of the United Nations Relief and Works Agency for Palestine Refugees in the Near East 1 July 1966–30 June 1967*, June 30, 1967, at 13, UN Document A/6713. Peter Dodd and Halim Barakat, *River without Bridges* (Beirut: Institute for Palestine Studies, 1969), at 57. Raz, *The Bride and the Dowry*, at 133.

35 *Country Reports on Human Rights Practices for 1990* (Washington, DC: US Department of State, 1991), at 1491.

36 Shabtai Rosenne, Directions for a Middle East Settlement – Some Underlying Legal Problems, *Law and Contemporary Problems*, vol. 33, 44, at 55 (1968).

37 Shabtai Rosenne, On Defining International Aggression – An Exercise in Futility, *Israel Law Review*, vol. 12, 401, at 403 (1977).

38 Eric Rouleau, Le général Rabin ne pense pas que Nasser voulait la guerre, *Le Monde*, February 29, 1968, at 1.

39 Abba Eban, *Voice of Israel* (New York: Horizon Press, 1969).

40 Mordecai Bentov, For whom and why are the settlements necessary?, *Al-Hamishmar*, April 14, 1972, at 3, translated in Amnon Kapeliouk, Israël était-il réellement menacé d'extermination?, *Le Monde*, June 3, 1972, at 4.

41 Asher Wallfish, Meir reveals text of cabinet decision, *Jerusalem Post*, June 5, 1972, at 1.

42 Wallfish, Meir reveals text of cabinet decision, at 1.

43 Jérusalem affirme que l'État hébreu était menace d'anéantissement en 1967, *Le Monde*, June 6, 1972, at 3.

44 Decision on 1967 war disclosed by Israelis, *Washington Post*, June 5, 1972, at A23.

45 Benjamin Geist, A Question of Survival, *International Journal* (Canadian International Council), vol. 28, no. 4, 630, at 631 (1973).
46 Id. at 631.
47 Moshe Dayan, *Story of My Life* (London: Weidenfeld and Nicolson, 1976), at 275.
48 Michael Oren, *Six Days of War: June 1967 and the Making of the Modern Middle East* (Oxford: Oxford University Press, 2002), at 97.
49 Dayan, *Story of My Life*, at 280–281.
50 Eban, *Abba Eban*, at 403.
51 Raz, *The Bride and the Dowry*, at 294.
52 Address by Prime Minister Begin at the National Defense College, 8 August 1982, *Israel's Foreign Relations: Selected Documents 1982–1984* (Jerusalem: Ministry of Foreign Affairs, 1990), vol. 8, 131, at 134. See also Excerpts from Begin Speech at National Defense College, *New York Times*, August 21, 1982, at 6.
53 Israel Ministry of Foreign Affairs, www.mfa.org ("frequently asked questions about status of territories"), as posted 2012.
54 U.S. again prods Israel and Arabs, *New York Times*, November 20, 1960, at 1. Kennedy offers Arab refugee plan: Ben-Gurion, *Chicago Tribune*, June 2, 1961, at 1.
55 Shay Hazkani, Catastrophic thinking: Did Ben-Gurion try to rewrite history? The file in the state archives contains clear evidence that the researchers at the time did not paint the full picture of Israel's role in creating the Palestinian refugee problem, *Ha-aretz*, May 16, 2013.
56 *Background Notes on Current Themes – No.6: Dir Yassin* (Jerusalem: Ministry for Foreign Affairs, Information Division, March 16, 1969).
57 UN General Assembly, 5th session, Ad Hoc Political Committee, 64th meeting, November 30, 1950, at 411, UN Document A/AC.38/SR.64.
58 David K. Shipler, Israel bars Rabin from relating '48 eviction of Arabs, *New York Times*, October 23, 1979, at 3.
59 Yitzhak Rabin, *The Rabin Memoirs* (Boston: Little, Brown, 1979), at 35.

20 AN ORGANIZATION TURNED SINISTER

1 UN General Assembly, Resolution 2443, December 19, 1968.
2 UN General Assembly, Resolution 3376, November 10, 1975.
3 UN General Assembly, Resolution 34/65D, para. 1, December 12, 1979.
4 Israel and International Organizations: Lecture by Shabtai Rosenne, February 13, 1984, *Bracton Law Journal*, vol. 17, 22, at 29 (1984).
5 Id. at 30.
6 UN General Assembly, Resolution 3379, November 10, 1975.
7 UN General Assembly, Resolution ES-9/1, February 5, 1982.
8 Credentials of Representatives to the Fortieth Session of the General Assembly, UN Document A/40/752/Rev.1, October 16, 1982.
9 Palestine National Council, Declaration of Independence, November 15, 1988, UN Document A/43/827, S/20278, Annex III.
10 UN General Assembly, Resolution 43/177, December 15, 1988.

11 UN General Assembly, 43rd session, 82nd meeting, December 15, 1988, at 56–60, UN Document A/43/PV.82.
12 UN General Assembly, Resolution 46/86, December 16, 1991.
13 UN *Commission on Human Rights, Resolution 1993/2 A, para. 4(a), UN Document E/CN.4/RES/1993 2 A.*
14 UN General Assembly, Resolution ES-10/14, December 8, 2003.
15 International Court of Justice, Legal Consequences of the Construction of a Wall in the Occupied Palestinian Territory, *Reports of Judgments, Advisory Opinions and Orders*, 2004, at 136.
16 See, e.g., US Supreme Court, *Zivotofsky v. Kerry*, No 13–628, US Reports, vol. 576 (2015).
17 Peaceful Settlement of the Question of Palestine, UN General Assembly, Resolution 68/15, November 26, 2013, para. 22.
18 UN General Assembly, 66th session, 19th meeting, September 23, 2011, UN Document A/66/PV.19.
19 Jodi Rudoren and Somini Sengupta, Both sides in Gaza war are faulted by U.N. panel, *New York Times*, June 23, 2015, at A4.

21 PREVARICATION PAYS

1 *Documents on Israeli-Soviet Relations 1941–1953: Part I: 1941-May 1949* (London: Frank Cass, 2000). *Sovetsko-izrail'skie otnosheniia: Sbornik dokumentov, Tom I 1941–1953: Kniga 1 1941-mai 1949* (Moscow: Mezhdunarodnie otnosheniia, 2000).
2 Ari Shavit, *My Promised Land: The Triumph and Tragedy of Israel* (New York: Spiegel and Grau, 2013), at 189.
3 Robert Malley and Hussein Agha, Camp David: The Tragedy of Error, *New York Review of Books*, August 9, 2001.
4 Gilead Sher, *The Israeli-Palestinian Peace Negotiations, 1999–2001: Within Reach* (London: Routledge, 2006), at 68. Charles Enderlin, *Shattered Dreams: The Failure of the Peace Process in the Middle East 1995–2002* (New York: Other Press, 2003), at 212. Dennis Ross, *The Missing Peace: The Inside Story of the Fight for the Middle East* (New York: Farrar, Straus and Giroux, 2004), at 655.
5 Raymond G. Helmick, *Negotiating Outside the Law: Why Camp David Failed* (London: Pluto Press, 2004), at 149. Clayton Swisher, *The Truth about Camp David: The Untold Story about the Collapse of the Middle East Peace Process* (New York: Nation Books, 2004), at 274–275.
6 Ehud Barak, The Myths Spread About Camp David Are Baseless, in Shimon Shamir and Bruce Maddy-Weitzman, *The Camp David Summit – What Went Wrong?: Americans, Israelis, and Palestinians Analyze the Failure of the Boldest Attempt Ever to Resolve the Palestinian-Israeli Conflict* (Brighton, UK: Sussex Academic Press, 2005), 117, at 130.
7 Barak, at 134.
8 Sher, *The Israeli-Palestinian Peace Negotiations, 1999–2001*, at 5.
9 Israel Ministry of Foreign Affairs, www.mfa.org, under "Foreign Policy," as posted 2015.

10 Israel Ministry of Foreign Affairs, www.mfa.org, under "Foreign Policy," as posted 2015.

11 John Mearsheimer, *Why Leaders Lie: The Truth about Lying in International Politics* (Oxford: Oxford University Press, 2010), at 99.

12 Gideon Levy, Israeli propaganda isn't fooling anyone – except Israelis, *Ha'aretz*, June 4, 2015.

Bibliography

Abu-Lughod, Ibrahim (ed.). *The Transformation of Palestine: Essays on the Origin and Development of the Arab-Israeli Conflict* (Evanston, IL: Northwestern University Press, 1971).

Abu Sitta, Salman, and Terry Rempel. The ICRC and the Detention of Palestinian Civilians in Israel's 1948 POW/Labor Camps, *Journal of Palestine Studies*, vol. 43, no. 4, Issue 172 (Summer 2014).

Alroey, Gur. *An Unpromising Land: Jewish Migration to Palestine in the Early Twentieth Century* (Stanford: Stanford University Press, 2014).

Arendt, Hannah. *The Jew as Pariah: Jewish Identity and Politics in the Modern Age* (New York: Random House, 1978).

Barbour, Nevill. *Palestine: Star or Crescent?* (New York: Odyssey Press, 1947).

Avnery, Uri. *My Friend, the Enemy* (Westport, CT: Lawrence Hill, 1986).

Banks, Lynne Reid. *Torn Country: An Oral History of the Israeli War of Independence* (New York: Franklin Watts, 1982).

Baron, Salo. *The Russian Jew Under Tsars and Soviets* (New York: Macmillan, 1976).

Barzilay, Dvorah, and Barnet Litvinoff. *The Letters and Papers of Chaim Weizmann* (New Brunswick, NJ: Transaction Books, 1977).

Bar-Zohar, Michael. *Ben-Gurion: A Biography* (New York: Delacorte Press, 1978).

Histoire secrète de la guerre d'Israël (Paris: Fayard, 1968).

Begin, Menachem. *The Revolt* (New York: Henry Schuman, 1951).

Ben-Dror, Elad. The Arab Struggle against Partition: The International Arena of Summer 1947, *Middle Eastern Studies*, vol. 43, issue 2 (2007).

Ralph Bunche and the Arab-Israeli Conflict: Mediation and the UN, 1947–1949 (London: Routledge, 2016).

Ben Gurion, David. *Rebirth and Destiny of Israel* (New York: Philosophical Library, 1954).

Berman, Aaron. *Nazism, the Jews and American Zionism 1933–1948* (Detroit, MI: Wayne State University Press, 1990).

Bloomfield, L.M. *Egypt, Israel and the Gulf of Aqaba in International Law* (Toronto: Carswell, 1957).

Bober, Arie (ed.). *The Other Israel: The Radical Case against Zionism* (Garden City, NY: Doubleday, 1972).

Bowett, Derek. Reprisals Involving Recourse to Armed Force, *American Journal of International Law*, vol. 66 (1972).

Brecher, Michael. *Decisions in Israel's Foreign Policy* (New Haven, CT: Yale University Press, 1975).

The Foreign Policy System of Israel: Setting, Images, Process (London: Oxford University Press, 1972).

Breitman, Richard, Barbara McDonald Stewart, and Severin Hochberg (eds.). *Refugees and Rescue: The Diaries and Papers of James G. McDonald 1935–1945* (Bloomington, IL: Indiana University Press, 2009).

Burns, E.L.M. *Between Arab and Israeli* (New York: Ivan Obolensky, 1962).

Busailah, Reja-e. The Fall of Lydda, 1948: Impressions and Reminiscences, *Arab Studies Quarterly*, vol. 3 (1981).

Cohen, Michael J. *Palestine and the Great Powers 1945–1948* (Princeton, NJ: Princeton University Press, 1982).

Cohn-Sherbok, Dan. *Introduction to Zionism and Israel: From Ideology to History* (London: Continuum, 2012).

Dayan, Moshe. *Diary of the Sinai Campaign* (Jerusalem: Steimatzky's, 1966).

Story of My Life (London: Weidenfeld and Nicolson, 1976).

Documents on Israeli-Soviet Relations 1941–1953: Part I: 1941–May 1949 (London: Frank Cass, 2000).

Documents on the Foreign Policy of Israel (Jerusalem: Israel State Archives) (multivolume, dates vary)

Dodd, Peter and Halim Barakat. *River without Bridges* (Beirut: Institute for Palestine Studies, 1969).

Drory, Ze'ev. *Israel's Reprisal Policy 1953–1956: The Dynamics of Military Retaliation* (London: Frank Cass, 2005).

Dubnow, S.M. *History of the Jews in Russia and Poland from the Earliest Times until the Present Day* (New York: Ktav Publishing House, 1975).

Eban, Abba. *Abba Eban: An Autobiography* (New York: Random House, 1977).

Obstacles to Autonomy, *New Outlook*, June/July 1982.

Our Place in the Human Scheme: A Presentation, *Congress Bi-Weekly*, vol. 40, no. 6 (March 30, 1973).

Ernst, Morris. *So Far So Good* (New York: Harper, 1948).

Esber, Rosemarie. *Under the Cover of War: The Zionist Expulsion of the Palestinians* (Alexandria, VA: Arabicus Books, 2008).

Eytan, Walter. *The First Ten Years: A Diplomatic History of Israel* (London: Weidenfeld and Nicolson, 1958).

Finer, Herman. *Dulles over Suez: The Theory and Practice of His Diplomacy* (Chicago, IL: Quadrangle Books, 1964).

Flapan, Simha. *Zionism and the Palestinians* (London: Croom Helm, 1979).

Friedman, Isaiah. *Germany, Turkey, and Zionism 1897–1918* (Oxford: Clarendon Press, 1977).

The Question of Palestine: British-Jewish-Arab Relations: 1914–1918 (London: Transaction Books, 1992).

Galili, Ziva and Boris Morozov. *Exiled to Palestine: The Emigration of Zionist Convicts from the Soviet Union, 1924–1934* (London: Routledge, 2006).

Gannon, M. Anina. *The Influence of the Permanent Mandates Commission in the Administration of the Class A Mandate* (New York: St. John's University dissertation, 1968).

García-Granados, Jorge. *The Birth of Israel: The Drama as I Saw It* (New York: Alfred A. Knopf, 1948).

Gibbons, Herbert Adams. Zionism and the World Peace, *The Century*, vol. 97 (1919).

Gilbert, Martin. *In Ishmael's House: A History of Jews in Muslim Lands* (New Haven, CT: Yale University Press, 2010).

Gilmour, David. *The Dispossessed: the Ordeal of the Palestinians* (London: Sphere Books, 1980).

Gluska, Ami. *The Israeli Military and the Origins of the 1967 War: Government, armed forces and defence policy 1963–1967* (London: Routledge, 2007).

Golani, Motti, *Israel in Search of a War: The Sinai Campaign, 1955–1956* (Brighton, UK: Sussex Academic Press, 1998).

Goldman, Guido. *Zionism under Soviet Rule (1917–1928)* (New York: Herzl Press, 1960).

Goodman, Paul (ed.). *Chaim Weizmann: A Tribute on His Seventieth Birthday* (London: Victor Gollancz, 1945).

Granott, A. *The Land System in Palestine: History and Structure* (London: Eyre and Spottiswoode, 1952).

Grauel, John. *Grauel: Reverend John Stanley Grauel: An Autobiography as Told to Eleanor Elfenbein* (Freehold, NJ: Ivory House, 1983).

Gruber, Ruth. *Exodus 1947: The Ship that Launched a Nation* (New York: Random House, 1999).

Halamish, Aviva. *The Exodus Affair: Holocaust Survivors and the Struggle for Palestine* (Syracuse, NY: Syracuse University Press, 1998).

Halevi, Ilan. *A History of the Jews: Ancient and Modern* (London: Zed Press, 1987).

Halpern, Ben. *The Idea of the Jewish State* (Cambridge, MA: Harvard University Press, 1969).

Heiman, Leo. All's Fair …, *Marine Corps Gazette*, June 1964.

Henry, Charles (ed.). *Ralph Bunche: Selected Speeches and Writings* (Ann Arbor: University of Michigan Press, 1995).

Horowitz, David. *State in the Making* (New York: Alfred A. Knopf, 1953).

Hirst, David. *The Gun and the Olive Branch: The Roots of Violence in the Middle East* (London: Faber and Faber, 1977).

Hutchison, E. H. *Violent Truce: A Military Observer Looks at the Arab-Israeli Conflict 1951–1955* (New York: Devin-Adair, 1956).

Ingrams, Doreen. *Palestine Papers 1917–1922* (London: John Murray, 1972).

Israel and the United Nations (Report of a Study Group Set Up by the Hebrew University of Jerusalem) (New York: Manhattan Publishing, 1956).

Israel's Foreign Relations: Selected Documents (Jerusalem: Ministry of Foreign Affairs) (multivolume, dates vary)

Judis, John. *Genesis: Truman, American Jews, and the Origins of the Arab-Israeli Conflict* (New York: Farrar, Straus and Giroux, 2014).

Junod, Dominique-D. *The Imperiled Red Cross and the Palestine-Eretz-Yisrael Conflict 1945–1952: The Influence of Institutional Concerns on a Humanitarian Operation* (London: Kegan Paul International, 1996).

Kamen, Charles. The Arab Population in Palestine and Israel, 1946–1951, *New Outlook*, vol. 27–28 (October–November 1984).

Khalidi, Walid. *All That Remains: The Palestinian Villages Occupied and Depopulated by Israel in 1948* (Washington, DC: Institute for Palestine Studies, 1992).

Kissinger, Henry. *White House Years* (Boston, MA: Little, Brown, 1979).

Klausner, Joseph. *Menahem Ussishkin: His Life and Work* (New York: Scopus, 1942).

Klieman, Aharon. *Statecraft in the Dark: Israel's Practice of Quiet Diplomacy* (Boulder, CO: Westview Press, 1988).

Kling, Simcha. *The Mighty Warrior: The Life Story of Menahem Ussishkin* (New York: Jonathan David, 1965).

Kochan, Lionel (ed.). *The Jews in Soviet Russia since 1917* (London: Oxford University Press, 1972).

Kolsky, Thomas. *Jews Against Zionism: The American Council for Judaism, 1942–1948* (Philadelphia, PA: Temple University Press, 2010).

Krammer, Arnold. *The Forgotten Friendship: Israel and the Soviet Bloc, 1947–53* (Urbana: University of Illinois Press, 1974).

Langer, William. *The Diplomacy of Imperialism 1890–1902* (New York: Alfred A. Knopf, 1935).

Lapidoth, Ruth and Moshe Hirsch (eds.). *The Jerusalem Question and Its Resolution: Selected Documents* (Dordrecht: Martinus Nijhoff Publishers, 1994).

Laqueur, Walter. *A History of Zionism* (New York: Schocken Books, 1976).

Lehn, Walter and Uri Davis, *The Jewish National Fund* (London: Routledge, 1988).

Lewis, Geoffrey. *Balfour and Weizmann: The Zionist, the Zealot and the Emergence of Israel* (London: Continuum, 2009).

Levin, Harry. *I Saw the Battle of Jerusalem* (New York: Schocken Books, 1950).

Lloyd George, David. *The Truth about the Peace Treaties* (London: Gallancz, 1938).

Locke, Richard and Antony Stewart, *Bantustan Gaza* (London: Zed Press, 1985).

Lorch, Netanel, *The Edge of the Sword: Israel's War of Independence, 1947–1949* (Jerusalem: Massada Press, 1968).

Lustick, Ian. Has Israel Annexed East Jerusalem? *Middle East Policy*, vol. 5, issue 1 (1997).

Masalha, Nur. *Expulsion of the Palestinians: The Concept of "Transfer" in Zionist Political Thought 1882–1948* (Washington, DC: Institute for Palestine Studies, 1992).

Mearsheimer, John. *Why Leaders Lie: The Truth about Lying in International Politics* (Oxford: Oxford University Press, 2010).

Menuhin, Moshe. *The Decadence of Judaism in Our Time* (New York: Exposition Press, 1965).

Metzer, Jacob. *The Divided Economy of Mandatory Palestine* (Cambridge: Cambridge University Press, 1998).

Miller, Rory (ed.). *Britain, Palestine, and Empire: The Mandate Years* (Farnham, UK: Ashgate, 2010).
Morris, Benny. *1948: A History of the First Arab-Israeli War* (New Haven, CT: Yale University Press, 2008).
The Birth of the Palestinian Refugee Problem, 1947–1949 (Cambridge: Cambridge University Press, 1989).
The Birth of the Palestinian Refugee Problem Revisited (Cambridge: Cambridge University Press, 2004).
The Causes and Character of the Arab Exodus from Palestine: The Israel Defence Forces Intelligence Branch Analysis of June 1948, *Middle Eastern Studies*, vol. 22 (1986).
Israel's Border Wars 1949–1956: Arab Infiltration, Israeli Retaliation, and the Countdown to the Suez War (Oxford: Oxford University Press, 1993).
Operation Dani and the Palestinian Exodus from Lydda and Ramle in 1948, *Middle East Journal*, vol. 40 (1986).
Righteous Victims: A History of the Zionist-Arab Conflict, 1881–1999 (New York: Alfred A. Knopf, 1999).
Nazzal, Nafez. The Zionist Occupation of Western Galilee, 1948, *Journal of Palestine Studies*, vol. 3, no. 3 (1974).
Neff, Donald. *Warriors at Suez: Eisenhower Takes America into the Middle East* (New York: Simon and Schuster, 1981).
Nutting, Anthony. *No End of a Lesson: The Story of Suez* (New York: Clarkson N. Potter, 1967).
O'Ballance, Edgar. *The Arab-Israeli War, 1948* (London: Faber and Faber, 1956).
Oden, David H. *Israel's Foreign Policy in the United Nations 1948–1967: Security Aspects*, Ph.D. dissertation, University of Pennsylvania (1970) (microfilm).
Oren, Michael. *Origins of the Second Arab-Israel War: Egypt, Israel and the Great Powers 1952–1956* (London: Frank Cass, 1992).
Six Days of War (Oxford: Oxford University Press, 2002).
Palumbo, Michael. *The Palestinian Catastrophe: The 1948 Expulsion of a People from Their Homeland* (London: Faber and Faber, 1987).
Pappé, Ilan. *The Ethnic Cleansing of Palestine* (Oxford: Oneworld, 2006).
A History of Modern Palestine, 2nd ed. (Cambridge: Cambridge University Press, 2006).
Parker, Richard (ed.). *The Six-Day War: A Retrospective* (Gainesville: University Press of Florida, 1996).
Patai, Raphael (ed.). *The Complete Diaries of Theodor Herzl* (New York: Herzl Press, 1960).
Nahum Goldmann: His Missions to the Gentiles (Tuscaloosa: University of Alabama Press, 1987).
Peres, Shimon. *Battling for Peace: A Memoir* (New York: Random House, 1995).
Pineau, Christian. *1956/Suez* (Paris: Robert Laffont, 1976).
Rabin, Yitzhak. *The Rabin Memoirs* (Boston, MA: Little, Brown, 1979).
Rafael, Gideon. *Destination Peace: Three Decades of Israeli Foreign Policy – A Personal Memoir* (New York: Stein and Day, 1981).
Raz, Avi. *The Bride and the Dowry: Israel, Jordan, and the Palestinians in the Aftermath of the June 1967 War* (New Haven, CT: Yale University Press, 2012).

Reinharz, Jehuda. *Chaim Weizmann: The Making of a Statesman* (New York: Oxford University Press, 1993).

Reynier, Jacques de. *1948 à Jérusalem* (Neuchatel: Editions de la Baconnière, 1969).

Richardson, John. *The West Bank: A Portrait* (Washington, DC: Middle East Institute, 1984).

Rikhye, Indar Jit. *The Sinai Blunder: Withdrawal of the United Nations Emergency Force Leading to the Six-Day War of June 1967* (London: Frank Cass, 1980).

Rodman, David. *Defense and Diplomacy in Israel's National Security Experience: Tactics, Partnerships, and Motives* (Brighton, UK: Sussex Academic Press, 2005).

Ro'i, Yaakov. *Jews and Jewish Life in Russia and the Soviet Union* (Ilford, UK: Frank Cass, 1995).

Soviet Decision Making in Practice: The USSR and Israel 1947–1954 (New Brunswick, NJ: Transaction Books, 1980).

Rokach, Livia. *Israel's Sacred Terrorism: A Study Based on Moshe Sharett's Personal Diary and Other Documents* (Belmont, MA: Association of Arab-American University Graduates Press, 1986).

Rose, Norman. *Chaim Weizmann: A Biography* (New York: Viking Penguin, 1986).

The Gentile Zionists: A Study in Anglo-Zionist Diplomacy 1929–1939 (London: Frank Cass, 1973).

Rosenne, Shabtai. Basic Elements of Israel's Foreign Policy, *India Quarterly*, vol. 17 (1961).

Directions for a Middle East Settlement – Some Underlying Legal Problems, *Law and Contemporary Problems*, vol. 33 (1968).

Israel and the United Nations: Changed Perspectives, 1945–1976, in *American Jewish Year Book 1978*, vol. 78 (Philadelphia, PA: American Jewish Committee, 1977).

The Israeli Nationality Law 5712–1952 and the Law of Return 5710–1950, *Journal du droit international*, vol. 81 (1954).

Israel's Armistice Agreements with the Arab States: A Juridical Interpretation (Tel Aviv: Blumstein's, 1951).

The Law and Practice of the International Court (Leyden: A.W. Sijthoff, 1965).

On Defining International Aggression – An Exercise in Futility, *Israel Law Review*, vol. 12 (1977).

Recognition of Israel by the Security Council in 1948, *Israel Yearbook on Human Rights*, vol. 13 (1983).

Rubenberg, Cheryl. *Israel and the American National Interest* (Urbana: University of Illinois Press, 1986).

St. John, Robert. *Ben-Gurion: A Biography* (Garden City, NY: Doubleday, 1971).

Eban (Garden City, NY: Doubleday, 1972).

Sacher, Harry. *A Jewish Palestine: The Jewish Case for a British Trusteeship* (London: Zionist Organization, 1919).

Sayigh, Rosemary. *Palestinians: From Peasants to Revolutionaries* (London: Zed Press, 1979).

Schechtman, Joseph. *Zionism and Zionists in Soviet Russia: Greatness and Drama* (New York: Zionist Organization of America, 1966).

Schiff, Ze'ev. *A History of the Israeli Army 1874 to the Present* (New York: Macmillan, 1985).
Segev, Tom. *1949: The First Israelis* (New York: Free Press, 1986).
1967: Israel, the War, and the Year that Transformed the Middle East (New York: Henry Holt, 2007).
One Palestine, Complete: Jews and Arabs under the British Mandate (New York: Henry Holt, 2000).
Sereni, Ada. *I clandestini del mare: L'emigrazione ebraica in terra d'Israele dal 1945 al 1948* (Milan: U. Mursia, 1973).
Sharon, Ariel. *Warrior: The Autobiography of Ariel Sharon* (New York: Simon and Schuster, 1989).
Sheffer, Gabriel. *Moshe Sharett: Biography of a Political Moderate* (Oxford: Clarendon Press, 1996).
Sherman, A.J. *Island Refuge: Britain and Refugees from the Third Reich 1933–1939* (Berkeley: University of California Press, 1973).
Shavit, Ari. *My Promised Land: The Triumph and Tragedy of Israel* (New York: Spiel and Grau, 2013).
Shlaim, Avi. *The Iron Wall: Israel and the Arab World* (New York: W.W. Norton, 2000).
The Politics of Partition: King Abdullah, the Zionists and Palestine 1921–1951 (New York: Columbia University Press, 1990).
The Protocol of Sevres, 1956: Anatomy of a War Plot, *International Affairs*, vol. 73, no. 2 (1997).
Simons, Chaim. *International Proposals to Transfer Arabs from Palestine 1895–1946: A Historical Survey* (Hoboken, NJ: Ktav Publishing House, 1988).
Sofer, Sasson. *Zionism and the Foundations of Israeli Diplomacy* (Cambridge: Cambridge University Press, 1998).
Sokolow, Nahum. *History of Zionism 1600–1918* (New York: Ktav Publishing House, 1969).
Stein, Kenneth. *The Land Question in Palestine, 1917–1939* (Chapel Hill, NC: University of North Carolina Press, 1984).
Stewart, Barbara McDonald. *United States Government Policy on Refugees from Nazism, 1933–1940* (New York: Garland, 1982).
Teveth, Shabtai. *Ben-Gurion and the Palestinian Arabs: From Peace to War* (Oxford: Oxford University Press, 1985).
Moshe Dayan: The Soldier, the Man, the Legend (Boston, MA: Houghton Mifflin, 1973).
The Tanks of Tammuz (London: Sphere Books, 1970).
Thomas, Abel. *Comment Israël fût sauvé: Les secrets de l'expédition de Suez* (Paris: Albin Michel, 1978).
Toynbee, Arnold. The Present Situation in Palestine, *International Affairs: Journal of the Royal Institute of International Affairs*, vol. 10, no. 1 (January 1931).
Trevor-Roper, Hugh. Jewish and Other Nationalisms, *Commentary*, January 1963.
Uris, Leon. *Exodus* (Garden City, NY: Doubleday, 1958).
Urquhart, Brian. *Ralph Bunche: An American Life* (New York: W.W. Norton, 1993).

Weizman, Ezer. *On Eagles' Wings: The Personal Story of the Leading Commander of the Israeli Air Force* (New York: Macmillan, 1976).
Weizmann, Chaim. *Trial and Error: The Autobiography of Chaim Weizmann* (New York: Schocken Books, 1966).
Wischnitzer, Mark. *To Dwell in Safety: The Story of Jewish Migration since 1800* (Philadelphia, PA: Jewish Publication Society of America, 1948).
Zertal, Idith. *From Catastrophe to Power: Holocaust Survivors and the Emergence of Israel* (Berkeley: University of California Press, 1998).

Index

Printed in Great Britain
by Amazon

29733345R10178